NEGIMA!

23

Ken Akamatsu

TRANSLATED AND ADAPTED BY
Alethea Nibley and Athena Nibley

LETTERING AND RETOUCH BY
Steve Palmer

BALLANTINE BOOKS • NEW YORK

Negima! volume 23 is a work of fiction. Names, characters, places, and incidents are the products of the author's imagination or are used fictitiously. Any resemblance to actual events, locales, or persons, living or dead, is entirely coincidental.

A Del Rey Manga/Kodansha Trade Paperback Original

Negima! volume 23 copyright © 2008 by Ken Akamatsu
English translation copyright © 2009 by Ken Akamatsu

All rights reserved.

Published in the United States by Del Rey, an imprint of The Random House Publishing Group, a division of Random House, Inc., New York.

DEL REY is a registered trademark and the Del Rey colophon is a trademark of Random House, Inc.

Publication rights arranged through Kodansha Ltd.

First published in Japan in 2008 by Kodansha Ltd., Tokyo

ISBN 978-0-345-51426-4

Printed in the United States of America

www.delreymanga.com

9 8 7 6 5 4 3 2 1

Translators/adapters: Alethea Nibley and Athena Nibley
Lettering and retouch: Steve Palmer

Honorifics Explained

Throughout the Del Rey Manga books, you will find Japanese honorifics left intact in the translations. For those not familiar with how the Japanese use honorifics and, more important, how they differ from American honorifics, we present this brief overview.

Politeness has always been a critical facet of Japanese culture. Ever since the feudal era, when Japan was a highly stratified society, use of honorifics—which can be defined as polite speech that indicates relationship or status—has played an essential role in the Japanese language. When addressing someone in Japanese, an honorific usually takes the form of a suffix attached to one's name (example: "Asuna-san"), is used as a title at the end of one's name, or appears in place of the name itself (example: "Negi-sensei," or simply "Sensei!").

Honorifics can be expressions of respect or endearment. In the context of manga and anime, honorifics give insight into the nature of the relationship between characters. Many English translations leave out these important honorifics and therefore distort the feel of the original Japanese. Because Japanese honorifics contain nuances that English honorifics lack, it is our policy at Del Rey not to translate them. Here, instead, is a guide to some of the honorifics you may encounter in Del Rey Manga.

-*san*: This is the most common honorific and is equivalent to Mr., Miss, Ms., or Mrs. It is the all-purpose honorific and can be used in any situation where politeness is required.

-*sama*: This is one level higher than "-san" and is used to confer great respect.

-*dono*: This comes from the word "tono," which means "lord." It is an even higher level than "-sama" and confers utmost respect.

-*kun*: This suffix is used at the end of boys' names to express familiarity or endearment. It is also sometimes used by men among friends, or when addressing someone younger or of a lower station.

-chan: This is used to express endearment, mostly toward girls. It is also used for little boys, pets, and even among lovers. It gives a sense of childish cuteness.

Bōzu: This is an informal way to refer to a boy, similar to the English terms "kid" and "squirt."

Sempai/Senpai: This title suggests that the addressee is one's senior in a group or organization. It is most often used in a school setting, where underclassmen refer to their upperclassmen as "sempai." It can also be used in the workplace, such as when a newer employee addresses an employee who has seniority in the company.

Kohai: This is the opposite of "sempai" and is used toward underclassmen in school or newcomers in the workplace. It connotes that the addressee is of a lower station.

Sensei: Literally meaning "one who has come before," this title is used for teachers, doctors, or masters of any profession or art.

Anesan (or *nesan*): A generic term for a girl, usually older, that means "sister."

Ojōsama: A way of referring to the daughter or sister of someone with high political or social status.

-[blank]: This is usually forgotten in these lists, but it is perhaps the most significant difference between Japanese and English. The lack of honorific means that the speaker has permission to address the person in a very intimate way. Usually, only family, spouses, or very close friends have this kind of permission. Known as *yobisute*, it can be gratifying when someone who has earned the intimacy starts to call one by one's name without an honorific. But when that intimacy hasn't been earned, it can be very insulting.

A Word from the Author

Presenting *Negima!* volume 23! While split up in the Magical World, each of the members of the Negi Party powers up. Meanwhile, our main character Negi...!?

There are still a lot of battles, but we're keeping track of the class-mates that stayed behind, too. (laugh) Because this is *Negima*, with its thirty-one classmates, after all. (^^)

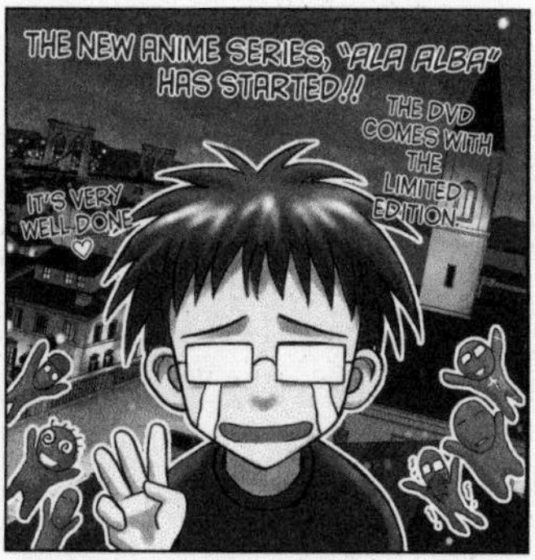
THE NEW ANIME SERIES, "ALA ALBA" HAS STARTED!!
THE DVD COMES WITH THE LIMITED EDITION.
IT'S VERY WELL DONE ♥

The new anime series, completely based on the manga, *Magister Negi Magi ~ Ala Alba ~* has started! DVDs come with the limited editions of volumes 23–25! For details, check my homepage.

Ken Akamatsu
www.ailove.net

魔法先生（まほうせんせい）ネギま！

MAGISTER NEGI MAGI

23

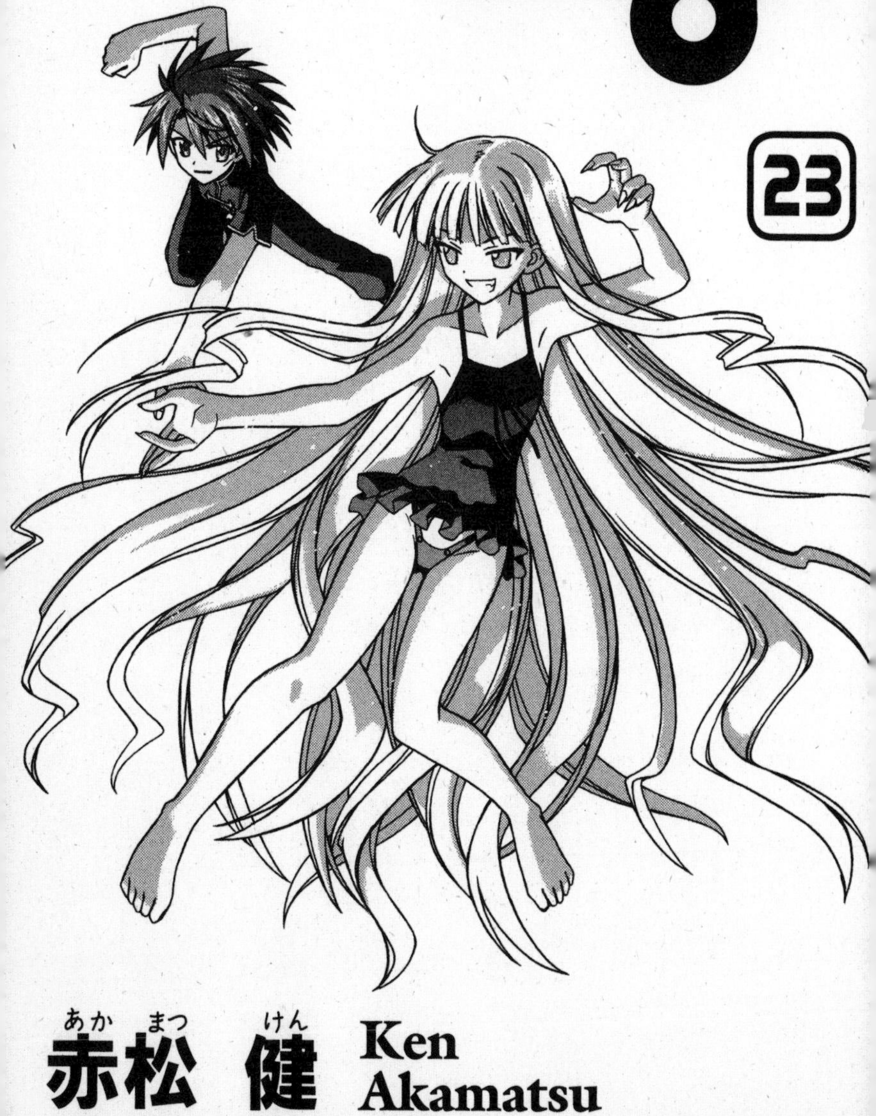

赤松（あかまつ） 健（けん） Ken Akamatsu

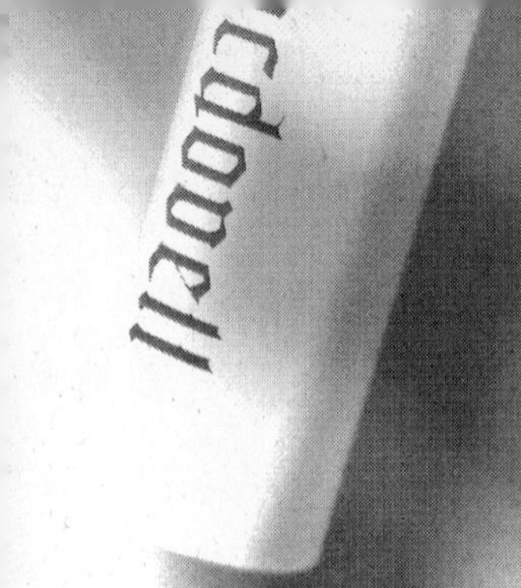
cdowell

CONTENTS

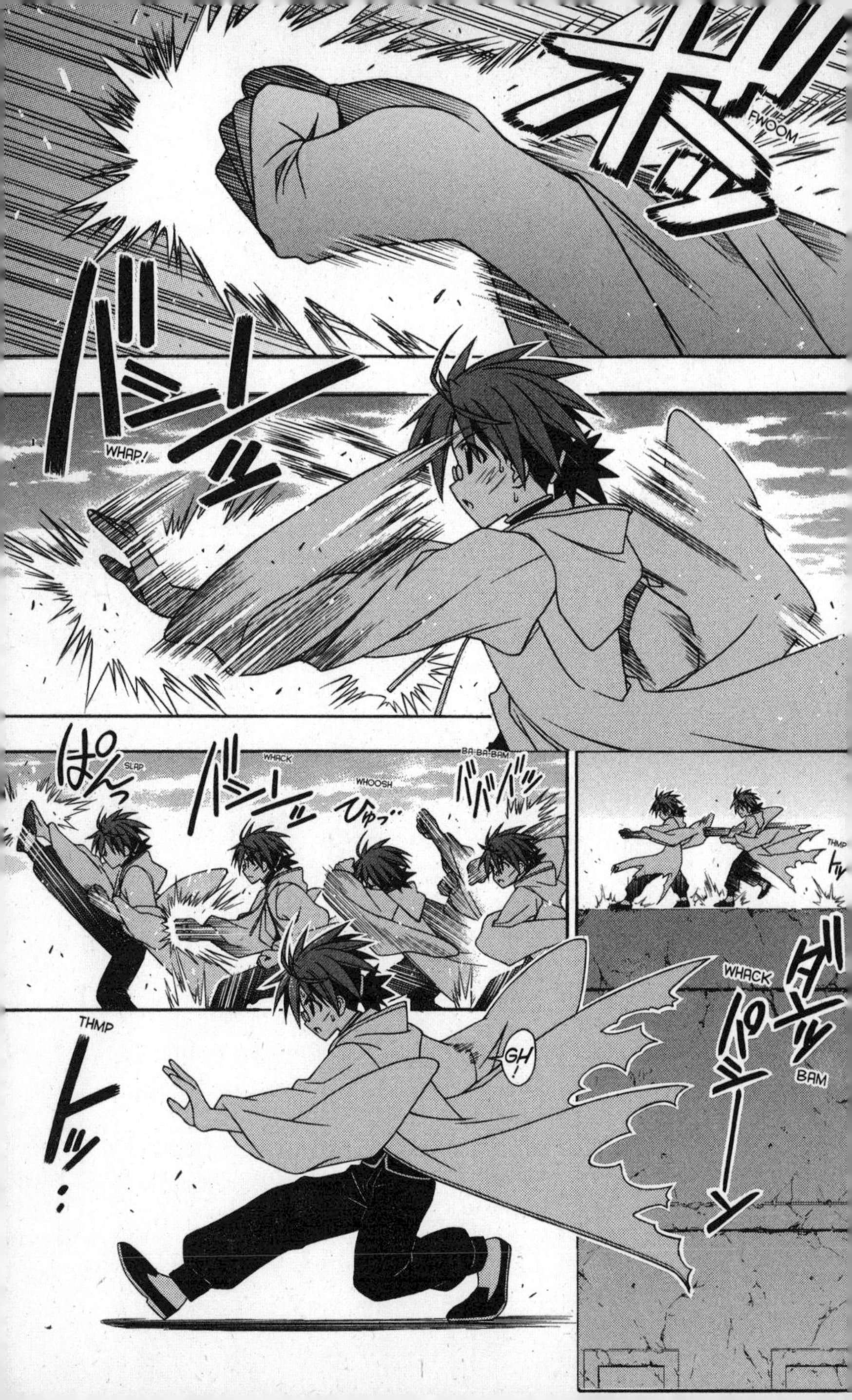
FWOOM
WHAP!
THMP
BA-BA-BAM
WHOOSH
WHACK
SLAP
GH!
BAM
WHACK
THMP

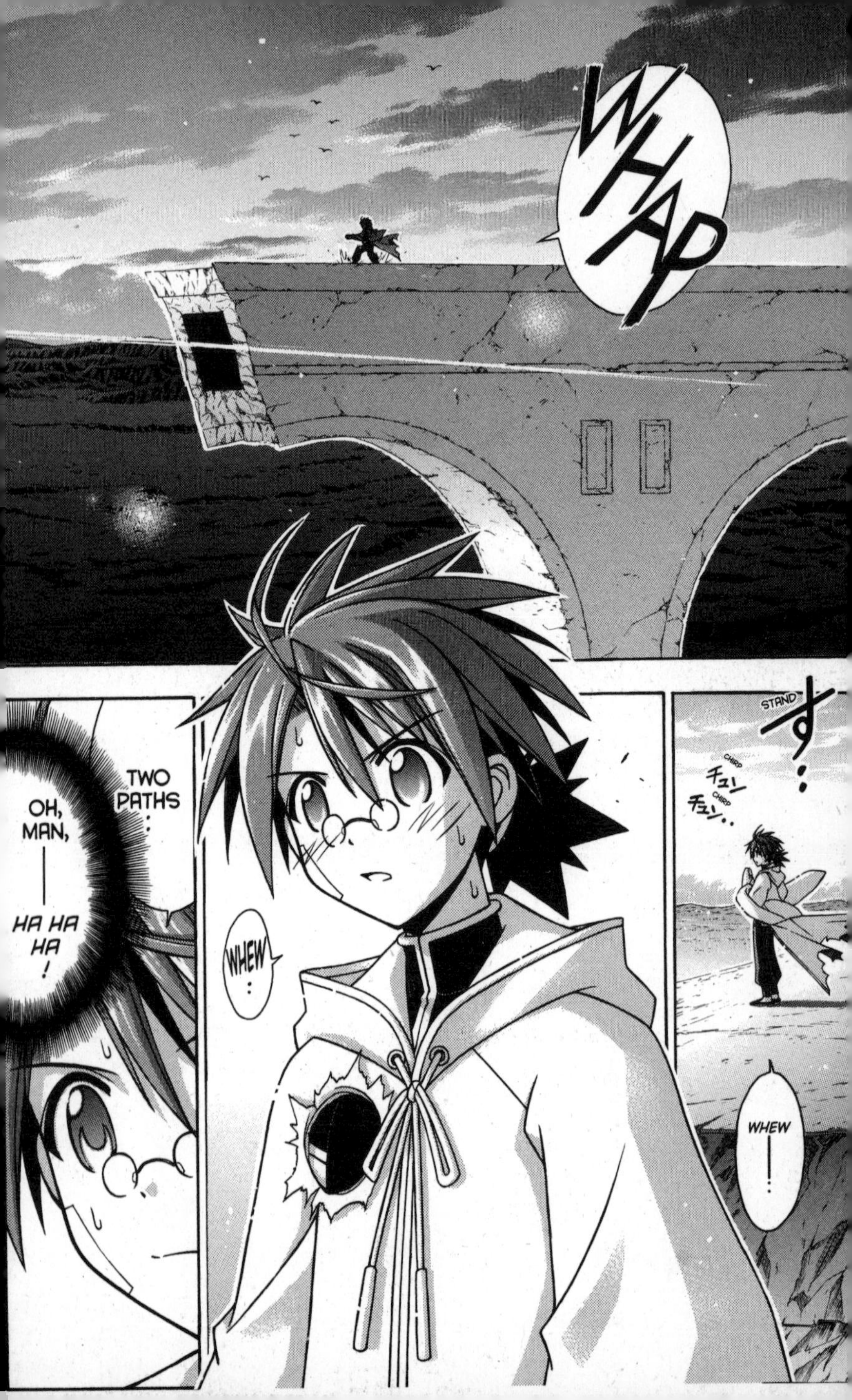
WHAP
STAND
す
CHIRP
チュン
CHIRP
チュン..
WHEW —!
WHEW...
TWO PATHS...
OH, MAN, — HA HA HA!

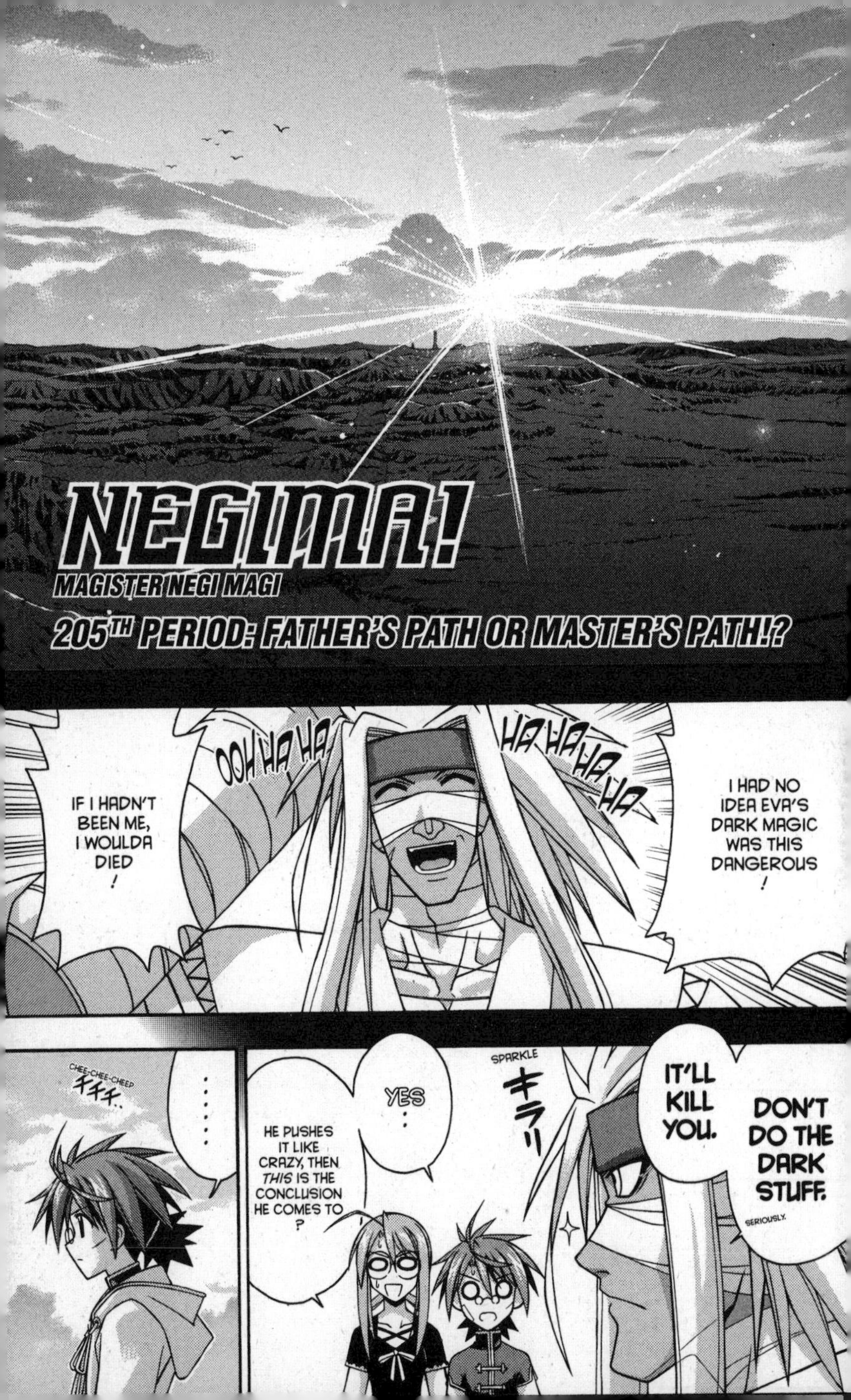

NEGIMA!
MAGISTER NEGI MAGI
205TH PERIOD: FATHER'S PATH OR MASTER'S PATH!?
HA HA HA HA HA
I HAD NO IDEA EVA'S DARK MAGIC WAS THIS DANGEROUS!
OOH HA HA
IF I HADN'T BEEN ME, I WOULDA DIED!
DON'T DO THE DARK STUFF.
IT'LL KILL YOU.
SERIOUSLY.
SPARKLE
キラリ
YES...
HE PUSHES IT LIKE CRAZY, THEN THIS IS THE CONCLUSION HE COMES TO?
......
CHEE-CHEE-CHEEP
チチチ...

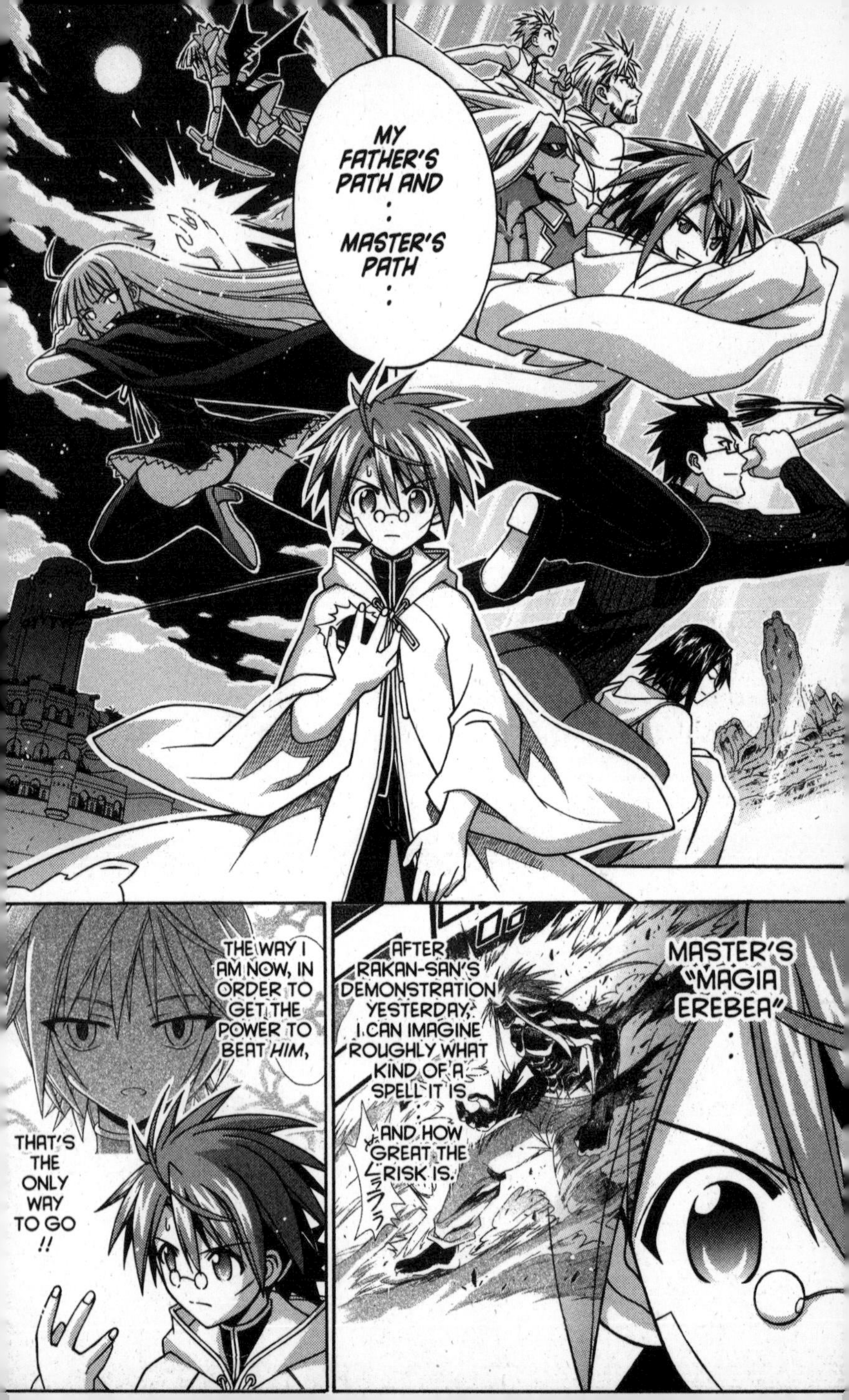
MY FATHER'S PATH AND . . . MASTER'S PATH . . .
MASTER'S "MAGIA EREBEA" . . .
AFTER RAKAN-SAN'S DEMONSTRATION YESTERDAY, I CAN IMAGINE ROUGHLY WHAT KIND OF A SPELL IT IS . . .
AND HOW GREAT THE RISK IS.
THE WAY I AM NOW, IN ORDER TO GET THE POWER TO BEAT HIM,
THAT'S THE ONLY WAY TO GO !!

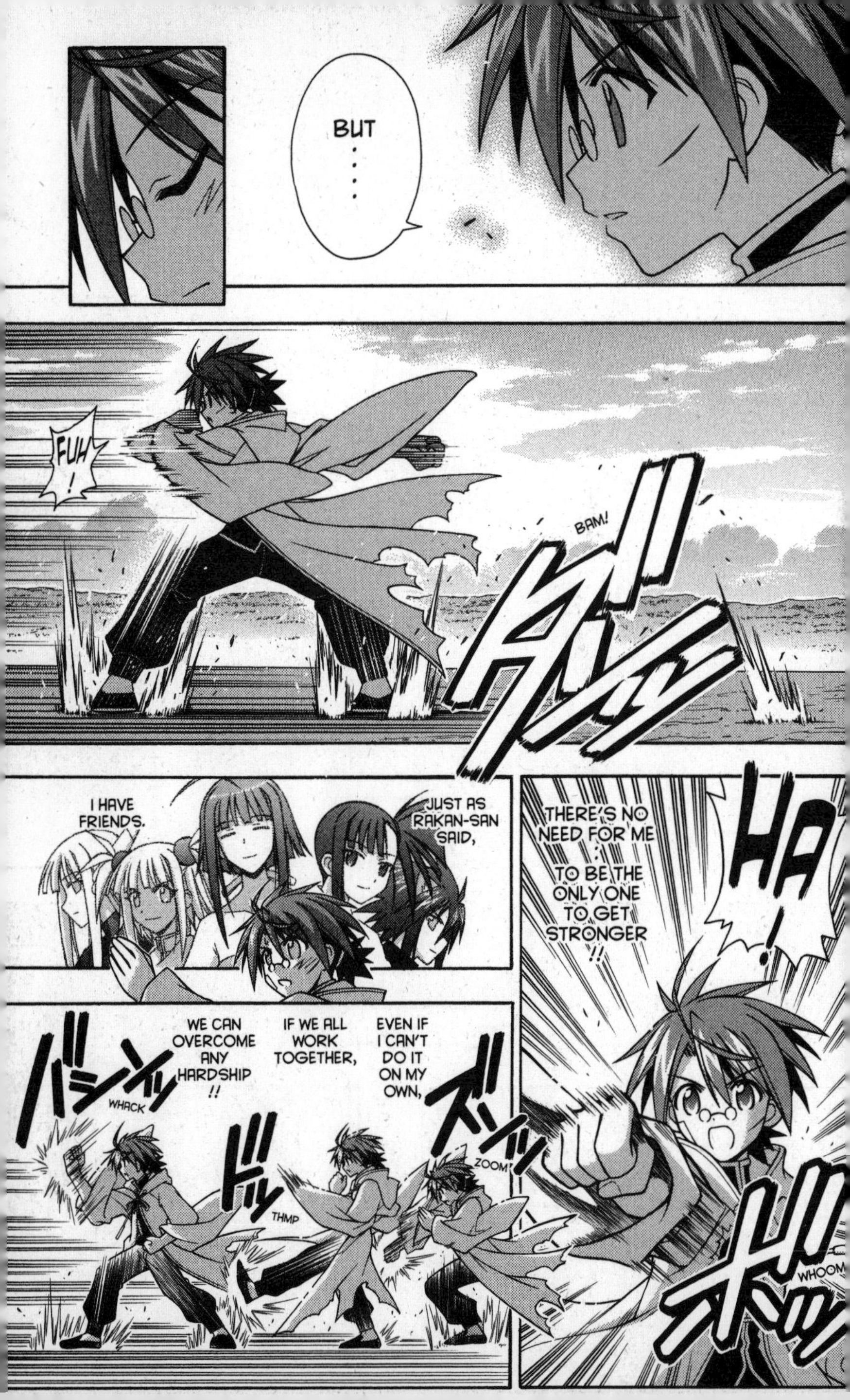
BUT ....
BAM!
FUH!
HA!
THERE'S NO NEED FOR ME... TO BE THE ONLY ONE TO GET STRONGER!!
WHOOM
JUST AS RAKAN-SAN SAID,
I HAVE FRIENDS.
EVEN IF I CAN'T DO IT ON MY OWN,
ZOOM
IF WE ALL WORK TOGETHER,
THMP
WE CAN OVERCOME ANY HARDSHIP!!
WHACK

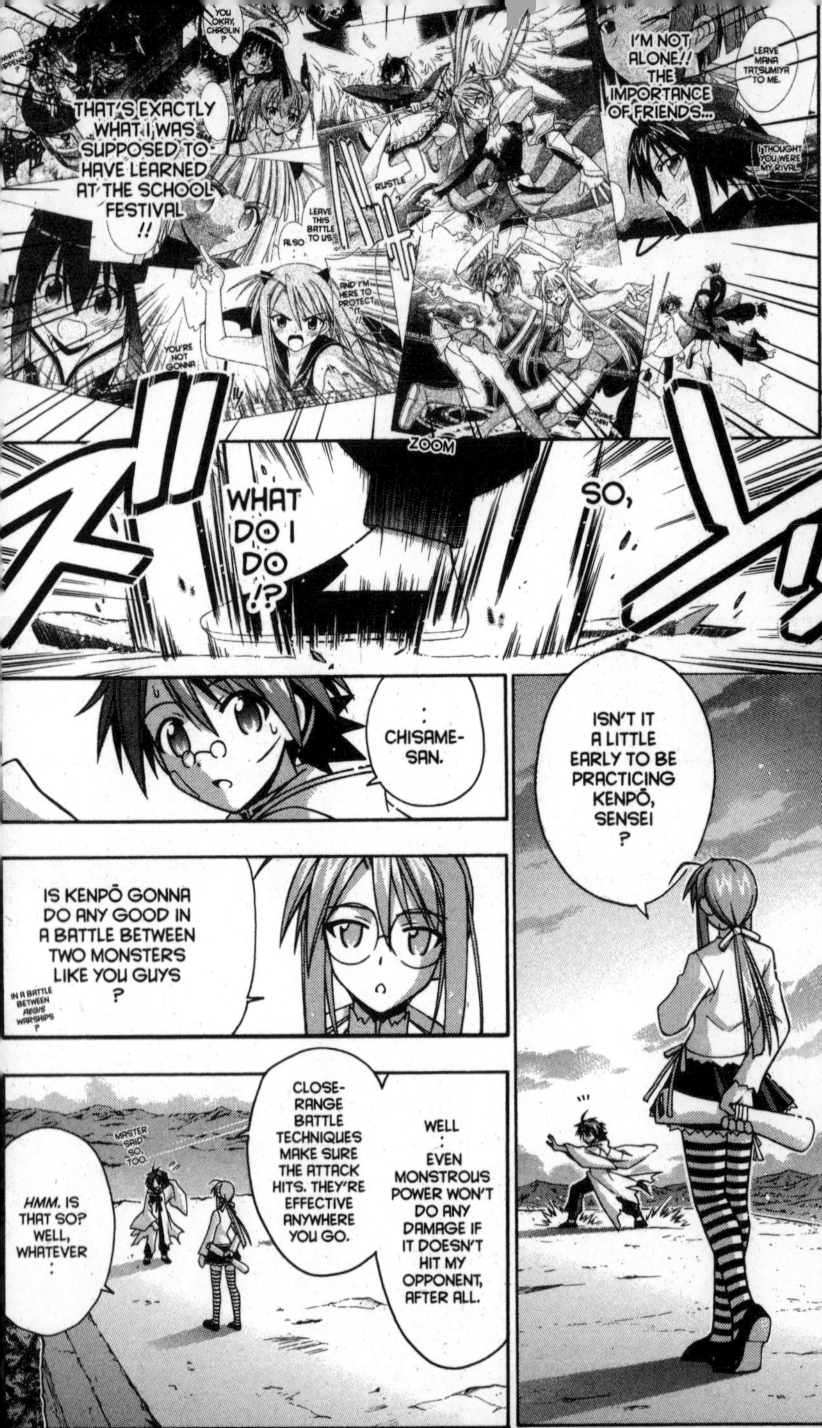
LEAVE MANA TATSUMIYA TO ME.
I'M NOT ALONE!! THE IMPORTANCE OF FRIENDS...
I THOUGHT YOU WERE MY RIVAL.
RUSTLE
YOU OKAY, CHAOLIN?
WHAT'S HAPPENING?
THAT'S EXACTLY WHAT I WAS SUPPOSED TO HAVE LEARNED AT THE SCHOOL FESTIVAL!!
LEAVE THIS BATTLE TO US.
ALSO...
AND I'M HERE TO PROTECT IT!!
YOU'RE NOT GONNA
CHISAME-CHAN
ZOOM
SO,
WHAT DO I DO!?
ISN'T IT A LITTLE EARLY TO BE PRACTICING KENPŌ, SENSEI?
...CHISAME-SAN.
IS KENPŌ GONNA DO ANY GOOD IN A BATTLE BETWEEN TWO MONSTERS LIKE YOU GUYS?
IN A BATTLE BETWEEN *AEGIS* WARSHIPS?
WELL... EVEN MONSTROUS POWER WON'T DO ANY DAMAGE IF IT DOESN'T HIT MY OPPONENT, AFTER ALL.
CLOSE-RANGE BATTLE TECHNIQUES MAKE SURE THE ATTACK HITS. THEY'RE EFFECTIVE ANYWHERE YOU GO.
MASTER SAID SO, TOO.
HMM. IS THAT SO? WELL, WHATEVER...

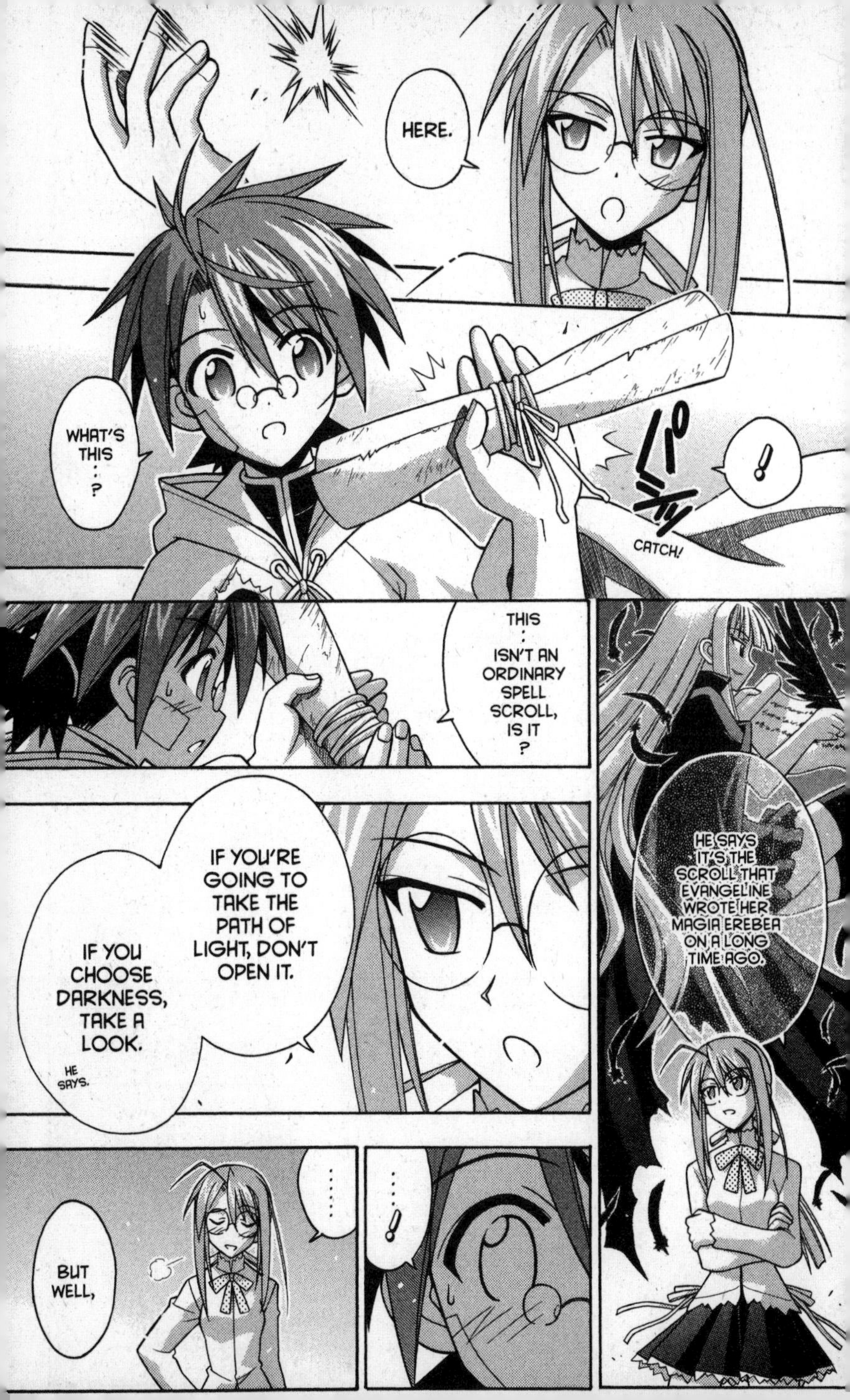
HERE.
!
CATCH!
WHAT'S THIS...?
HE SAYS IT'S THE SCROLL THAT EVANGELINE WROTE HER MAGIA EREBEA ON A LONG TIME AGO.
THIS... ISN'T AN ORDINARY SPELL SCROLL, IS IT?
IF YOU'RE GOING TO TAKE THE PATH OF LIGHT, DON'T OPEN IT.
IF YOU CHOOSE DARKNESS, TAKE A LOOK.
HE SAYS.
......!
......
BUT WELL,

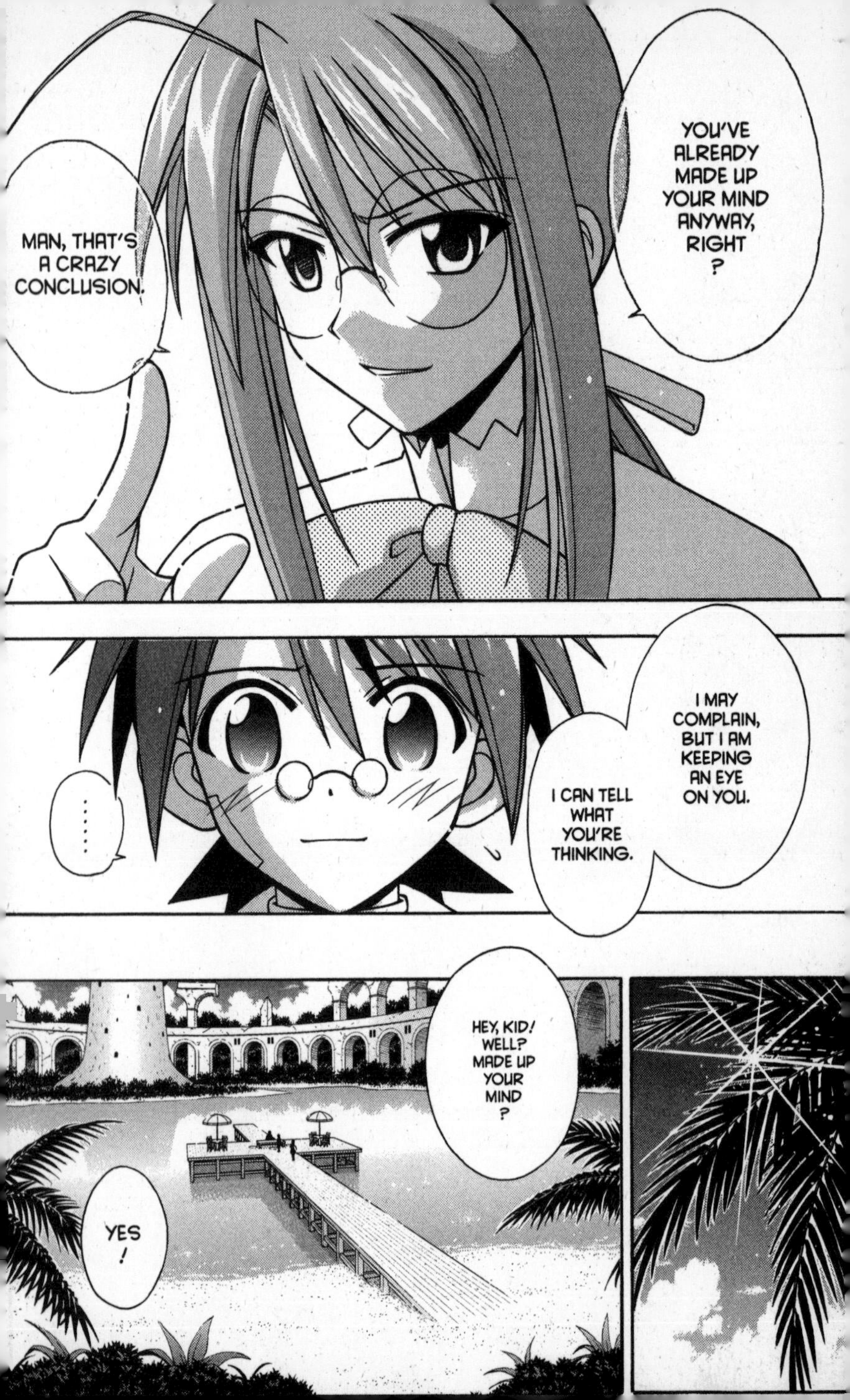
YOU'VE ALREADY MADE UP YOUR MIND ANYWAY, RIGHT?
MAN, THAT'S A CRAZY CONCLUSION.
I MAY COMPLAIN, BUT I AM KEEPING AN EYE ON YOU.
I CAN TELL WHAT YOU'RE THINKING.
......
HEY, KID! WELL? MADE UP YOUR MIND?
YES!

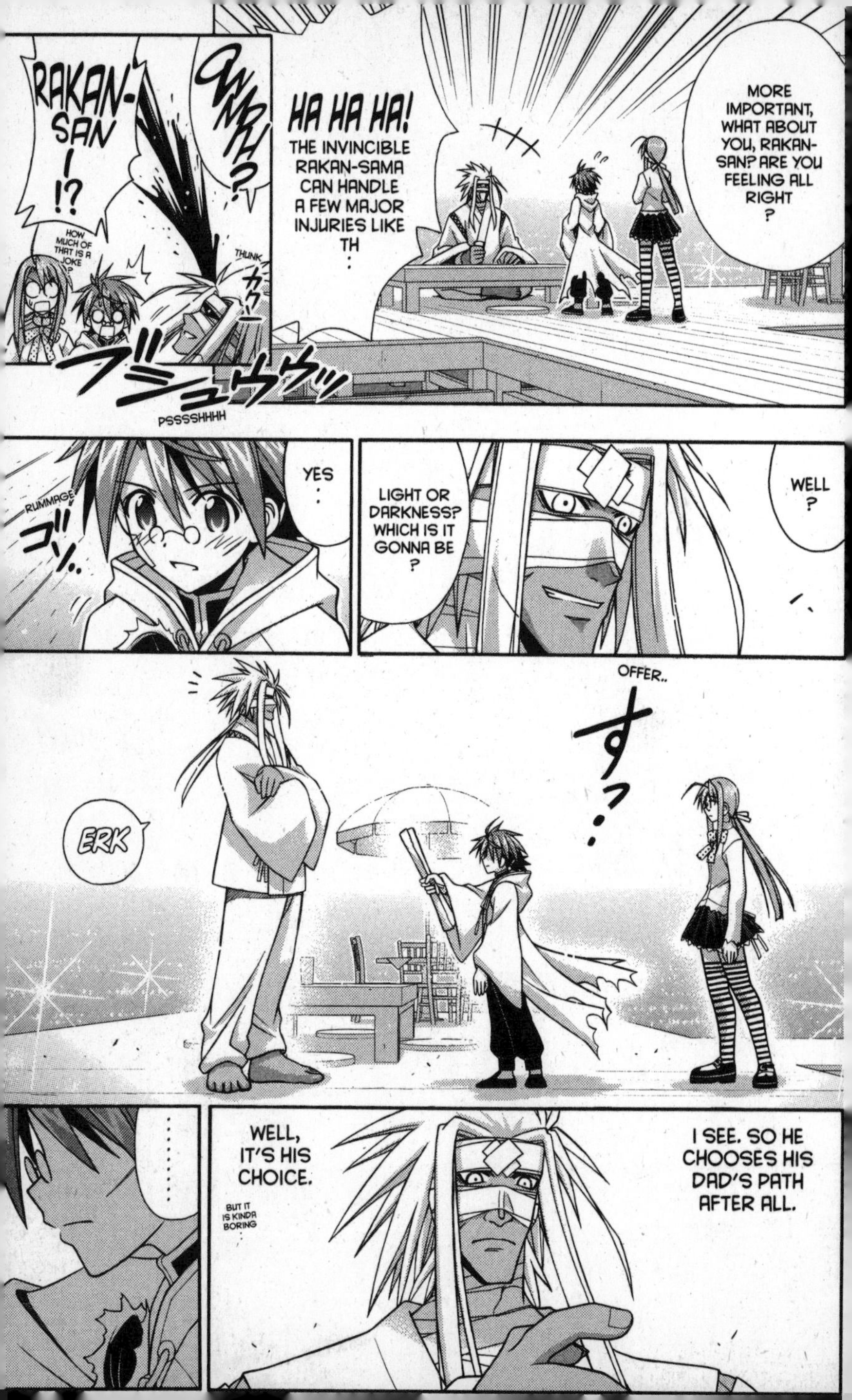
MORE IMPORTANT, WHAT ABOUT YOU, RAKAN-SAN? ARE YOU FEELING ALL RIGHT?
HA HA HA! THE INVINCIBLE RAKAN-SAMA CAN HANDLE A FEW MAJOR INJURIES LIKE TH...
THUNK
RAKAN-SAN!?
HOW MUCH OF THAT IS A JOKE?
PSSSSHHHH
WELL?
LIGHT OR DARKNESS? WHICH IS IT GONNA BE?
YES...
RUMMAGE
OFFER..
ERK
I SEE. SO HE CHOOSES HIS DAD'S PATH AFTER ALL.
WELL, IT'S HIS CHOICE.
BUT IT IS KINDA BORING
......

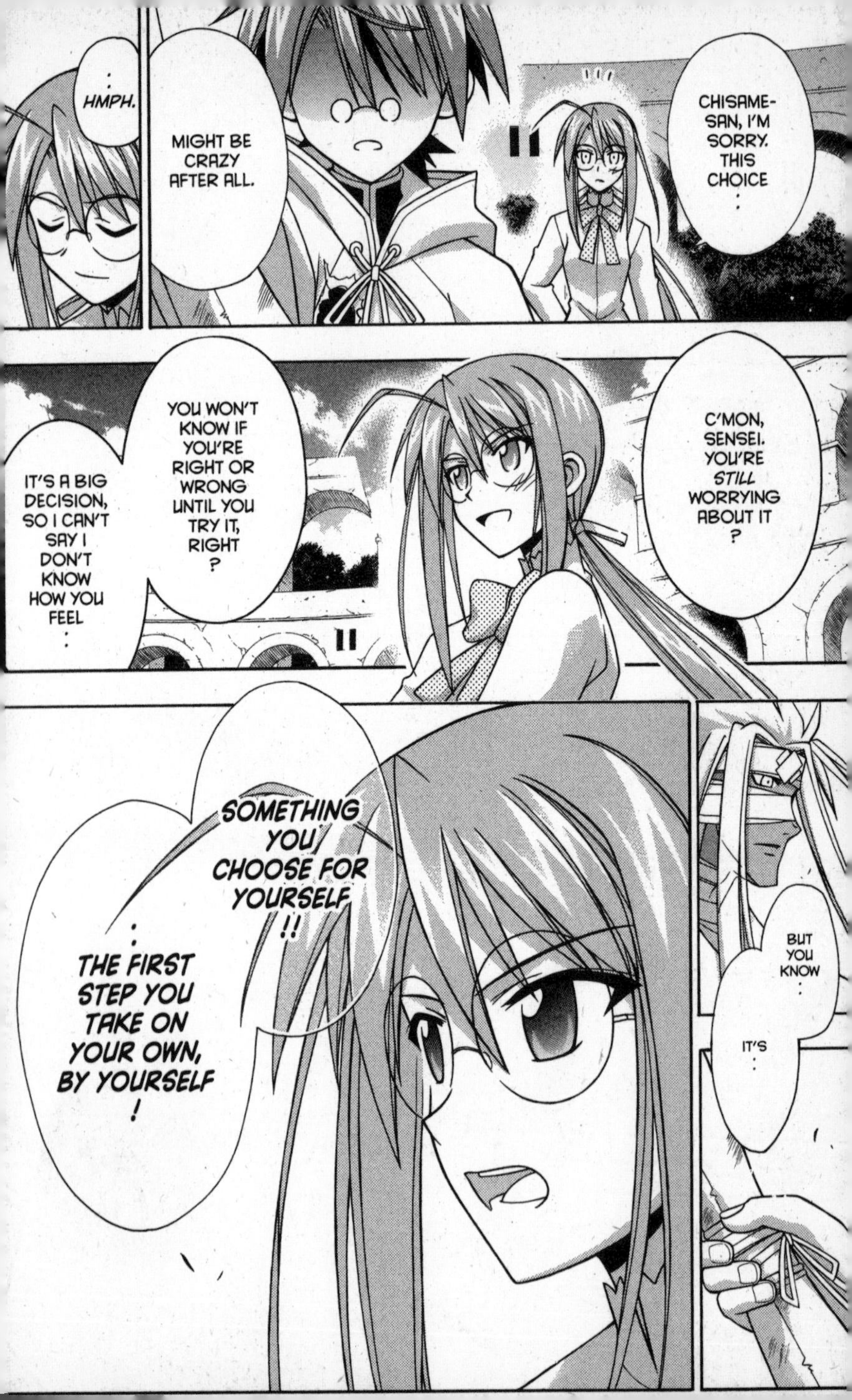

CHISAME-SAN, I'M SORRY. THIS CHOICE...
MIGHT BE CRAZY AFTER ALL.
...HMPH.
C'MON, SENSEI. YOU'RE *STILL* WORRYING ABOUT IT?
YOU WON'T KNOW IF YOU'RE RIGHT OR WRONG UNTIL YOU TRY IT, RIGHT?
IT'S A BIG DECISION, SO I CAN'T SAY I DON'T KNOW HOW YOU FEEL...
BUT YOU KNOW...
IT'S...
SOMETHING YOU CHOOSE FOR YOURSELF!!
...THE FIRST STEP YOU TAKE ON YOUR OWN, BY YOURSELF!

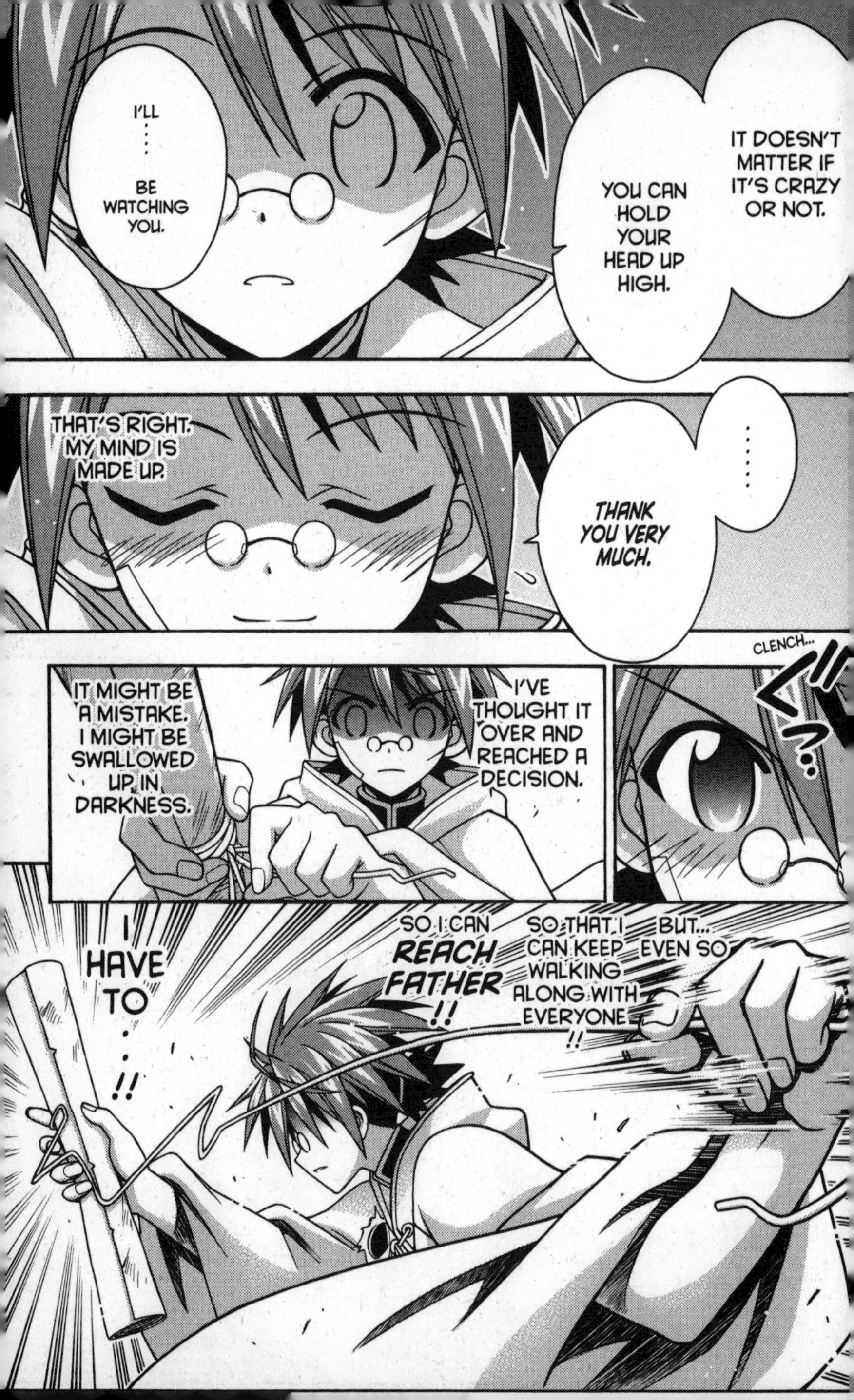
IT DOESN'T MATTER IF IT'S CRAZY OR NOT.
YOU CAN HOLD YOUR HEAD UP HIGH.
I'LL ... BE WATCHING YOU.
...... THANK YOU VERY MUCH.
THAT'S RIGHT. MY MIND IS MADE UP.
CLENCH...
I'VE THOUGHT IT OVER AND REACHED A DECISION.
IT MIGHT BE A MISTAKE. I MIGHT BE SWALLOWED UP IN DARKNESS.
BUT... EVEN SO
SO THAT I CAN KEEP WALKING ALONG WITH EVERYONE!!
SO I CAN REACH FATHER!!
I HAVE TO...!!

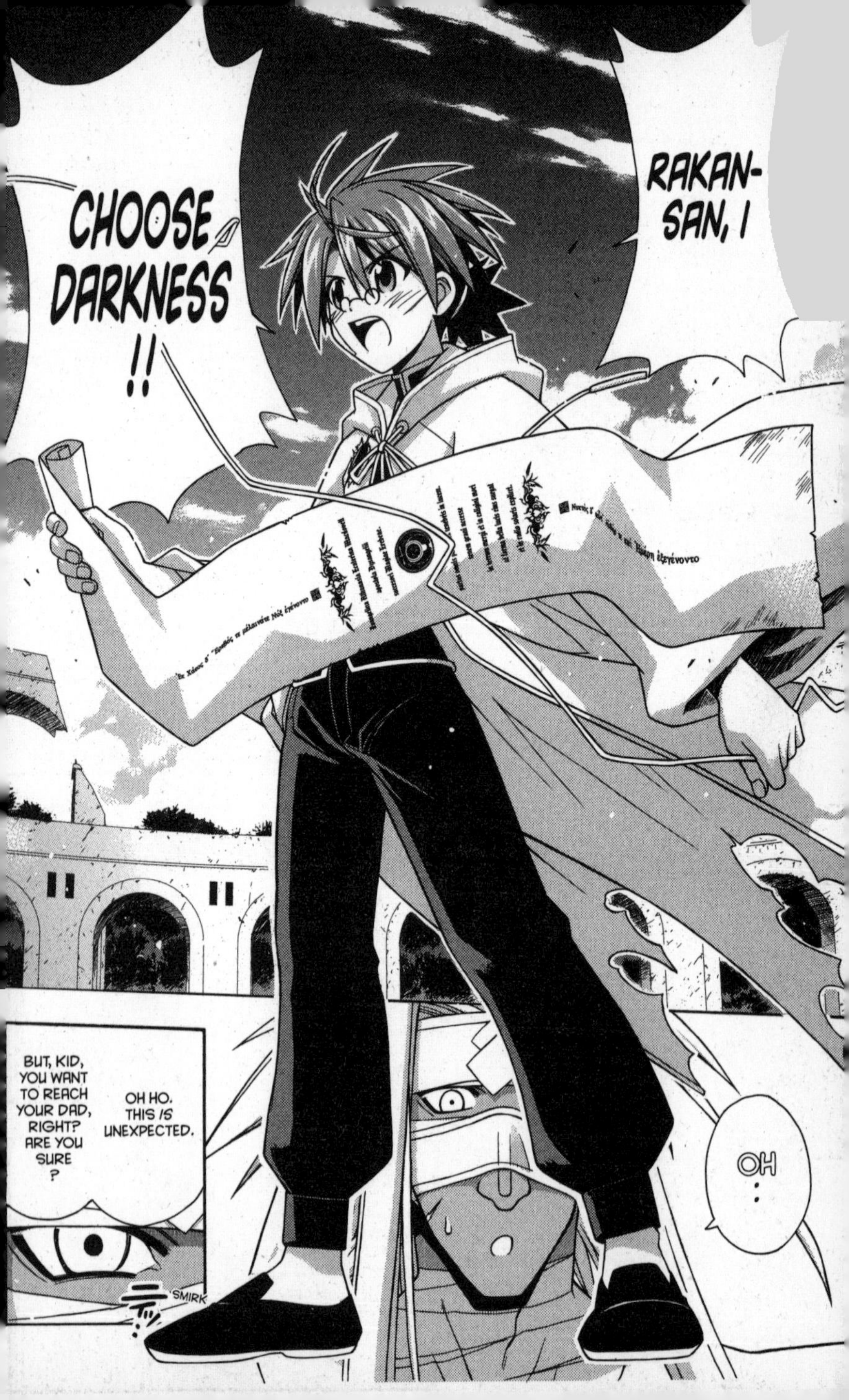
RAKAN-SAN, I
CHOOSE DARKNESS !!
OH . .
OH HO. THIS IS UNEXPECTED.
BUT, KID, YOU WANT TO REACH YOUR DAD, RIGHT? ARE YOU SURE ?
SMIRK

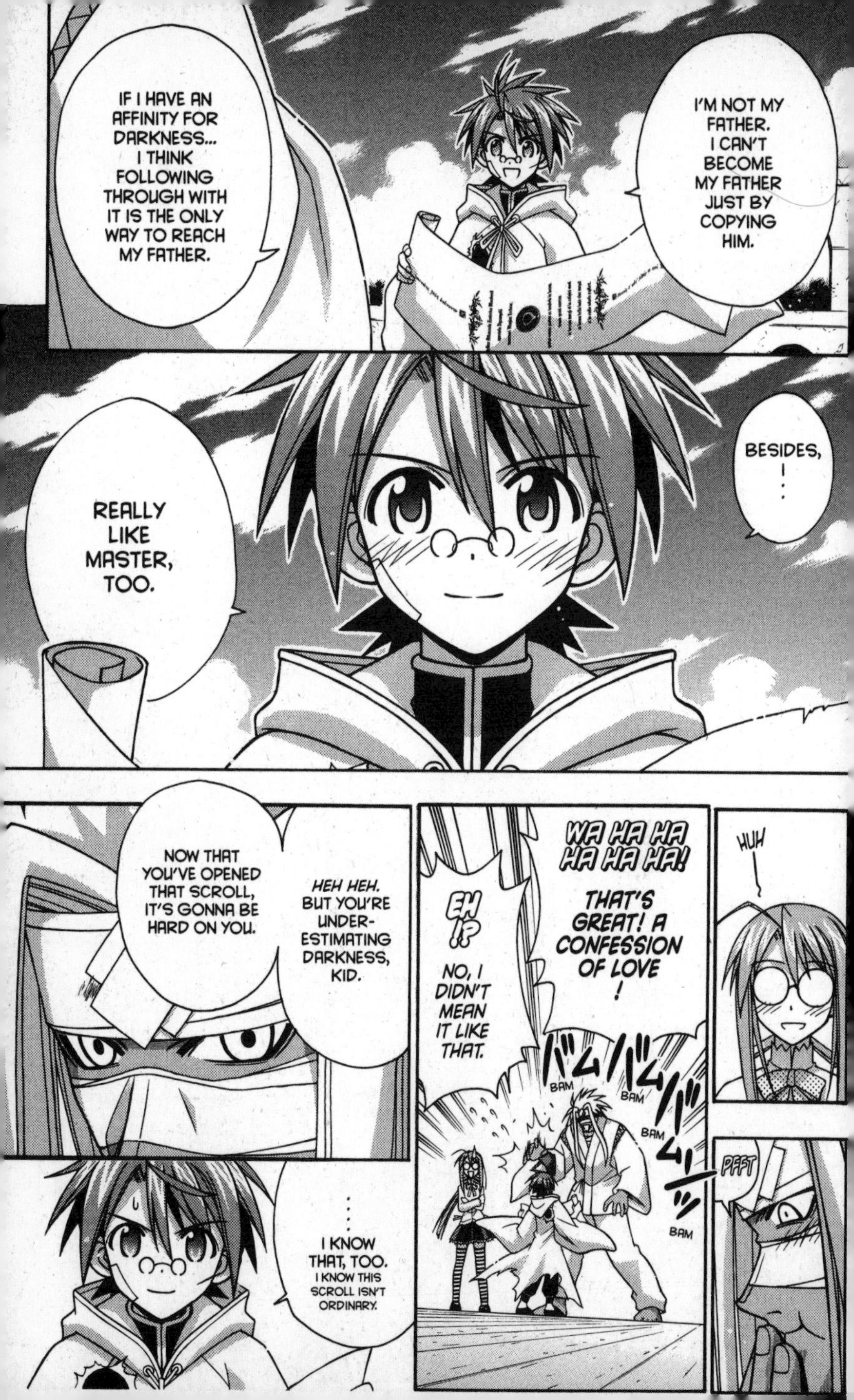

I'M NOT MY FATHER. I CAN'T BECOME MY FATHER JUST BY COPYING HIM.
IF I HAVE AN AFFINITY FOR DARKNESS... I THINK FOLLOWING THROUGH WITH IT IS THE ONLY WAY TO REACH MY FATHER.
BESIDES, !..
REALLY LIKE MASTER, TOO.
HUH!
PFFT
WA HA HA HA HA HA!
THAT'S GREAT! A CONFESSION OF LOVE!
EH!?
NO, I DIDN'T MEAN IT LIKE THAT.
BAM
BAM
BAM
BAM
HEH HEH. BUT YOU'RE UNDER-ESTIMATING DARKNESS, KID.
NOW THAT YOU'VE OPENED THAT SCROLL, IT'S GONNA BE HARD ON YOU.
... I KNOW THAT, TOO. I KNOW THIS SCROLL ISN'T ORDINARY.

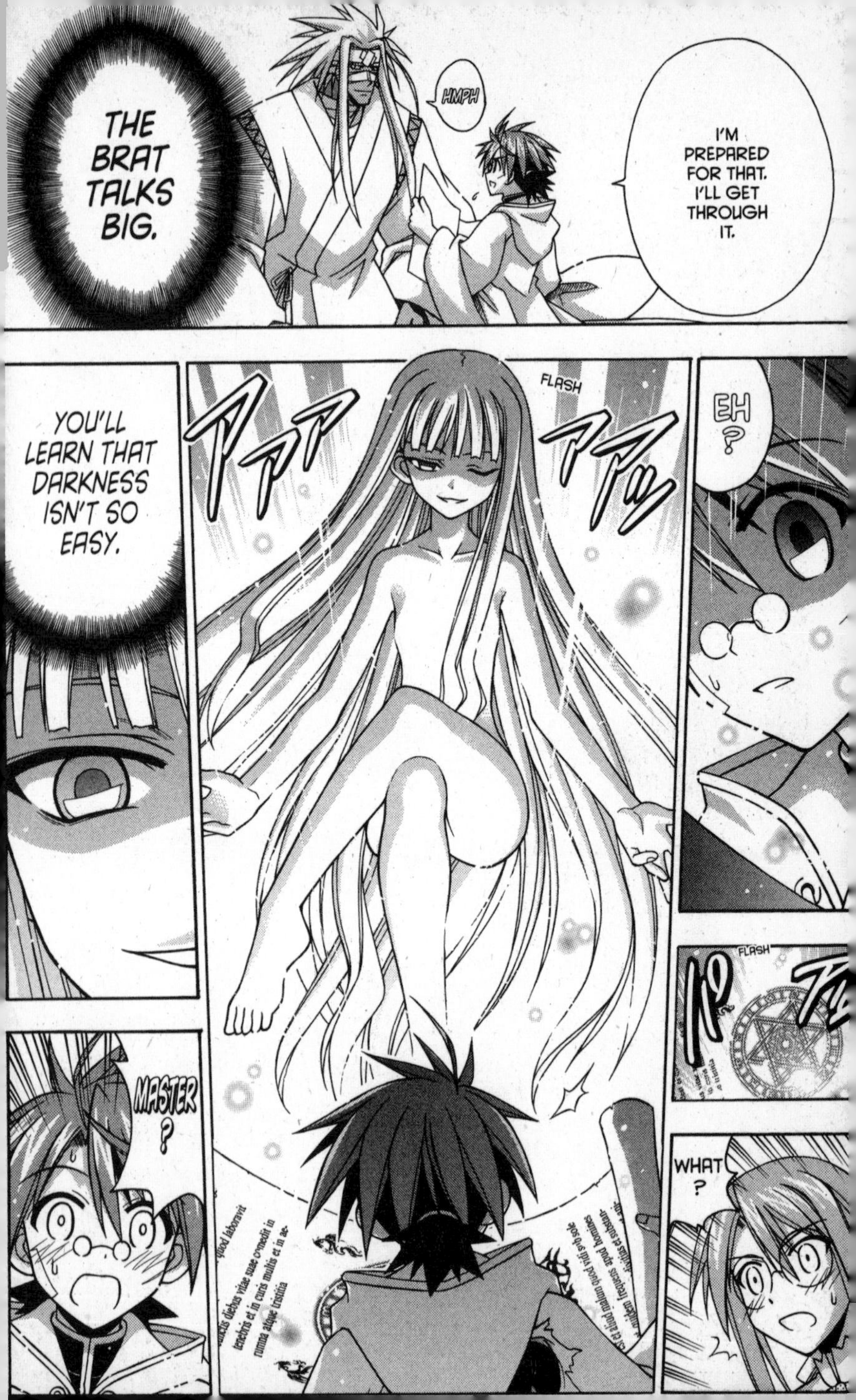
I'M PREPARED FOR THAT. I'LL GET THROUGH IT.
HMPH
THE BRAT TALKS BIG.
EH?
FLASH
アアア
アアッ
YOU'LL LEARN THAT DARKNESS ISN'T SO EASY.
FLASH
WHAT?
MASTER?

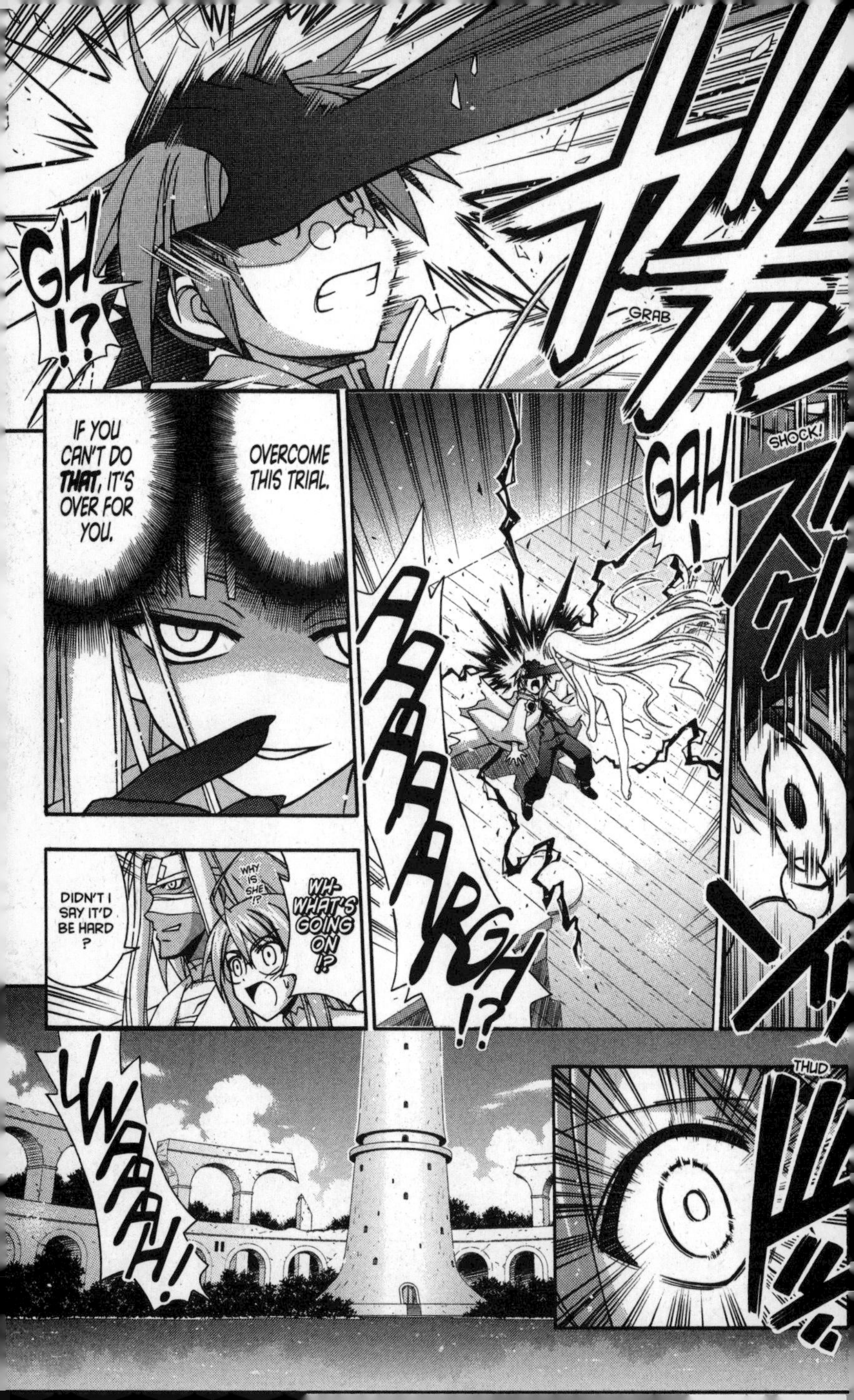
GRAB
GH!?
SHOCK!
GAH!
AAAAAARGH!?
OVERCOME THIS TRIAL.
IF YOU CAN'T DO THAT, IT'S OVER FOR YOU.
WH-WHAT'S GOING ON!?
WHY IS SHE!?
DIDN'T I SAY IT'D BE HARD?
THUD
UWAAAAH!

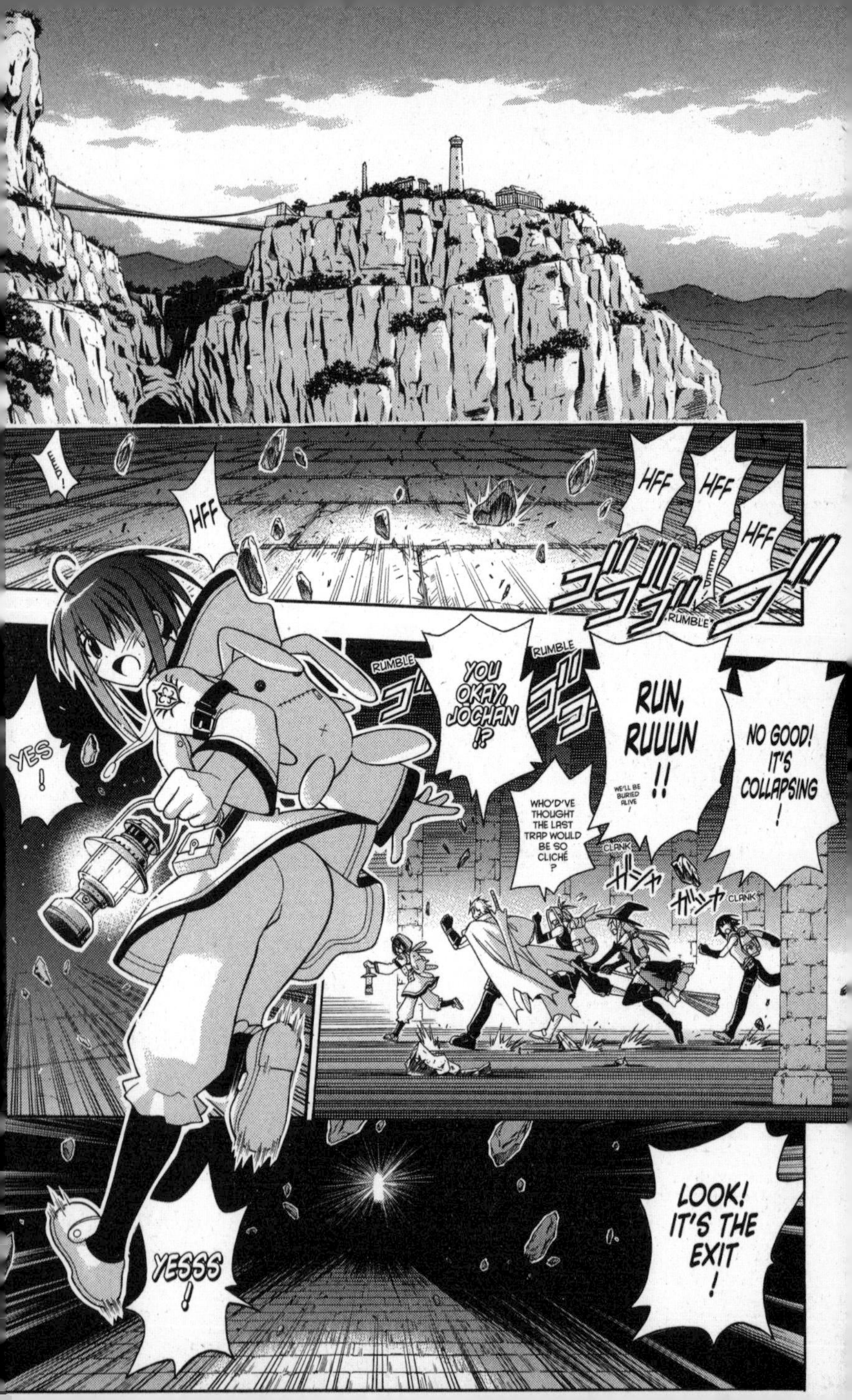
HFF
HFF
HFF
EEEP!
RUMBLE
HFF
EEEP!
NO GOOD! IT'S COLLAPSING!
RUN, RUUUN!!
WE'LL BE BURIED ALIVE!
RUMBLE
YOU OKAY, JOCHAN!?
RUMBLE
YES!
WHO'D'VE THOUGHT THE LAST TRAP WOULD BE SO CLICHÉ?
CLANK
CLANK
LOOK! IT'S THE EXIT!
YESSS!

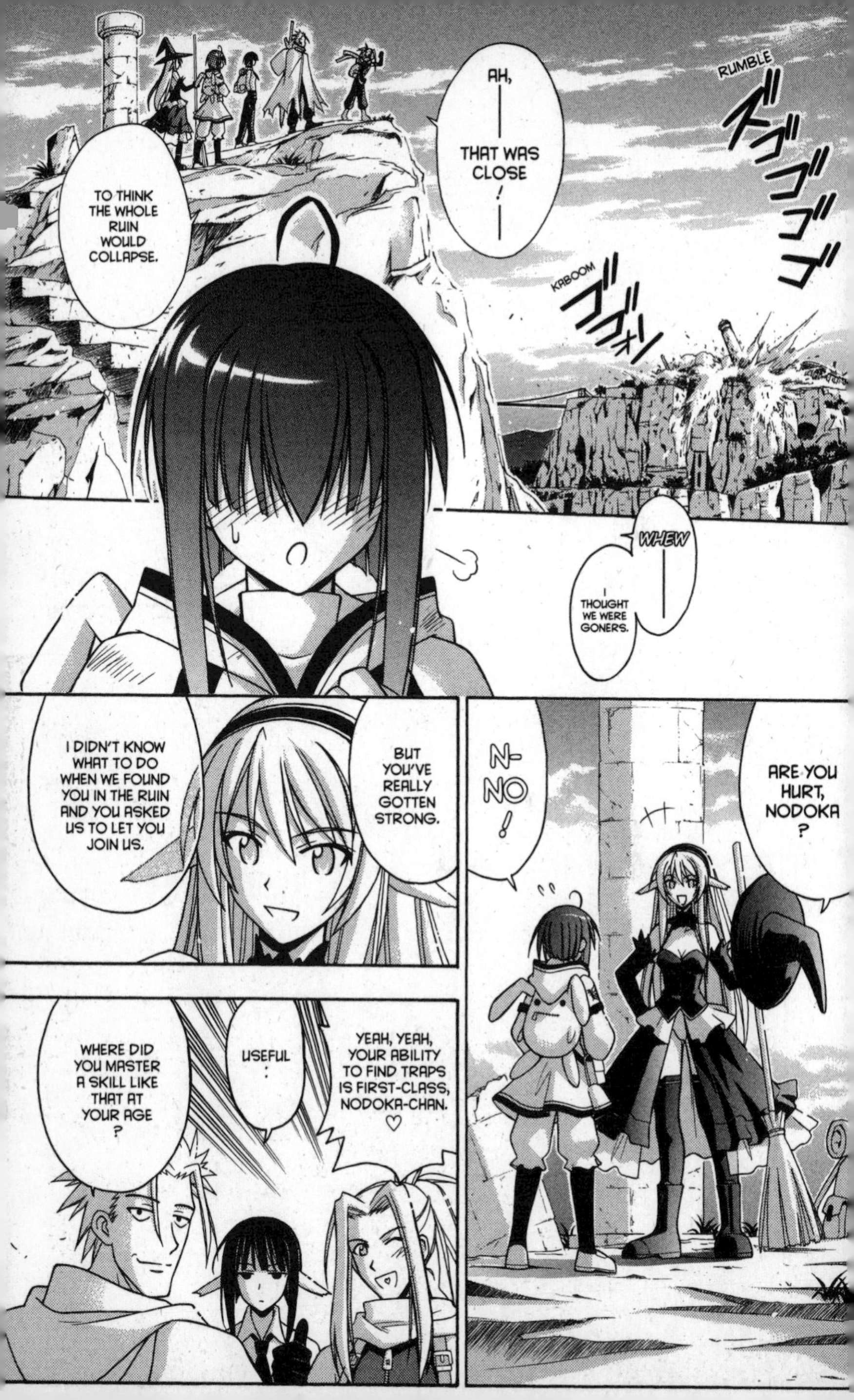
RUMBLE
AH, — THAT WAS CLOSE! —
KABOOM
TO THINK THE WHOLE RUIN WOULD COLLAPSE.
WHEW
— I THOUGHT WE WERE GONERS.
ARE YOU HURT, NODOKA?
N-NO!
BUT YOU'VE REALLY GOTTEN STRONG.
I DIDN'T KNOW WHAT TO DO WHEN WE FOUND YOU IN THE RUIN AND YOU ASKED US TO LET YOU JOIN US.
YEAH, YEAH, YOUR ABILITY TO FIND TRAPS IS FIRST-CLASS, NODOKA-CHAN. ♡
USEFUL:
WHERE DID YOU MASTER A SKILL LIKE THAT AT YOUR AGE?

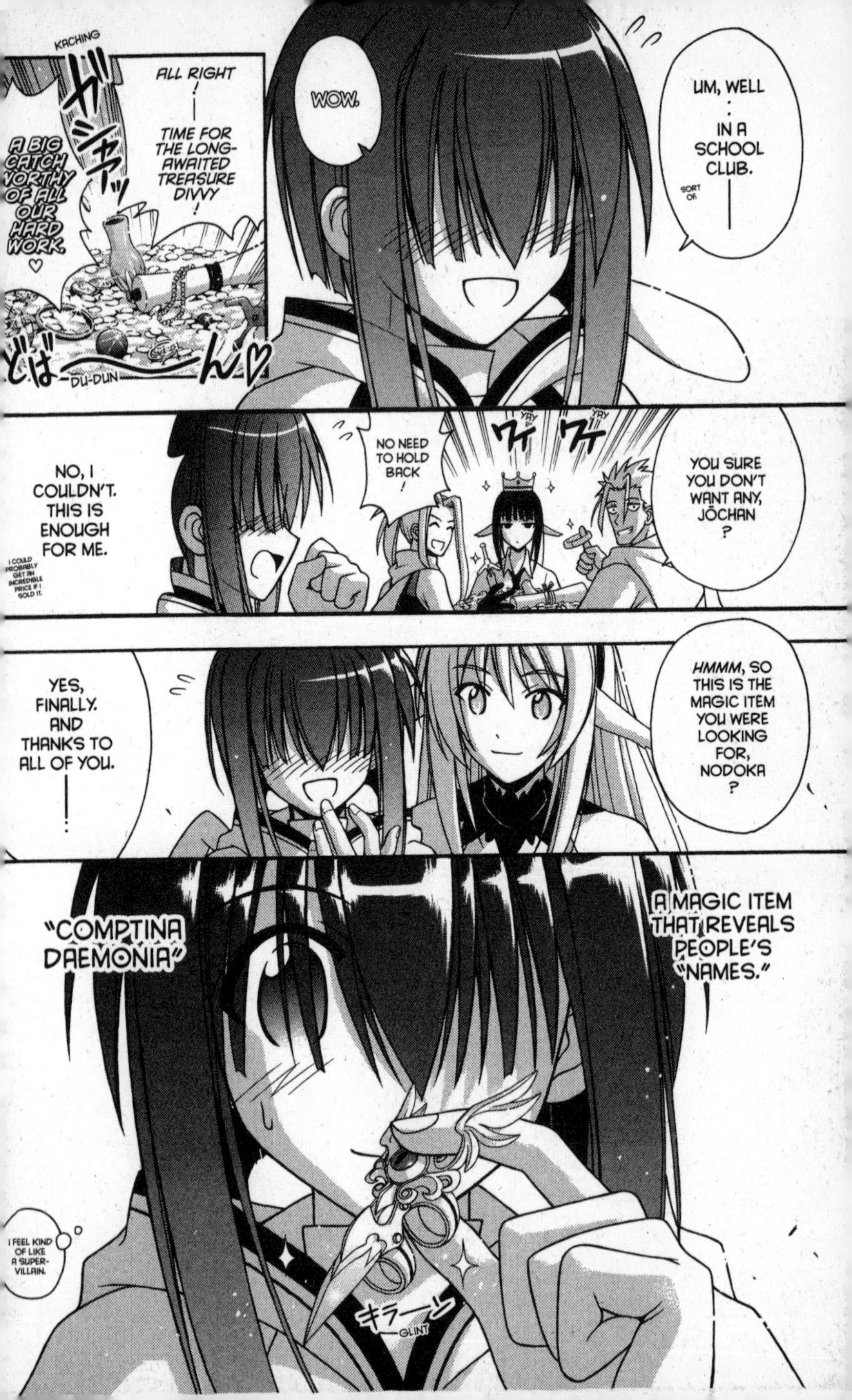
UM, WELL : IN A SCHOOL CLUB.
SORT OF.
WOW.
ALL RIGHT! TIME FOR THE LONG-AWAITED TREASURE DIVVY!
KACHING
A BIG CATCH WORTHY OF ALL OUR HARD WORK. ♥
DU-DUN
YOU SURE YOU DON'T WANT ANY, JŌCHAN?
YAY
YAY
NO NEED TO HOLD BACK!
NO, I COULDN'T. THIS IS ENOUGH FOR ME.
I COULD PROBABLY GET AN INCREDIBLE PRICE IF I SOLD IT.
HMMM, SO THIS IS THE MAGIC ITEM YOU WERE LOOKING FOR, NODOKA?
YES, FINALLY. AND THANKS TO ALL OF YOU—!
A MAGIC ITEM THAT REVEALS PEOPLE'S "NAMES."
"COMPTINA DAEMONIA"
I FEEL KIND OF LIKE A SUPER-VILLAIN.
GLINT

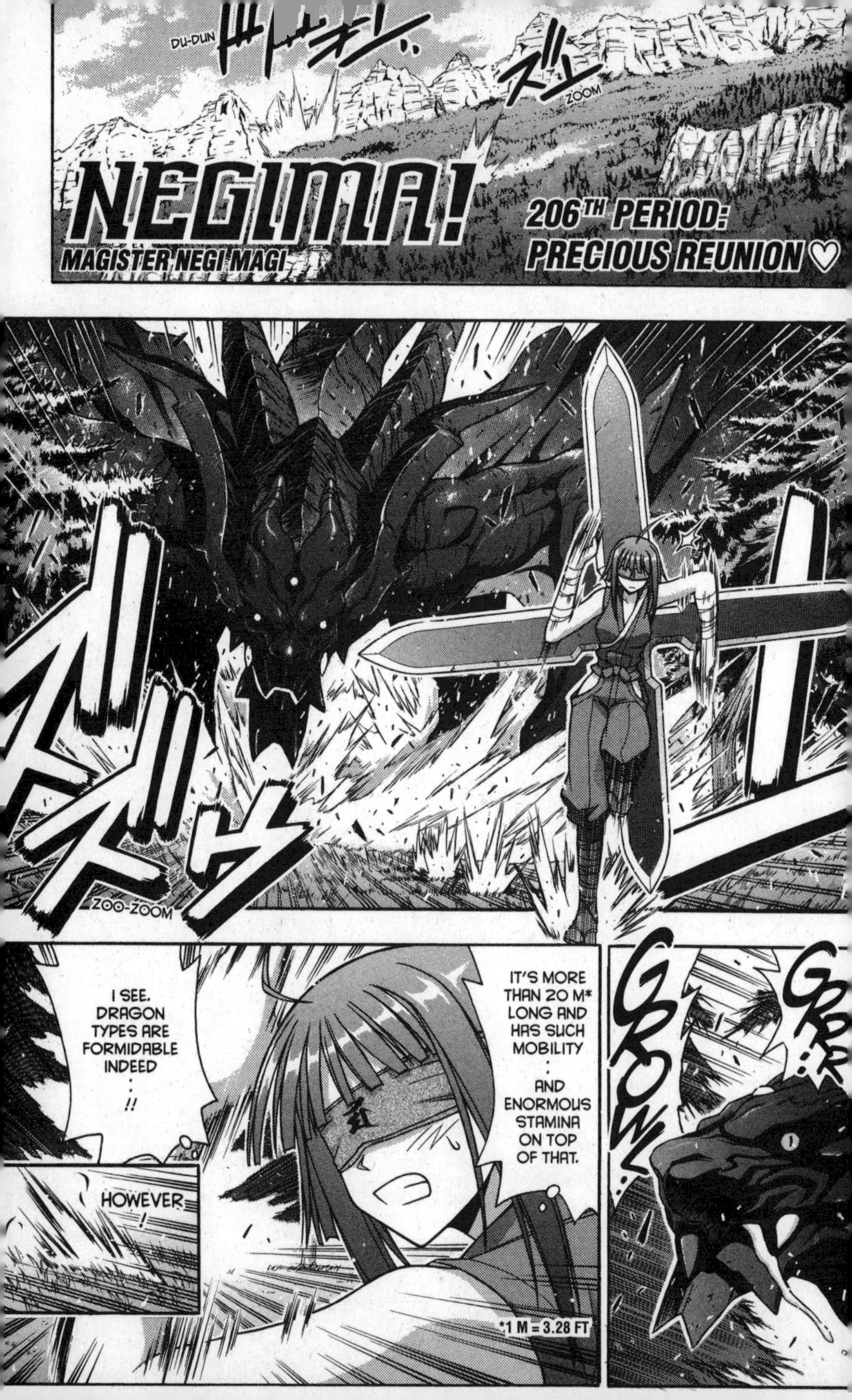

DU-DUN
ZOOM
NEGIMA!
MAGISTER NEGI MAGI
206TH PERIOD: PRECIOUS REUNION ♡
ZOO-ZOOM
GRRR...
GROWL...
IT'S MORE THAN 20 M* LONG AND HAS SUCH MOBILITY... AND ENORMOUS STAMINA ON TOP OF THAT.
I SEE. DRAGON TYPES ARE FORMIDABLE INDEED...!!
HOWEVER!
*1 M = 3.28 FT

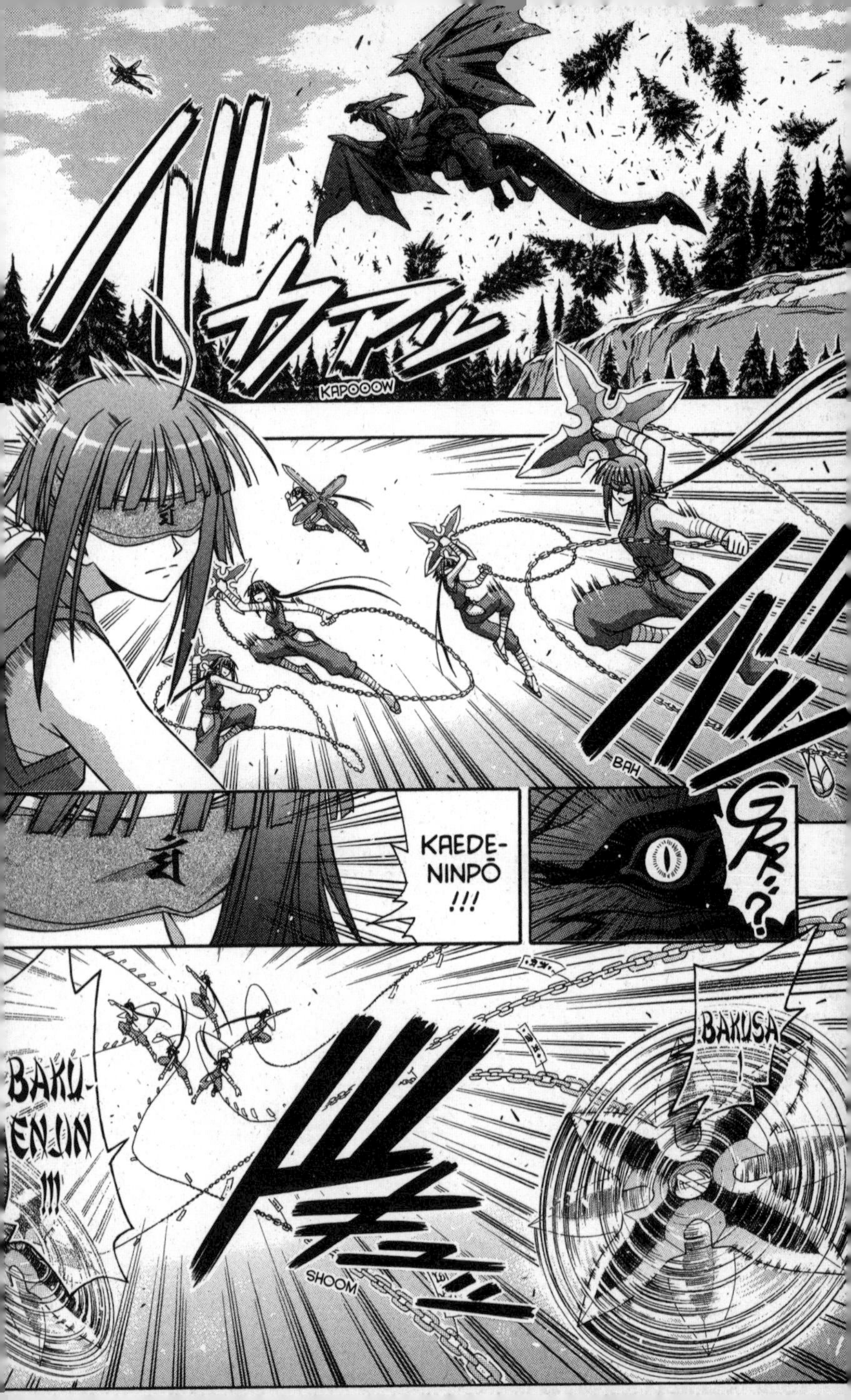
KAPOOOW
BAH
GR...?
KAEDE-NINPŌ
!!!
BAKUSA
BAKU-ENJIN
!!!
SHOOM

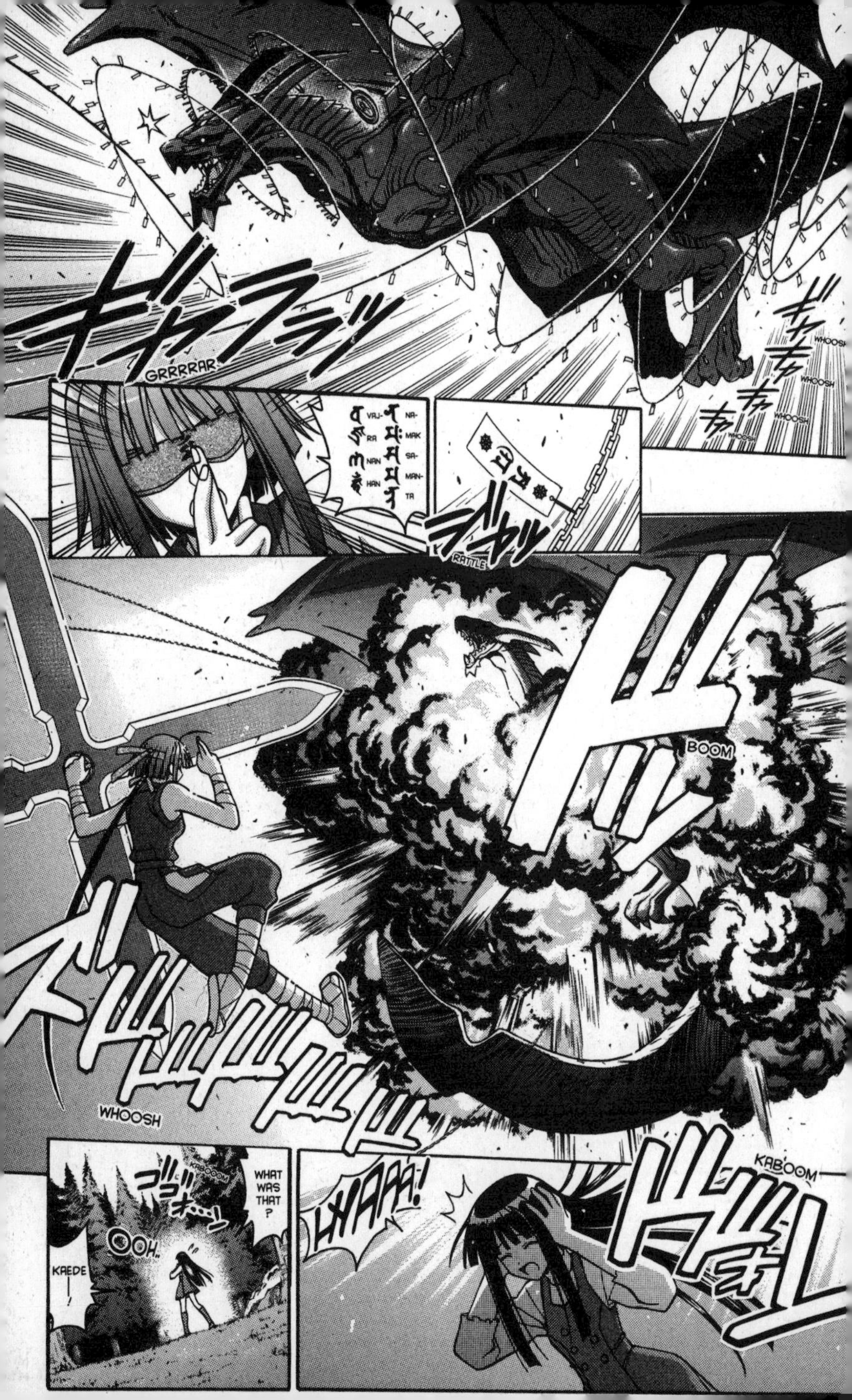
GRRRRAR
WHOOSH
WHOOSH
WHOOSH
WHOOSH
RATTLE
NA-MAK SA-MAN-TA
VAJ-RA NAN HAN
BOOM
WHOOSH
KABOOM
WHAAA!
KABOOOM
WHAT WAS THAT?
OOH..
KAEDE!

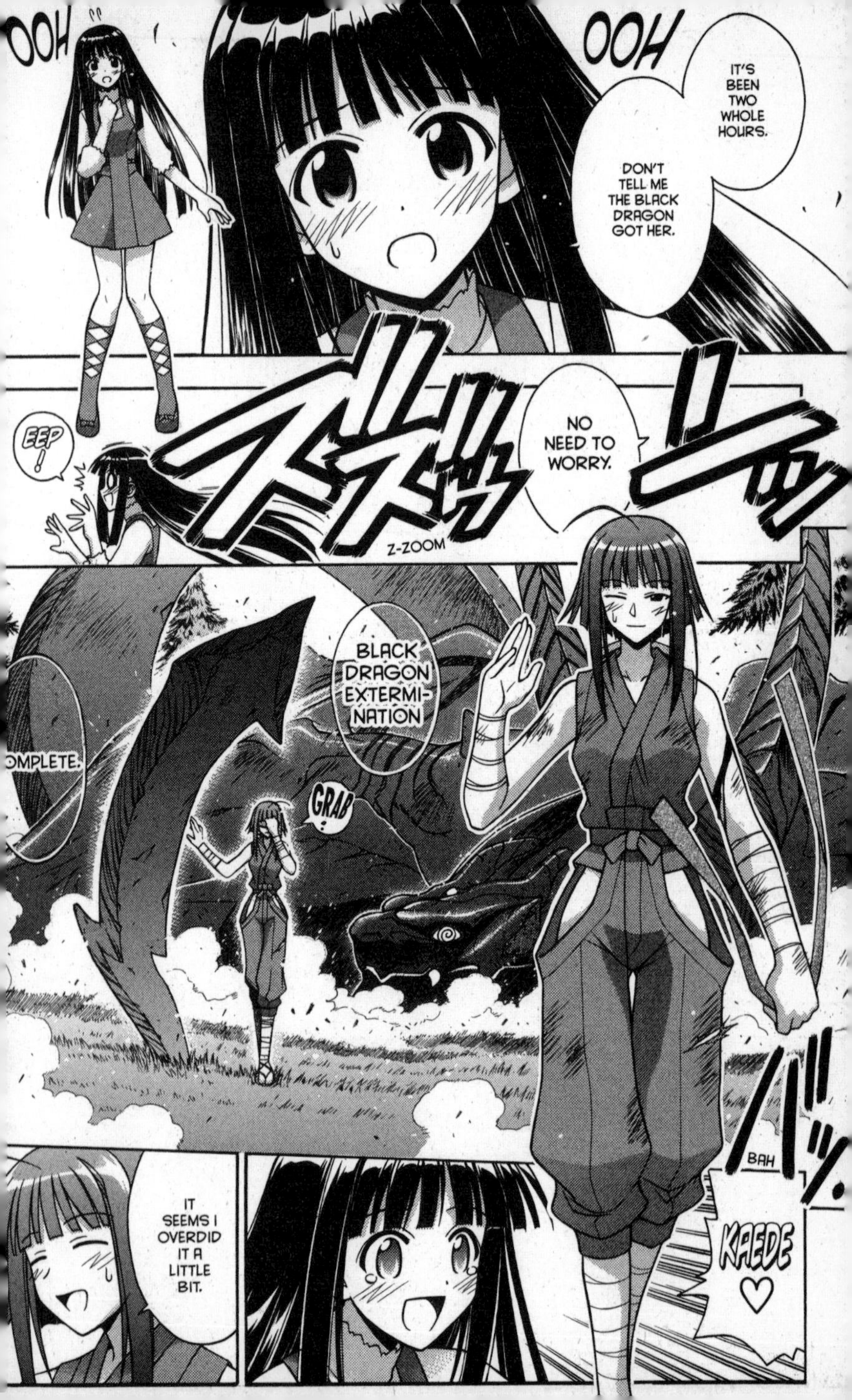
OOH
IT'S BEEN TWO WHOLE HOURS.
DON'T TELL ME THE BLACK DRAGON GOT HER.
OOH
NO NEED TO WORRY.
Z-ZOOM
EEP!
BLACK DRAGON EXTERMI-NATION
OMPLETE.
GRAB
BAH
KAEDE ♥
IT SEEMS I OVERDID IT A LITTLE BIT.

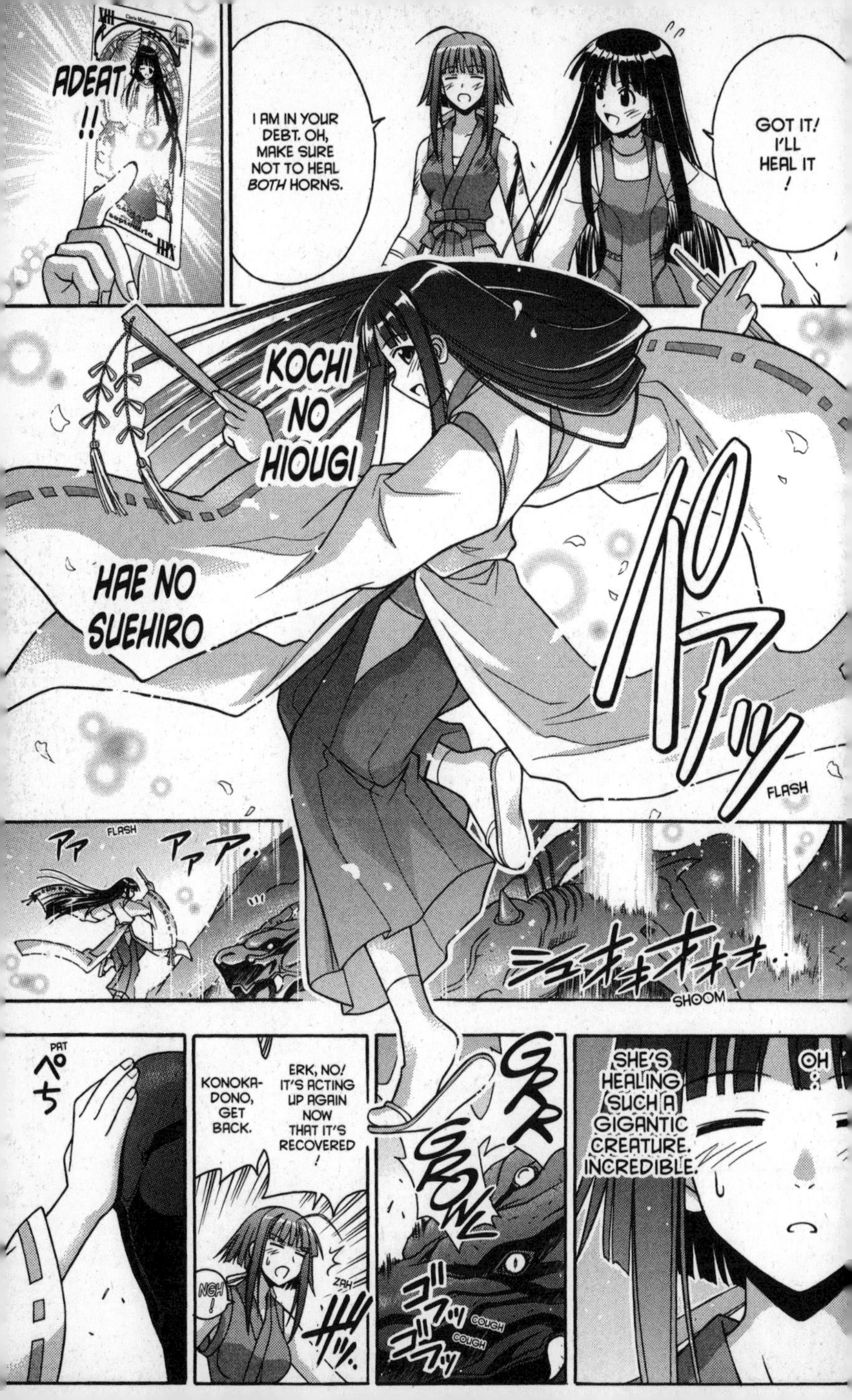
GOT IT! I'LL HEAL IT!
I AM IN YOUR DEBT. OH, MAKE SURE NOT TO HEAL BOTH HORNS.
ADEAT!!
FLASH
KOCHI NO HIOUGI
HAE NO SUEHIRO
SHOOM
FLASH
OH...
SHE'S HEALING SUCH A GIGANTIC CREATURE. INCREDIBLE.
GRR
GROWL
COUGH
COUGH
ERK, NO! IT'S ACTING UP AGAIN NOW THAT IT'S RECOVERED!
KONOKA-DONO, GET BACK.
NGH!
ZAH
PAT

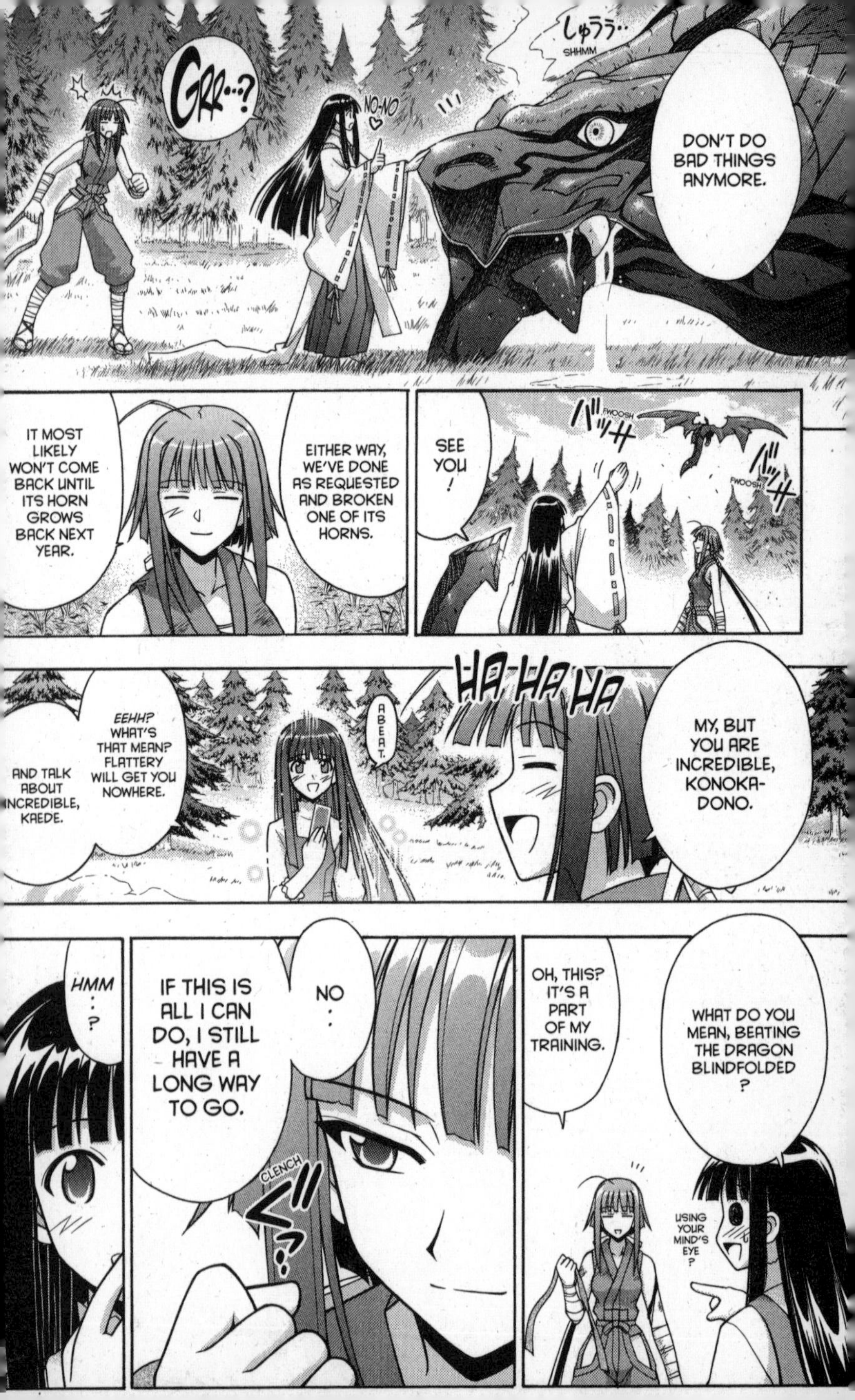
しゅララ..
SHHMM
DON'T DO BAD THINGS ANYMORE.
NO-NO
GRR...?
FWOOSH
FWOOSH
SEE YOU!
EITHER WAY, WE'VE DONE AS REQUESTED AND BROKEN ONE OF ITS HORNS.
IT MOST LIKELY WON'T COME BACK UNTIL ITS HORN GROWS BACK NEXT YEAR.
MY, BUT YOU ARE INCREDIBLE, KONOKA-DONO.
HA HA HA
A BEAT.
EEHH? WHAT'S THAT MEAN? FLATTERY WILL GET YOU NOWHERE.
AND TALK ABOUT INCREDIBLE, KAEDE.
WHAT DO YOU MEAN, BEATING THE DRAGON BLINDFOLDED?
USING YOUR MIND'S EYE?
OH, THIS? IT'S A PART OF MY TRAINING.
NO...
IF THIS IS ALL I CAN DO, I STILL HAVE A LONG WAY TO GO.
CLENCH
HMM...?

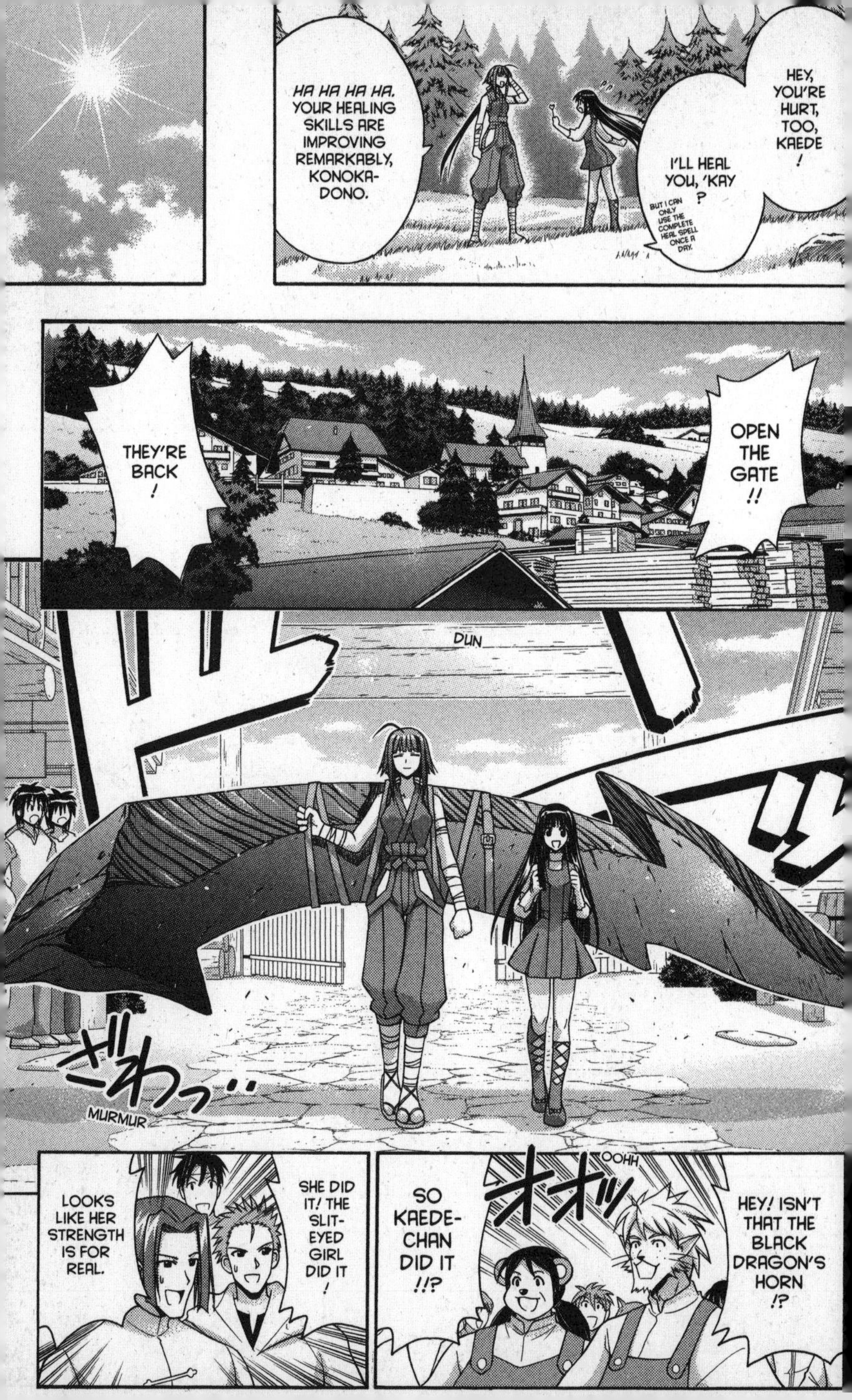
HEY, YOU'RE HURT, TOO, KAEDE!
I'LL HEAL YOU, 'KAY?
BUT I CAN ONLY USE THE COMPLETE HEAL SPELL ONCE A DAY.
HA HA HA HA. YOUR HEALING SKILLS ARE IMPROVING REMARKABLY, KONOKA-DONO.
OPEN THE GATE!!
THEY'RE BACK!
DUN
ざわっ…
MURMUR
HEY! ISN'T THAT THE BLACK DRAGON'S HORN!?
オオッ
OOHH
SO KAEDE-CHAN DID IT!!?
SHE DID IT! THE SLIT-EYED GIRL DID IT!
LOOKS LIKE HER STRENGTH IS FOR REAL.

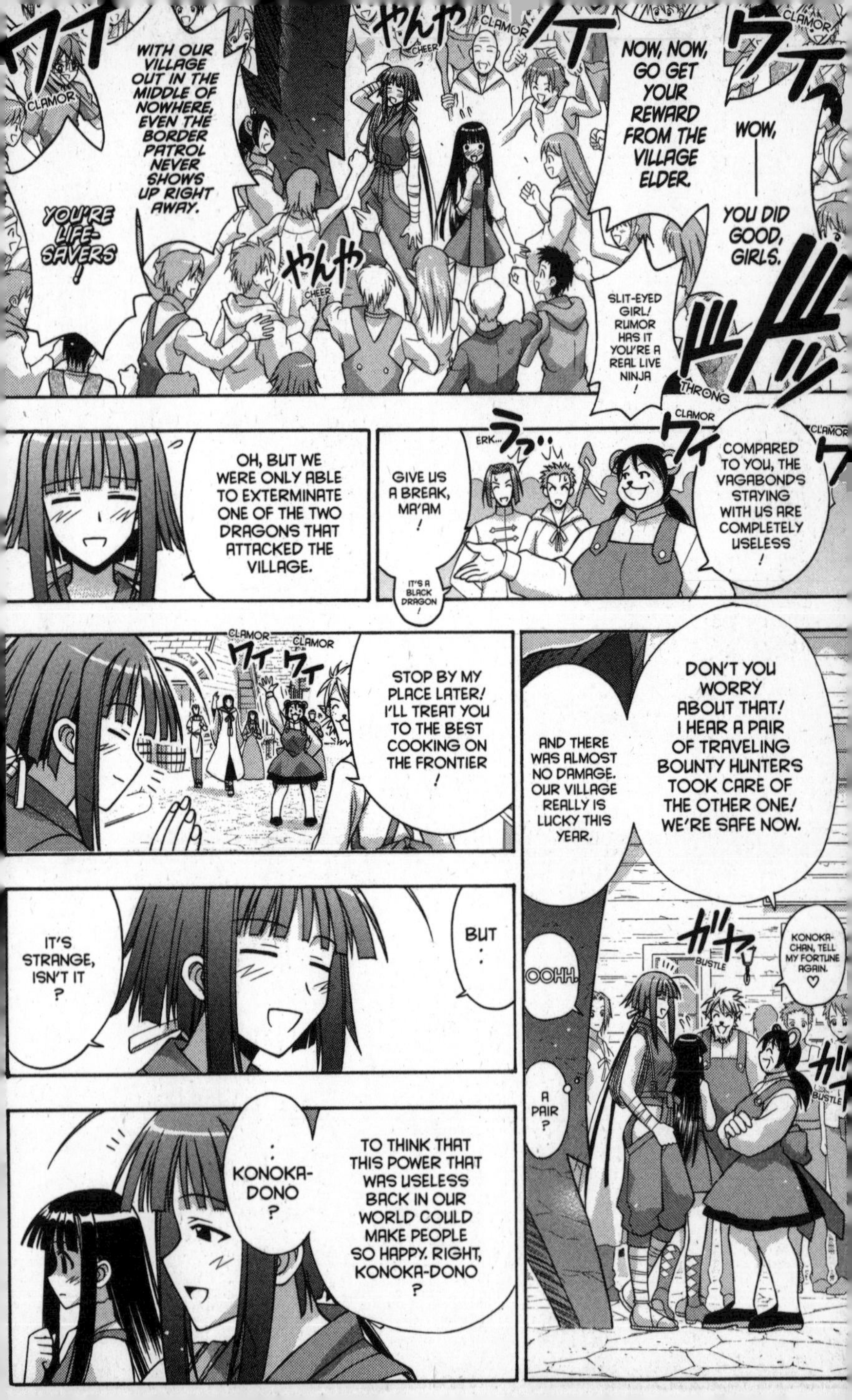
CLAMOR
NOW, NOW, GO GET YOUR REWARD FROM THE VILLAGE ELDER.
WOW, — YOU DID GOOD, GIRLS.
CLAMOR
やんや
CHEER
WITH OUR VILLAGE OUT IN THE MIDDLE OF NOWHERE, EVEN THE BORDER PATROL NEVER SHOWS UP RIGHT AWAY.
CLAMOR
YOU'RE LIFE-SAVERS!
SLIT-EYED GIRL! RUMOR HAS IT YOU'RE A REAL LIVE NINJA!
THRONG
やんや
CHEER
CLAMOR
CLAMOR
COMPARED TO YOU, THE VAGABONDS STAYING WITH US ARE COMPLETELY USELESS!
ERK...
GIVE US A BREAK, MA'AM!
IT'S A BLACK DRAGON!
OH, BUT WE WERE ONLY ABLE TO EXTERMINATE ONE OF THE TWO DRAGONS THAT ATTACKED THE VILLAGE.
DON'T YOU WORRY ABOUT THAT! I HEAR A PAIR OF TRAVELING BOUNTY HUNTERS TOOK CARE OF THE OTHER ONE! WE'RE SAFE NOW.
AND THERE WAS ALMOST NO DAMAGE. OUR VILLAGE REALLY IS LUCKY THIS YEAR.
BUSTLE
KONOKA-CHAN, TELL MY FORTUNE AGAIN. ♡
OOHH.
BUSTLE
A PAIR?
CLAMOR
CLAMOR
STOP BY MY PLACE LATER! I'LL TREAT YOU TO THE BEST COOKING ON THE FRONTIER!
BUT...
IT'S STRANGE, ISN'T IT?
TO THINK THAT THIS POWER THAT WAS USELESS BACK IN OUR WORLD COULD MAKE PEOPLE SO HAPPY. RIGHT, KONOKA-DONO?
...KONOKA-DONO?

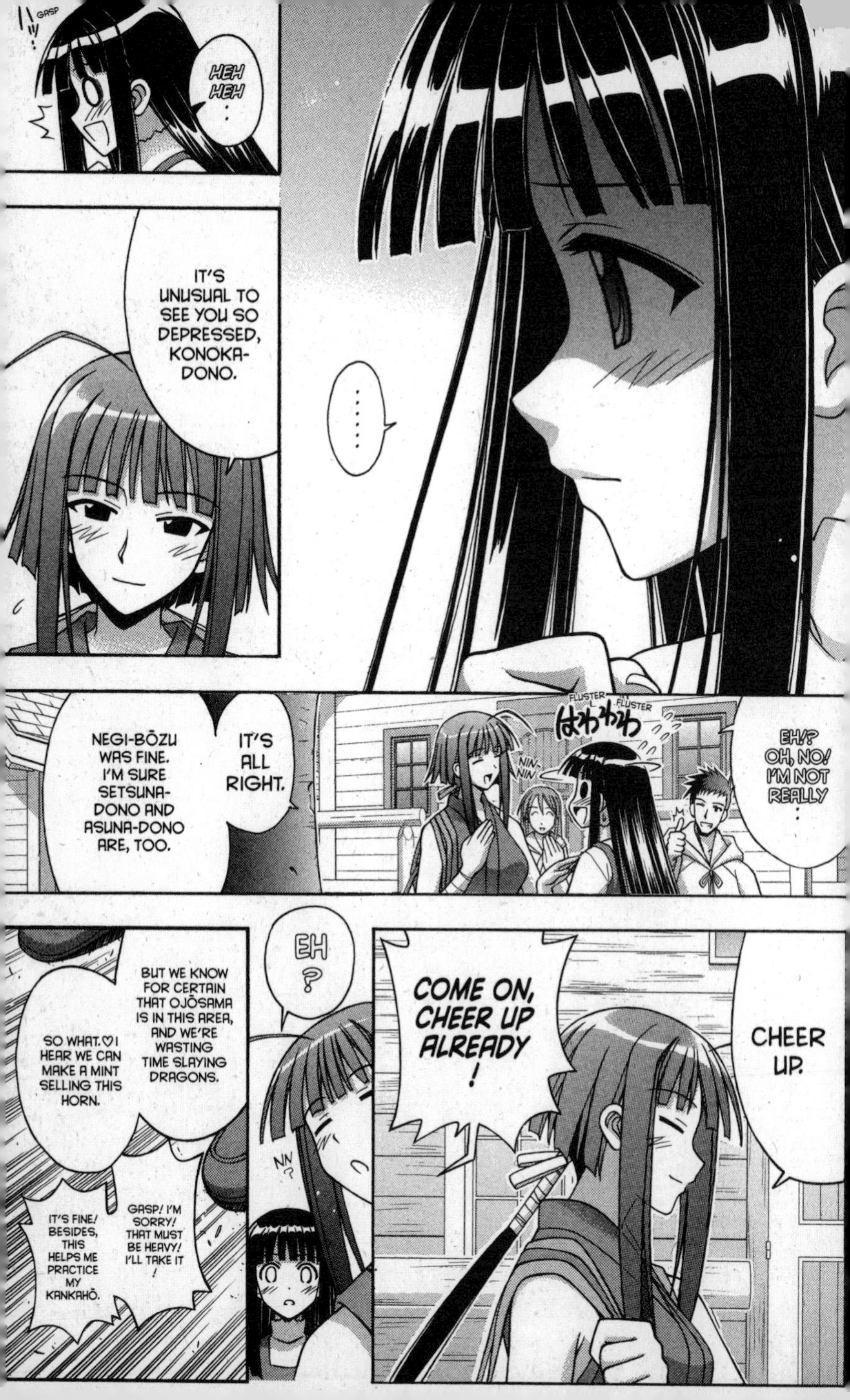
......
GASP
HEH HEH...
IT'S UNUSUAL TO SEE YOU SO DEPRESSED, KONOKA-DONO.
EH!? OH, NO! I'M NOT REALLY...
FLUSTER FLUSTER
はわわわ
NIN-NIN
IT'S ALL RIGHT.
NEGI-BŌZU WAS FINE. I'M SURE SETSUNA-DONO AND ASUNA-DONO ARE, TOO.
CHEER UP.
COME ON, CHEER UP ALREADY!
EH?
NN?
BUT WE KNOW FOR CERTAIN THAT OJŌSAMA IS IN THIS AREA, AND WE'RE WASTING TIME SLAYING DRAGONS.
SO WHAT.♡ I HEAR WE CAN MAKE A MINT SELLING THIS HORN.
GASP! I'M SORRY! THAT MUST BE HEAVY! I'LL TAKE IT!
IT'S FINE! BESIDES, THIS HELPS ME PRACTICE MY KANKAHŌ.

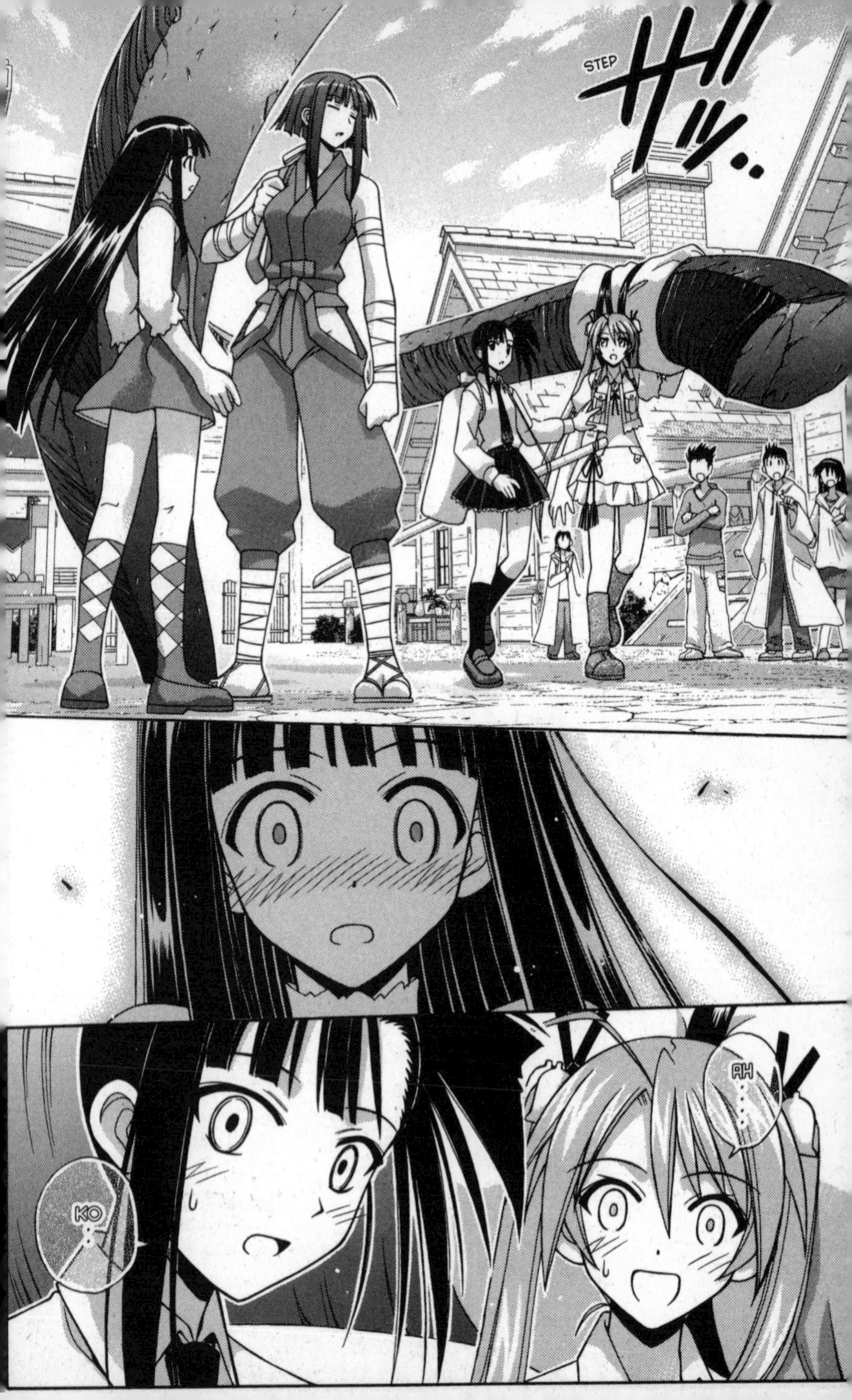
STEP
AH.......
KO..

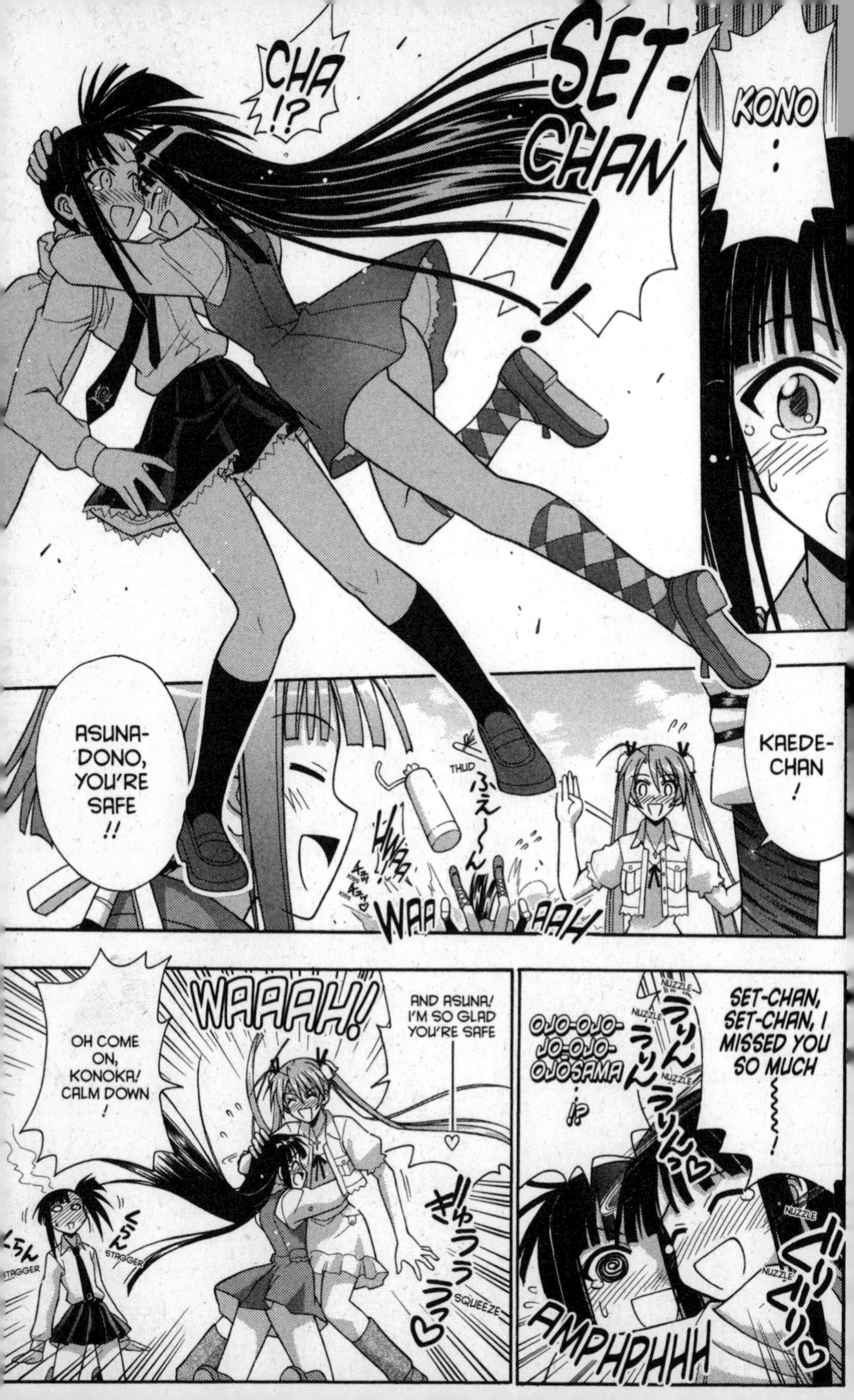

KONO : :
SET-CHAN!!
CHA !?
KAEDE-CHAN!
ASUNA-DONO, YOU'RE SAFE!!
THUD
ふえ〜ん
HWAA
WAA AAH
SET-CHAN, SET-CHAN, I MISSED YOU SO MUCH~~~!
OJO-OJO-JO-OJO-OJOSAMA!?
NUZZLE
NUZZLE
NUZZLE
NUZZLE
NUZZLE
AMPHPHHH
WAAAH!
AND ASUNA! I'M SO GLAD YOU'RE SAFE♡
SQUEEZE
OH COME ON, KONOKA! CALM DOWN!
STAGGER
STAGGER

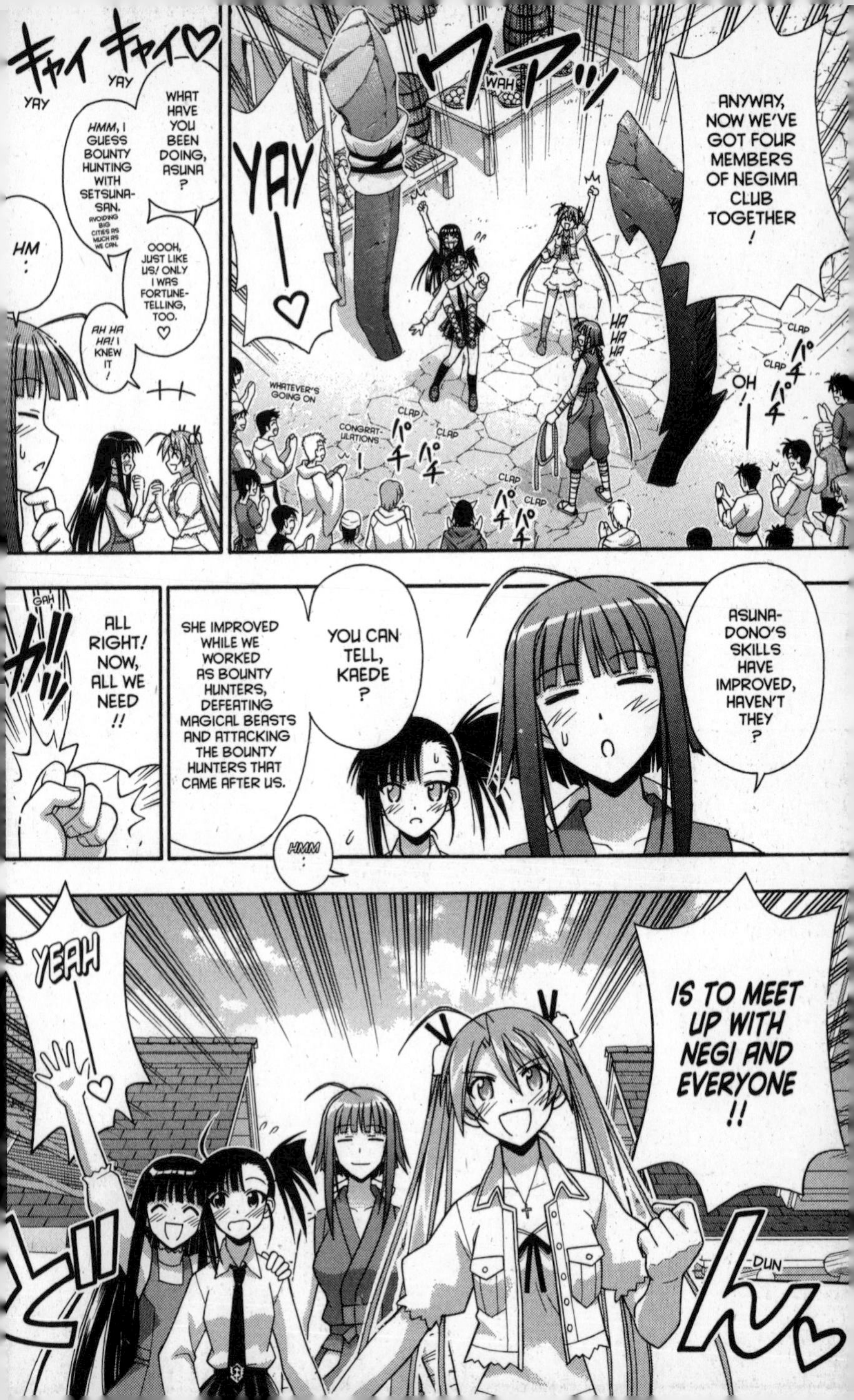
ANYWAY, NOW WE'VE GOT FOUR MEMBERS OF NEGIMA CLUB TOGETHER!
ワァッ
WAH
YAY! ♡
HA HA HA HA
CLAP パチ CLAP パチ
OH!
WHATEVER'S GOING ON!
CONGRATULATIONS!
CLAP パチ CLAP パチ
CLAP パチ CLAP パチ
キャイ キャイ♡
YAY YAY
WHAT HAVE YOU BEEN DOING, ASUNA?
HMM, I GUESS BOUNTY HUNTING WITH SETSUNA-SAN.
AVOIDING BIG CITIES AS MUCH AS WE CAN.
OOOH, JUST LIKE US! ONLY I WAS FORTUNE-TELLING, TOO. ♡
HM...
AH HA HA! I KNEW IT!
ASUNA-DONO'S SKILLS HAVE IMPROVED, HAVEN'T THEY?
YOU CAN TELL, KAEDE?
SHE IMPROVED WHILE WE WORKED AS BOUNTY HUNTERS, DEFEATING MAGICAL BEASTS AND ATTACKING THE BOUNTY HUNTERS THAT CAME AFTER US.
HMM...
ガッ
GAH
ALL RIGHT! NOW, ALL WE NEED!!
IS TO MEET UP WITH NEGI AND EVERYONE!!
YEAH ♡
-DUN

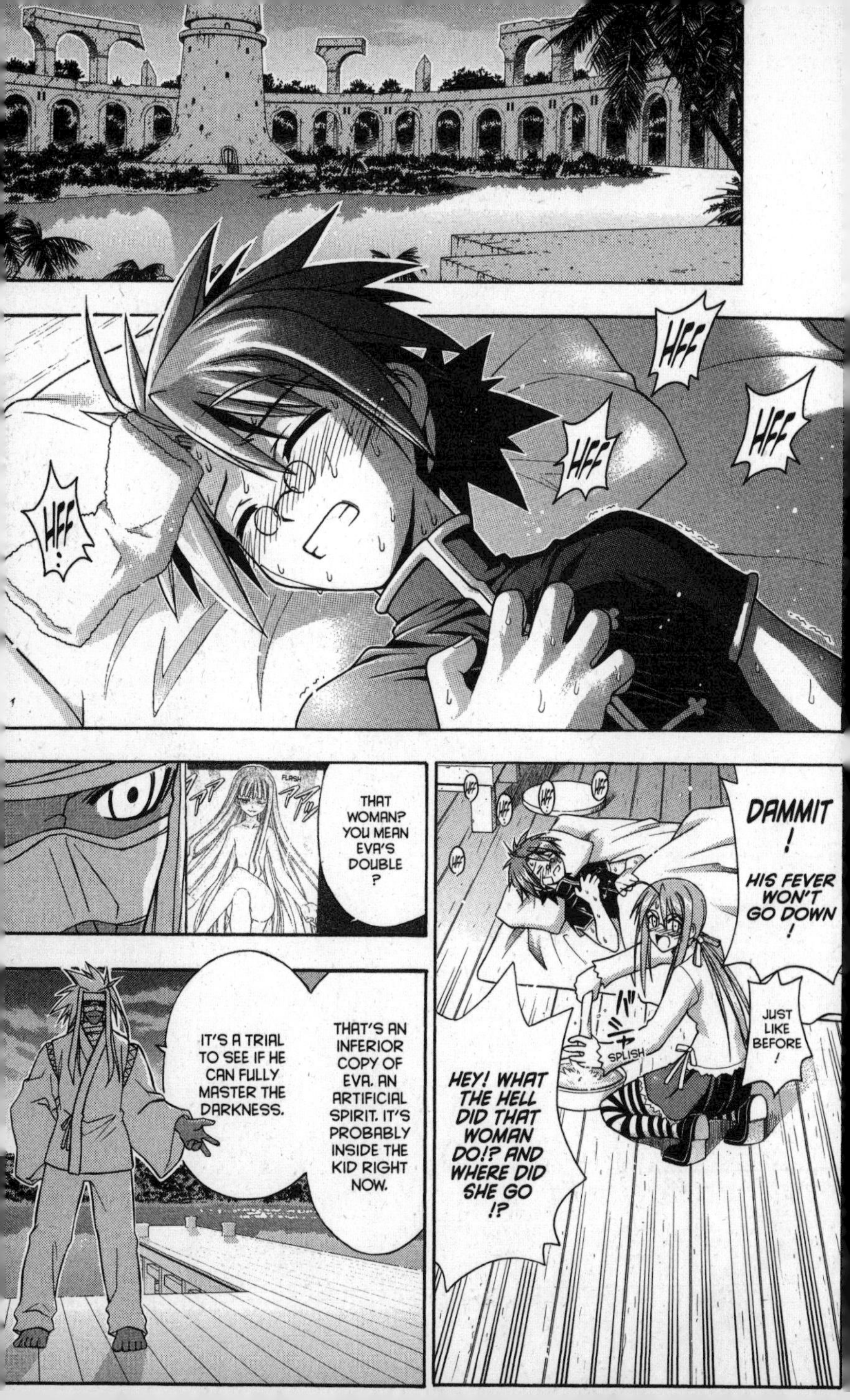

HFF
HFF
HFF
HFF
HFF
HFF
HFF
HFF
HFF
DAMMIT!
HIS FEVER WON'T GO DOWN!
JUST LIKE BEFORE!
SPLISH
HEY! WHAT THE HELL DID THAT WOMAN DO!? AND WHERE DID SHE GO!?
FLASH
THAT WOMAN? YOU MEAN EVA'S DOUBLE?
THAT'S AN INFERIOR COPY OF EVA. AN ARTIFICIAL SPIRIT. IT'S PROBABLY INSIDE THE KID RIGHT NOW.
IT'S A TRIAL TO SEE IF HE CAN FULLY MASTER THE DARKNESS.

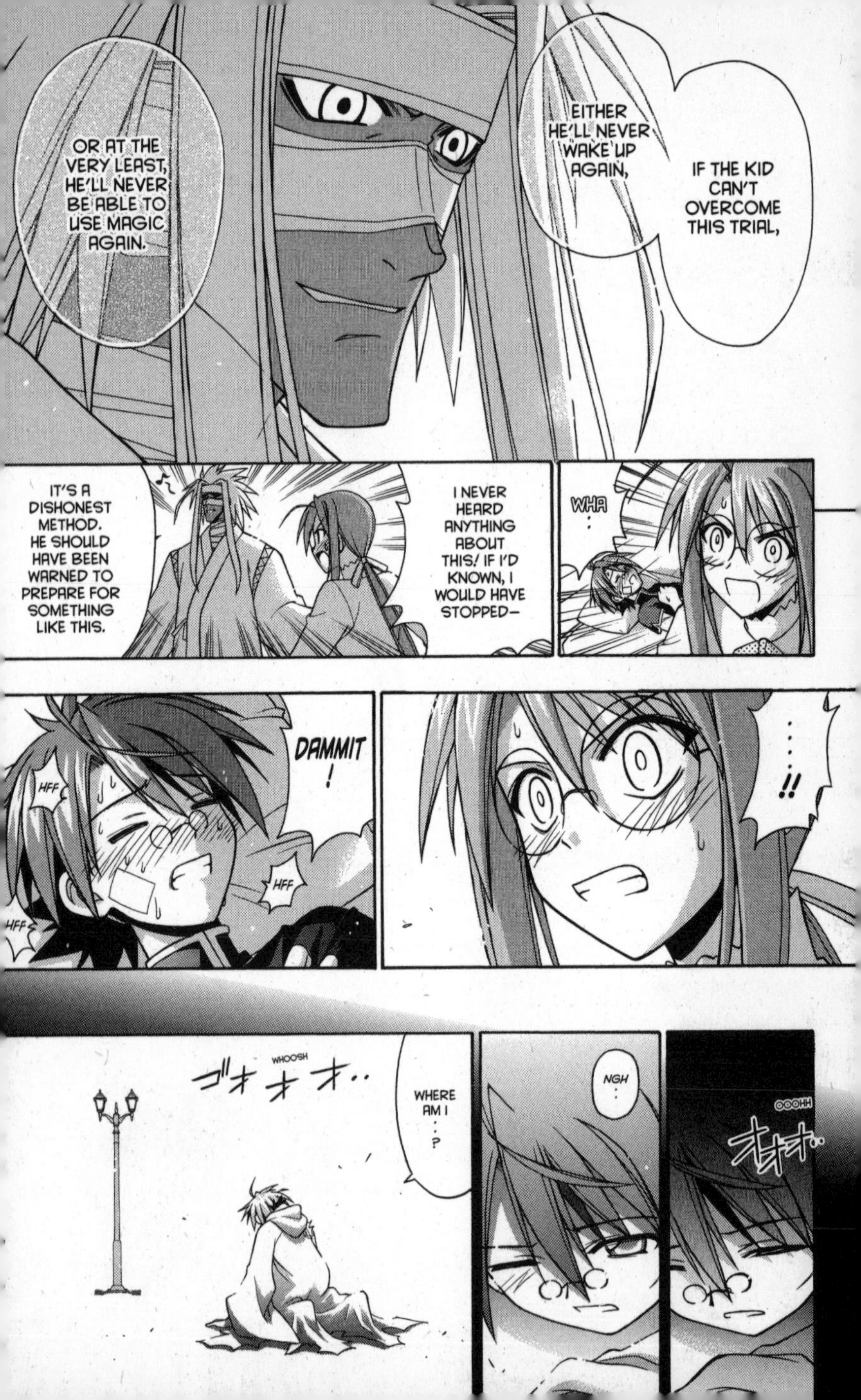
IF THE KID CAN'T OVERCOME THIS TRIAL,
EITHER HE'LL NEVER WAKE UP AGAIN,
OR AT THE VERY LEAST, HE'LL NEVER BE ABLE TO USE MAGIC AGAIN.
WHA...
I NEVER HEARD ANYTHING ABOUT THIS! IF I'D KNOWN, I WOULD HAVE STOPPED—
IT'S A DISHONEST METHOD. HE SHOULD HAVE BEEN WARNED TO PREPARE FOR SOMETHING LIKE THIS.
.....!!
DAMMIT!
HFF
HFF
HFF
OOOHH
オオオ..
NGH...
WHERE AM I...?
WHOOSH
ゴオオオ..

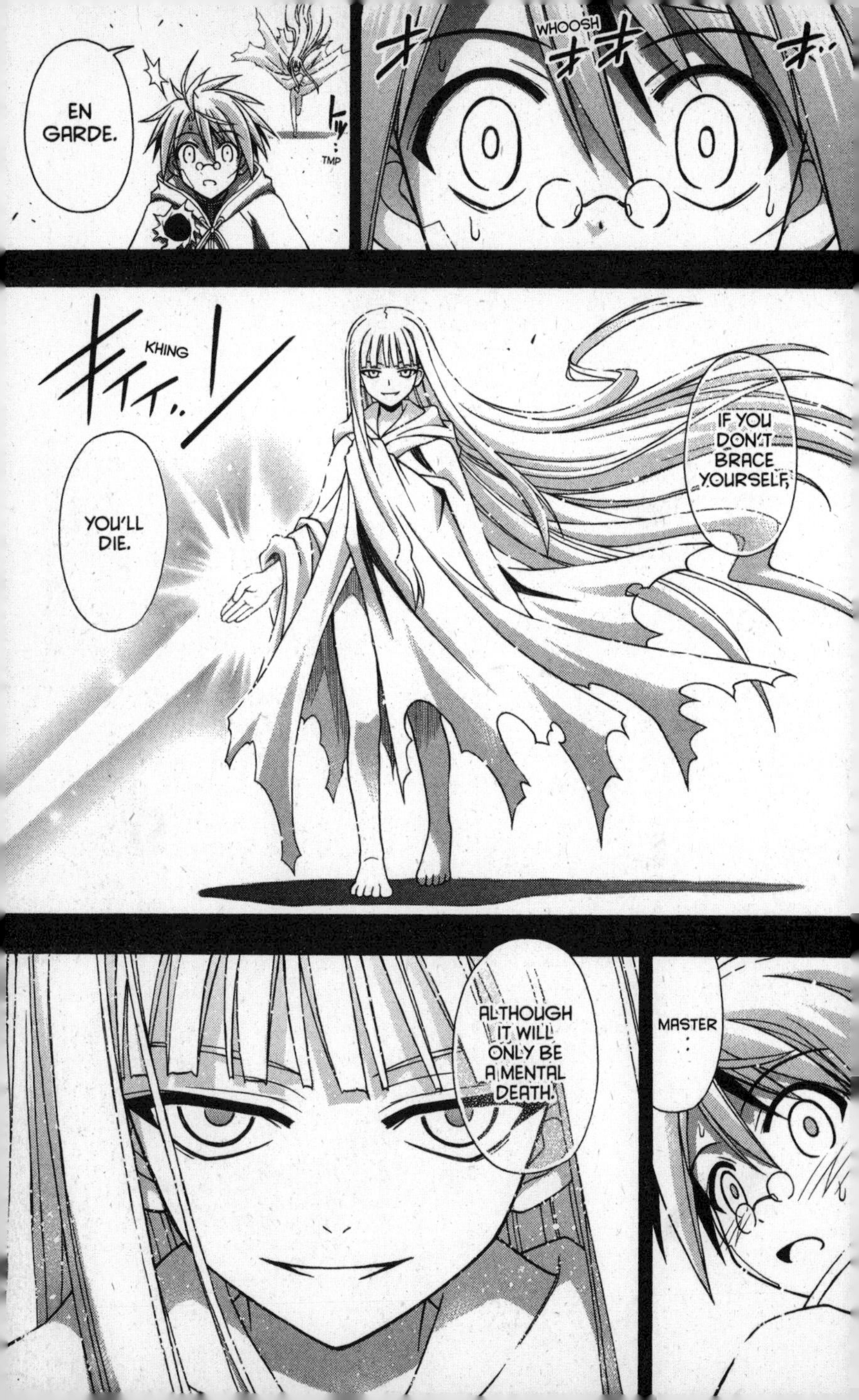
WHOOSH
EN GARDE.
TMP
KHING
IF YOU DON'T BRACE YOURSELF,
YOU'LL DIE.
MASTER . . .
ALTHOUGH IT WILL ONLY BE A MENTAL DEATH.

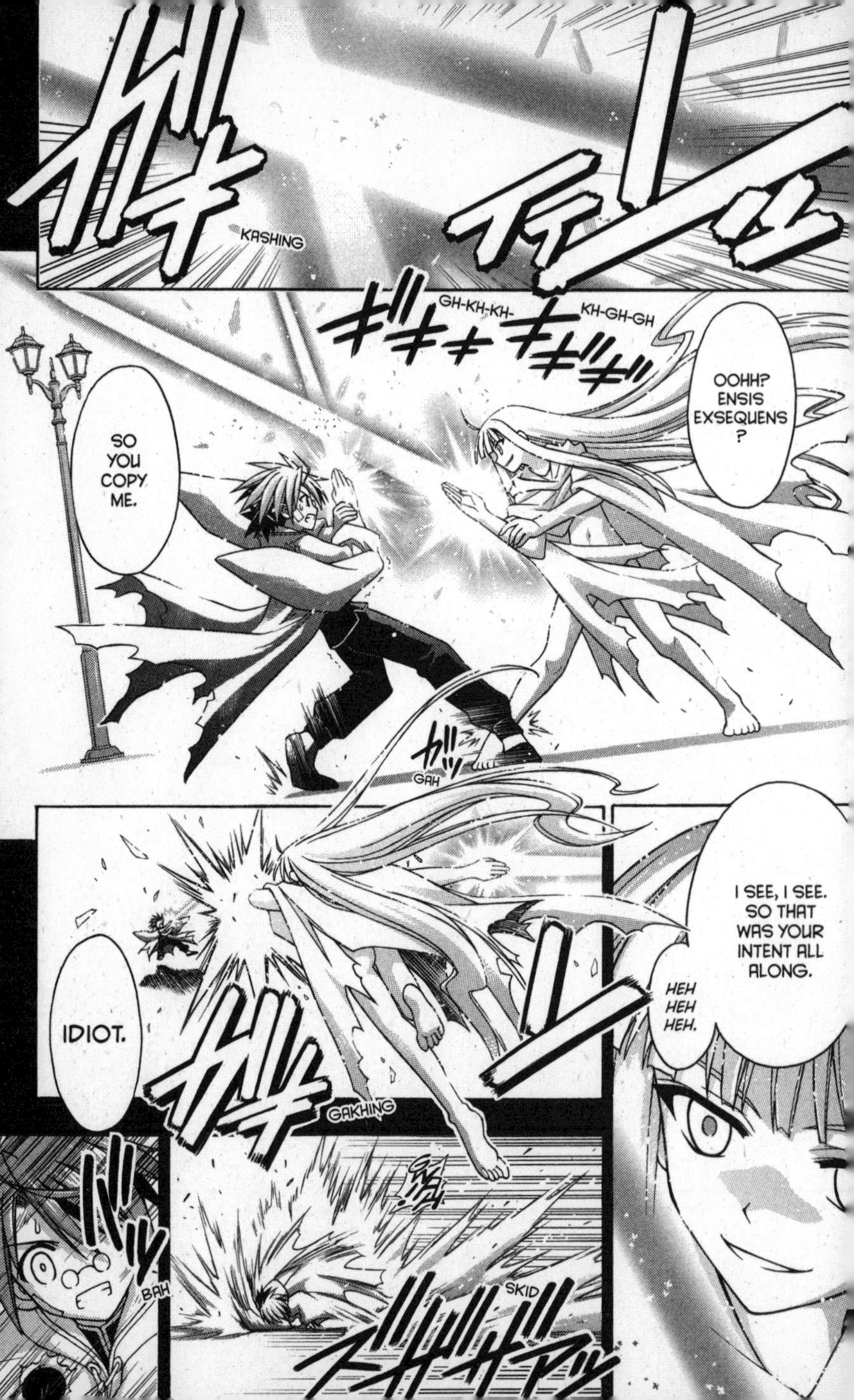
KASHING
KH-GH-GH
GH-KH-KH-
OOHH? ENSIS EXSEQUENS ?
SO YOU COPY ME.
GAH
I SEE, I SEE. SO THAT WAS YOUR INTENT ALL ALONG.
HEH HEH HEH.
IDIOT.
GAKHING
SKID
BAH

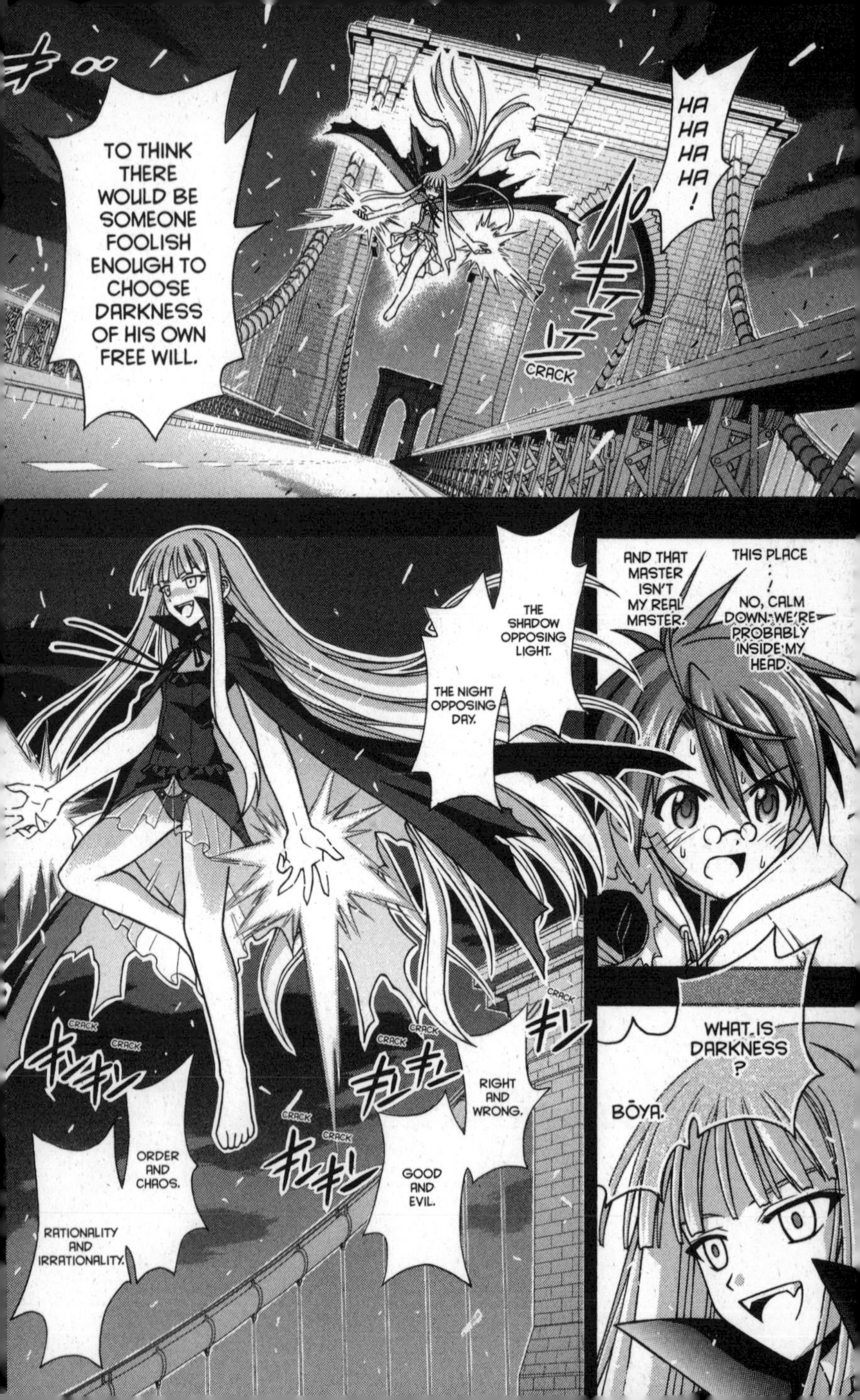
HA HA HA HA!
CRACK
TO THINK THERE WOULD BE SOMEONE FOOLISH ENOUGH TO CHOOSE DARKNESS OF HIS OWN FREE WILL.
THIS PLACE...!
NO, CALM DOWN. WE'RE PROBABLY INSIDE MY HEAD.
AND THAT MASTER ISN'T MY REAL MASTER.
WHAT IS DARKNESS?
BŌYA.
THE SHADOW OPPOSING LIGHT.
THE NIGHT OPPOSING DAY.
CRACK
RIGHT AND WRONG.
CRACK
CRACK
GOOD AND EVIL.
CRACK
CRACK
CRACK
CRACK
ORDER AND CHAOS.
RATIONALITY AND IRRATIONALITY.

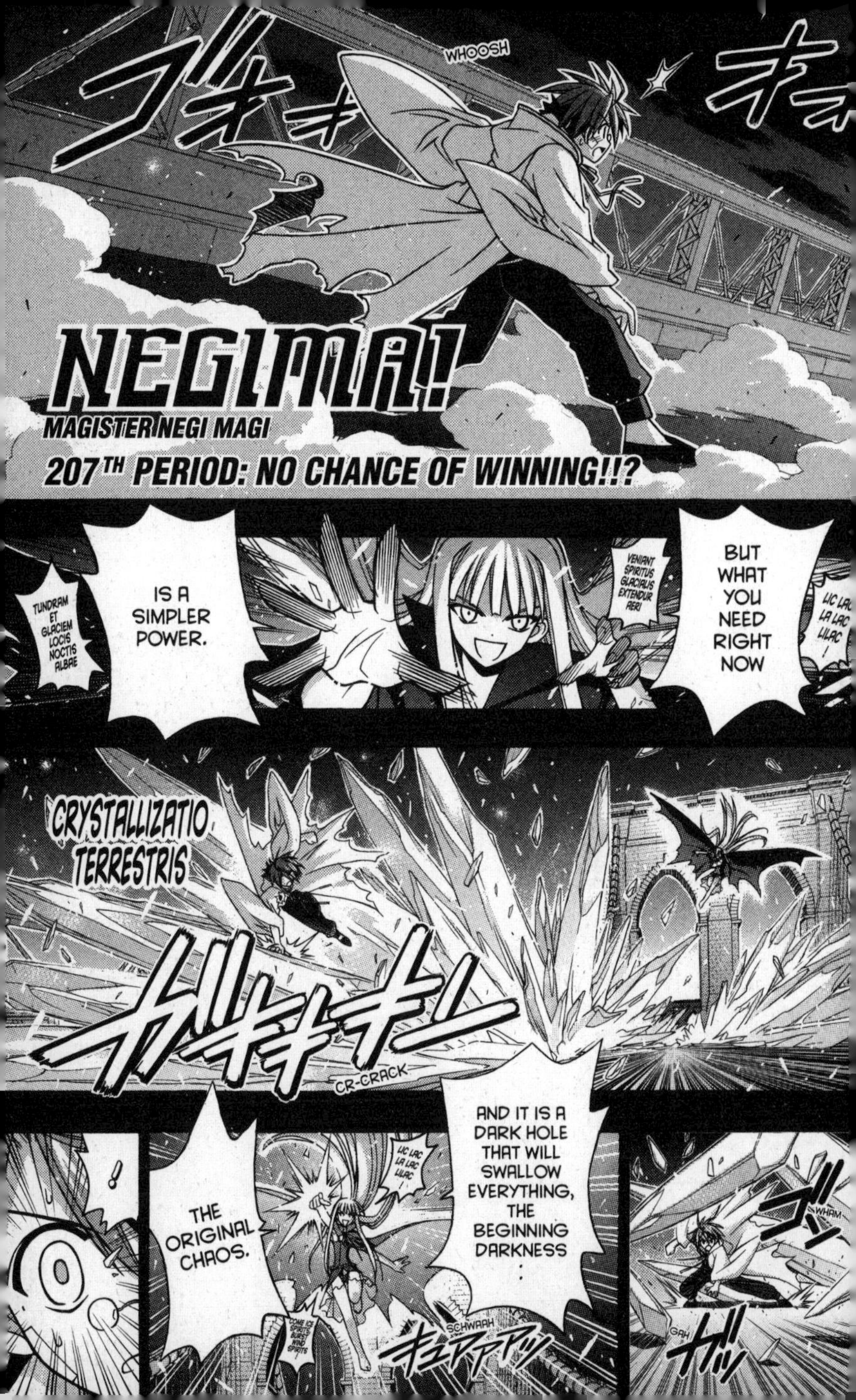
WHOOSH
NEGIMA!
MAGISTER NEGI MAGI
207TH PERIOD: NO CHANCE OF WINNING!!?
LIC LAC LA LAC LILAC!
BUT WHAT YOU NEED RIGHT NOW
VENIANT SPIRITUS GLACIALIS EXTENDUR AERI
IS A SIMPLER POWER.
TUNDRAM ET GLACIEM LOCIS NOCTIS ALBAE
CRYSTALLIZATIO TERRESTRIS
CR-CRACK
WHAM
GAH
AND IT IS A DARK HOLE THAT WILL SWALLOW EVERYTHING, THE BEGINNING DARKNESS
LIC LAC LA LAC LILAC!
THE ORIGINAL CHAOS.
COME ICE SPIRITS AND WIND SPIRITS
SCHWAAH
!

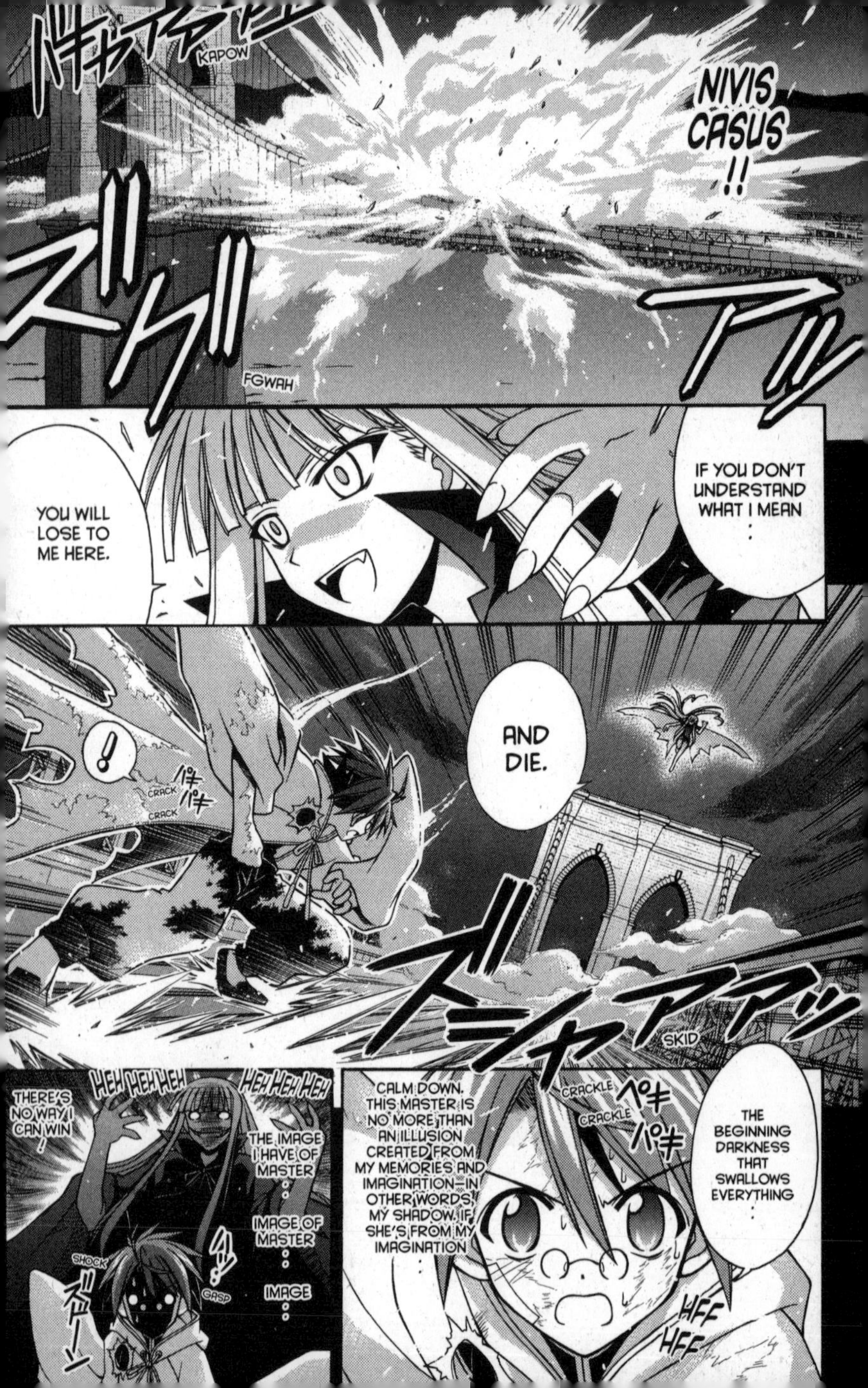
NIVIS CASUS !!
KAPOW
FGWAH
IF YOU DON'T UNDERSTAND WHAT I MEAN :
YOU WILL LOSE TO ME HERE.
AND DIE.
!
CRACK
CRACK
SKID
THE BEGINNING DARKNESS THAT SWALLOWS EVERYTHING :
CRACKLE
CRACKLE
CALM DOWN. THIS MASTER IS NO MORE THAN AN ILLUSION CREATED FROM MY MEMORIES AND IMAGINATION—IN OTHER WORDS, MY SHADOW. IF SHE'S FROM MY IMAGINATION
HFF
HFF
HEH HEH HEH
THE IMAGE I HAVE OF MASTER ...
IMAGE OF MASTER ...
IMAGE ...
HEH HEH HEH
THERE'S NO WAY I CAN WIN !
SHOCK
GASP

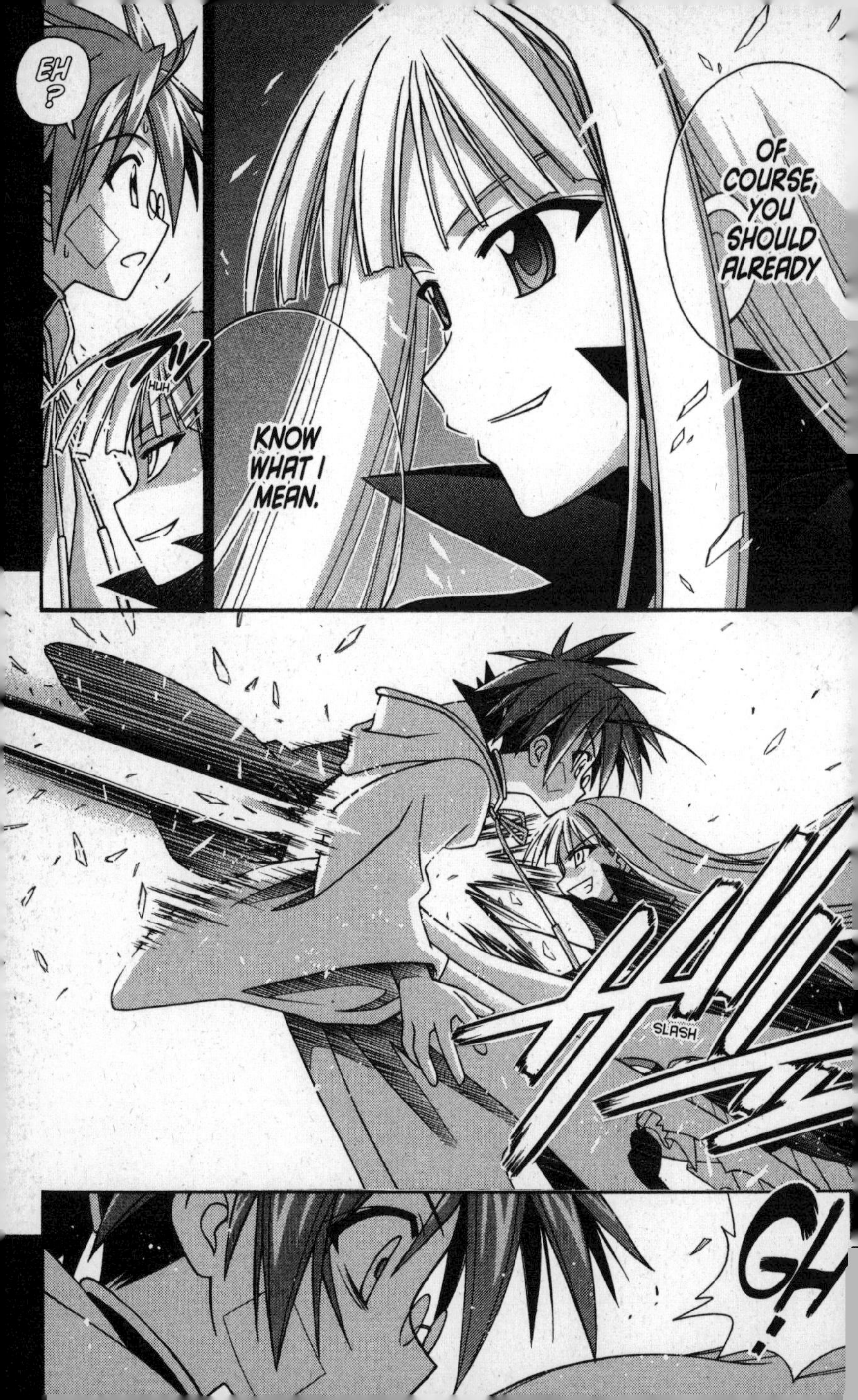
OF COURSE, YOU SHOULD ALREADY
KNOW WHAT I MEAN.
EH?
HUH
SLASH
GH

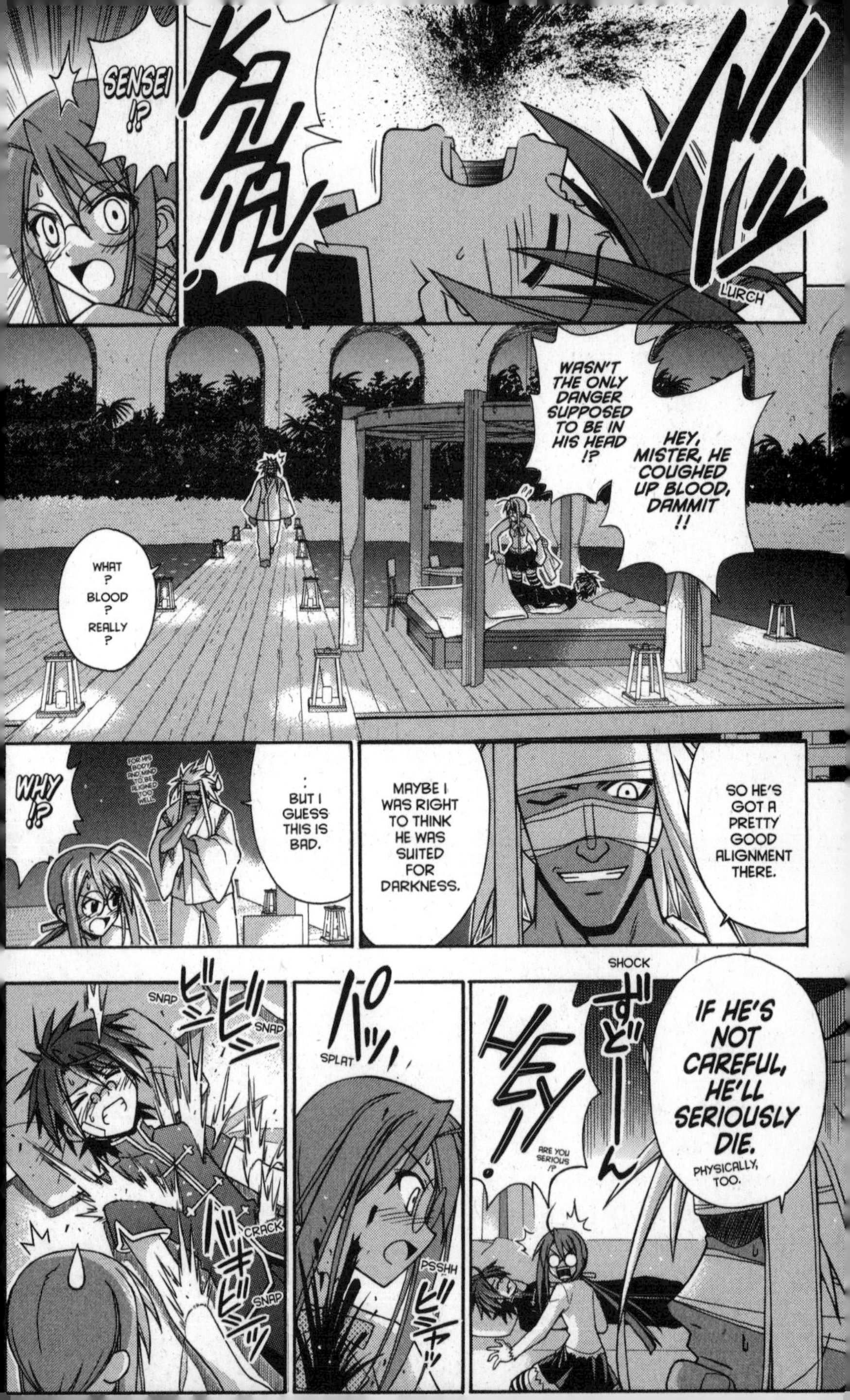
KAHAH!
LURCH
SENSEI !?
HEY, MISTER, HE COUGHED UP BLOOD, DAMMIT !!
WASN'T THE ONLY DANGER SUPPOSED TO BE IN HIS HEAD !?
WHAT ? BLOOD ? REALLY ?
SO HE'S GOT A PRETTY GOOD ALIGNMENT THERE.
MAYBE I WAS RIGHT TO THINK HE WAS SUITED FOR DARKNESS.
...BUT I GUESS THIS IS BAD.
FOR HIS BODY AND MIND TO BE ALIGNED TOO WELL.
WHY !?
IF HE'S NOT CAREFUL, HE'LL SERIOUSLY DIE.
PHYSICALLY, TOO.
SHOCK
HEY!
ARE YOU SERIOUS !?
SPLAT
PSSHH
SNAP
SNAP
CRACK
SNAP

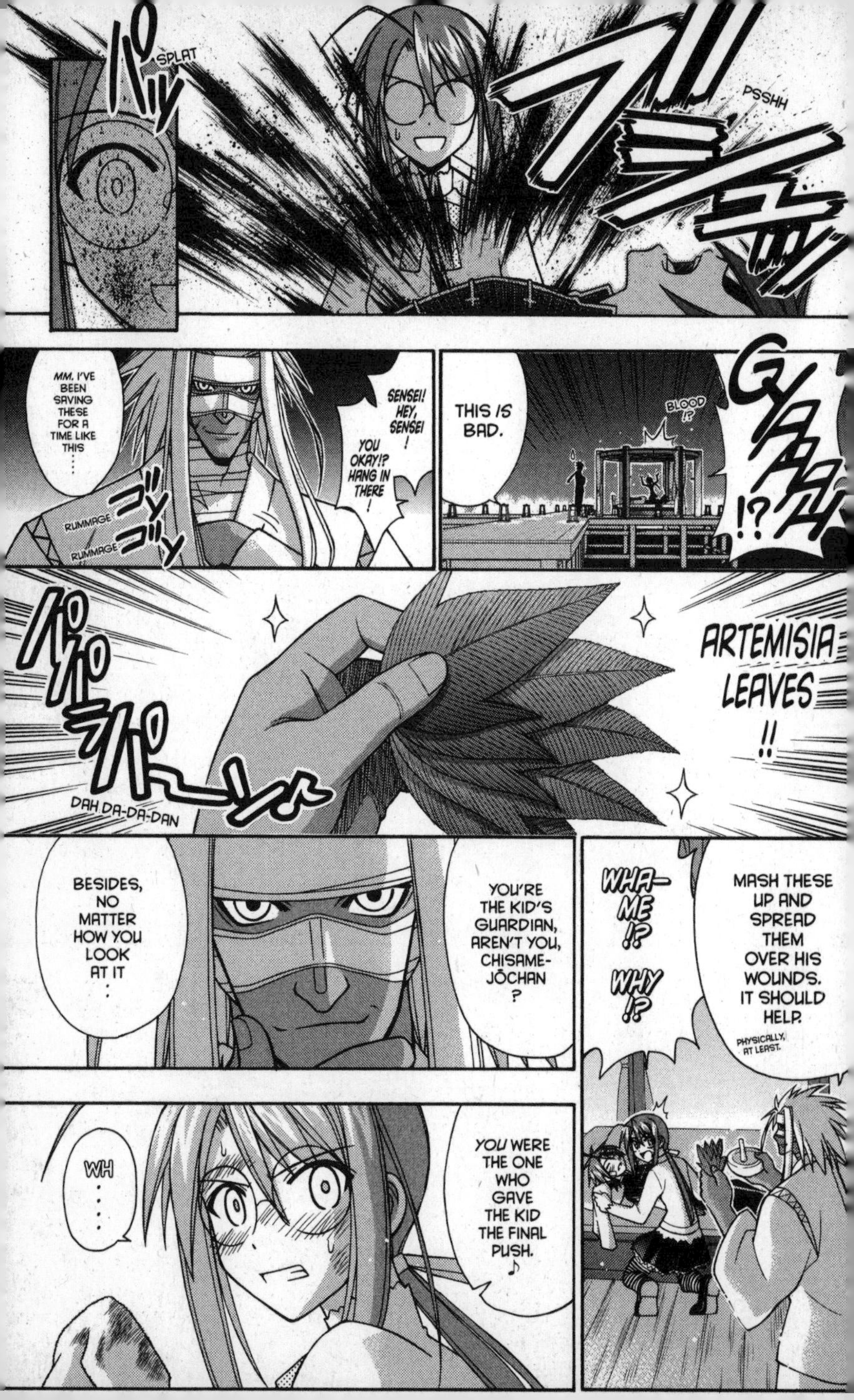
PSSHH
SPLAT
GYAAAAH!?
BLOOD!?
THIS IS BAD.
SENSEI! HEY, SENSEI! YOU OKAY!? HANG IN THERE!
MM. I'VE BEEN SAVING THESE FOR A TIME LIKE THIS...
RUMMAGE
RUMMAGE
ARTEMISIA LEAVES!!
DAH DA-DA-DAN
MASH THESE UP AND SPREAD THEM OVER HIS WOUNDS. IT SHOULD HELP.
PHYSICALLY, AT LEAST.
WHA-ME!? WHY!?
YOU'RE THE KID'S GUARDIAN, AREN'T YOU, CHISAME-JŌCHAN?
BESIDES, NO MATTER HOW YOU LOOK AT IT...
YOU WERE THE ONE WHO GAVE THE KID THE FINAL PUSH. ♪
WH...

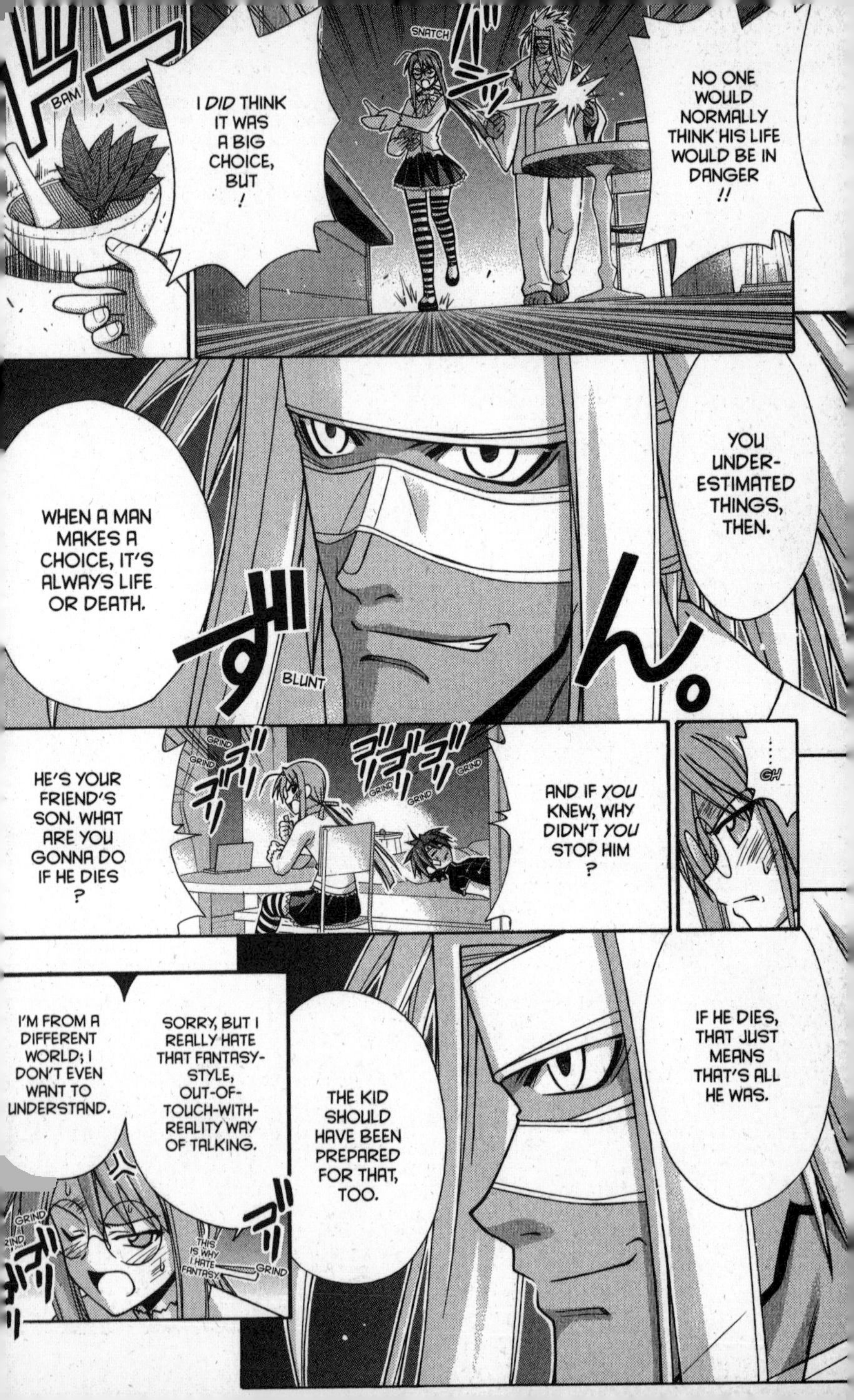

NO ONE WOULD NORMALLY THINK HIS LIFE WOULD BE IN DANGER !!
SNATCH
I *DID* THINK IT WAS A BIG CHOICE, BUT !
BAM
YOU UNDER-ESTIMATED THINGS, THEN.
WHEN A MAN MAKES A CHOICE, IT'S ALWAYS LIFE OR DEATH.
BLUNT
......
GH
AND IF *YOU* KNEW, WHY DIDN'T *YOU* STOP HIM ?
GRIND GRIND GRIND GRIND
HE'S YOUR FRIEND'S SON. WHAT ARE YOU GONNA DO IF HE DIES ?
IF HE DIES, THAT JUST MEANS THAT'S ALL HE WAS.
THE KID SHOULD HAVE BEEN PREPARED FOR THAT, TOO.
SORRY, BUT I REALLY HATE THAT FANTASY-STYLE, OUT-OF-TOUCH-WITH-REALITY WAY OF TALKING.
I'M FROM A DIFFERENT WORLD; I DON'T EVEN WANT TO UNDERSTAND.
THIS IS WHY I HATE FANTASY
GRIND
GRIND

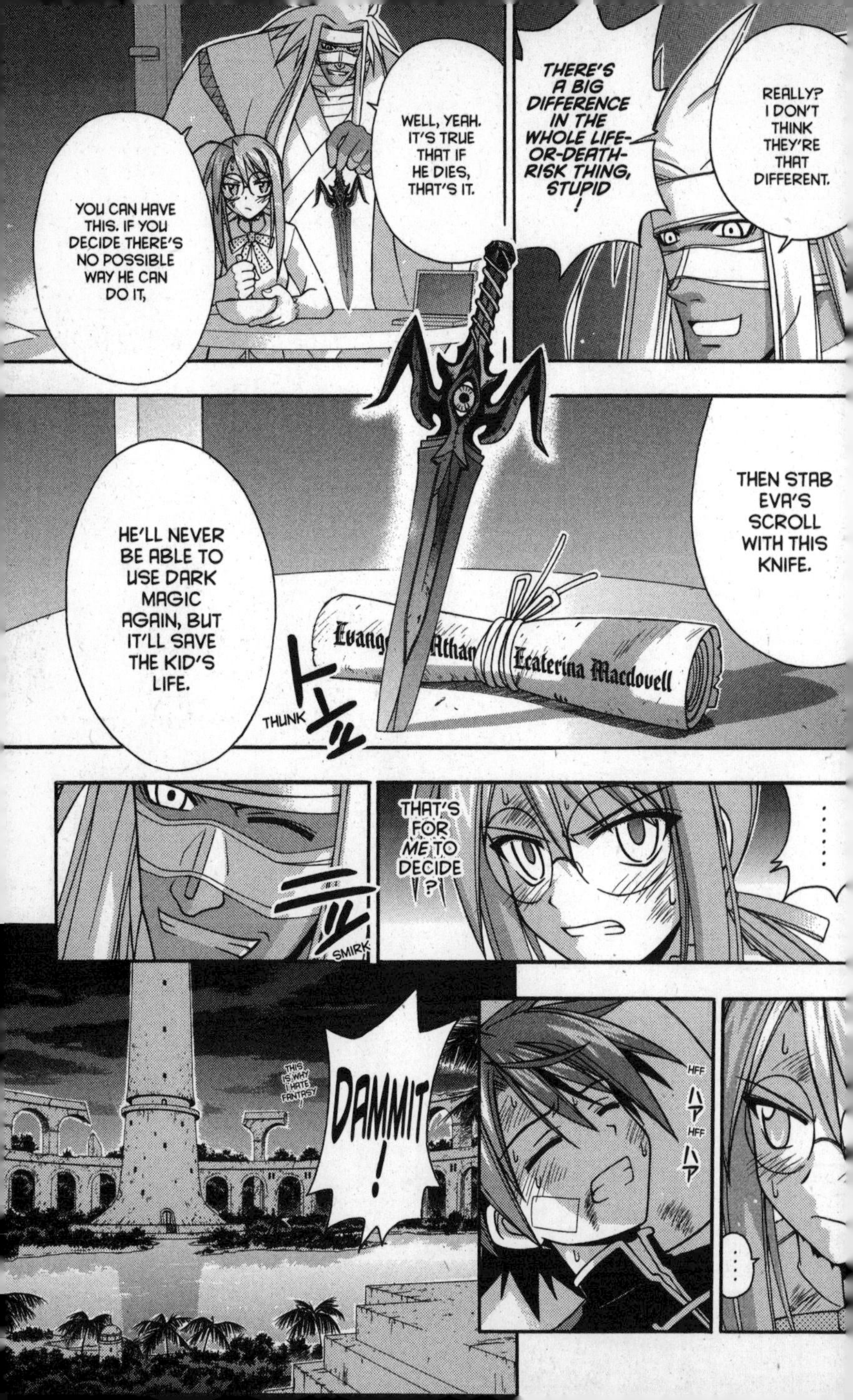
REALLY? I DON'T THINK THEY'RE THAT DIFFERENT.
THERE'S A BIG DIFFERENCE IN THE WHOLE LIFE-OR-DEATH-RISK THING, STUPID!
WELL, YEAH. IT'S TRUE THAT IF HE DIES, THAT'S IT.
YOU CAN HAVE THIS. IF YOU DECIDE THERE'S NO POSSIBLE WAY HE CAN DO IT,
THEN STAB EVA'S SCROLL WITH THIS KNIFE.
HE'LL NEVER BE ABLE TO USE DARK MAGIC AGAIN, BUT IT'LL SAVE THE KID'S LIFE.
Ecaterina Macdovell
THUNK
......
THAT'S FOR ME TO DECIDE?
SMIRK
...
HFF
HFF
DAMMIT!
THIS IS WHY I HATE FANTASY!

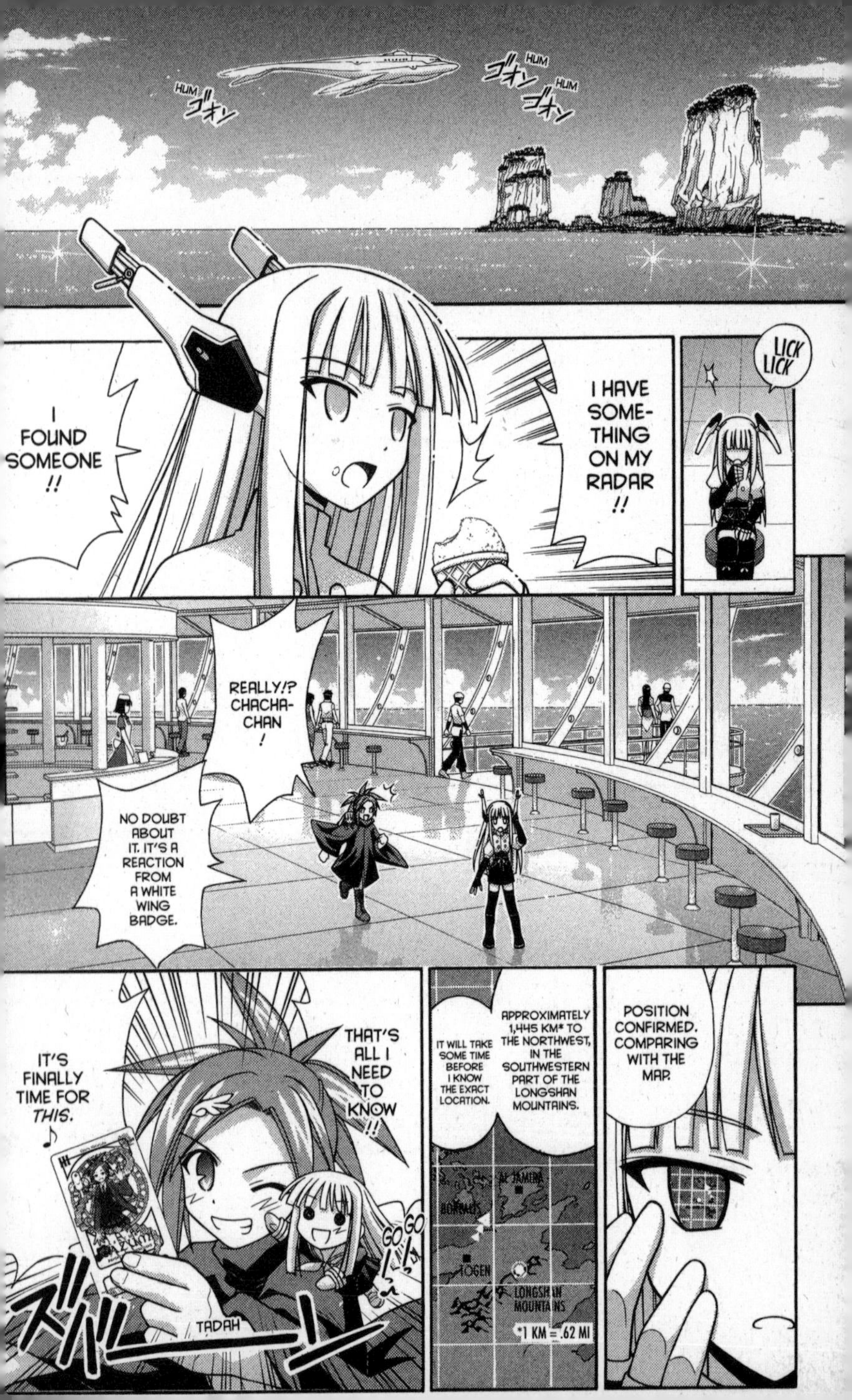
HUM
ゴオン
HUM
ゴオン
HUM
ゴオン
LICK LICK
I HAVE SOMETHING ON MY RADAR!!
I FOUND SOMEONE!!
REALLY!? CHACHA-CHAN!
NO DOUBT ABOUT IT. IT'S A REACTION FROM A WHITE WING BADGE.
POSITION CONFIRMED. COMPARING WITH THE MAP.
APPROXIMATELY 1,445 KM* TO THE NORTHWEST, IN THE SOUTHWESTERN PART OF THE LONGSHAN MOUNTAINS.
IT WILL TAKE SOME TIME BEFORE I KNOW THE EXACT LOCATION.
TOGEN
LONGSHAN MOUNTAINS
*1 KM = .62 MI
THAT'S ALL I NEED TO KNOW!!
IT'S FINALLY TIME FOR THIS. ♪
GO GO!
TADAH

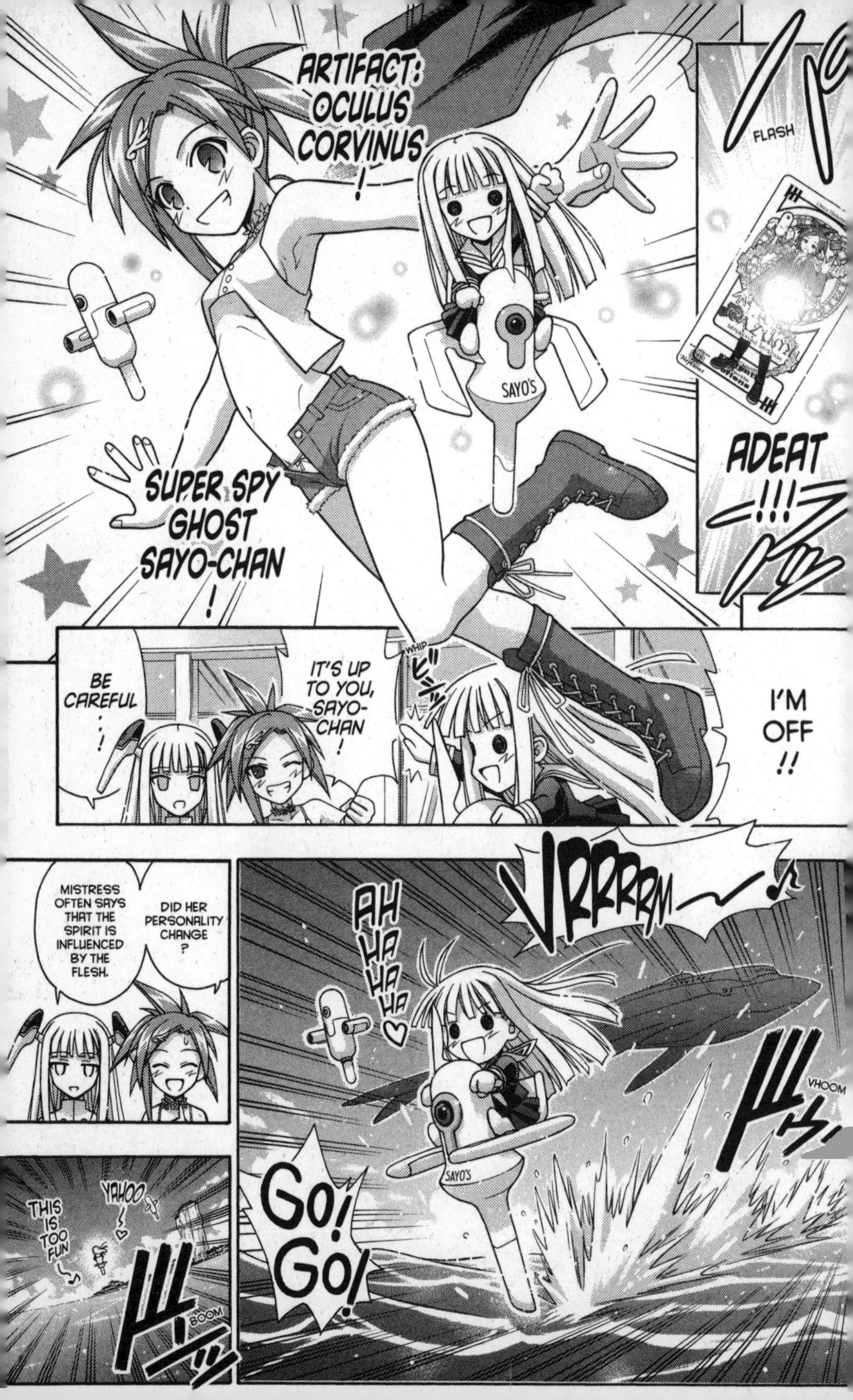
FLASH
ADEAT!!!
ARTIFACT: OCULUS CORVINUS!
SAYO'S
SUPER SPY GHOST SAYO-CHAN!
I'M OFF!!
WHIP
IT'S UP TO YOU, SAYO-CHAN!
BE CAREFUL...!
VRRRRM
AH HA HA HA HA ♡
VHOOM
SAYO'S
GO! GO!
DID HER PERSONALITY CHANGE?
MISTRESS OFTEN SAYS THAT THE SPIRIT IS INFLUENCED BY THE FLESH.
YAHOO ♡
THIS IS TOO FUN ♪
BOOM

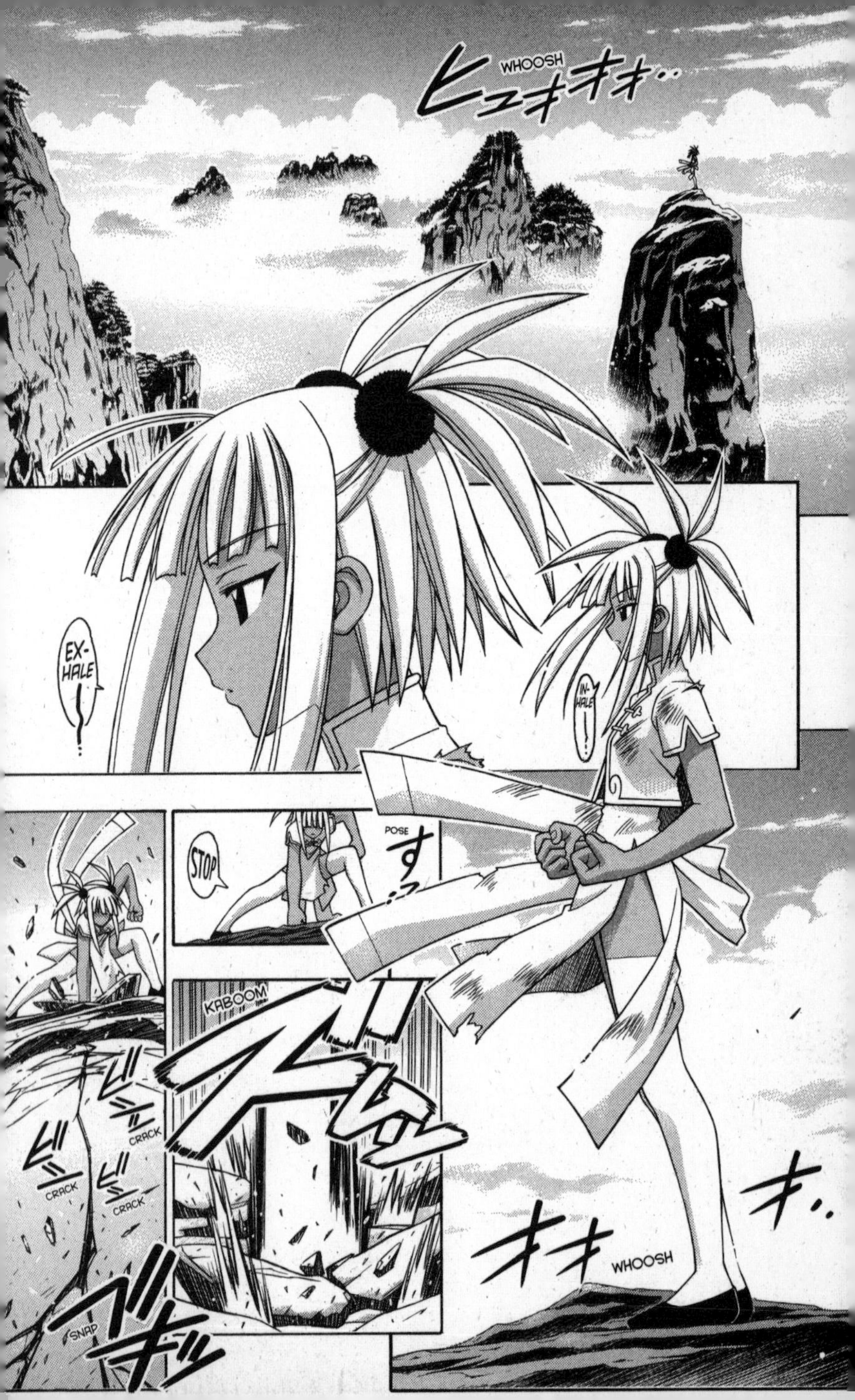

WHOOSH
ヒュオオオ‥
IN-HALE!
EX-HALE~!
POSE
すっ
STOP
KABOOM
CRACK
CRACK
CRACK
SNAP
オオオ‥
WHOOSH

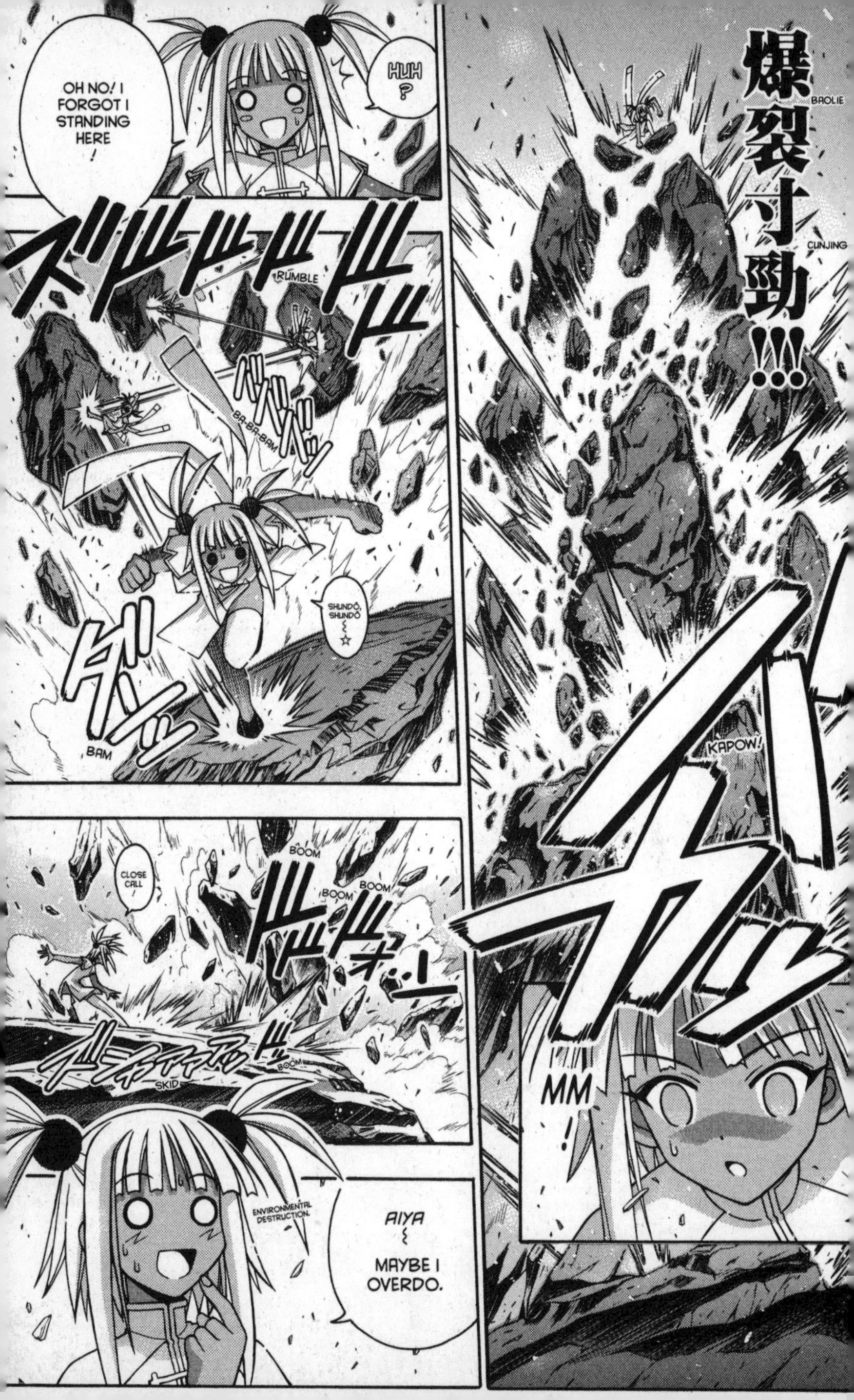

爆裂寸勁!!!
BAOLIE
CUNJING
KAPOW!
MM
!
HUH
?
OH NO! I FORGOT I STANDING HERE
!
RUMBLE
BA-BA-BAM
SHUNDŌ, SHUNDŌ ~☆
BAM
CLOSE CALL
!
BOOM
BOOM
BOOM
BOOM
SKID
ENVIRONMENTAL DESTRUCTION.
AIYA ~
MAYBE I OVERDO.

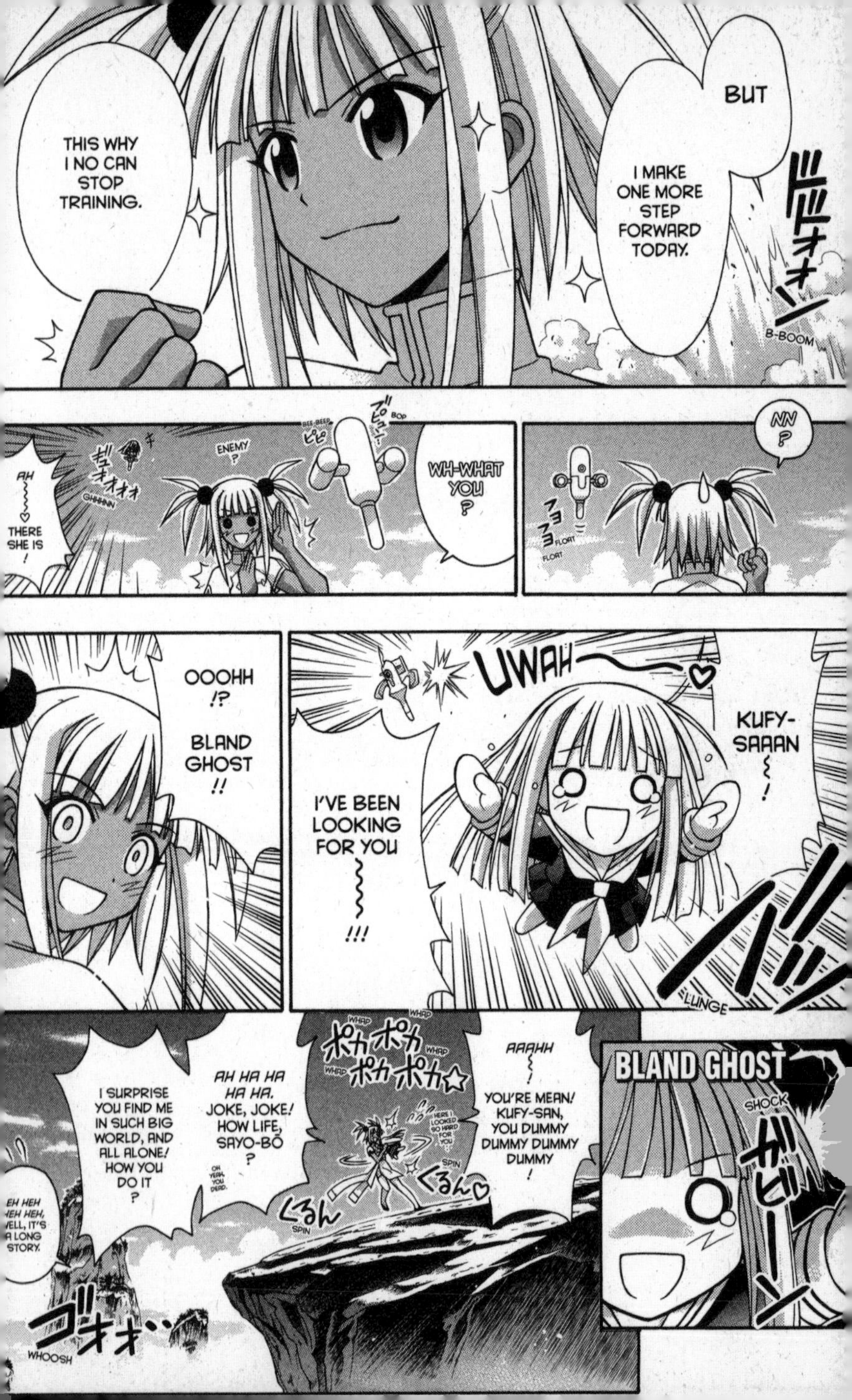
THIS WHY I NO CAN STOP TRAINING.
BUT
I MAKE ONE MORE STEP FORWARD TODAY.
B-BOOM
NN?
FLOAT
FLOAT
WH-WHAT YOU?
BEE-BEEP
BOP
ENEMY?
GHHHNN
AH~ THERE SHE IS!
UWAH~♥
KUFY-SAAAN~!
I'VE BEEN LOOKING FOR YOU~!!!
LUNGE
OOOHH!?
BLAND GHOST!!
BLAND GHOST
SHOCK
AAAHH~!
YOU'RE MEAN! KUFY-SAN, YOU DUMMY DUMMY DUMMY DUMMY!
WHAP WHAP WHAP WHAP
HERE I LOOKED SO HARD FOR YOU
SPIN
SPIN
AH HA HA HA HA. JOKE, JOKE! HOW LIFE, SAYO-BŌ?
OH YEAH, YOU DEAD.
I SURPRISE YOU FIND ME IN SUCH BIG WORLD, AND ALL ALONE! HOW YOU DO IT?
EH HEH HEH HEH, WELL, IT'S A LONG STORY.
WHOOSH

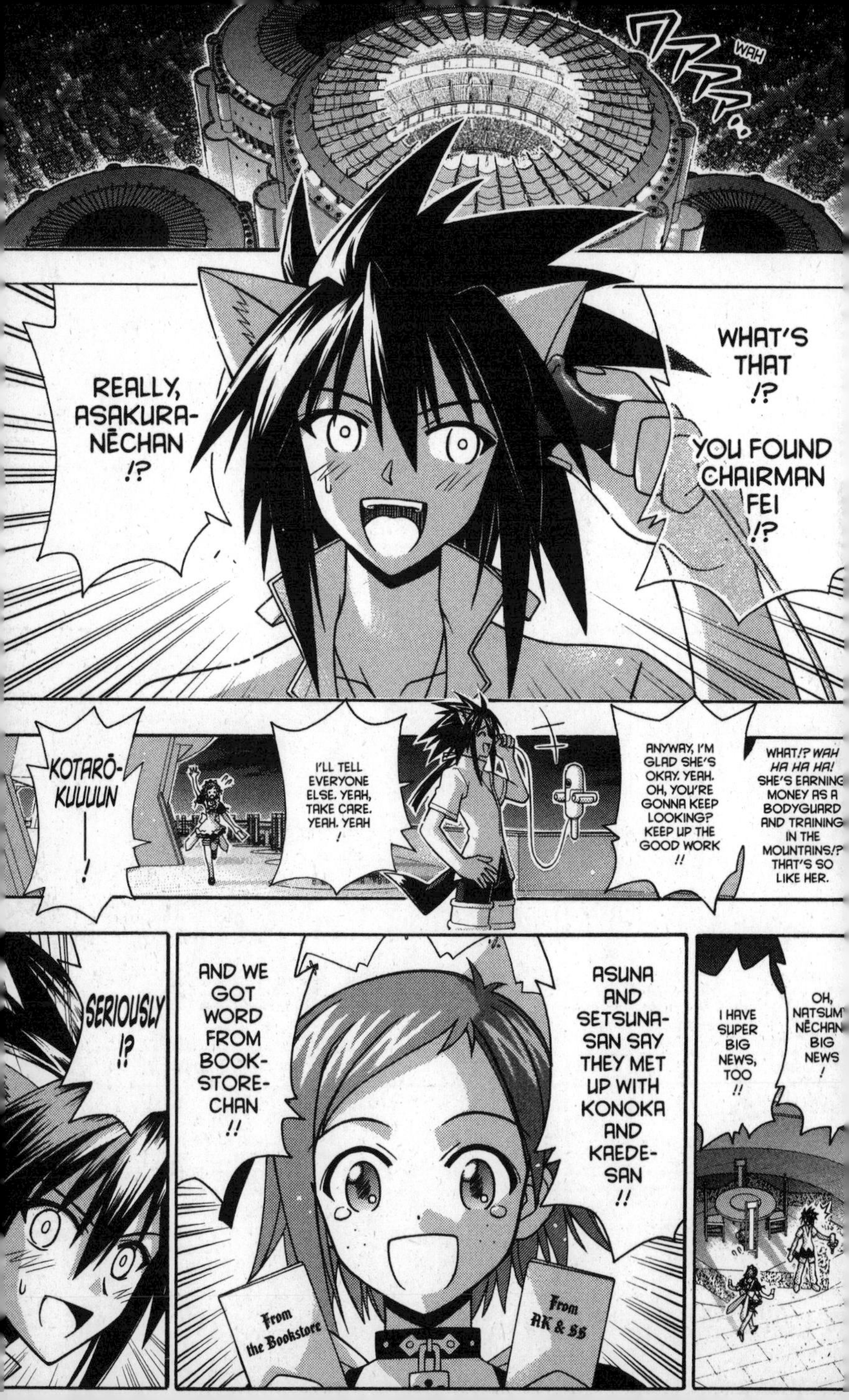
WAH
WHAT'S THAT !? YOU FOUND CHAIRMAN FEI !?
REALLY, ASAKURA-NĒCHAN !?
WHAT!? WAH HA HA HA! SHE'S EARNING MONEY AS A BODYGUARD AND TRAINING IN THE MOUNTAINS!? THAT'S SO LIKE HER.
ANYWAY, I'M GLAD SHE'S OKAY. YEAH. OH, YOU'RE GONNA KEEP LOOKING? KEEP UP THE GOOD WORK !!
I'LL TELL EVERYONE ELSE. YEAH, TAKE CARE. YEAH. YEAH !
KOTARŌ-KUUUUN !
OH, NATSUMI NĒCHAN BIG NEWS !
I HAVE SUPER BIG NEWS, TOO !!
ASUNA AND SETSUNA-SAN SAY THEY MET UP WITH KONOKA AND KAEDE-SAN !!
AND WE GOT WORD FROM BOOK-STORE-CHAN !!
From AK & SS
From the Bookstore
SERIOUSLY !?

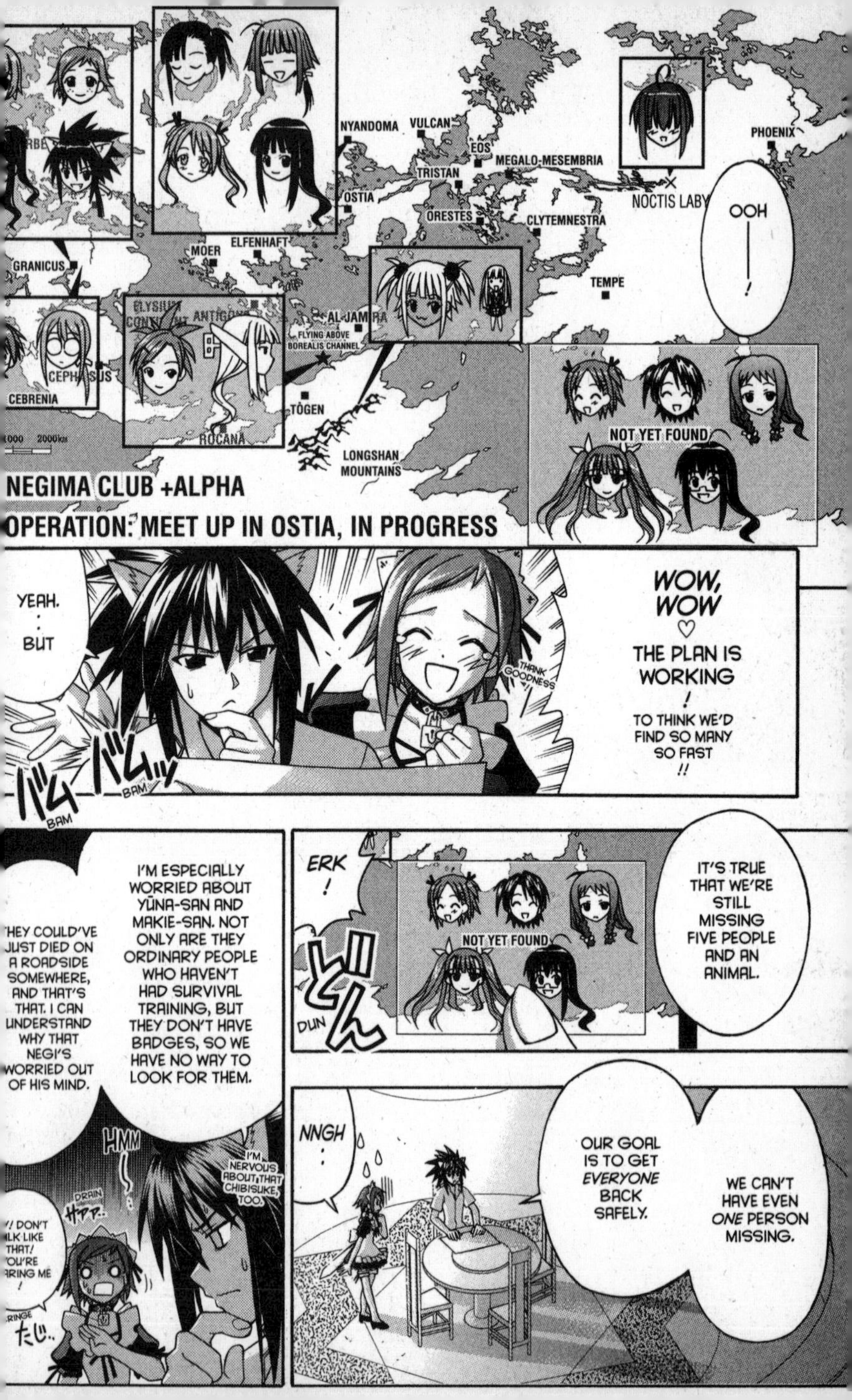
NYANDOMA
VULCAN
EOS
MEGALO-MESEMBRIA
PHOENIX
TRISTAN
NOCTIS LABY
OSTIA
ORESTES
CLYTEMNESTRA
ELFENHAFT
MOER
GRANICUS
TEMPE
AL-JAMIRA
FLYING ABOVE BOREALIS CHANNEL
CEPHISSUS
CEBRENIA
TŌGEN
ROCANA
LONGSHAN MOUNTAINS
2000km
NOT YET FOUND
OOH—!
NEGIMA CLUB +ALPHA
OPERATION: MEET UP IN OSTIA, IN PROGRESS
WOW, WOW ♡ THE PLAN IS WORKING!
TO THINK WE'D FIND SO MANY SO FAST!!
THANK GOODNESS
YEAH... BUT
BAM
BAM
IT'S TRUE THAT WE'RE STILL MISSING FIVE PEOPLE AND AN ANIMAL.
NOT YET FOUND
ERK!
DUN
WE CAN'T HAVE EVEN ONE PERSON MISSING.
OUR GOAL IS TO GET EVERYONE BACK SAFELY.
NNGH...
I'M ESPECIALLY WORRIED ABOUT YŪNA-SAN AND MAKIE-SAN. NOT ONLY ARE THEY ORDINARY PEOPLE WHO HAVEN'T HAD SURVIVAL TRAINING, BUT THEY DON'T HAVE BADGES, SO WE HAVE NO WAY TO LOOK FOR THEM.
THEY COULD'VE JUST DIED ON A ROADSIDE SOMEWHERE, AND THAT'S THAT. I CAN UNDERSTAND WHY THAT NEGI'S WORRIED OUT OF HIS MIND.
HMM...
I'M NERVOUS ABOUT THAT CHIBISUKE, TOO.
DRAIN
! DON'T ALK LIKE THAT! OU'RE ARING ME !
RINGE

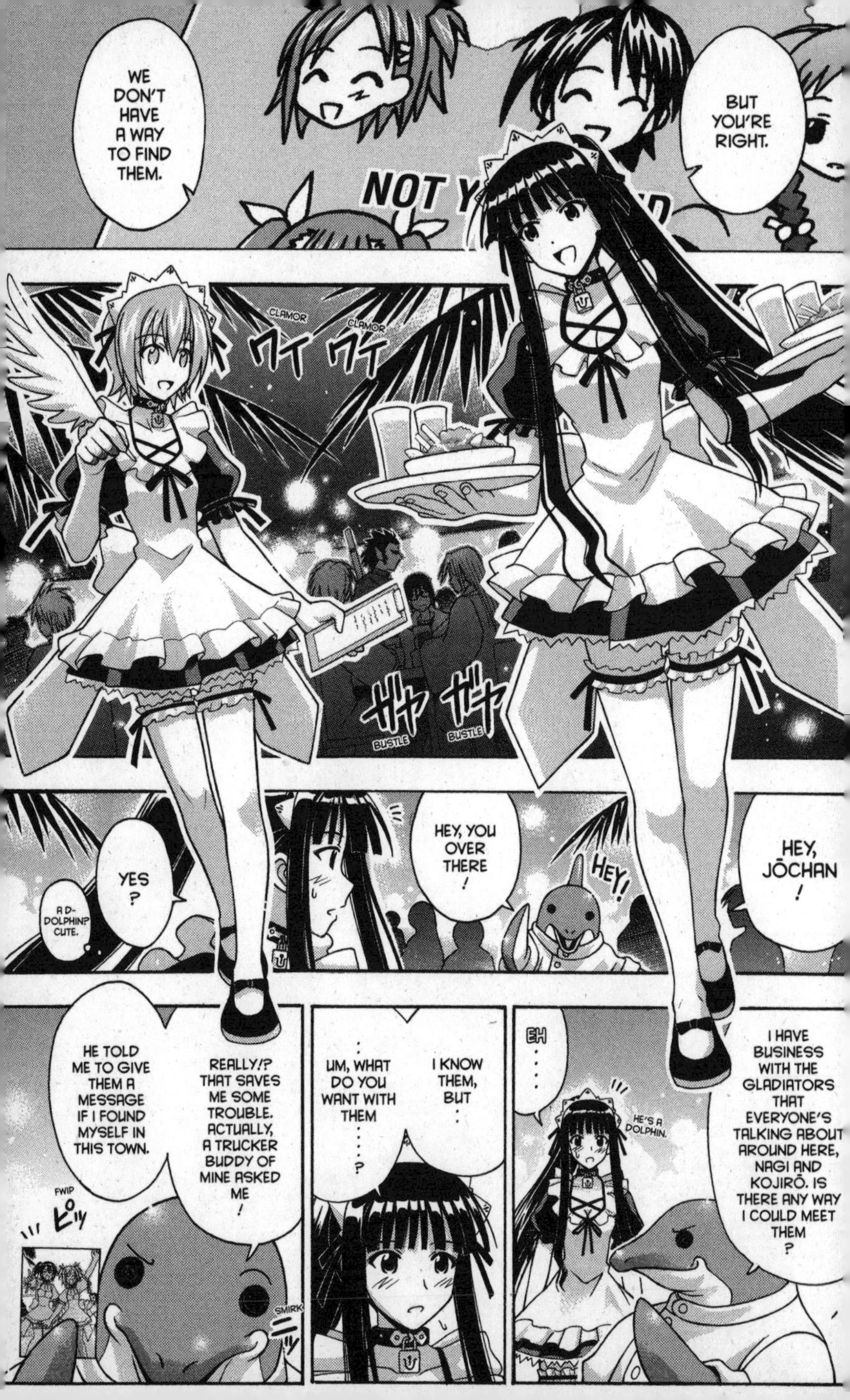
BUT YOU'RE RIGHT.
WE DON'T HAVE A WAY TO FIND THEM.
ワイ ワイ
CLAMOR CLAMOR
ガヤ ガヤ
BUSTLE BUSTLE
HEY, JŌCHAN!
HEY!
HEY, YOU OVER THERE!
YES?
A D-DOLPHIN? CUTE.
I HAVE BUSINESS WITH THE GLADIATORS THAT EVERYONE'S TALKING ABOUT AROUND HERE, NAGI AND KOJIRŌ. IS THERE ANY WAY I COULD MEET THEM?
EH...
HE'S A DOLPHIN.
I KNOW THEM, BUT...
UM, WHAT DO YOU WANT WITH THEM...?
REALLY!? THAT SAVES ME SOME TROUBLE. ACTUALLY, A TRUCKER BUDDY OF MINE ASKED ME!
HE TOLD ME TO GIVE THEM A MESSAGE IF I FOUND MYSELF IN THIS TOWN.
FWIP
ピッ
SMIRK
ニッ

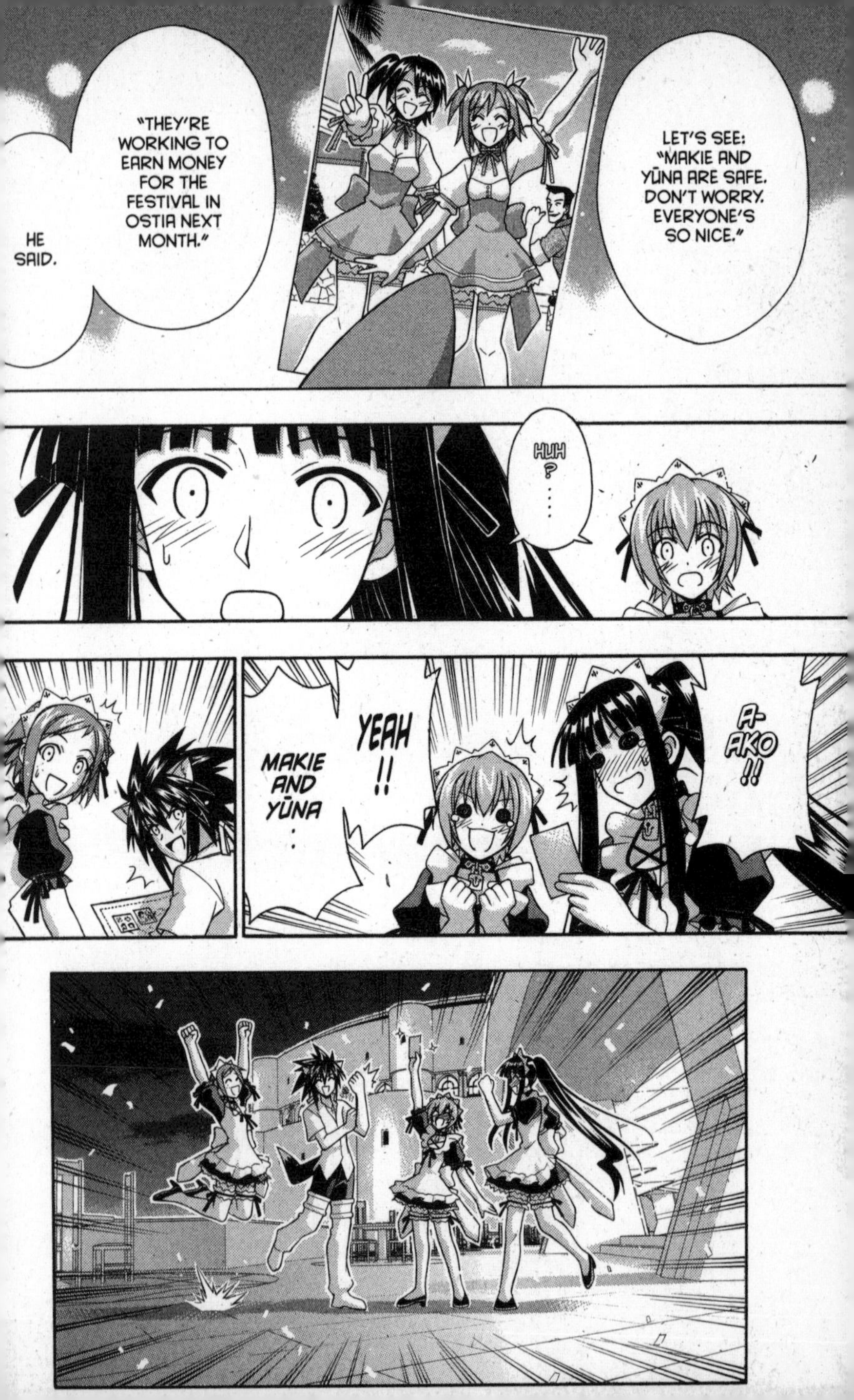
LET'S SEE: "MAKIE AND YŪNA ARE SAFE. DON'T WORRY. EVERYONE'S SO NICE."
"THEY'RE WORKING TO EARN MONEY FOR THE FESTIVAL IN OSTIA NEXT MONTH."
HE SAID.
HUH? ....
A-AKO!!
YEAH!!
MAKIE AND YŪNA...

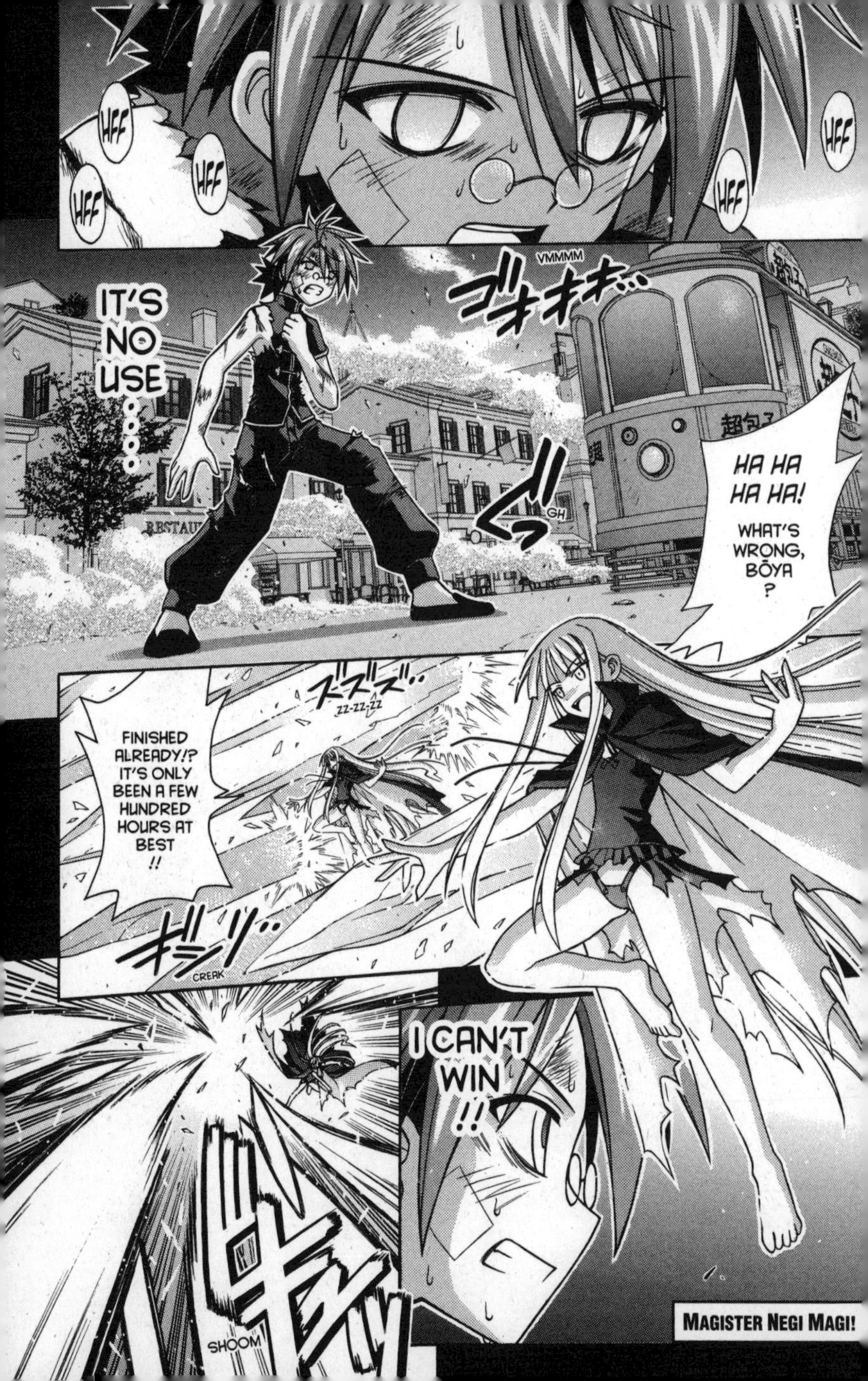
HFF
HFF
HFF
HFF
HFF
VMMMM
IT'S NO USE.....
GH
HA HA HA HA!
WHAT'S WRONG, BŌYA?
ZZ-ZZ-ZZ
FINISHED ALREADY!? IT'S ONLY BEEN A FEW HUNDRED HOURS AT BEST!!
CREAK
I CAN'T WIN!!
SHOOM
MAGISTER NEGI MAGI!

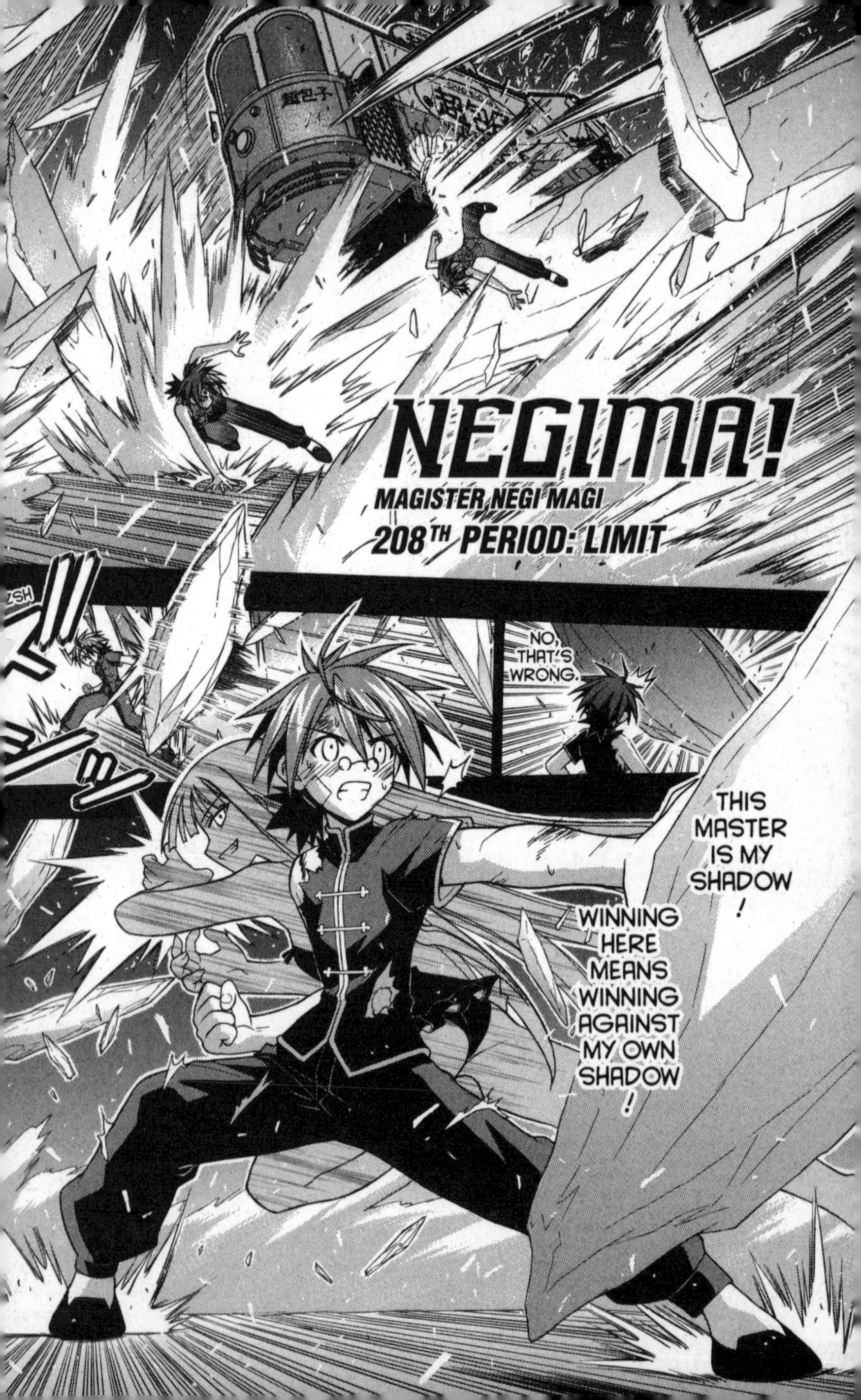
超包子
NEGIMA!
MAGISTER NEGI MAGI
208TH PERIOD: LIMIT
ZSH
NO, THAT'S WRONG.
THIS MASTER IS MY SHADOW!
WINNING HERE MEANS WINNING AGAINST MY OWN SHADOW!

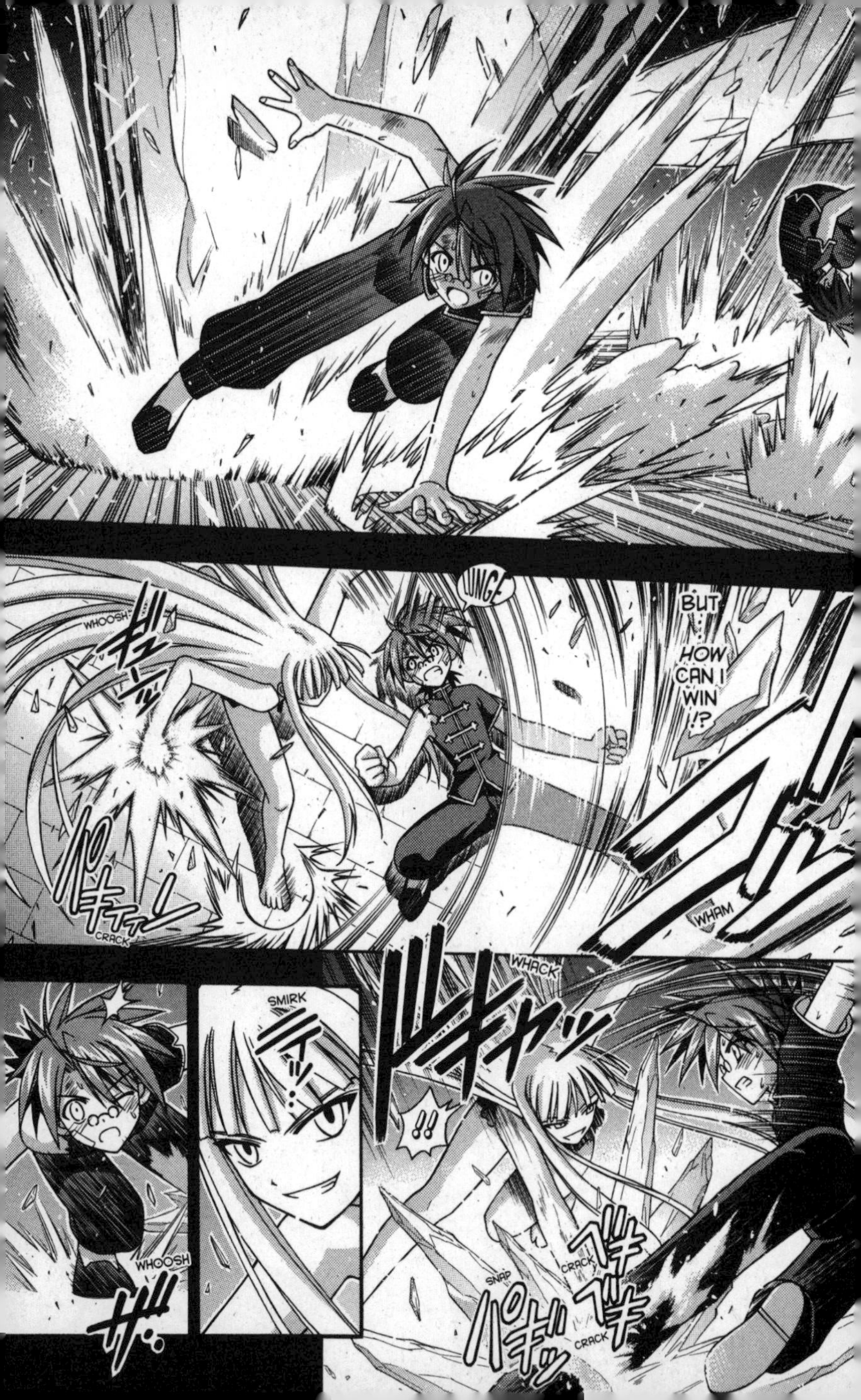

BUT... HOW CAN I WIN!?
WHAM
LUNGE
WHOOSH
CRACK
WHACK
!!
CRACK
CRACK
SNAP
SMIRK
WHOOSH

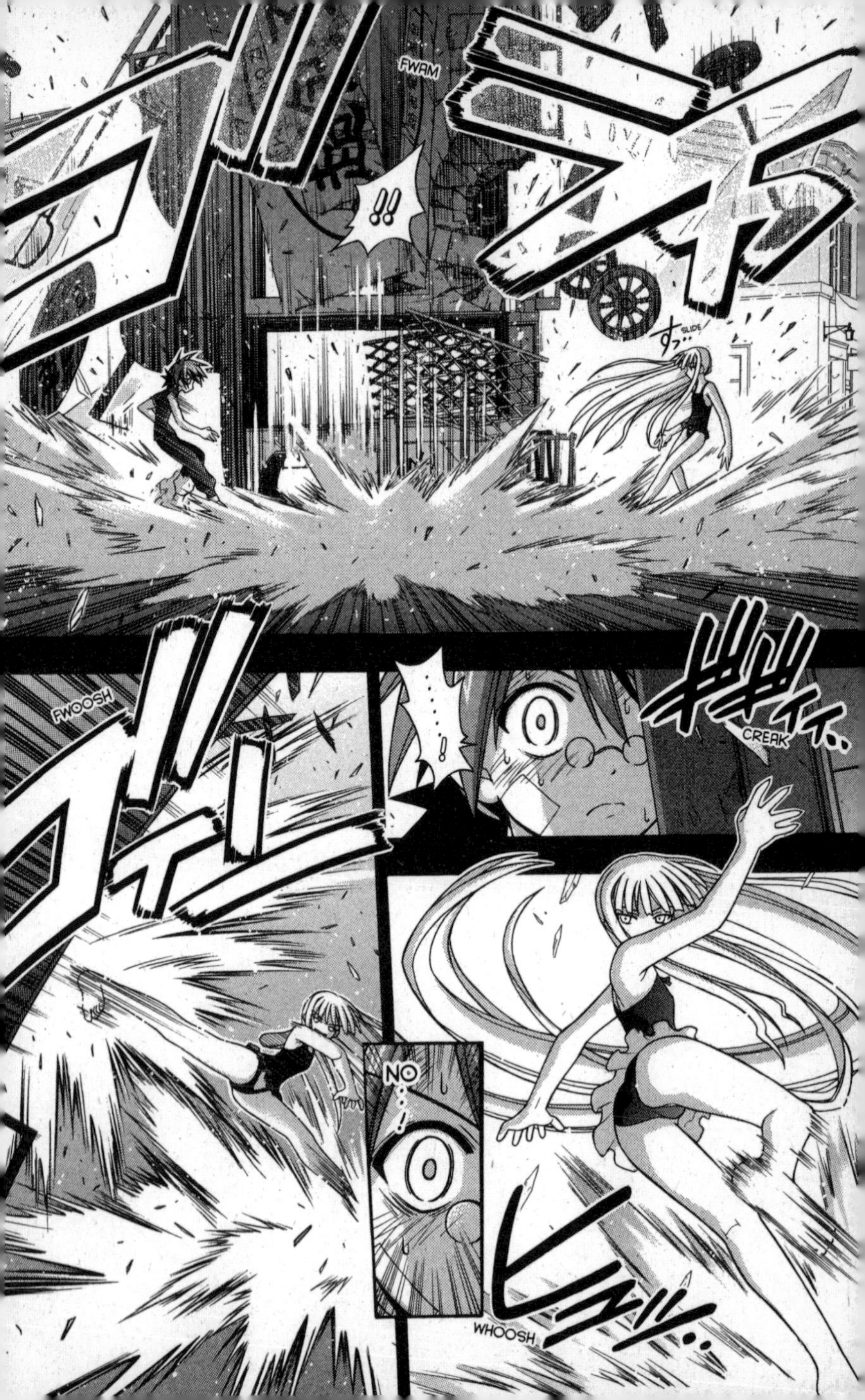
FWAM
!!
SLIDE
CREAK
. . . !
NO . . . !
WHOOSH
FWOOSH

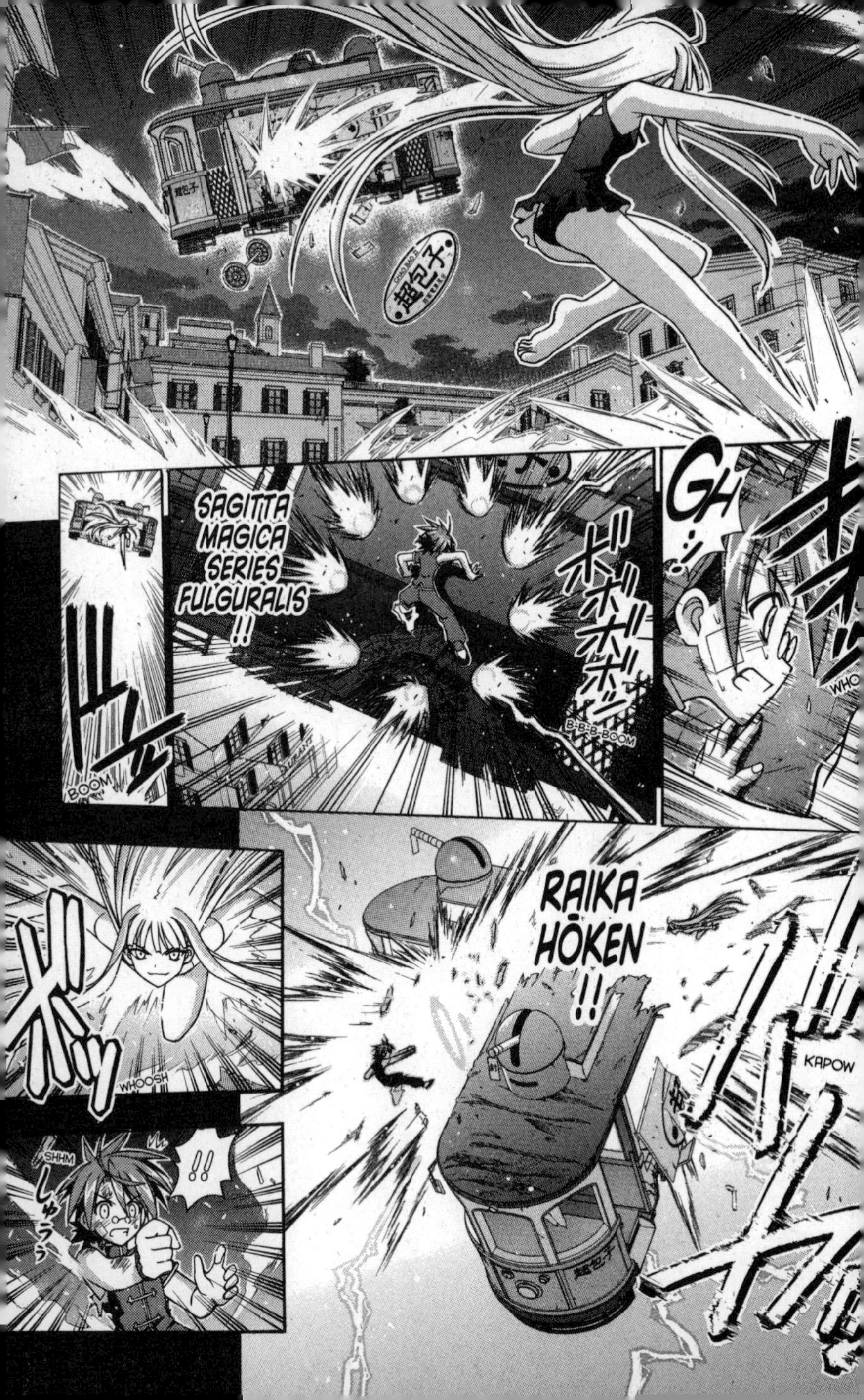

超包子
GH...!
SAGITTA MAGICA SERIES FULGURALIS!!
B-B-B-BOOM
BOOM
RAIKA HÖKEN!!
KAPOW
WHOOSH
SHHM
!!

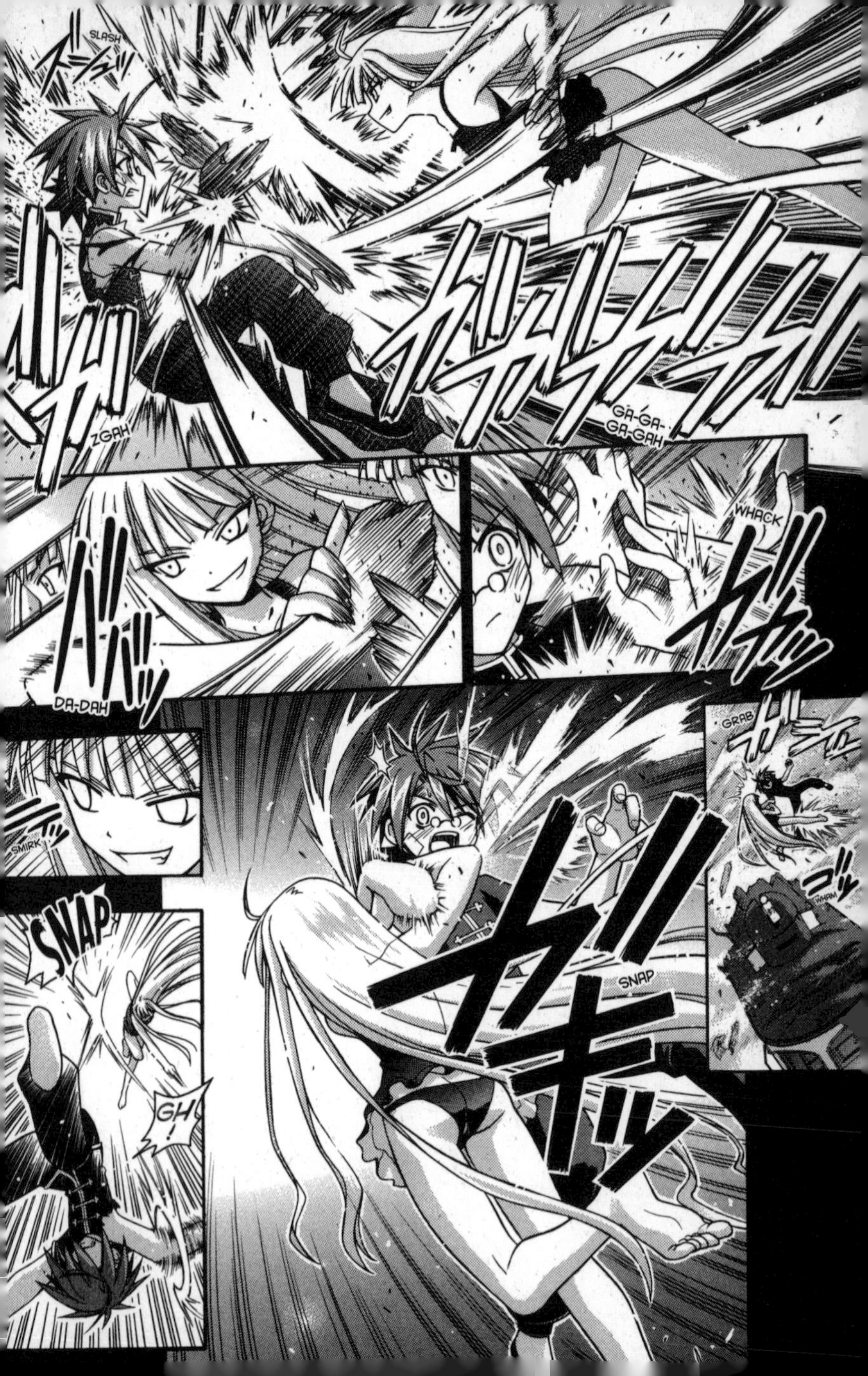
SLASH
GA-GA-GA-GAH
ZGAH
WHACK
DA-DAH
GRAB
WHAM
SNAP
SMIRK
SNAP
GH!

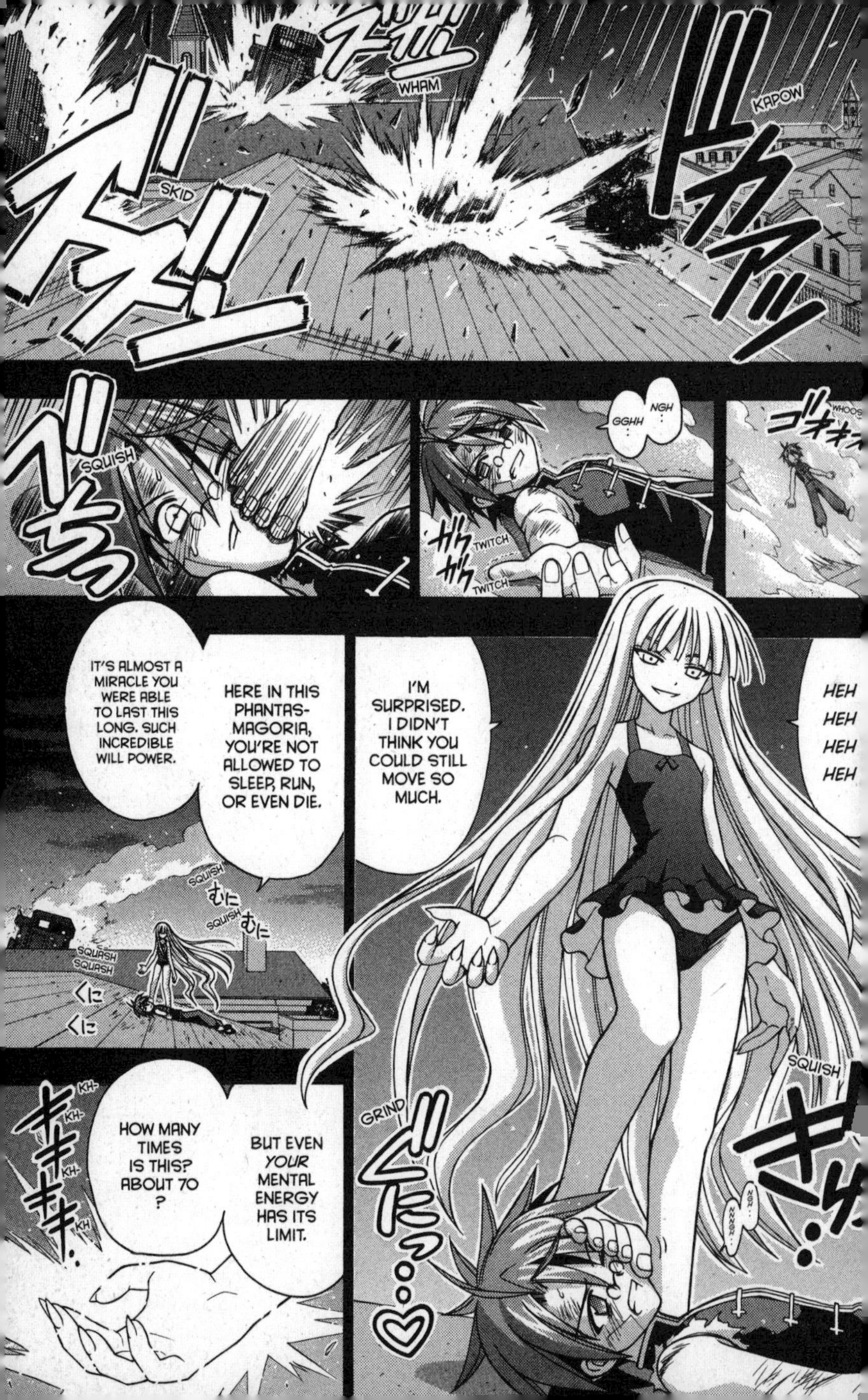

KAPOW
WHAM
SKID
WHOOS
NGH...
GGHH...
TWITCH
TWITCH
SQUISH
HEH HEH HEH HEH
I'M SURPRISED. I DIDN'T THINK YOU COULD STILL MOVE SO MUCH.
SQUISH
GRIND
NGH...
NNGH...
HERE IN THIS PHANTAS-MAGORIA, YOU'RE NOT ALLOWED TO SLEEP, RUN, OR EVEN DIE.
IT'S ALMOST A MIRACLE YOU WERE ABLE TO LAST THIS LONG. SUCH INCREDIBLE WILL POWER.
SQUISH むに
SQUISH むに
SQUASH くに
SQUASH くに
BUT EVEN *YOUR* MENTAL ENERGY HAS ITS LIMIT.
HOW MANY TIMES IS THIS? ABOUT 70?
KH-
KH-
KH-
KH

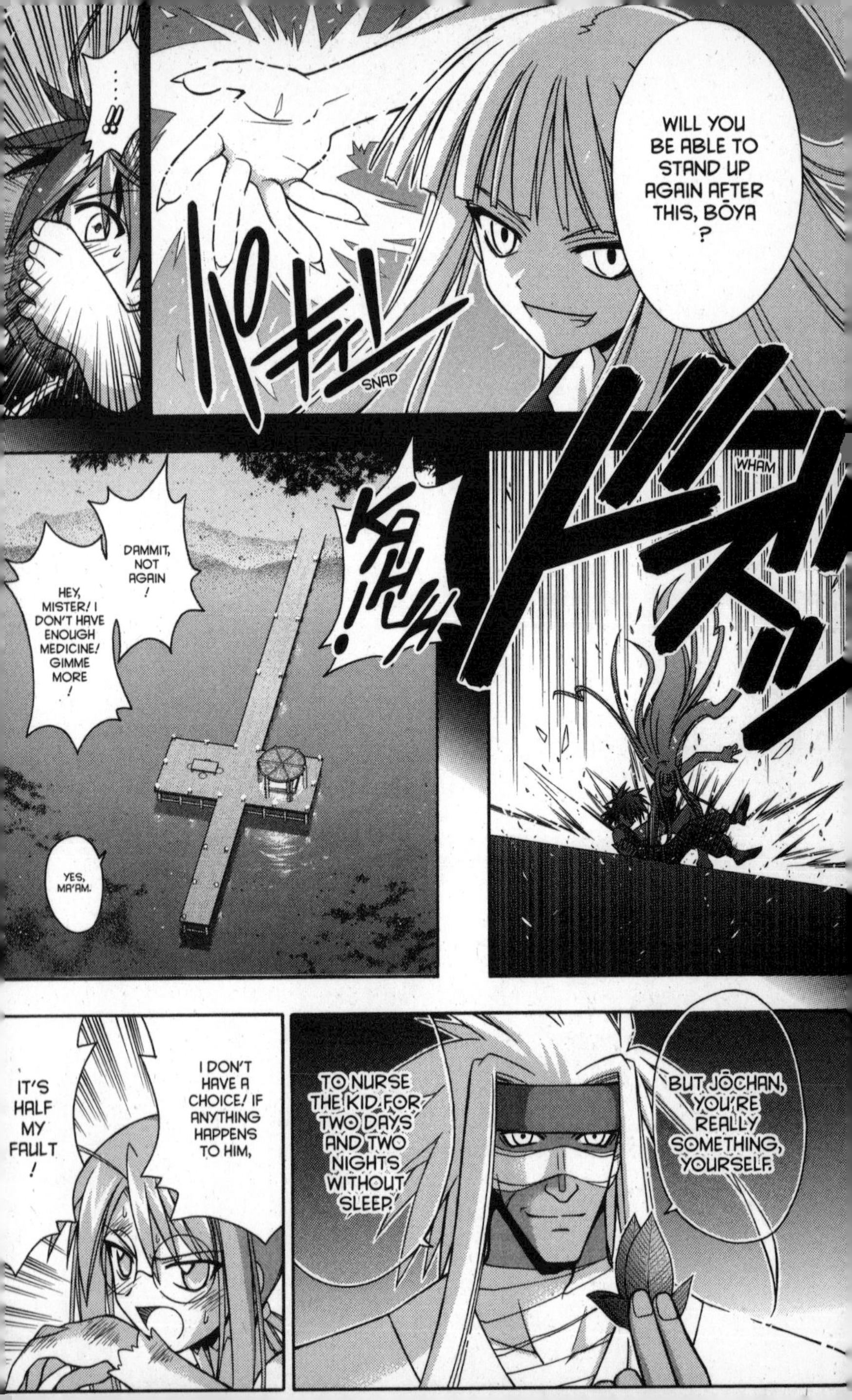
WILL YOU BE ABLE TO STAND UP AGAIN AFTER THIS, BŌYA?
SNAP
...!!
WHAM
KRUSH!
DAMMIT, NOT AGAIN!
HEY, MISTER! I DON'T HAVE ENOUGH MEDICINE! GIMME MORE!
YES, MA'AM.
BUT JŌCHAN, YOU'RE REALLY SOMETHING, YOURSELF.
TO NURSE THE KID FOR TWO DAYS AND TWO NIGHTS WITHOUT SLEEP.
I DON'T HAVE A CHOICE! IF ANYTHING HAPPENS TO HIM,
IT'S HALF MY FAULT!

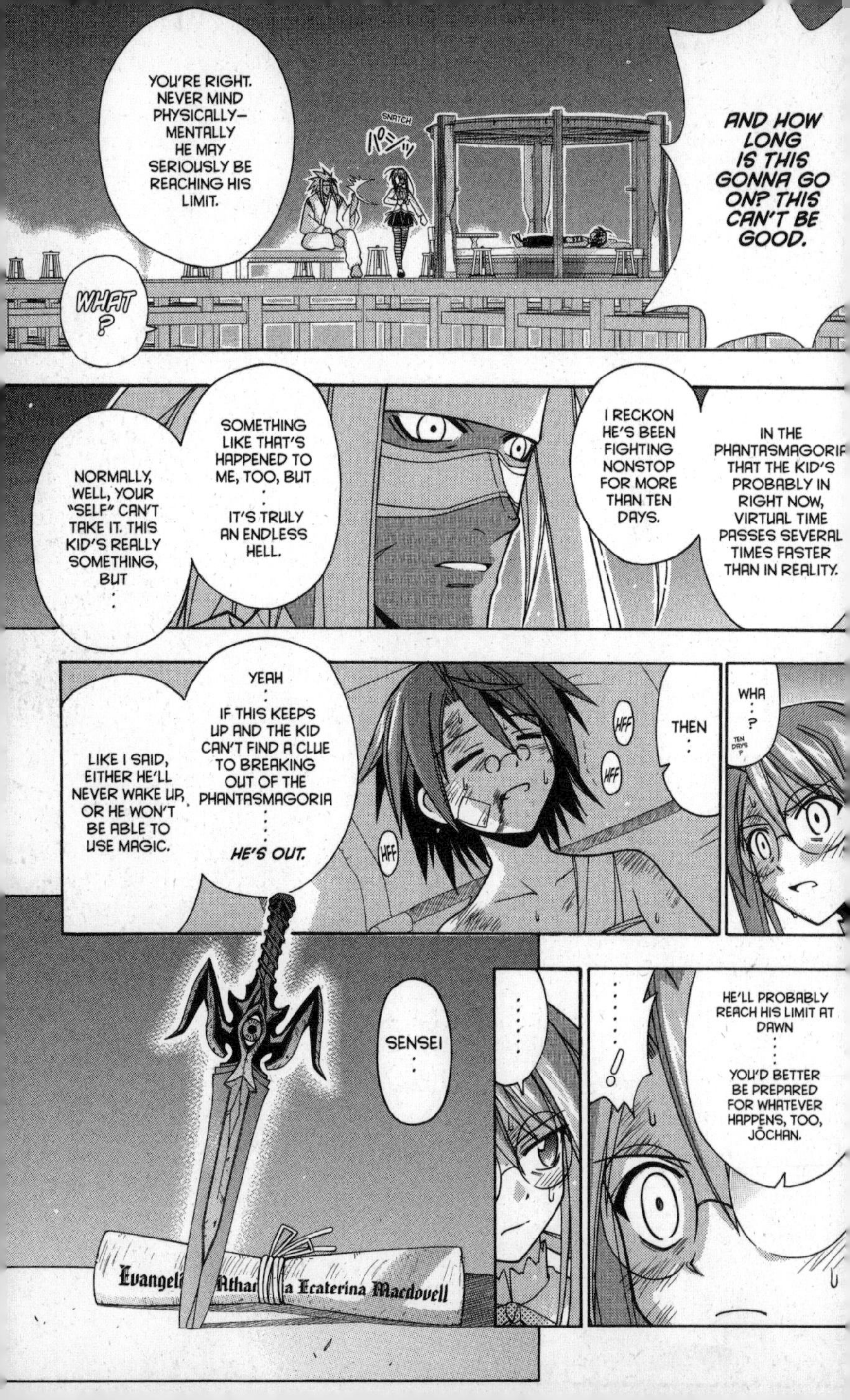

AND HOW LONG IS THIS GONNA GO ON? THIS CAN'T BE GOOD.
SNATCH
YOU'RE RIGHT. NEVER MIND PHYSICALLY— MENTALLY HE MAY SERIOUSLY BE REACHING HIS LIMIT.
WHAT?
IN THE PHANTASMAGORIA THAT THE KID'S PROBABLY IN RIGHT NOW, VIRTUAL TIME PASSES SEVERAL TIMES FASTER THAN IN REALITY.
I RECKON HE'S BEEN FIGHTING NONSTOP FOR MORE THAN TEN DAYS.
SOMETHING LIKE THAT'S HAPPENED TO ME, TOO, BUT . . . IT'S TRULY AN ENDLESS HELL.
NORMALLY, WELL, YOUR "SELF" CAN'T TAKE IT. THIS KID'S REALLY SOMETHING, BUT . . .
WHA . . ?
TEN DAYS?
THEN . . .
HFF
HFF
HFF
YEAH . . . IF THIS KEEPS UP AND THE KID CAN'T FIND A CLUE TO BREAKING OUT OF THE PHANTASMAGORIA . . . HE'S OUT.
LIKE I SAID, EITHER HE'LL NEVER WAKE UP, OR HE WON'T BE ABLE TO USE MAGIC.
HE'LL PROBABLY REACH HIS LIMIT AT DAWN . . . YOU'D BETTER BE PREPARED FOR WHATEVER HAPPENS, TOO, JŌCHAN.
. . . . . . !
. . . . . .
SENSEI . . .
Evangel Athan a Ecaterina Macdovell

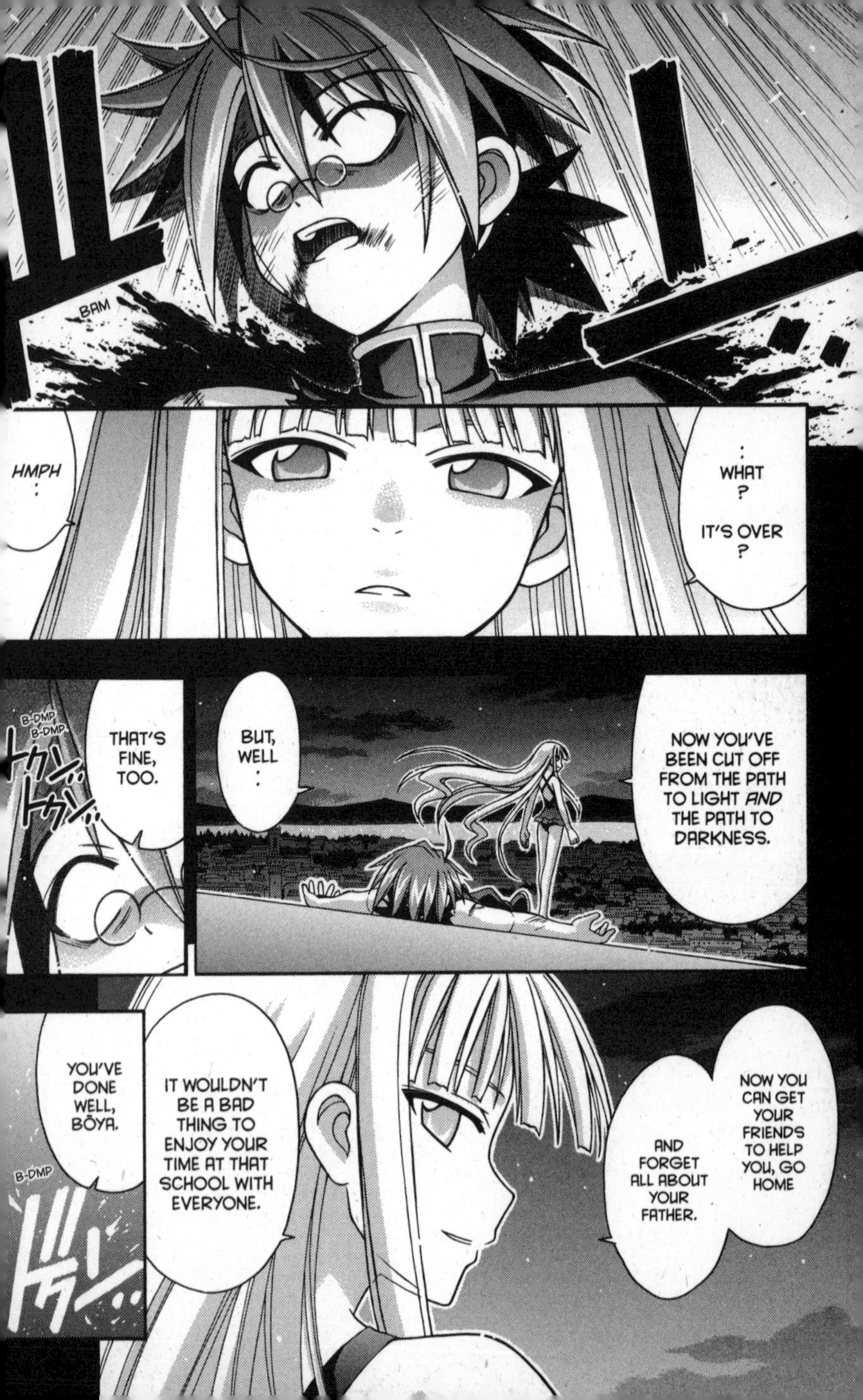
BAM
: WHAT? IT'S OVER?
HMPH :
NOW YOU'VE BEEN CUT OFF FROM THE PATH TO LIGHT *AND* THE PATH TO DARKNESS.
BUT, WELL :
THAT'S FINE, TOO.
B-DMP B-DMP
NOW YOU CAN GET YOUR FRIENDS TO HELP YOU, GO HOME
AND FORGET ALL ABOUT YOUR FATHER.
IT WOULDN'T BE A BAD THING TO ENJOY YOUR TIME AT THAT SCHOOL WITH EVERYONE.
YOU'VE DONE WELL, BŌYA.
B-DMP

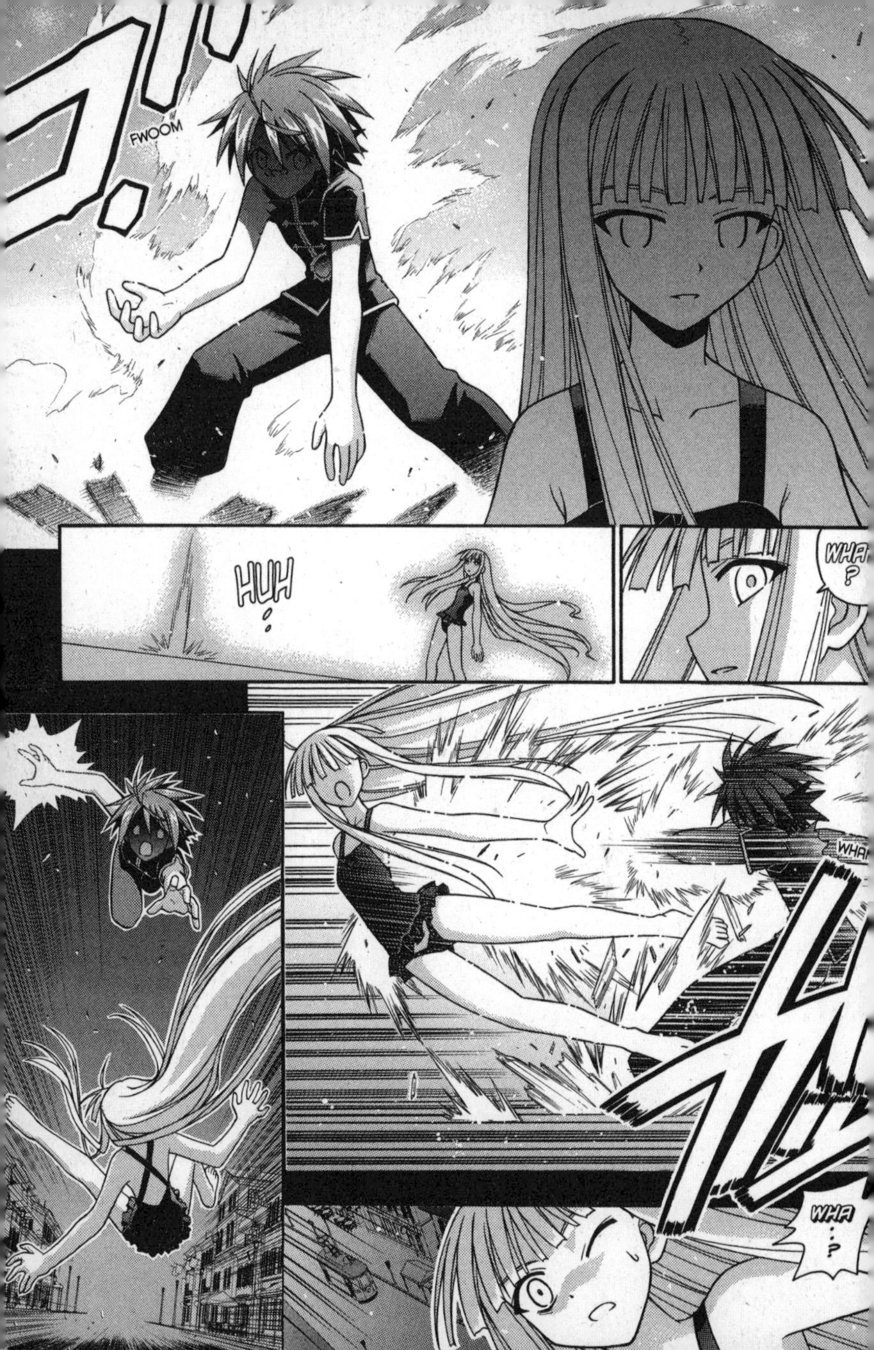

FWOOM
WHA ?
HUH
WHA
WHA ...?

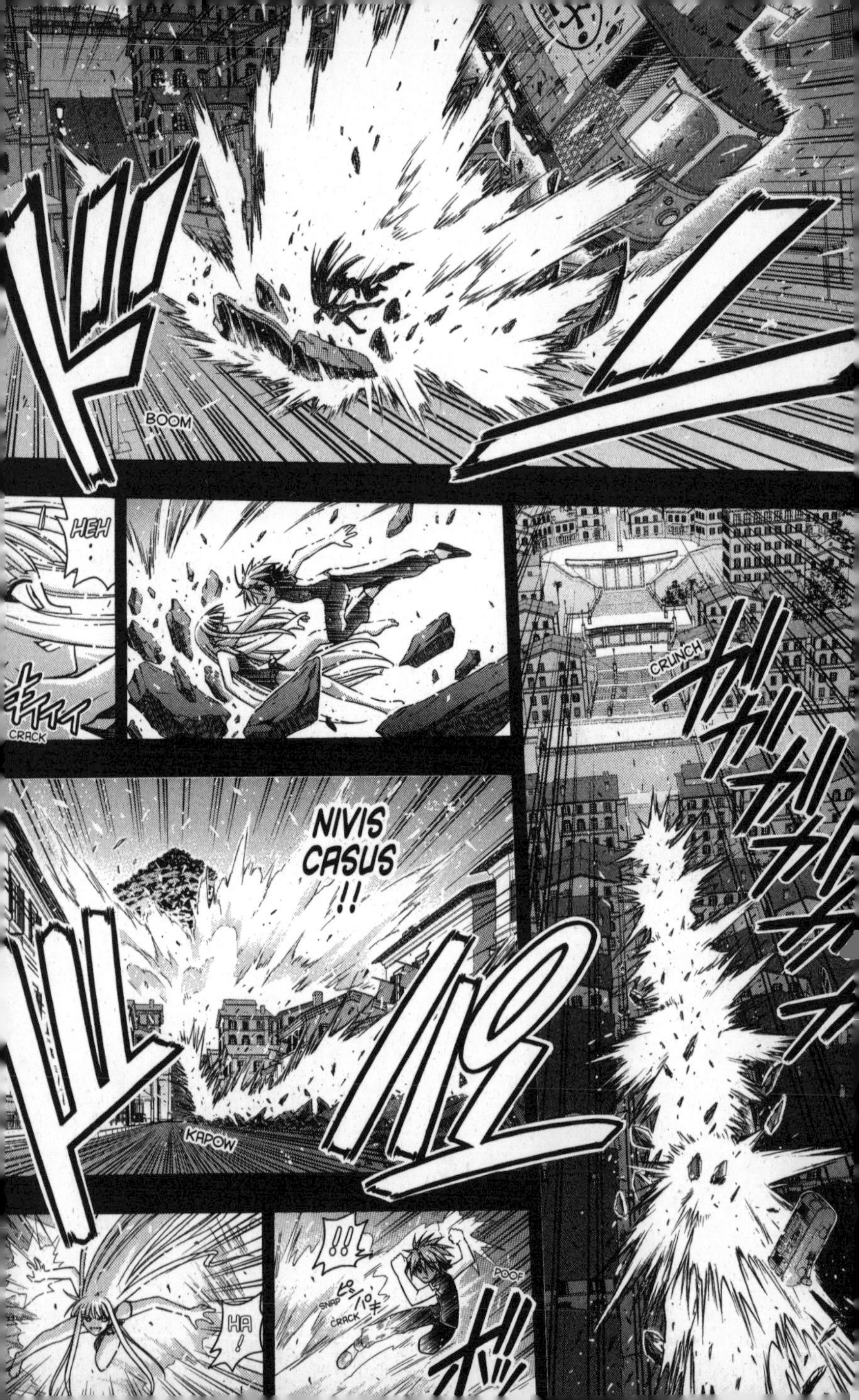
BOOM
CRUNCH
HEH
CRACK
NIVIS CASUS!!
KAPOW
!!
POOF
SNAP
CRACK
HA!

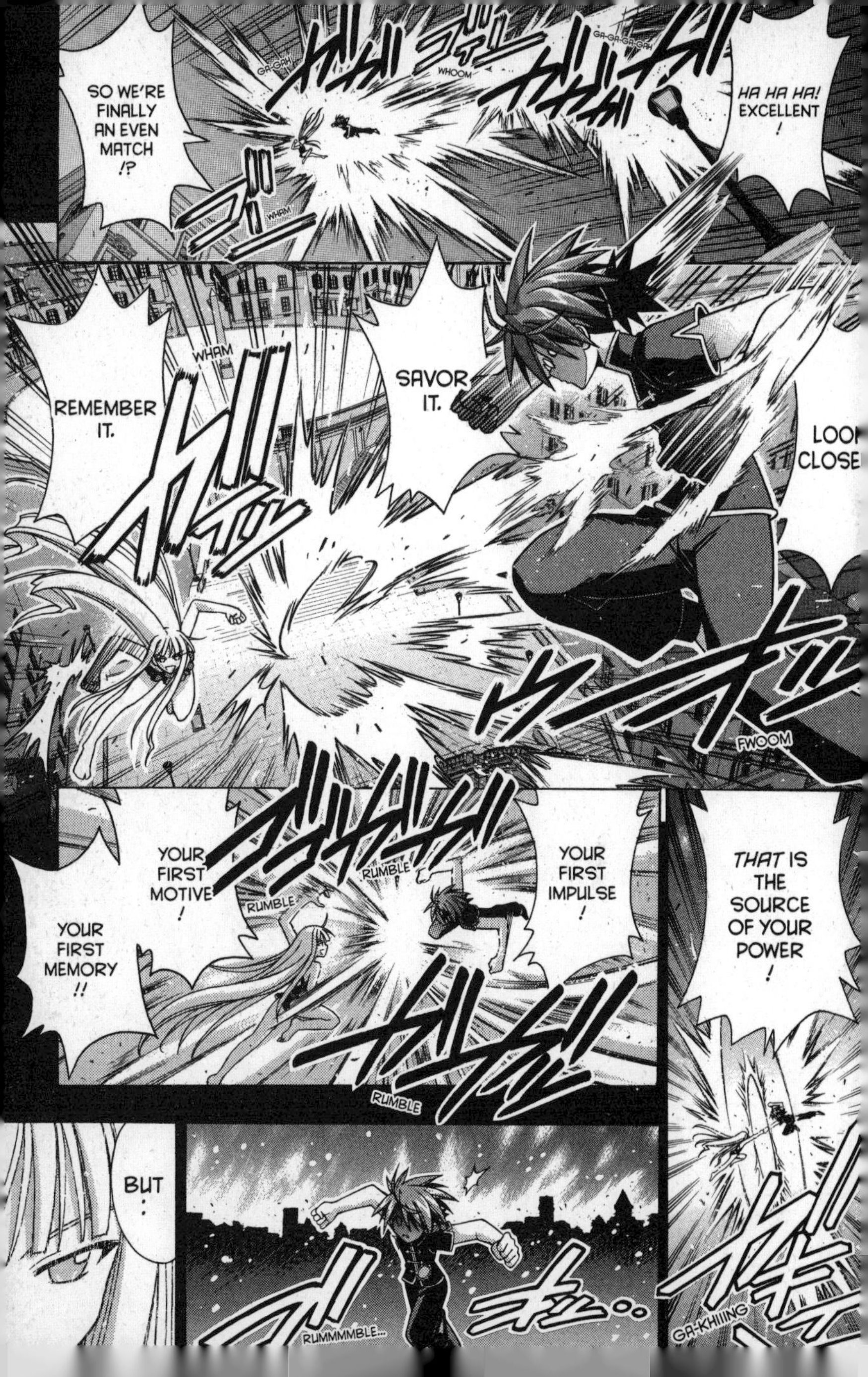
HA HA HA! EXCELLENT!
GA-GA-GA-GAH
WHOOM
GA-GAH
SO WE'RE FINALLY AN EVEN MATCH!?
WHAM
LOO
CLOSE
SAVOR IT.
WHAM
REMEMBER IT.
FWOOM
THAT IS THE SOURCE OF YOUR POWER!
GA-KHIIING
YOUR FIRST IMPULSE!
RUMBLE
YOUR FIRST MOTIVE!
RUMBLE
YOUR FIRST MEMORY!!
RUMBLE
BUT...
RUMMMMBLE...

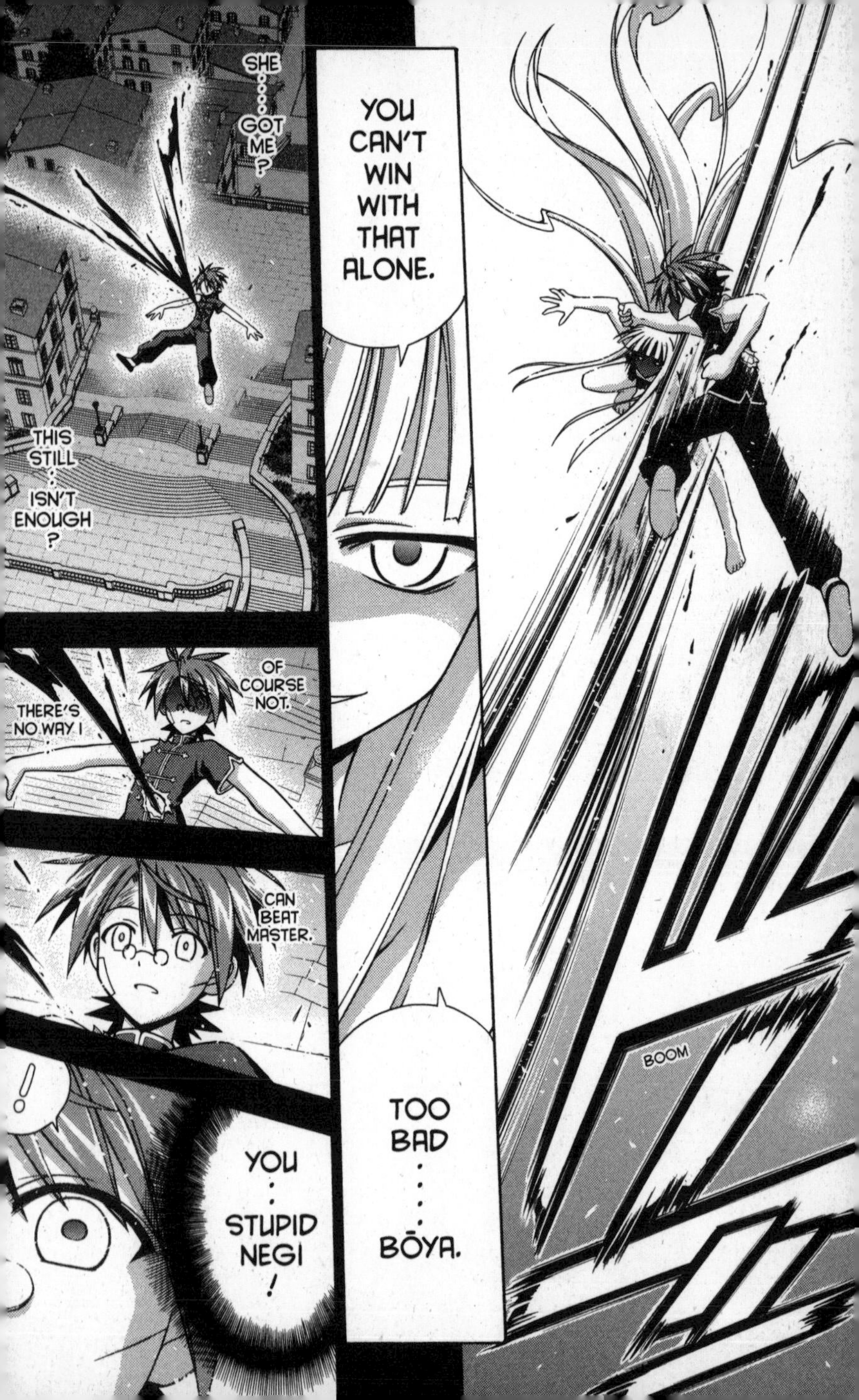
BOOM
YOU CAN'T WIN WITH THAT ALONE.
TOO BAD . . . . BŌYA.
SHE . . . . GOT ME?
THIS STILL . . . ISN'T ENOUGH?
OF COURSE NOT.
THERE'S NO WAY I . . .
CAN BEAT MASTER.
!
YOU . . . STUPID NEGI!

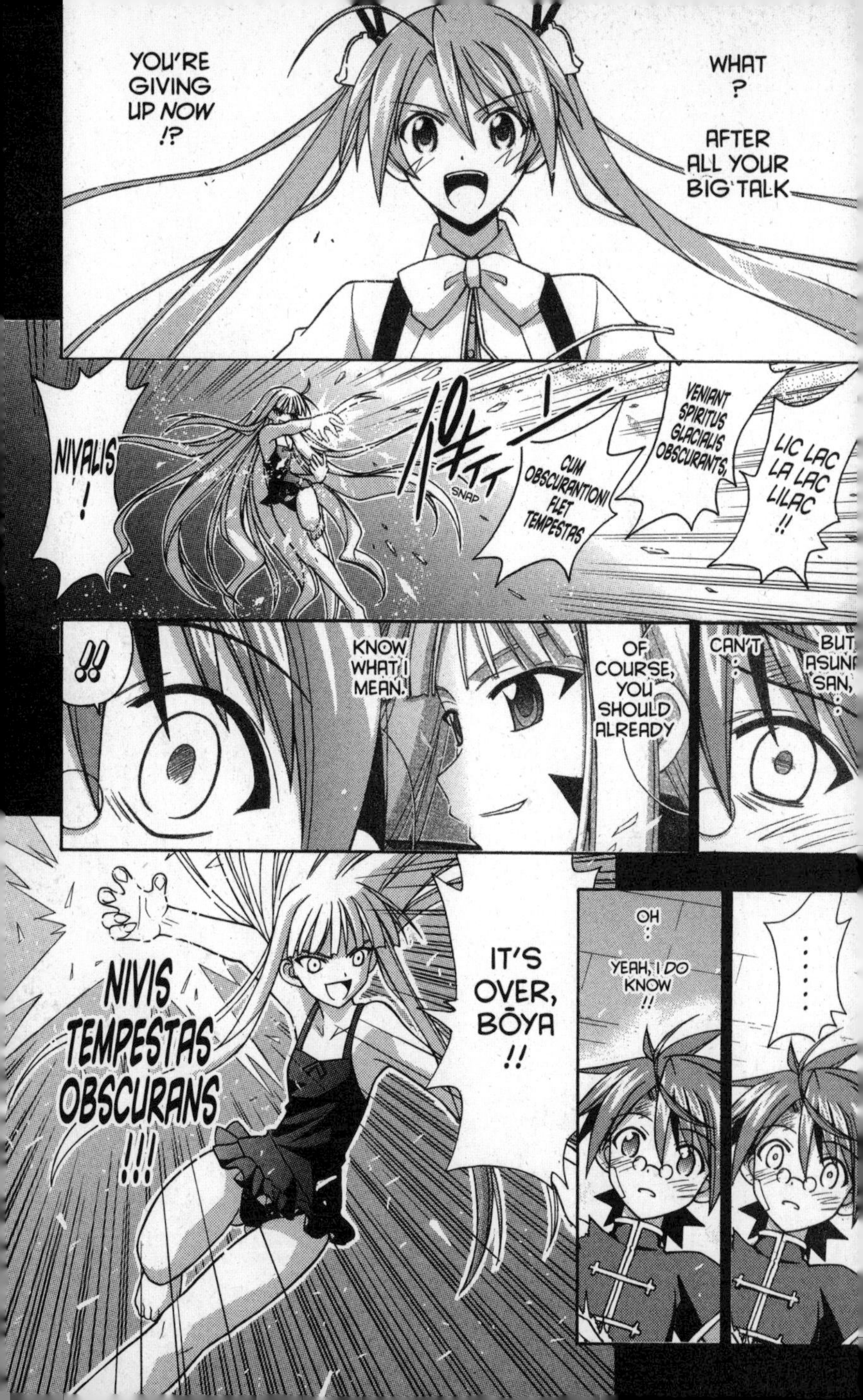
WHAT ?
AFTER ALL YOUR BIG TALK
YOU'RE GIVING UP NOW !?
LIC LAC LA LAC LILAC !!
VENIANT SPIRITUS GLACIALIS OBSCURANTS,
CUM OBSCURANTIONI FLET TEMPESTAS
SNAP
NIVALIS !
BUT ASUNA-SAN, ...
CAN'T ...
OF COURSE, YOU SHOULD ALREADY
KNOW WHAT I MEAN.
!!
......
OH ...
YEAH, I DO KNOW !!
IT'S OVER, BŌYA !!
NIVIS TEMPESTAS OBSCURANS !!!

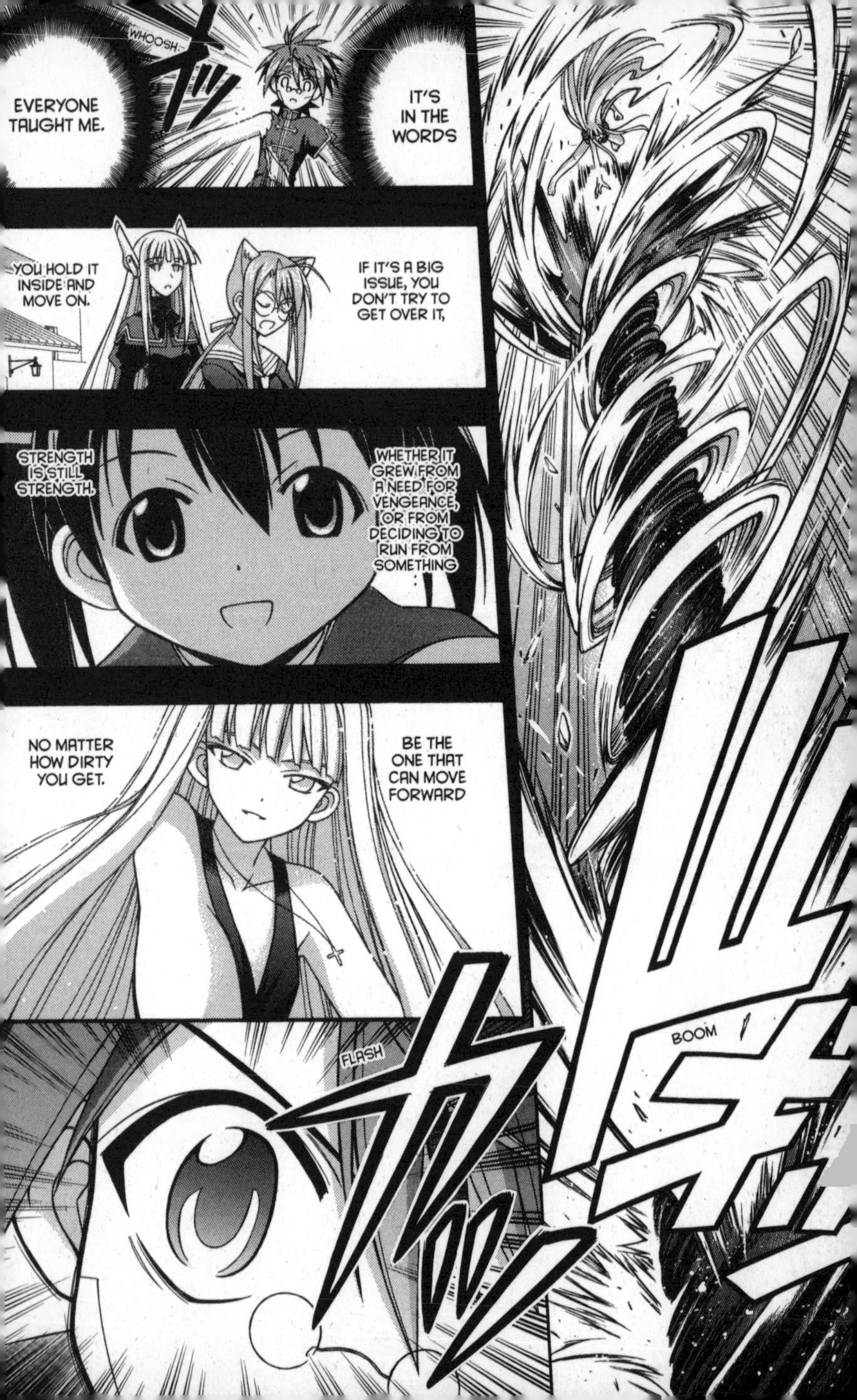
WHOOSH
IT'S IN THE WORDS
EVERYONE TAUGHT ME.
IF IT'S A BIG ISSUE, YOU DON'T TRY TO GET OVER IT,
YOU HOLD IT INSIDE AND MOVE ON.
WHETHER IT GREW FROM A NEED FOR VENGEANCE, OR FROM DECIDING TO RUN FROM SOMETHING
STRENGTH IS STILL STRENGTH.
BE THE ONE THAT CAN MOVE FORWARD
NO MATTER HOW DIRTY YOU GET.
BOOM
FLASH

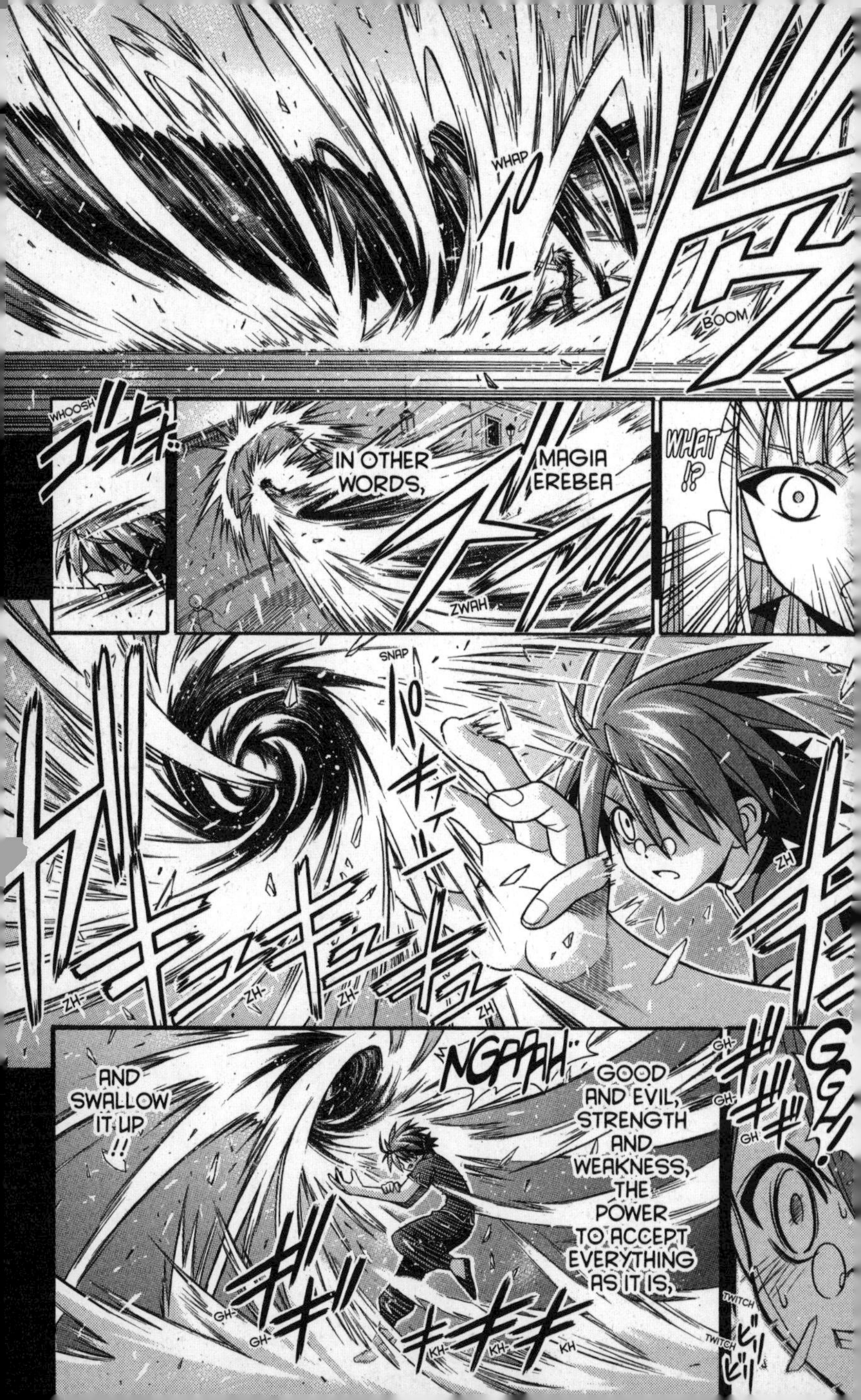
WHAP
BOOM
WHAT !?
MAGIA EREBEA
IN OTHER WORDS,
ZWAH
WHOOSH
SNAP
ZH
ZH-
ZH-
ZH-
ZH
GH-
GH-
GH
GOOD AND EVIL, STRENGTH AND WEAKNESS, THE POWER TO ACCEPT EVERYTHING AS IT IS,
NGAAAH
AND SWALLOW IT UP !!
GH-
GH-
KH-
KH-
KH
TWITCH
TWITCH

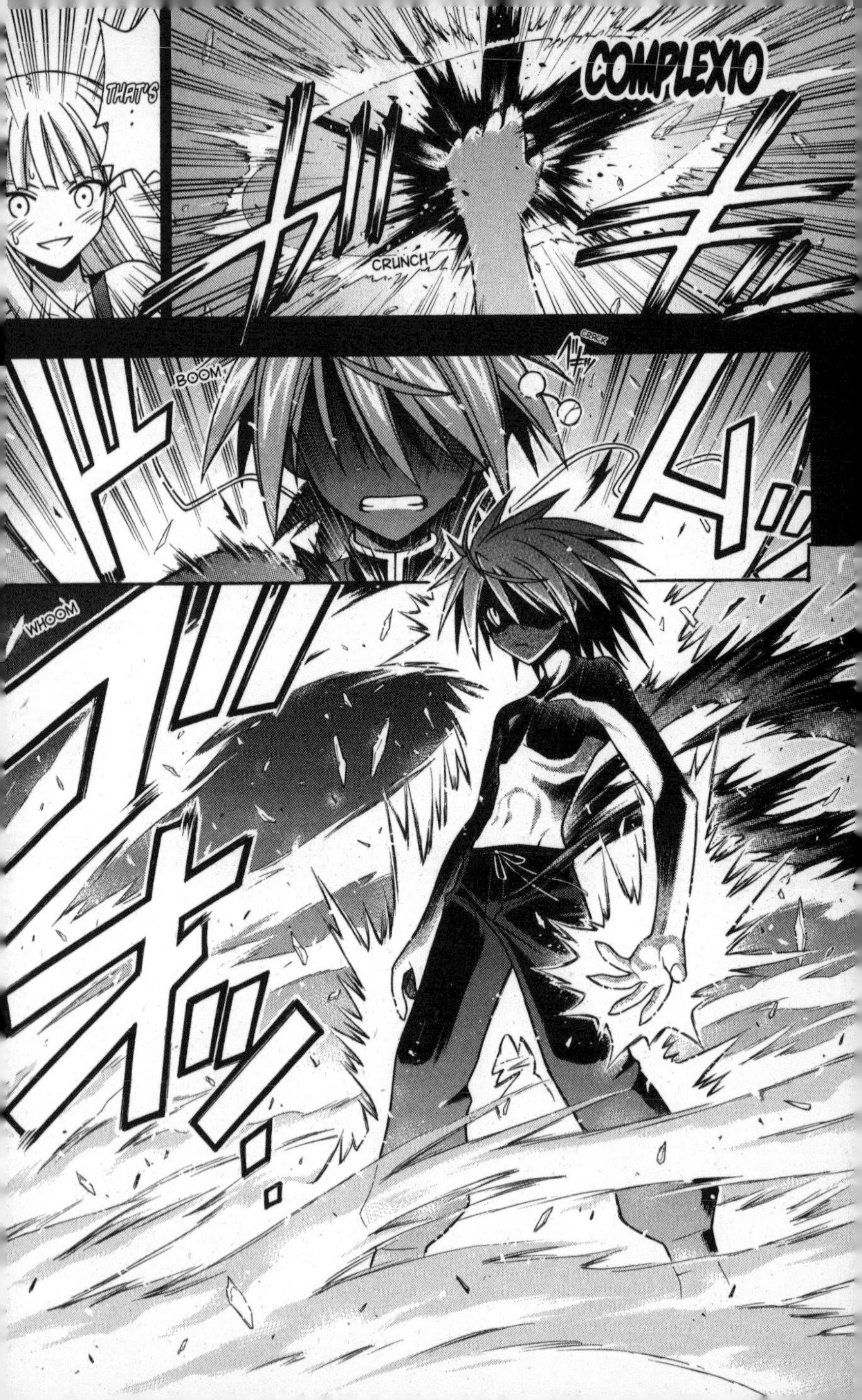
COMPLEXIO
CRUNCH
THAT'S
CRACK
BOOM
WHOOM

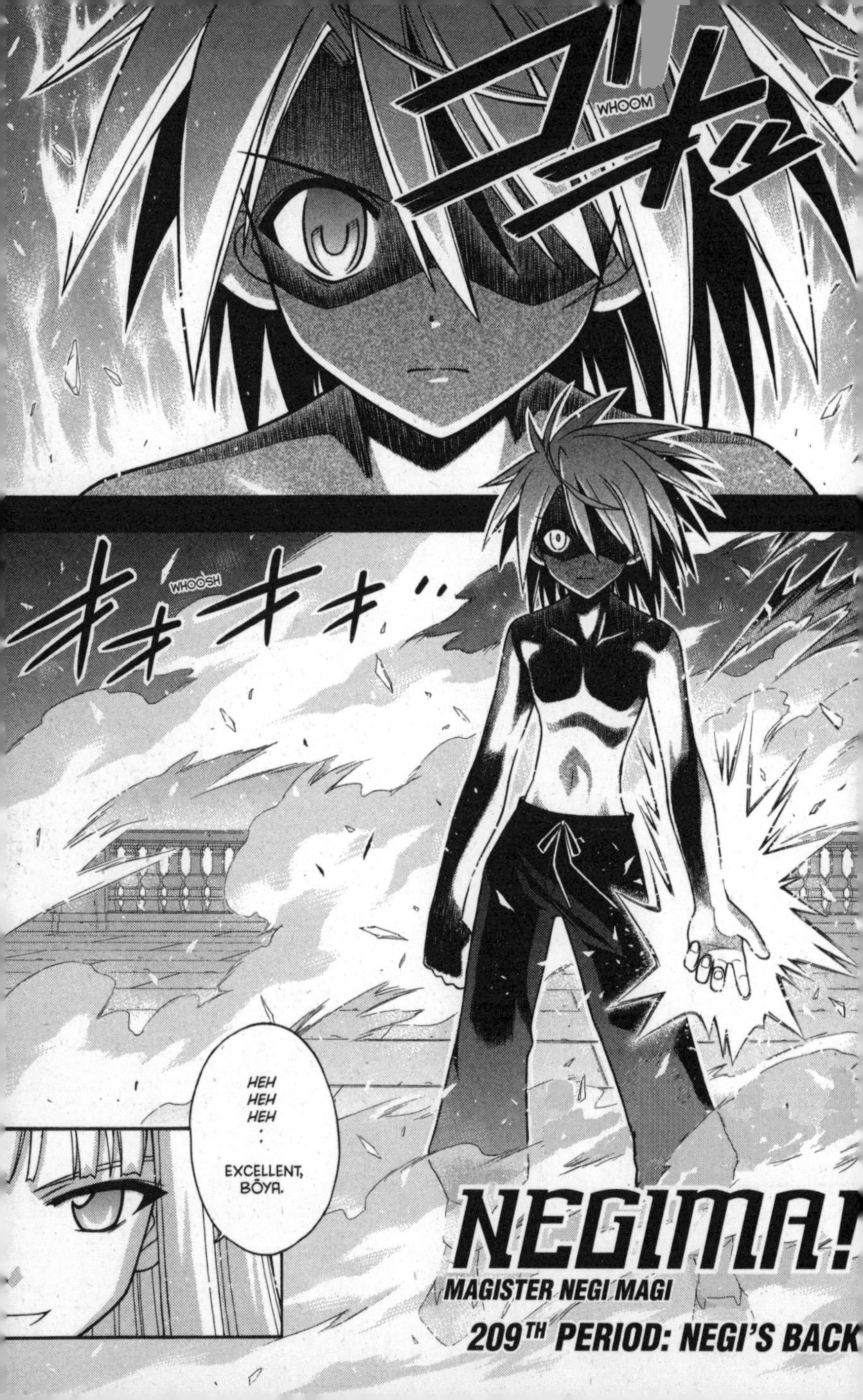
WHOOM
WHOOSH
HEH HEH HEH : EXCELLENT, BŌYA.
NEGIMA!
MAGISTER NEGI MAGI
209TH PERIOD: NEGI'S BACK

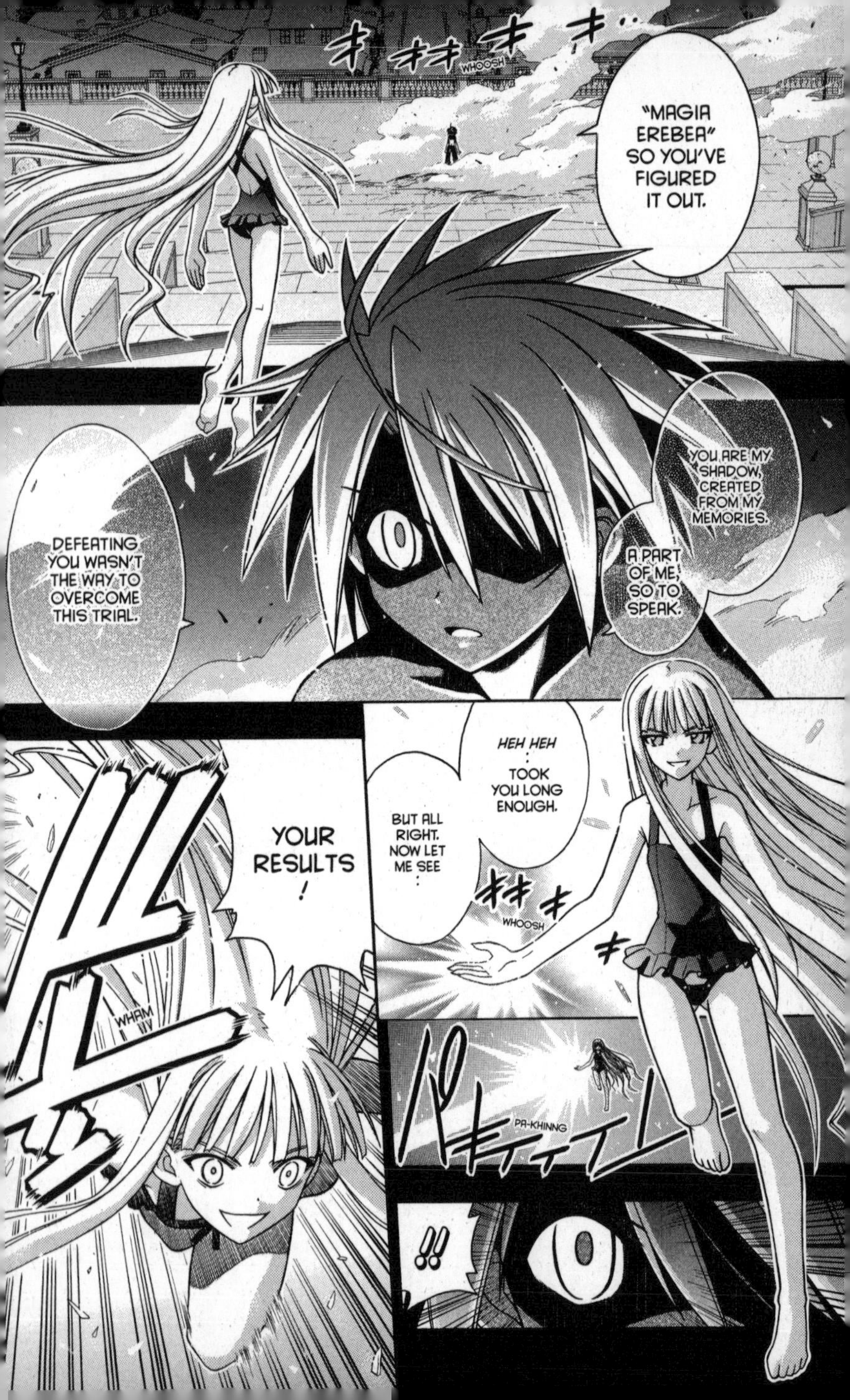
WHOOSH
"MAGIA EREBEA" SO YOU'VE FIGURED IT OUT.
YOU ARE MY SHADOW, CREATED FROM MY MEMORIES.
A PART OF ME, SO TO SPEAK.
DEFEATING YOU WASN'T THE WAY TO OVERCOME THIS TRIAL.
HEH HEH : TOOK YOU LONG ENOUGH.
BUT ALL RIGHT. NOW LET ME SEE :
WHOOSH
PA-KHINNG
!!
YOUR RESULTS !
WHAM

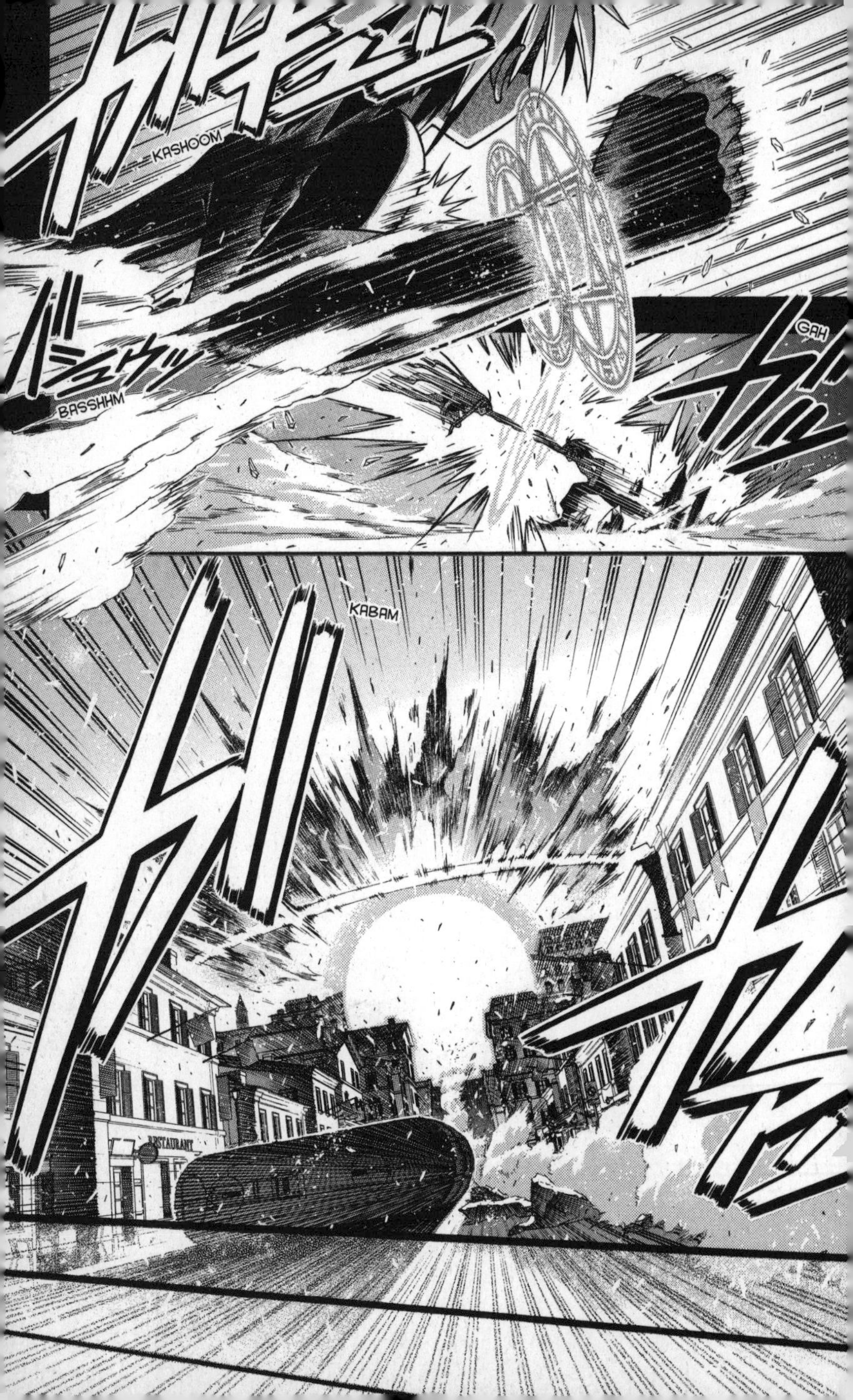
KASHOOM
GAH
BASSHHM
KABAM

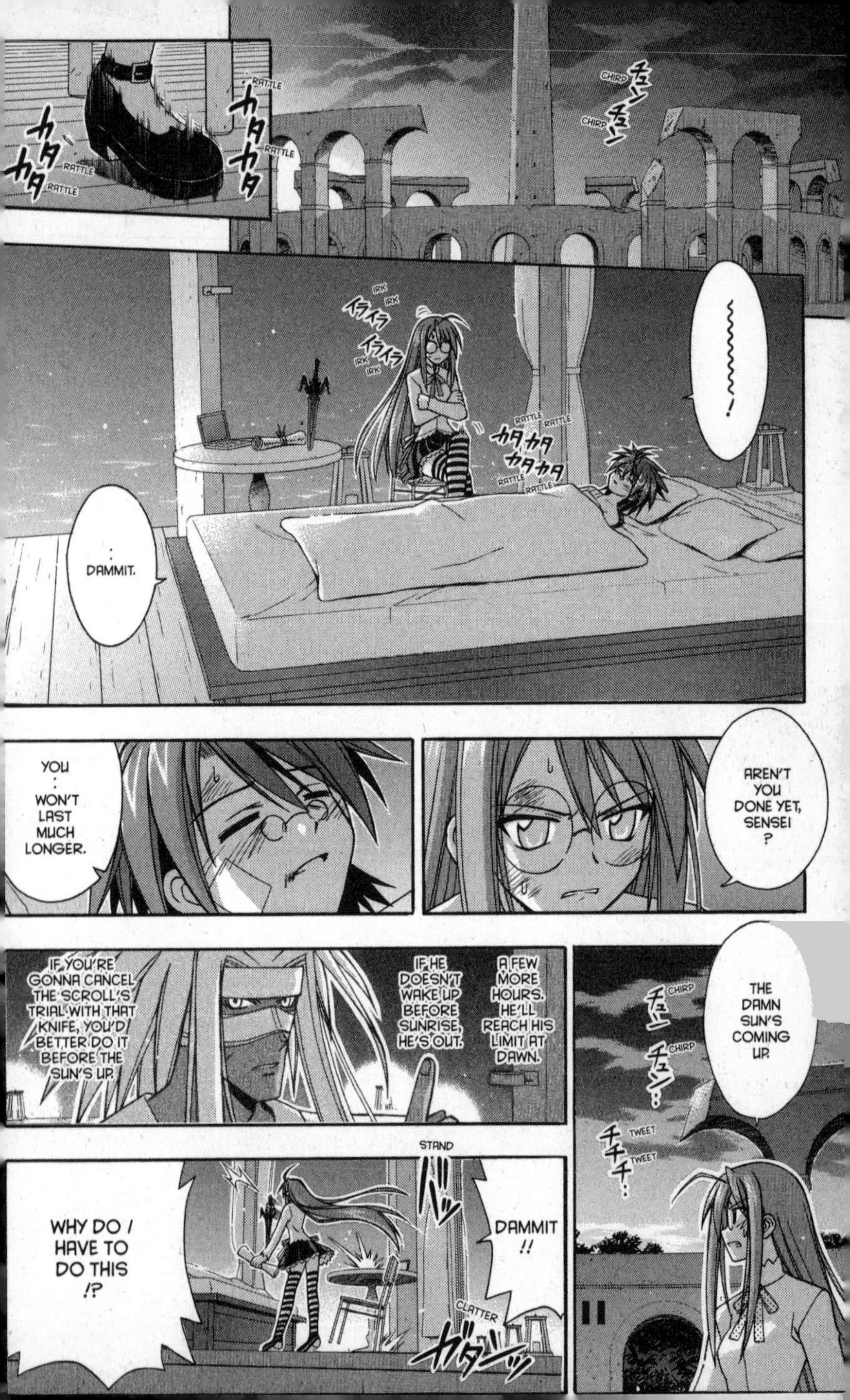
CHIRP
CHIRP
RATTLE
RATTLE
RATTLE
RATTLE
~~~~~!
IRK IRK
IRK IRK
RATTLE RATTLE
RATTLE RATTLE
... DAMMIT.
AREN'T YOU DONE YET, SENSEI?
YOU... WON'T LAST MUCH LONGER.
THE DAMN SUN'S COMING UP.
CHIRP
CHIRP
TWEET
TWEET
A FEW MORE HOURS. HE'LL REACH HIS LIMIT AT DAWN.
IF HE DOESN'T WAKE UP BEFORE SUNRISE, HE'S OUT.
IF YOU'RE GONNA CANCEL THE SCROLL'S TRIAL WITH THAT KNIFE, YOU'D BETTER DO IT BEFORE THE SUN'S UP.
STAND
DAMMIT!!
CLATTER
WHY DO I HAVE TO DO THIS!?
~~~~~

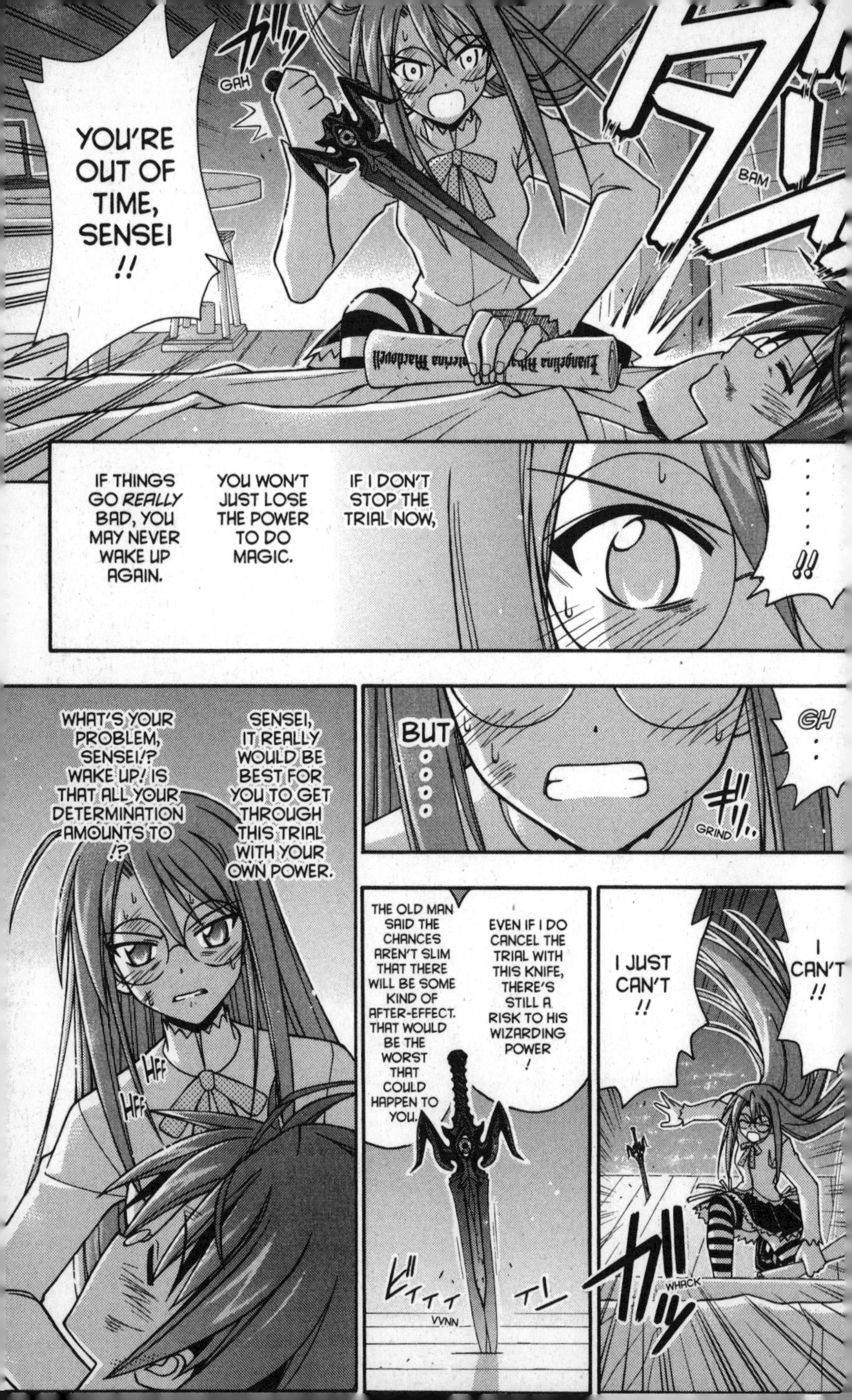
BAM
GAH
YOU'RE OUT OF TIME, SENSEI !!
......!!
IF I DON'T STOP THE TRIAL NOW,
YOU WON'T JUST LOSE THE POWER TO DO MAGIC.
IF THINGS GO *REALLY* BAD, YOU MAY NEVER WAKE UP AGAIN.
GH ..
BUT ....
GRIND
I CAN'T !!
I JUST CAN'T !!
WHACK
EVEN IF I DO CANCEL THE TRIAL WITH THIS KNIFE, THERE'S STILL A RISK TO HIS WIZARDING POWER !
THE OLD MAN SAID THE CHANCES AREN'T SLIM THAT THERE WILL BE SOME KIND OF AFTER-EFFECT. THAT WOULD BE THE WORST THAT COULD HAPPEN TO YOU.
VVNN
SENSEI, IT REALLY WOULD BE BEST FOR YOU TO GET THROUGH THIS TRIAL WITH YOUR OWN POWER.
WHAT'S YOUR PROBLEM, SENSEI!? WAKE UP! IS THAT ALL YOUR DETERMINATION AMOUNTS TO !?
HFF
HFF

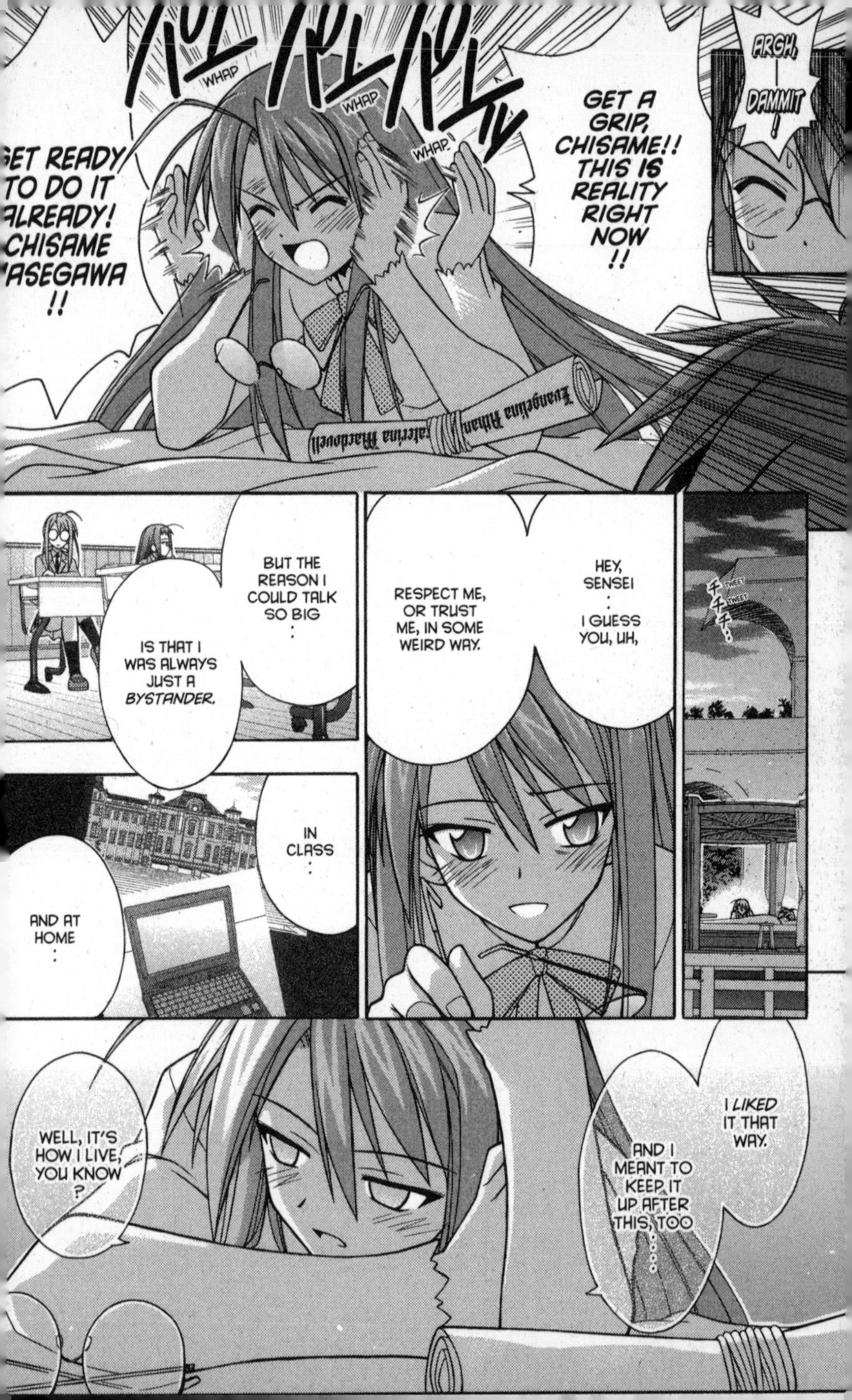
ARGH, DAMMIT!
GET A GRIP, CHISAME!! THIS IS REALITY RIGHT NOW!!
WHAP WHAP WHAP
GET READY TO DO IT ALREADY! CHISAME HASEGAWA!!
TWEET TWEET
HEY, SENSEI... I GUESS YOU, UH,
RESPECT ME, OR TRUST ME, IN SOME WEIRD WAY.
BUT THE REASON I COULD TALK SO BIG...
IS THAT I WAS ALWAYS JUST A *BYSTANDER.*
IN CLASS...
AND AT HOME...
I *LIKED* IT THAT WAY.
AND I MEANT TO KEEP IT UP AFTER THIS, TOO.....
WELL, IT'S HOW I LIVE, YOU KNOW?

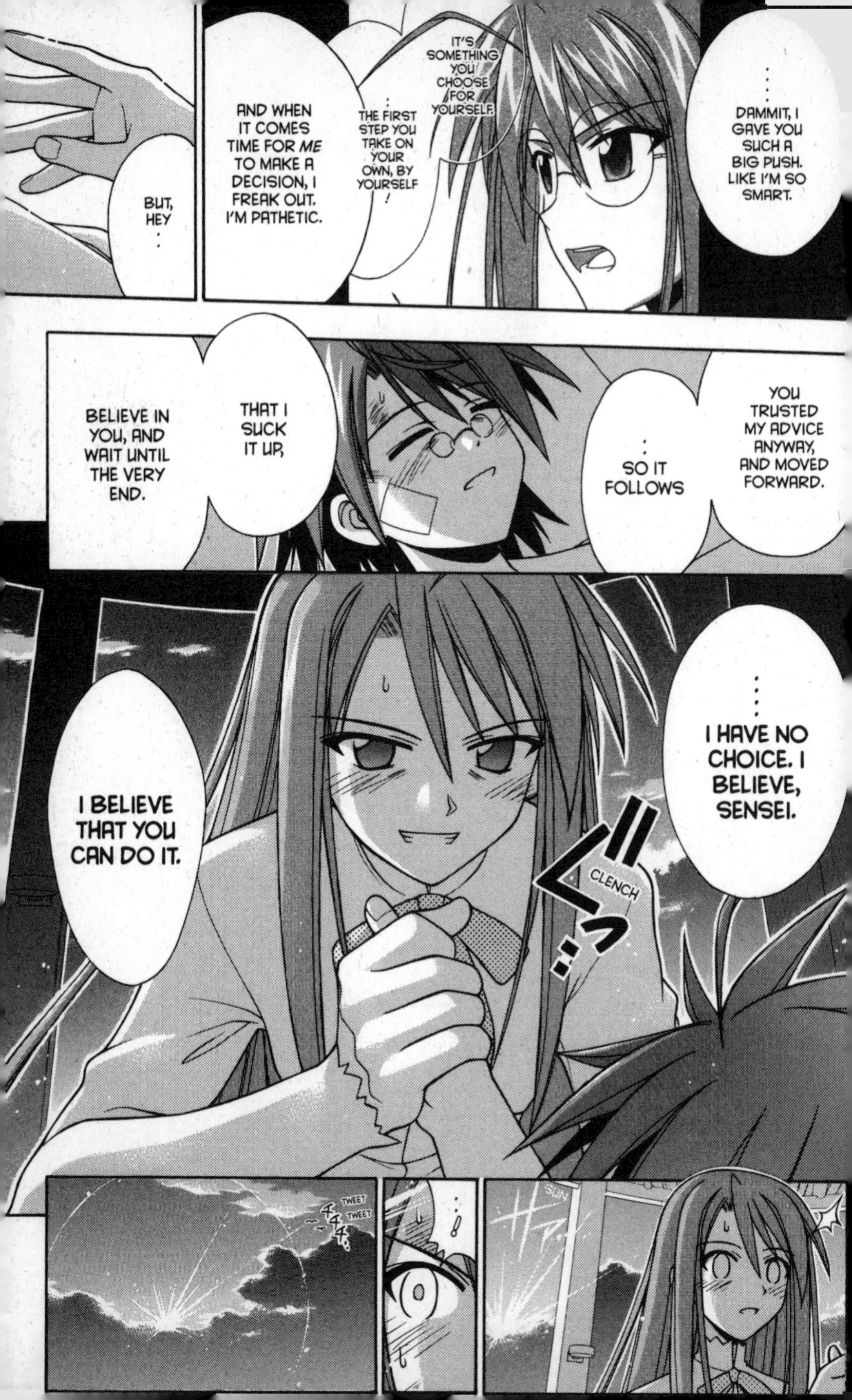

... DAMMIT, I GAVE YOU SUCH A BIG PUSH. LIKE I'M SO SMART.
IT'S SOMETHING YOU CHOOSE FOR YOURSELF.
... THE FIRST STEP YOU TAKE ON YOUR OWN, BY YOURSELF!
AND WHEN IT COMES TIME FOR *ME* TO MAKE A DECISION, I FREAK OUT. I'M PATHETIC.
BUT, HEY...
YOU TRUSTED MY ADVICE ANYWAY, AND MOVED FORWARD.
...SO IT FOLLOWS
THAT I SUCK IT UP,
BELIEVE IN YOU, AND WAIT UNTIL THE VERY END.
... I HAVE NO CHOICE. I BELIEVE, SENSEI.
CLENCH
I BELIEVE THAT YOU CAN DO IT.
SUN
...!
TWEET
TWEET

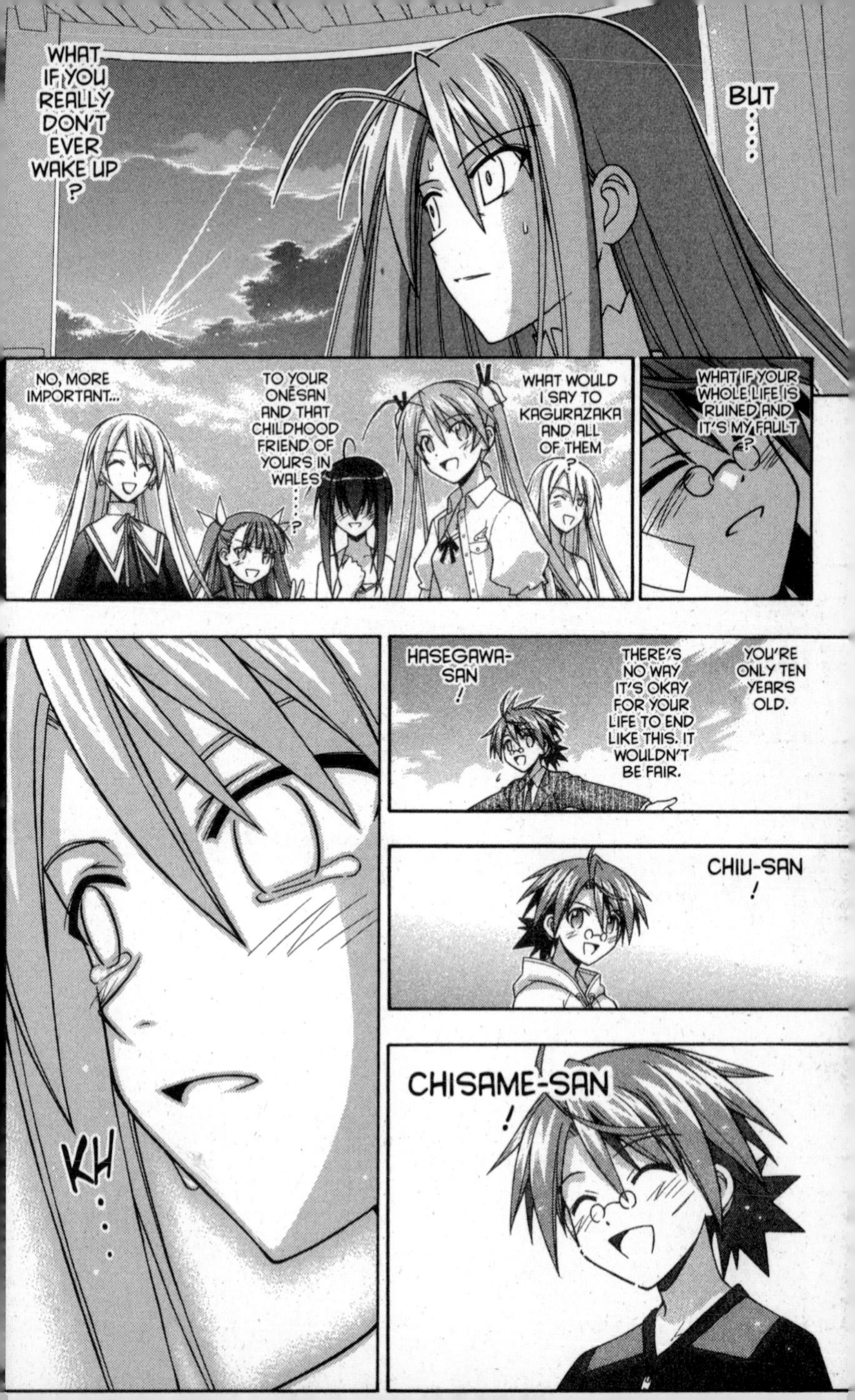
BUT....
WHAT IF YOU REALLY DON'T EVER WAKE UP?
WHAT IF YOUR WHOLE LIFE IS RUINED AND IT'S MY FAULT?
WHAT WOULD I SAY TO KAGURAZAKA AND ALL OF THEM?
TO YOUR ONĒSAN AND THAT CHILDHOOD FRIEND OF YOURS IN WALES...?
NO, MORE IMPORTANT...
YOU'RE ONLY TEN YEARS OLD.
THERE'S NO WAY IT'S OKAY FOR YOUR LIFE TO END LIKE THIS. IT WOULDN'T BE FAIR.
HASEGAWA-SAN!
CHIU-SAN!
CHISAME-SAN!
KH...

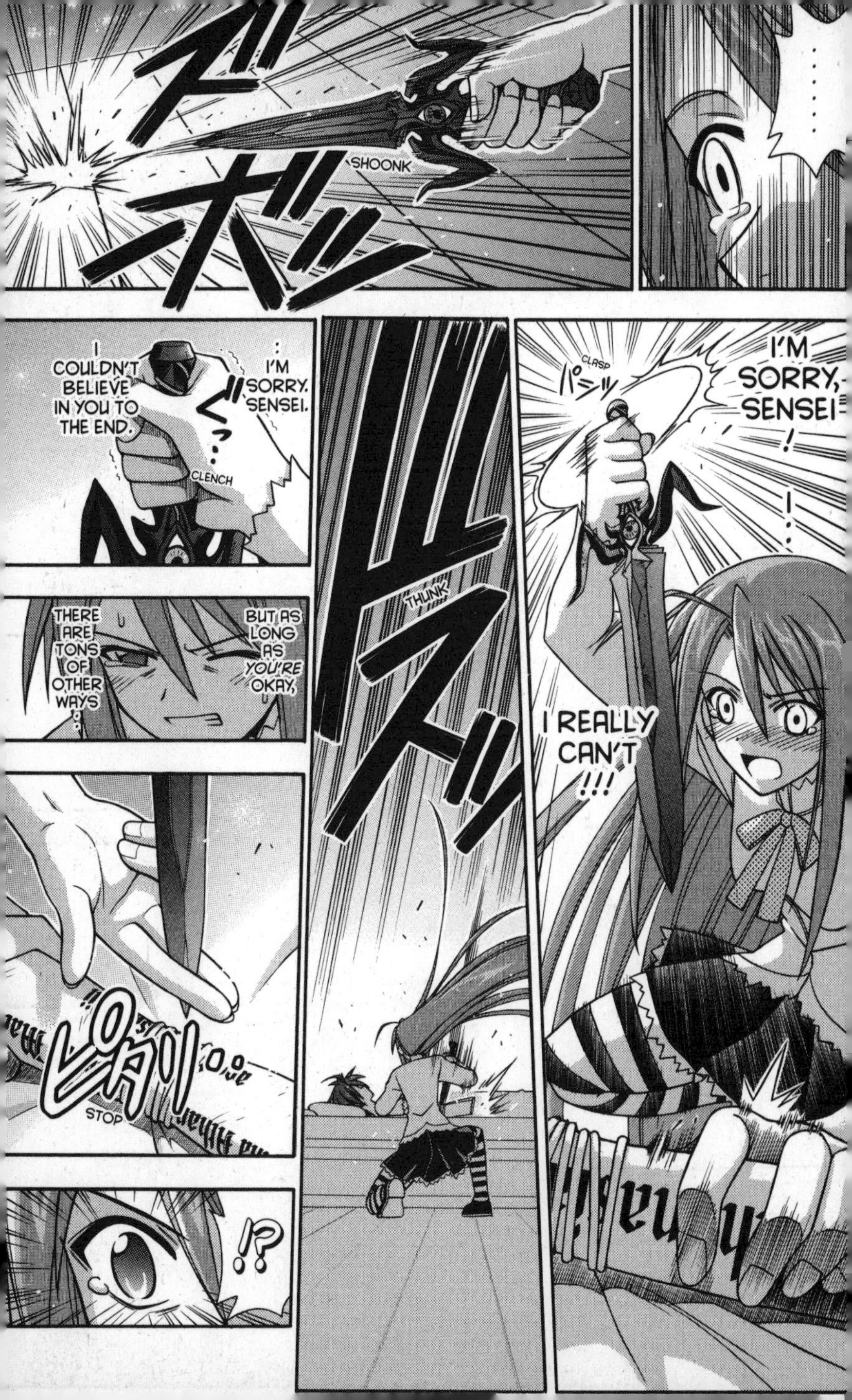

SHOONK
CLASP
I'M SORRY, SENSEI!
I REALLY CAN'T!!!
THUNK
I'M SORRY. SENSEI.
I COULDN'T BELIEVE IN YOU TO THE END.
CLENCH
BUT AS LONG AS YOU'RE OKAY,
THERE ARE TONS OF OTHER WAYS...
STOP
!?

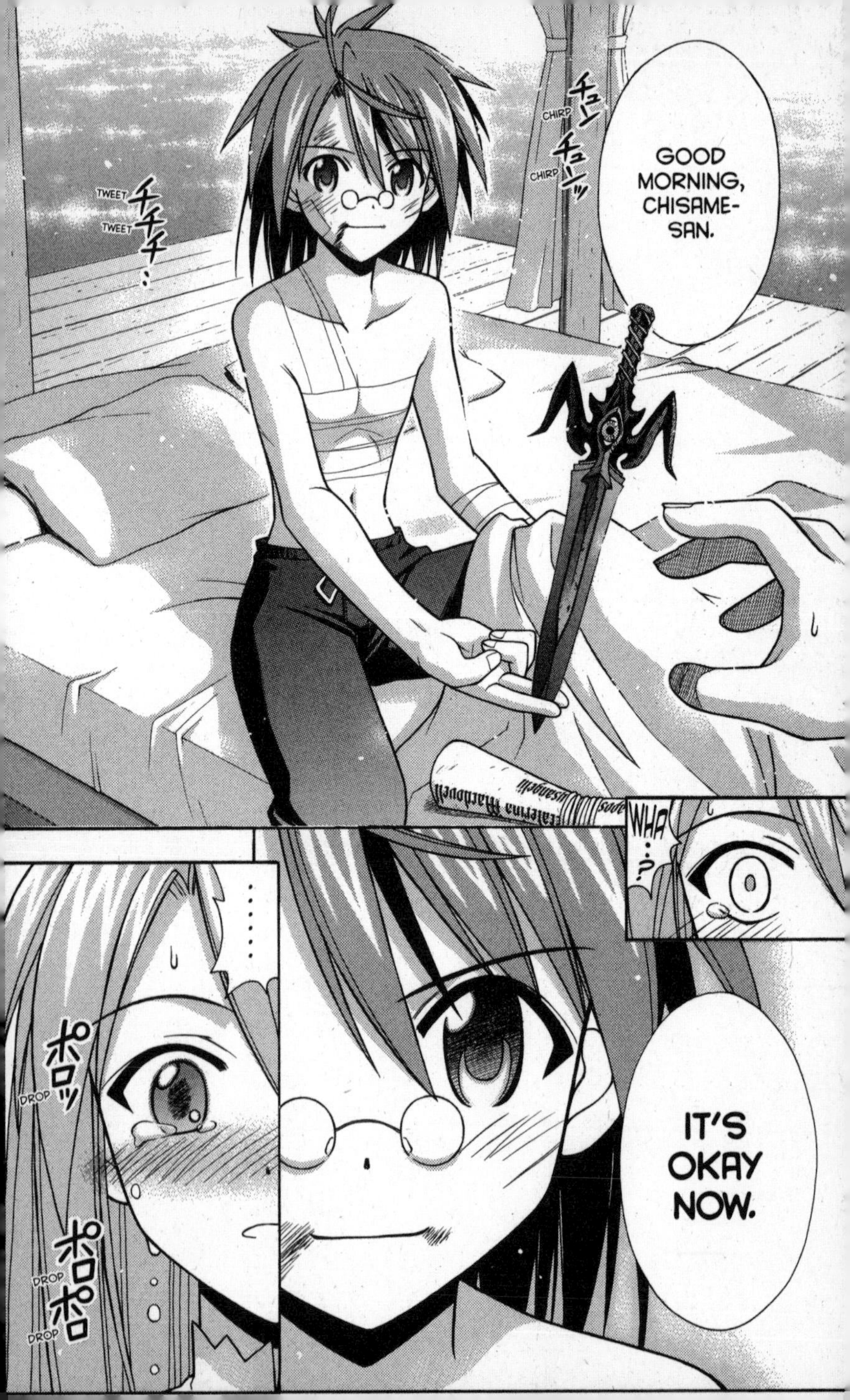
GOOD MORNING, CHISAME-SAN.
チュン
CHIRP
チュンッ
CHIRP
チチチ・・
TWEET
TWEET
WHA...?
IT'S OKAY NOW.
......
ポロッ
DROP
ポロポロ
DROP
DROP

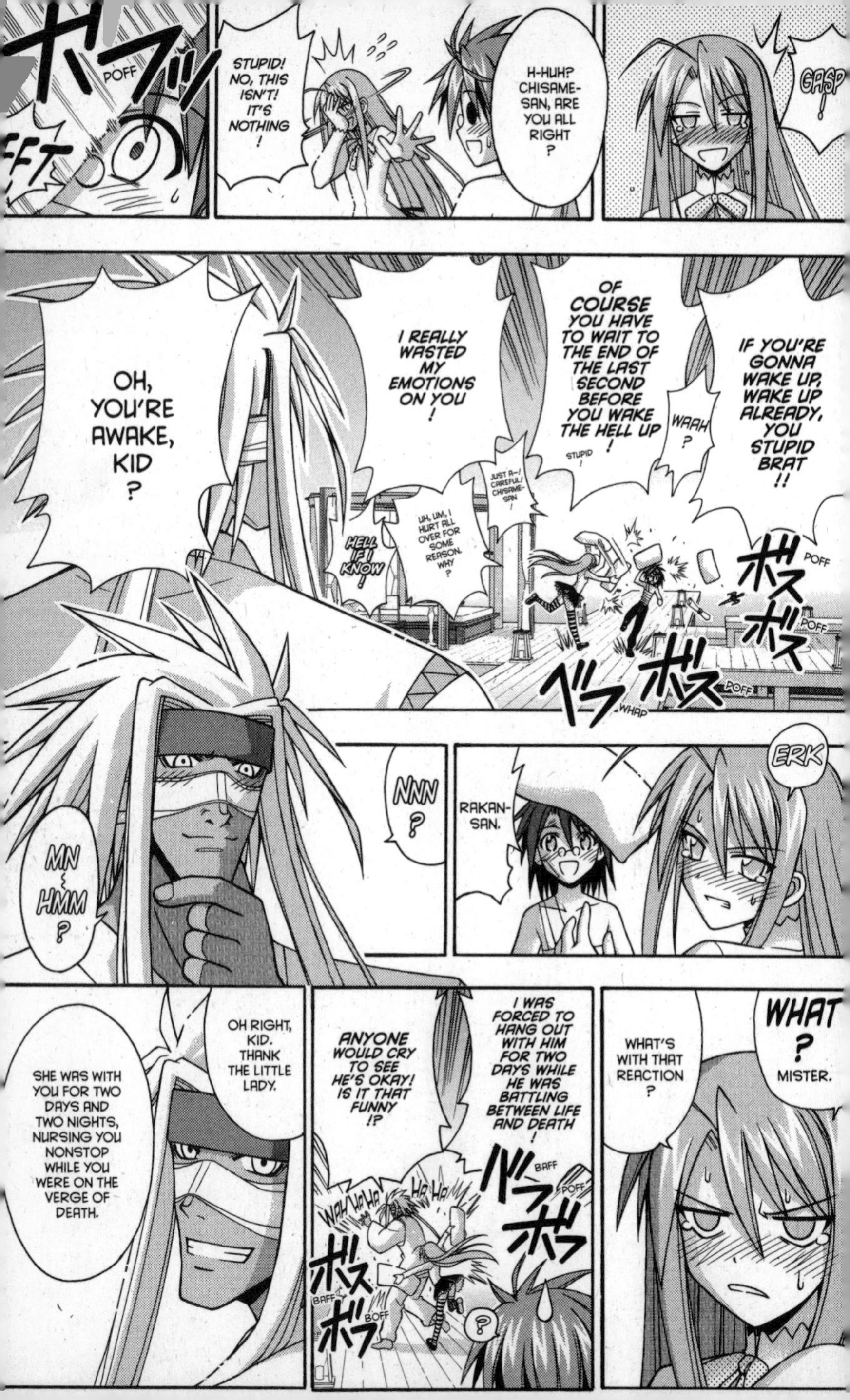
GASP!
H-HUH? CHISAME-SAN, ARE YOU ALL RIGHT?
STUPID! NO, THIS ISN'T! IT'S NOTHING!
POFF
IF YOU'RE GONNA WAKE UP, WAKE UP ALREADY, YOU STUPID BRAT!!
WAAH?
OF COURSE YOU HAVE TO WAIT TO THE END OF THE LAST SECOND BEFORE YOU WAKE THE HELL UP!
STUPID!
JUST A-! CAREFUL! CHISAME-SAN!
I REALLY WASTED MY EMOTIONS ON YOU!
UH, UM, I HURT ALL OVER FOR SOME REASON. WHY?
HELL IF I KNOW!
POFF
POFF
POFF
WHAP
OH, YOU'RE AWAKE, KID?
ERK
RAKAN-SAN.
NNN?
MN~HMM?
WHAT? MISTER.
WHAT'S WITH THAT REACTION?
I WAS FORCED TO HANG OUT WITH HIM FOR TWO DAYS WHILE HE WAS BATTLING BETWEEN LIFE AND DEATH!
ANYONE WOULD CRY TO SEE HE'S OKAY! IS IT THAT FUNNY!?
BAFF
POFF
HA HA
WAH HA HA
BAFF
BOFF
?
OH RIGHT, KID. THANK THE LITTLE LADY.
SHE WAS WITH YOU FOR TWO DAYS AND TWO NIGHTS, NURSING YOU NONSTOP WHILE YOU WERE ON THE VERGE OF DEATH.

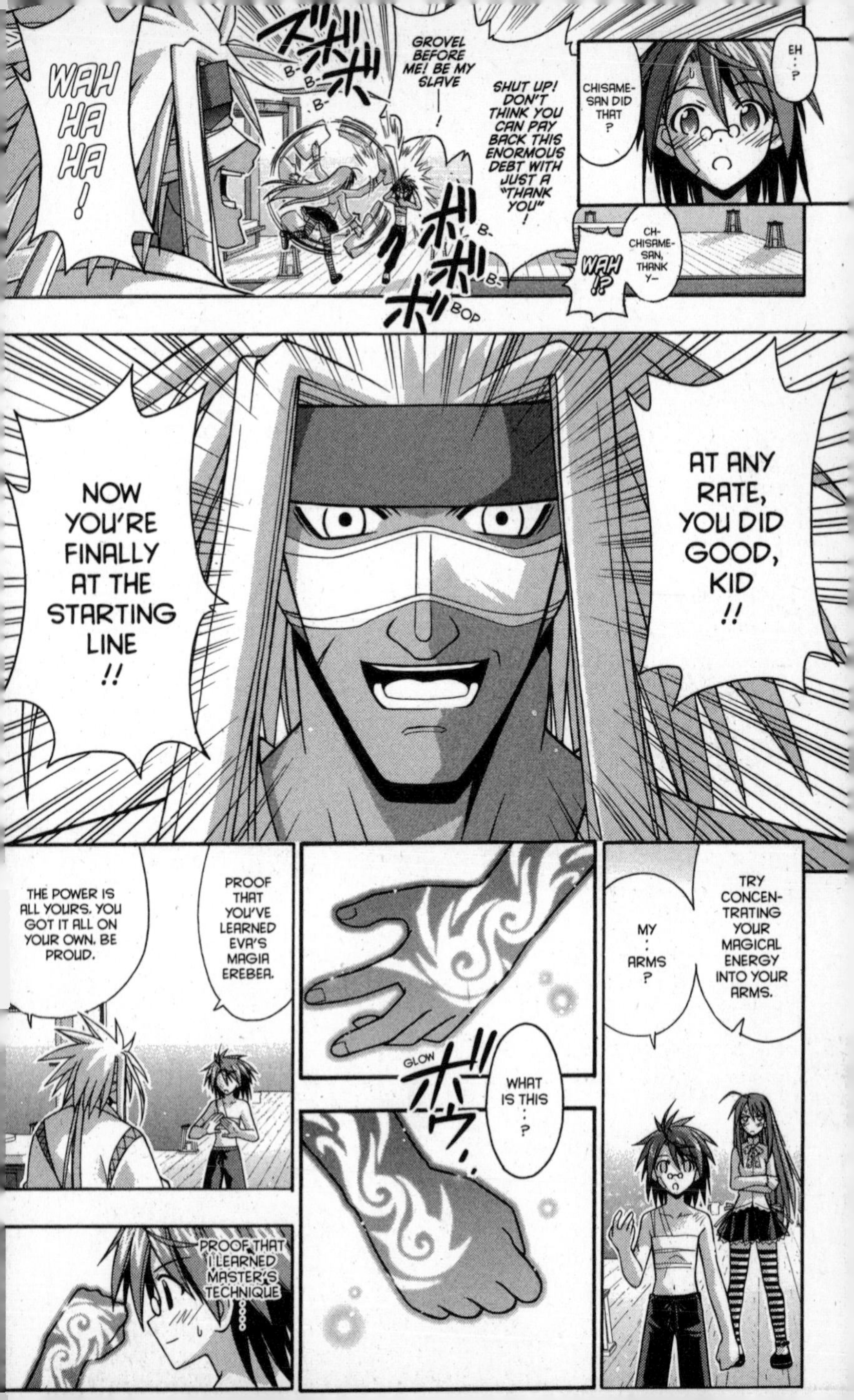
EH . . ?
CHISAME-SAN DID THAT?
CH-CHISAME-SAN, THANK Y—
WAH !?
WAH HA HA!
SHUT UP! DON'T THINK YOU CAN PAY BACK THIS ENORMOUS DEBT WITH JUST A "THANK YOU"!
GROVEL BEFORE ME! BE MY SLAVE!
B-B-B-
B-B-BOP
AT ANY RATE, YOU DID GOOD, KID!!
NOW YOU'RE FINALLY AT THE STARTING LINE!!
TRY CONCENTRATING YOUR MAGICAL ENERGY INTO YOUR ARMS.
MY . . ARMS?
GLOW
WHAT IS THIS . . . ?
PROOF THAT YOU'VE LEARNED EVA'S MAGIA EREBEA.
THE POWER IS ALL YOURS. YOU GOT IT ALL ON YOUR OWN. BE PROUD.
PROOF THAT I LEARNED MASTER'S TECHNIQUE

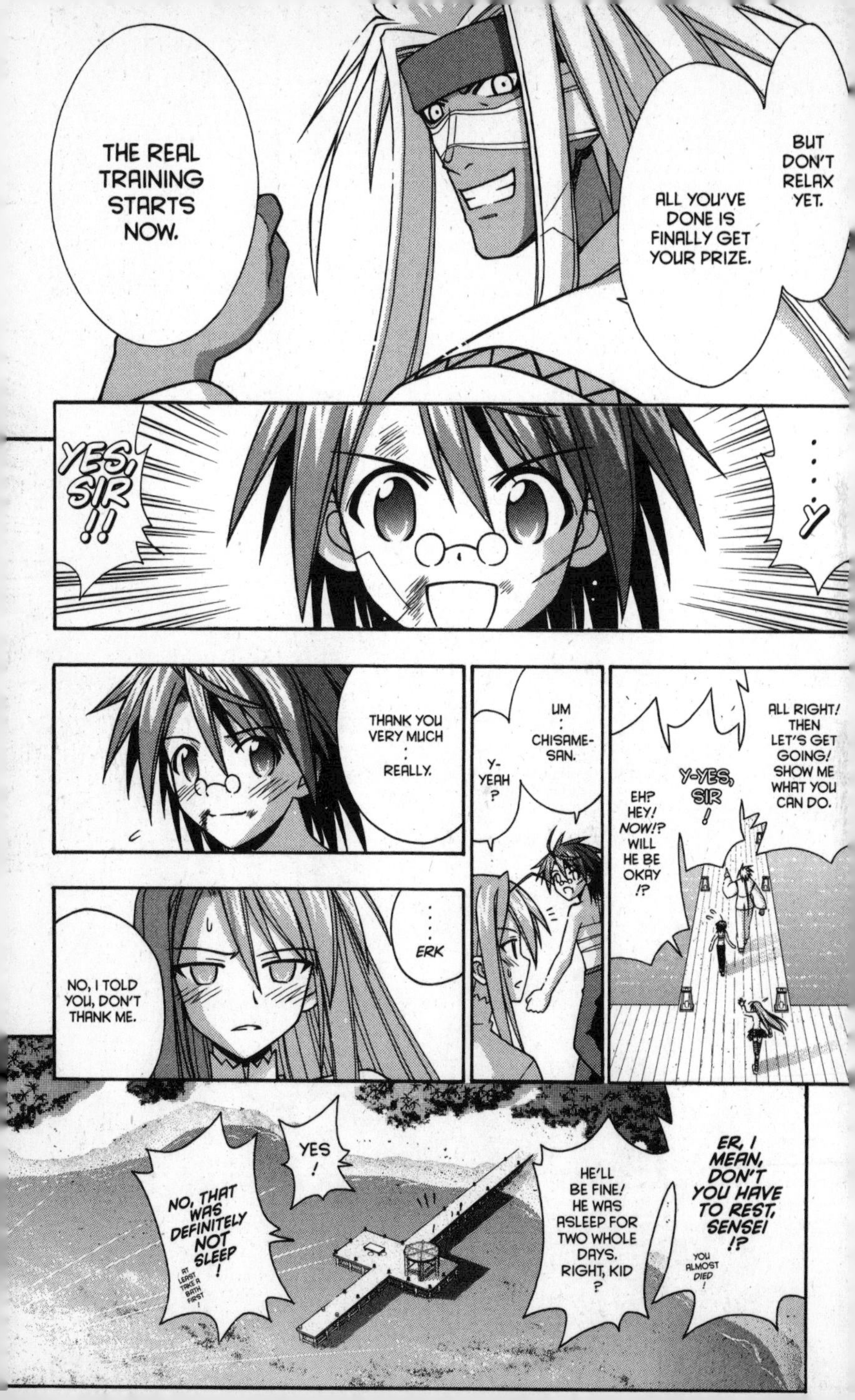
BUT DON'T RELAX YET.
ALL YOU'VE DONE IS FINALLY GET YOUR PRIZE.
THE REAL TRAINING STARTS NOW.
...Y
YES, SIR!!
ALL RIGHT! THEN LET'S GET GOING! SHOW ME WHAT YOU CAN DO.
Y-YES, SIR!
EH? HEY! NOW!? WILL HE BE OKAY!?
UM... CHISAME-SAN.
Y-YEAH?
THANK YOU VERY MUCH... REALLY.
...ERK
NO, I TOLD YOU, DON'T THANK ME.
ER, I MEAN, DON'T YOU HAVE TO REST, SENSEI!?
YOU ALMOST DIED!
HE'LL BE FINE! HE WAS ASLEEP FOR TWO WHOLE DAYS. RIGHT, KID?
YES!
NO, THAT WAS DEFINITELY NOT SLEEP!
AT LEAST TAKE A BATH FIRST!

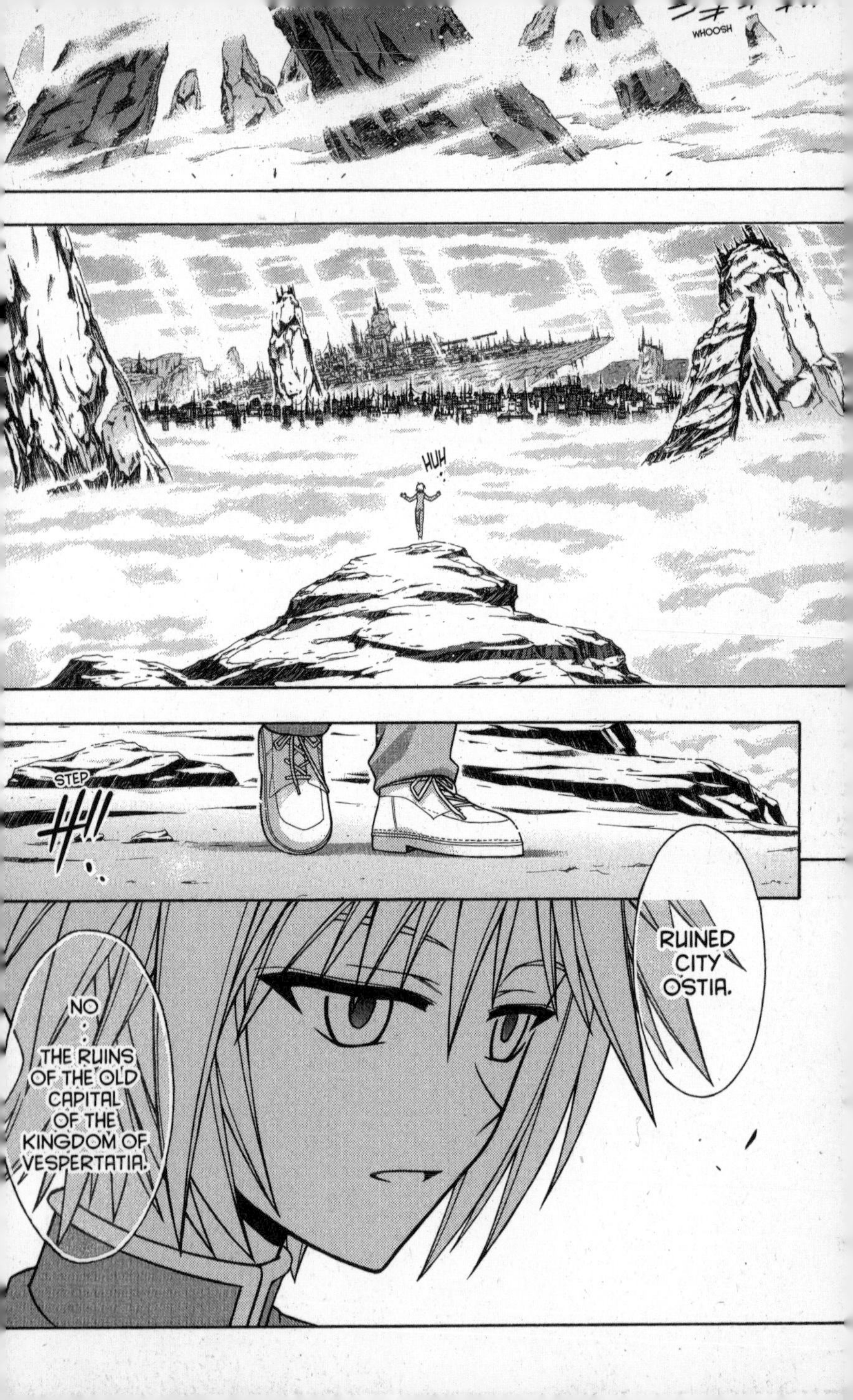
WHOOSH
HUH
STEP
RUINED CITY OSTIA.
NO... THE RUINS OF THE OLD CAPITAL OF THE KINGDOM OF VESPERTATIA.

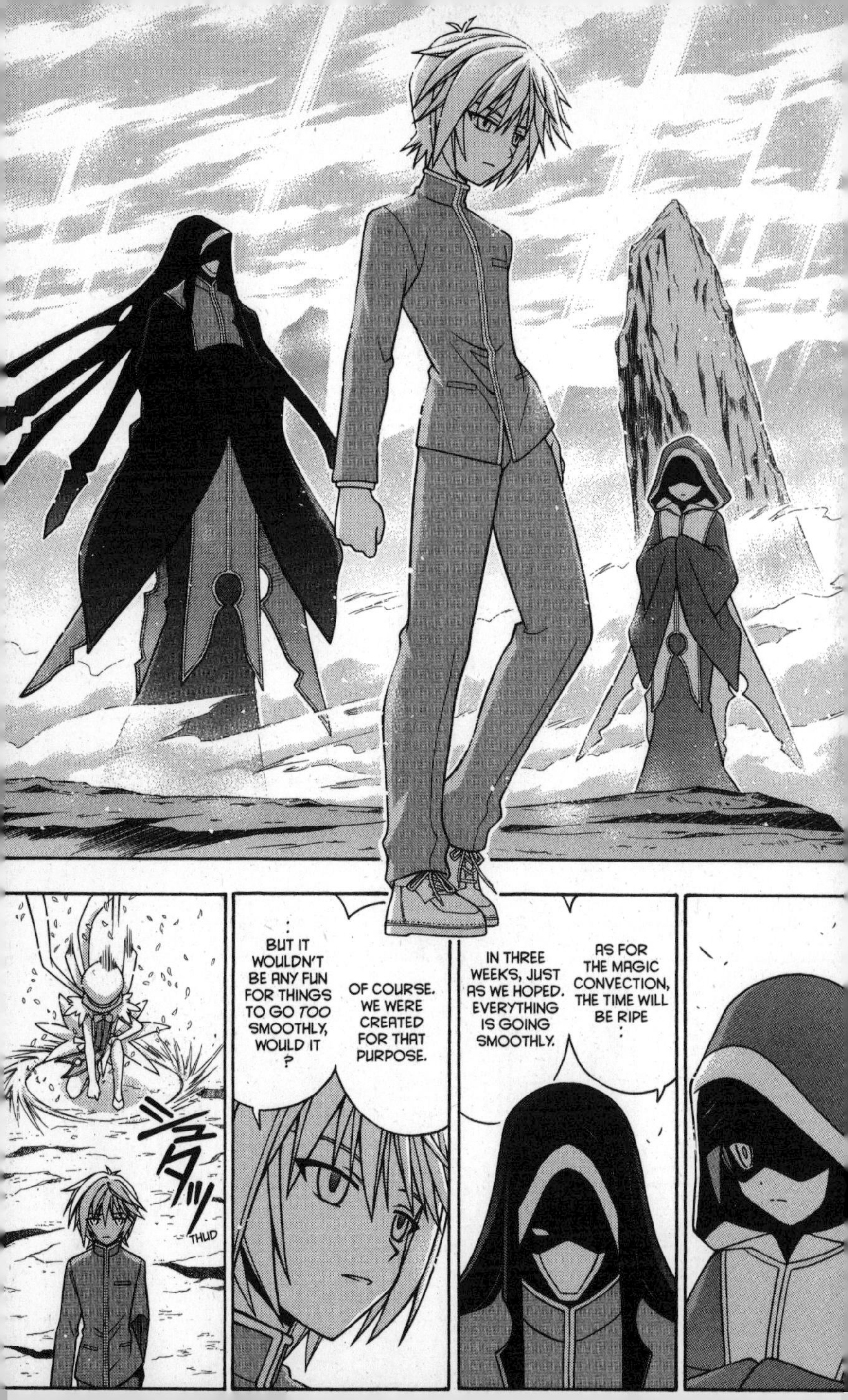
AS FOR THE MAGIC CONVECTION, THE TIME WILL BE RIPE :
IN THREE WEEKS, JUST AS WE HOPED. EVERYTHING IS GOING SMOOTHLY.
OF COURSE. WE WERE CREATED FOR THAT PURPOSE.
: BUT IT WOULDN'T BE ANY FUN FOR THINGS TO GO *TOO* SMOOTHLY, WOULD IT ?
シュタッ
THUD

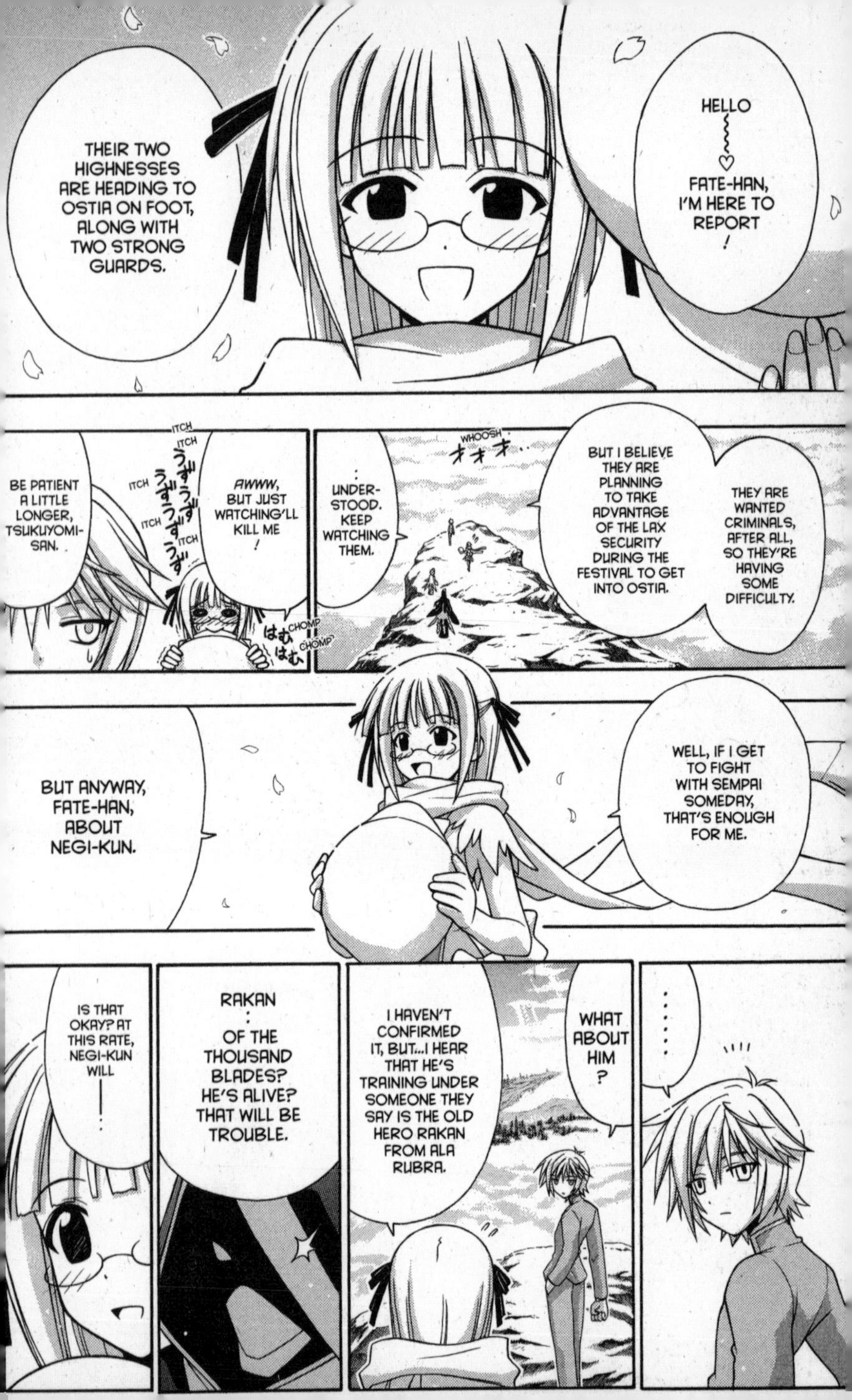
HELLO~♥ FATE-HAN, I'M HERE TO REPORT!
THEIR TWO HIGHNESSES ARE HEADING TO OSTIA ON FOOT, ALONG WITH TWO STRONG GUARDS.
THEY ARE WANTED CRIMINALS, AFTER ALL, SO THEY'RE HAVING SOME DIFFICULTY.
BUT I BELIEVE THEY ARE PLANNING TO TAKE ADVANTAGE OF THE LAX SECURITY DURING THE FESTIVAL TO GET INTO OSTIA.
WHOOSH オオオ…
…UNDER-STOOD. KEEP WATCHING THEM.
ITCH うず ITCH うず ITCH うず ITCH うず ITCH うず
AWWW, BUT JUST WATCHING'LL KILL ME!
はむ CHOMP はむ CHOMP
BE PATIENT A LITTLE LONGER, TSUKUYOMI-SAN.
WELL, IF I GET TO FIGHT WITH SEMPAI SOMEDAY, THAT'S ENOUGH FOR ME.
BUT ANYWAY, FATE-HAN, ABOUT NEGI-KUN.
……
WHAT ABOUT HIM?
I HAVEN'T CONFIRMED IT, BUT…I HEAR THAT HE'S TRAINING UNDER SOMEONE THEY SAY IS THE OLD HERO RAKAN FROM ALA RUBRA.
RAKAN… OF THE THOUSAND BLADES? HE'S ALIVE? THAT WILL BE TROUBLE.
IS THAT OKAY? AT THIS RATE, NEGI-KUN WILL—…

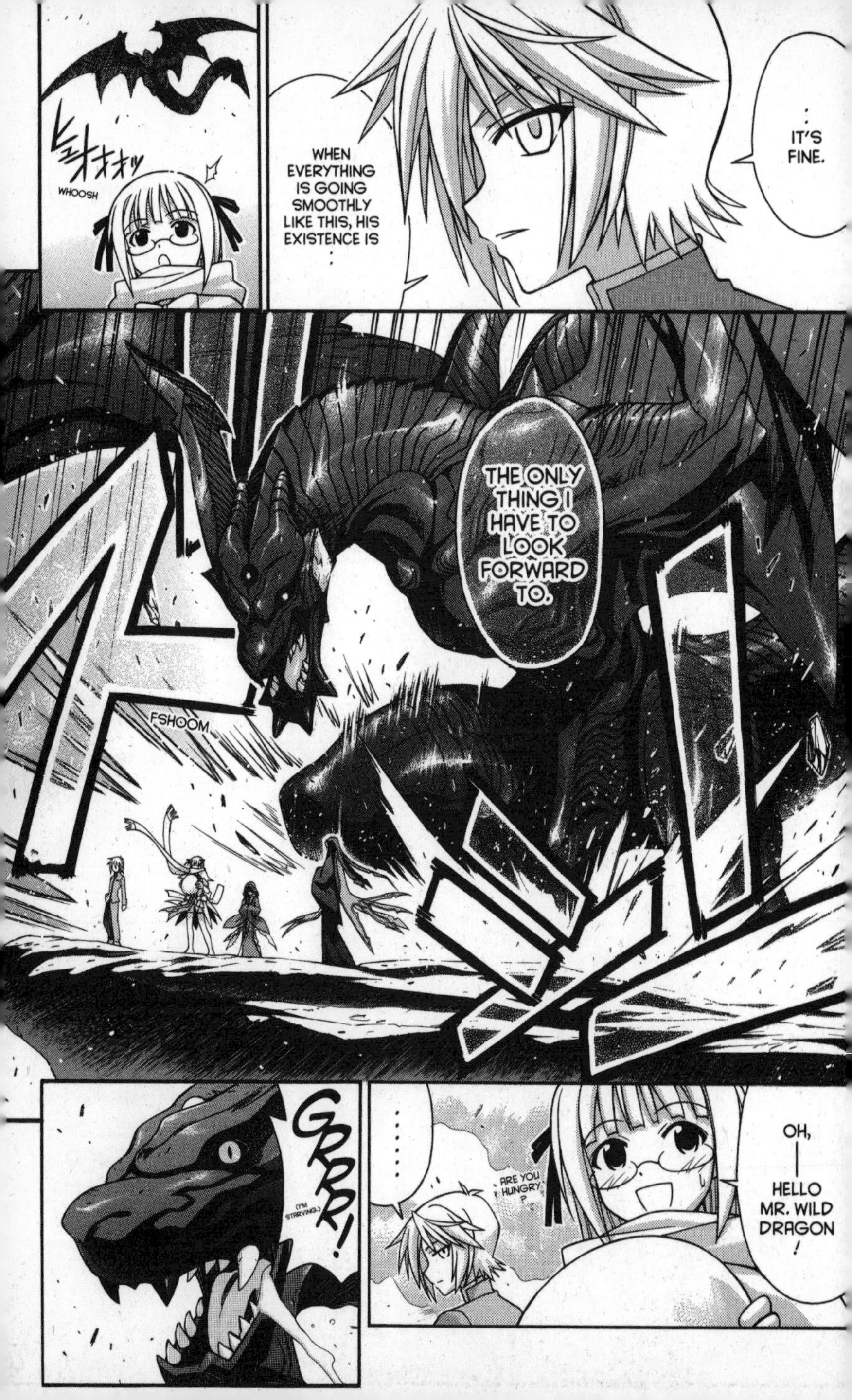
... IT'S FINE.
WHEN EVERYTHING IS GOING SMOOTHLY LIKE THIS, HIS EXISTENCE IS ...
ヒュオオオッ
WHOOSH
THE ONLY THING I HAVE TO LOOK FORWARD TO.
FSHOOM
OH, — HELLO MR. WILD DRAGON!
ARE YOU HUNGRY?
......
GRRR!
(I'M STARVING.)

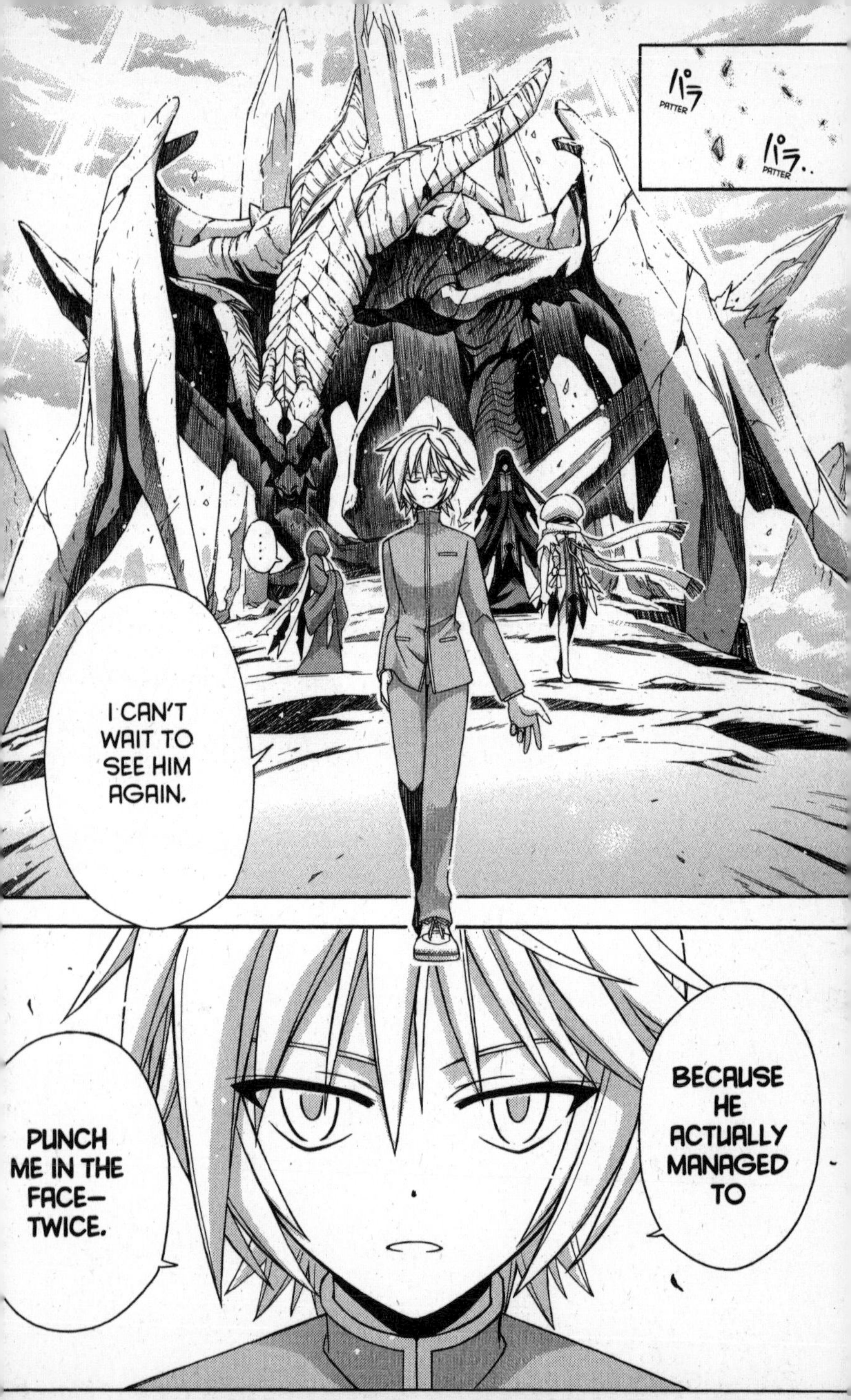
パラ
PATTER
パラ..
PATTER
I CAN'T WAIT TO SEE HIM AGAIN.
BECAUSE HE ACTUALLY MANAGED TO
PUNCH ME IN THE FACE—TWICE.

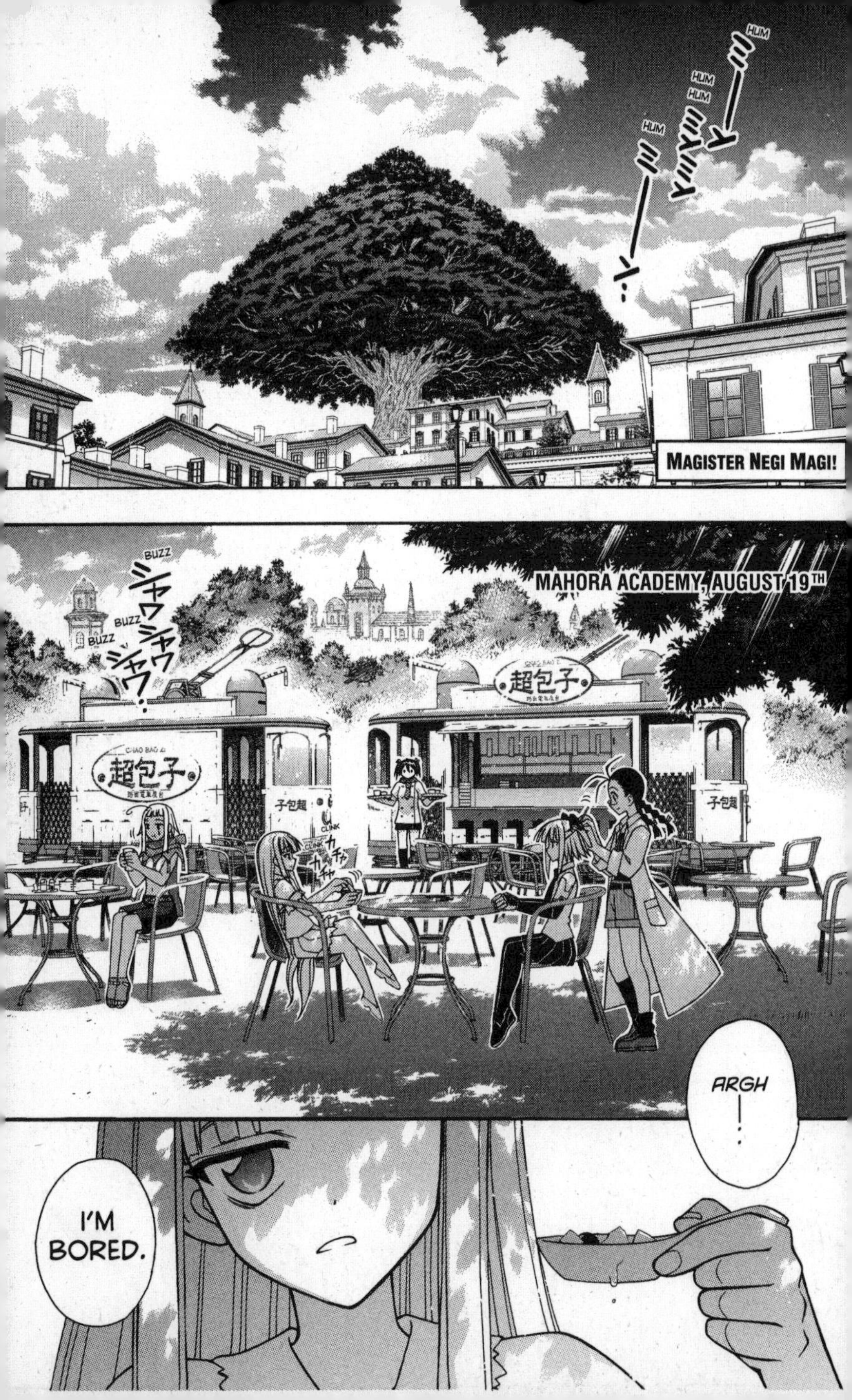
HUM
HUM HUM
HUM
ミーン ミンミンミ ミーン…
MAGISTER NEGI MAGI!
MAHORA ACADEMY, AUGUST 19TH
CHAO BAO ZI
超包子
BUZZ BUZZ BUZZ
シャワシャワシャワ…
CHAO BAO ZI
超包子
子包超
子包超
CLINK CLINK
カチャ カチャ
ARGH…!
I'M BORED.

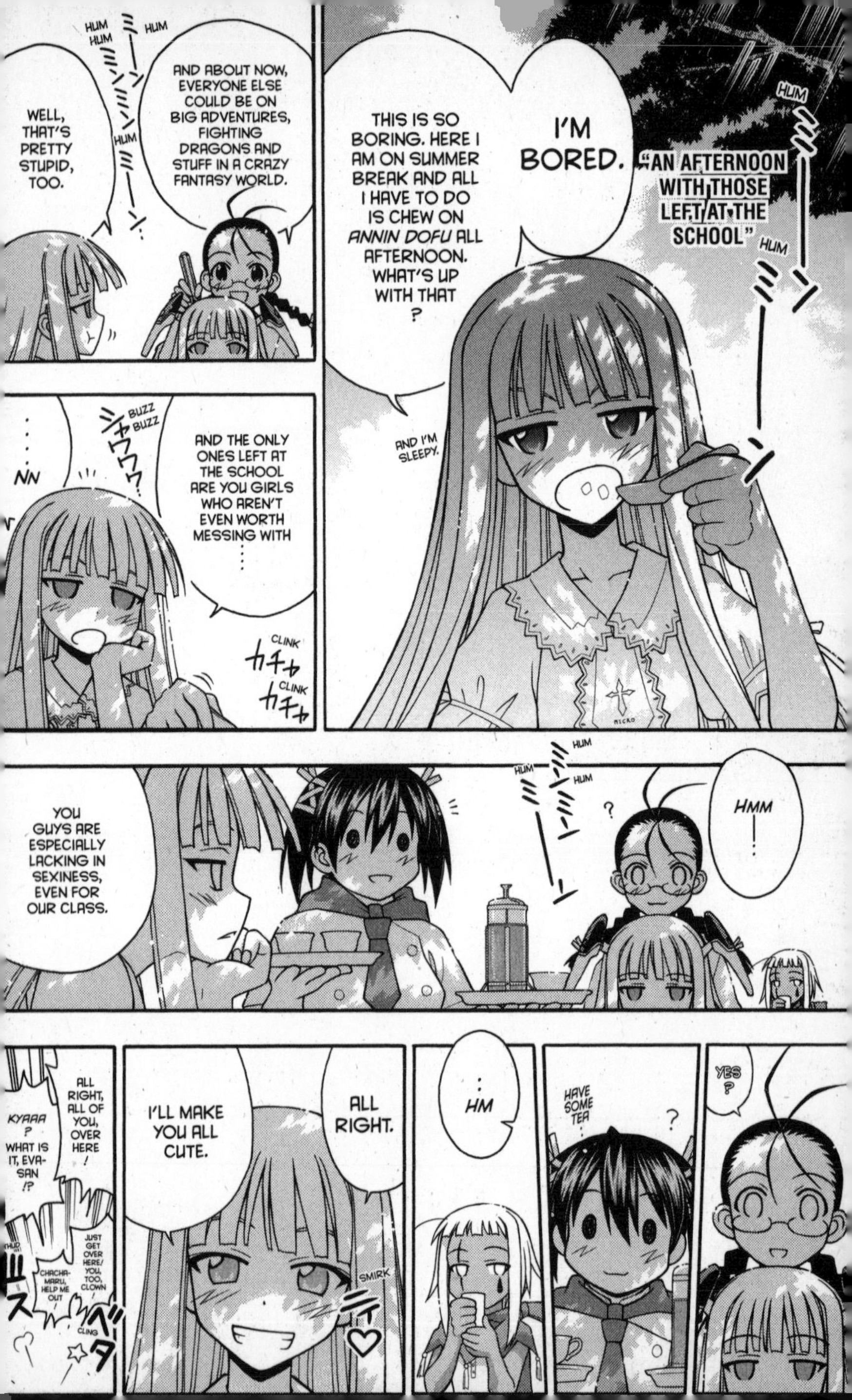
HUM
HUM
"AN AFTERNOON WITH THOSE LEFT AT THE SCHOOL"
I'M BORED.
THIS IS SO BORING. HERE I AM ON SUMMER BREAK AND ALL I HAVE TO DO IS CHEW ON *ANNIN DOFU* ALL AFTERNOON. WHAT'S UP WITH THAT?
AND I'M SLEEPY.
HUM HUM HUM HUM
AND ABOUT NOW, EVERYONE ELSE COULD BE ON BIG ADVENTURES, FIGHTING DRAGONS AND STUFF IN A CRAZY FANTASY WORLD.
WELL, THAT'S PRETTY STUPID, TOO.
BUZZ BUZZ
AND THE ONLY ONES LEFT AT THE SCHOOL ARE YOU GIRLS WHO AREN'T EVEN WORTH MESSING WITH...
...NN
CLINK
CLINK
HUM HUM HUM
HMM!
YOU GUYS ARE ESPECIALLY LACKING IN SEXINESS, EVEN FOR OUR CLASS.
YES?
HAVE SOME TEA...
:HM
ALL RIGHT.
I'LL MAKE YOU ALL CUTE.
SMIRK
ALL RIGHT, ALL OF YOU, OVER HERE!
KYAAA? WHAT IS IT, EVA-SAN!?
JUST GET OVER HERE/ YOU, TOO, CLOWN!
CHACHAMARU, HELP ME OUT!
THUD
CLING

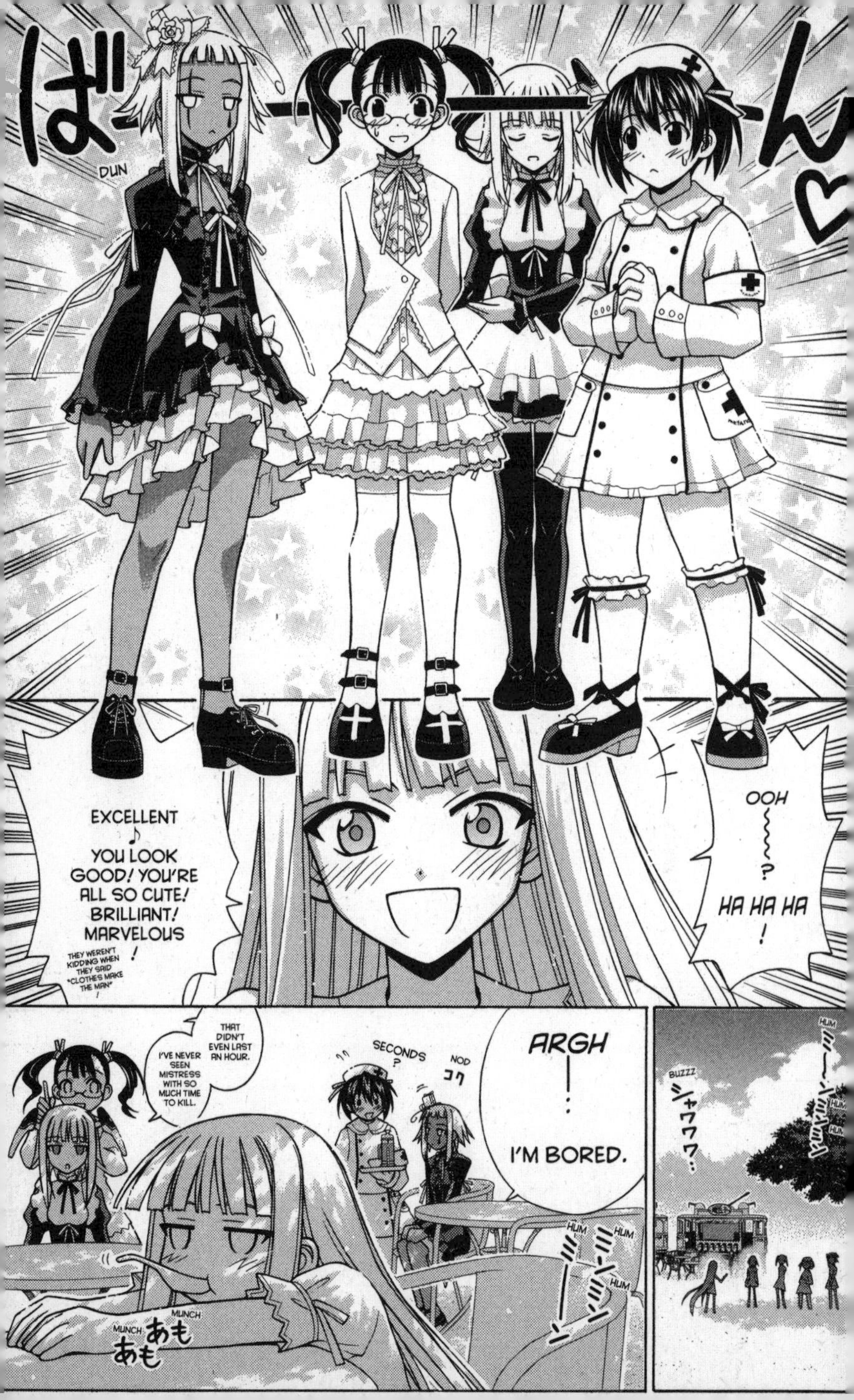
ばーーん♡
DUN
OOH~~~? HA HA HA!
EXCELLENT ♪ YOU LOOK GOOD! YOU'RE ALL SO CUTE! BRILLIANT! MARVELOUS!
THEY WEREN'T KIDDING WHEN THEY SAID "CLOTHES MAKE THE MAN"!
HUM ミ~ンミンミン HUM HUM
BUZZZ シャワワ…
ARGH… I'M BORED.
HUM ミーンミン HUM
HUM ミーー
SECONDS?
NOD コク
THAT DIDN'T EVEN LAST AN HOUR.
I'VE NEVER SEEN MISTRESS WITH SO MUCH TIME TO KILL.
MUNCH あも
MUNCH あも

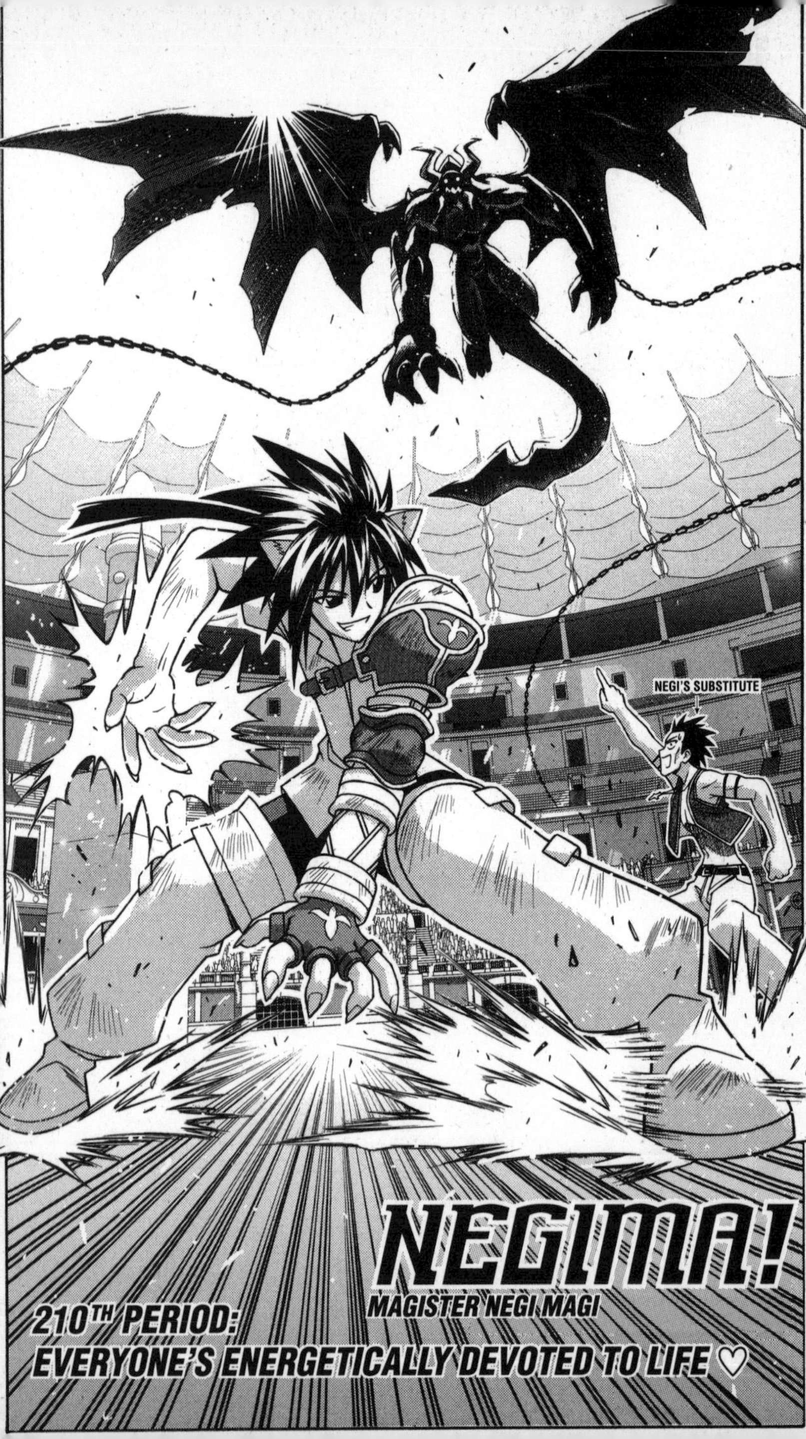
NEGI'S SUBSTITUTE
NEGIMA!
MAGISTER NEGI MAGI
210TH PERIOD:
EVERYONE'S ENERGETICALLY DEVOTED TO LIFE ♡

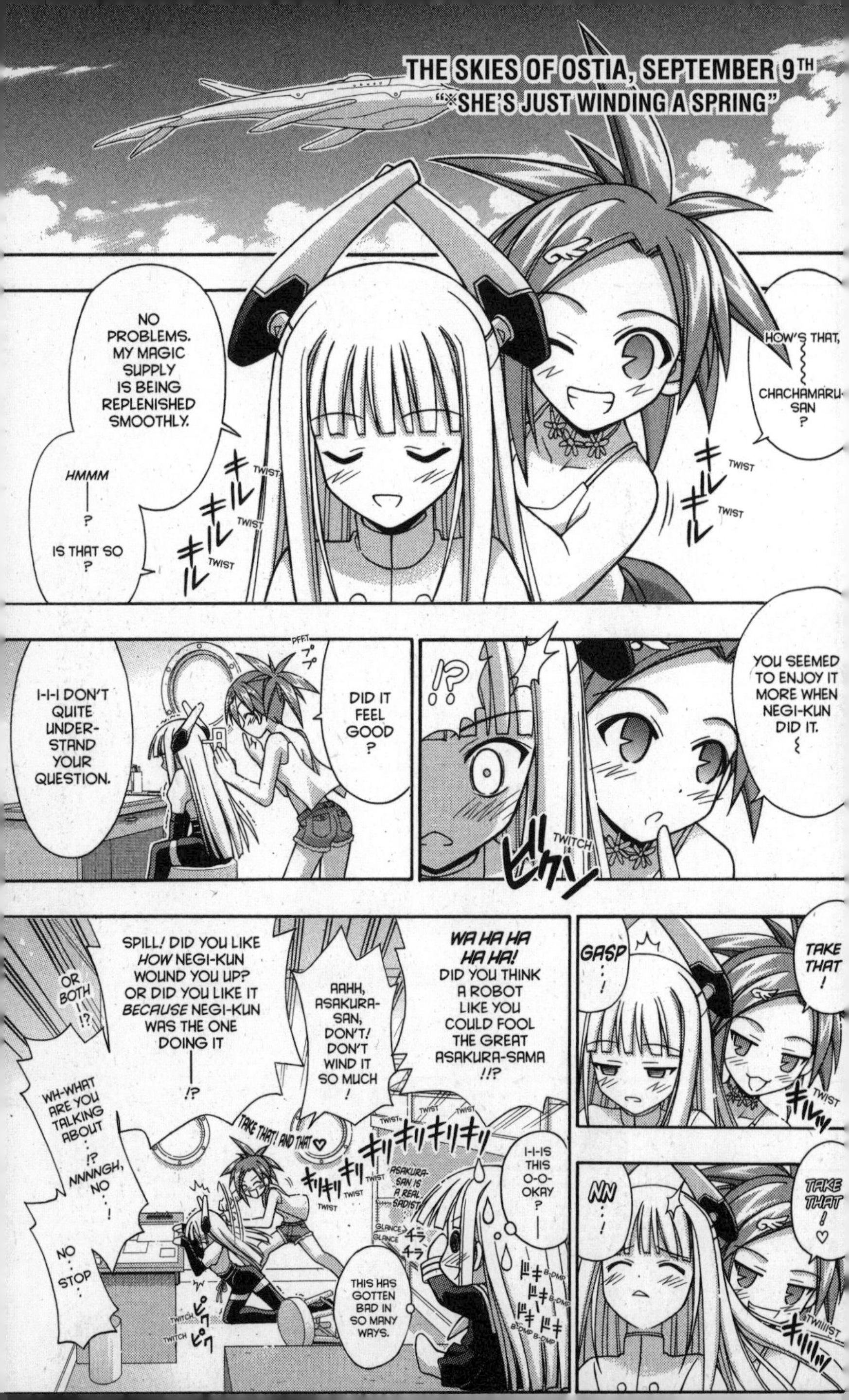
THE SKIES OF OSTIA, SEPTEMBER 9TH
"※SHE'S JUST WINDING A SPRING"
HOW'S THAT, CHACHAMARU-SAN?
TWIST
TWIST
NO PROBLEMS. MY MAGIC SUPPLY IS BEING REPLENISHED SMOOTHLY.
TWIST
TWIST
TWIST
HMMM—? IS THAT SO?
YOU SEEMED TO ENJOY IT MORE WHEN NEGI-KUN DID IT.
!?
TWITCH
DID IT FEEL GOOD?
PFFT
I-I-I DON'T QUITE UNDER-STAND YOUR QUESTION.
TAKE THAT!
GASP...!
TWIST
TAKE THAT! ♡
NN...!
TWIIIST
WA HA HA HA HA! DID YOU THINK A ROBOT LIKE YOU COULD FOOL THE GREAT ASAKURA-SAMA!!?
AAHH, ASAKURA-SAN, DON'T! DON'T WIND IT SO MUCH!
SPILL! DID YOU LIKE HOW NEGI-KUN WOUND YOU UP? OR DID YOU LIKE IT BECAUSE NEGI-KUN WAS THE ONE DOING IT—!?
OR BOTH!?
TAKE THAT! AND THAT ♡
TWIST TWIST TWIST TWIST TWIST
I-I-IS THIS O-O-OKAY?—
ASAKURA-SAN IS A REAL SADIST
GLANCE GLANCE
B-DMP B-DMP B-DMP B-DMP
THIS HAS GOTTEN BAD IN SO MANY WAYS.
WH-WHAT ARE YOU TALKING ABOUT...!? NNNNGH, NO...!
NO... STOP...
TWITCH TWITCH

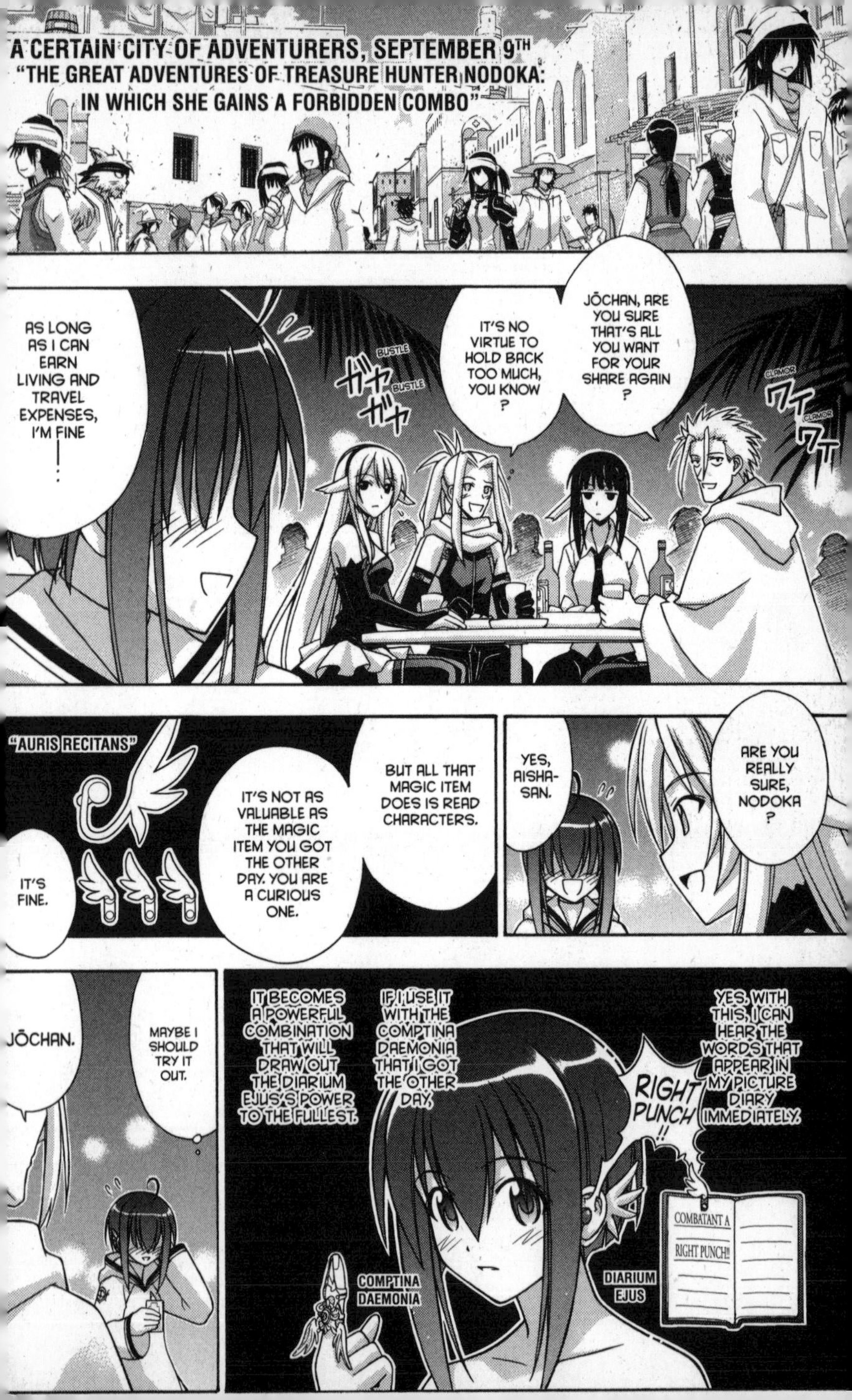
A CERTAIN CITY OF ADVENTURERS, SEPTEMBER 9TH
"THE GREAT ADVENTURES OF TREASURE HUNTER NODOKA: IN WHICH SHE GAINS A FORBIDDEN COMBO"
JŌCHAN, ARE YOU SURE THAT'S ALL YOU WANT FOR YOUR SHARE AGAIN?
CLAMOR CLAMOR
IT'S NO VIRTUE TO HOLD BACK TOO MUCH, YOU KNOW?
BUSTLE BUSTLE
AS LONG AS I CAN EARN LIVING AND TRAVEL EXPENSES, I'M FINE...!
ARE YOU REALLY SURE, NODOKA?
YES, AISHA-SAN.
BUT ALL THAT MAGIC ITEM DOES IS READ CHARACTERS.
IT'S NOT AS VALUABLE AS THE MAGIC ITEM YOU GOT THE OTHER DAY. YOU ARE A CURIOUS ONE.
"AURIS RECITANS"
IT'S FINE.
YES. WITH THIS, I CAN HEAR THE WORDS THAT APPEAR IN MY PICTURE DIARY IMMEDIATELY.
IF I USE IT WITH THE COMPTINA DAEMONIA THAT I GOT THE OTHER DAY,
IT BECOMES A POWERFUL COMBINATION THAT WILL DRAW OUT THE DIARIUM EJUS'S POWER TO THE FULLEST.
RIGHT PUNCH!!
COMBATANT A RIGHT PUNCH!!
DIARIUM EJUS
COMPTINA DAEMONIA
MAYBE I SHOULD TRY IT OUT.
JŌCHAN.

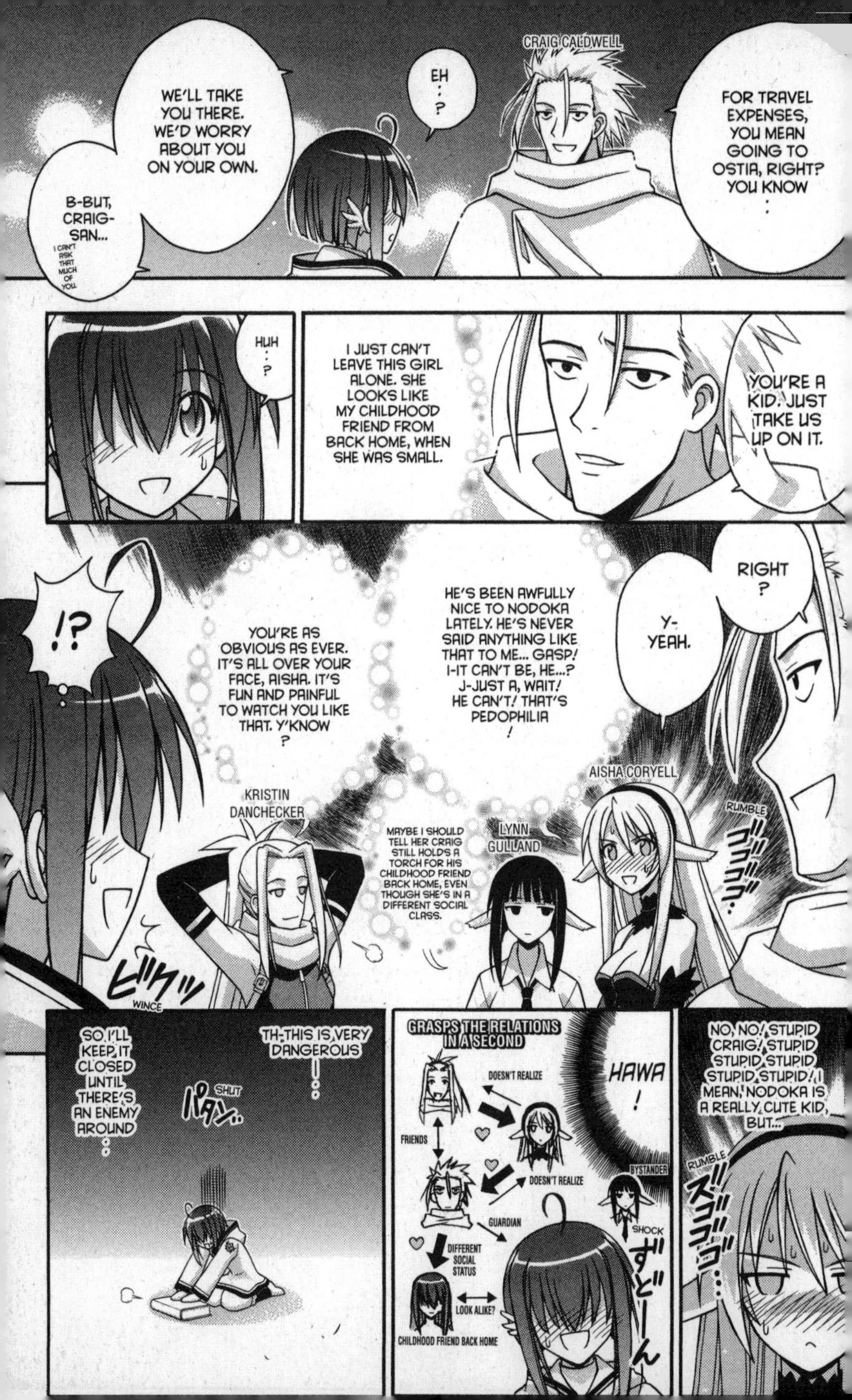
FOR TRAVEL EXPENSES, YOU MEAN GOING TO OSTIA, RIGHT? YOU KNOW...
CRAIG CALDWELL
EH...?
WE'LL TAKE YOU THERE. WE'D WORRY ABOUT YOU ON YOUR OWN.
B-BUT, CRAIG-SAN...
I CAN'T ASK THAT MUCH OF YOU
YOU'RE A KID. JUST TAKE US UP ON IT.
I JUST CAN'T LEAVE THIS GIRL ALONE. SHE LOOKS LIKE MY CHILDHOOD FRIEND FROM BACK HOME, WHEN SHE WAS SMALL.
HUH...?
RIGHT?
Y-YEAH.
HE'S BEEN AWFULLY NICE TO NODOKA LATELY. HE'S NEVER SAID ANYTHING LIKE THAT TO ME... GASP! I-IT CAN'T BE, HE...? J-JUST A, WAIT! HE CAN'T! THAT'S PEDOPHILIA!
AISHA CORYELL
RUMBLE
YOU'RE AS OBVIOUS AS EVER. IT'S ALL OVER YOUR FACE, AISHA. IT'S FUN AND PAINFUL TO WATCH YOU LIKE THAT. Y'KNOW?
KRISTIN DANCHECKER
MAYBE I SHOULD TELL HER CRAIG STILL HOLDS A TORCH FOR HIS CHILDHOOD FRIEND BACK HOME, EVEN THOUGH SHE'S IN A DIFFERENT SOCIAL CLASS.
LYNN GULLAND
!?
WINCE
NO, NO! STUPID CRAIG! STUPID STUPID STUPID STUPID STUPID! I MEAN, NODOKA IS A REALLY CUTE KID, BUT...
RUMBLE
GRASPS THE RELATIONS IN A SECOND
DOESN'T REALIZE
FRIENDS
DOESN'T REALIZE
BYSTANDER
GUARDIAN
DIFFERENT SOCIAL STATUS
LOOK ALIKE?
CHILDHOOD FRIEND BACK HOME
HAWA!
SHOCK
TH-THIS IS VERY DANGEROUS...!
SO I'LL KEEP IT CLOSED UNTIL THERE'S AN ENEMY AROUND...
SHUT

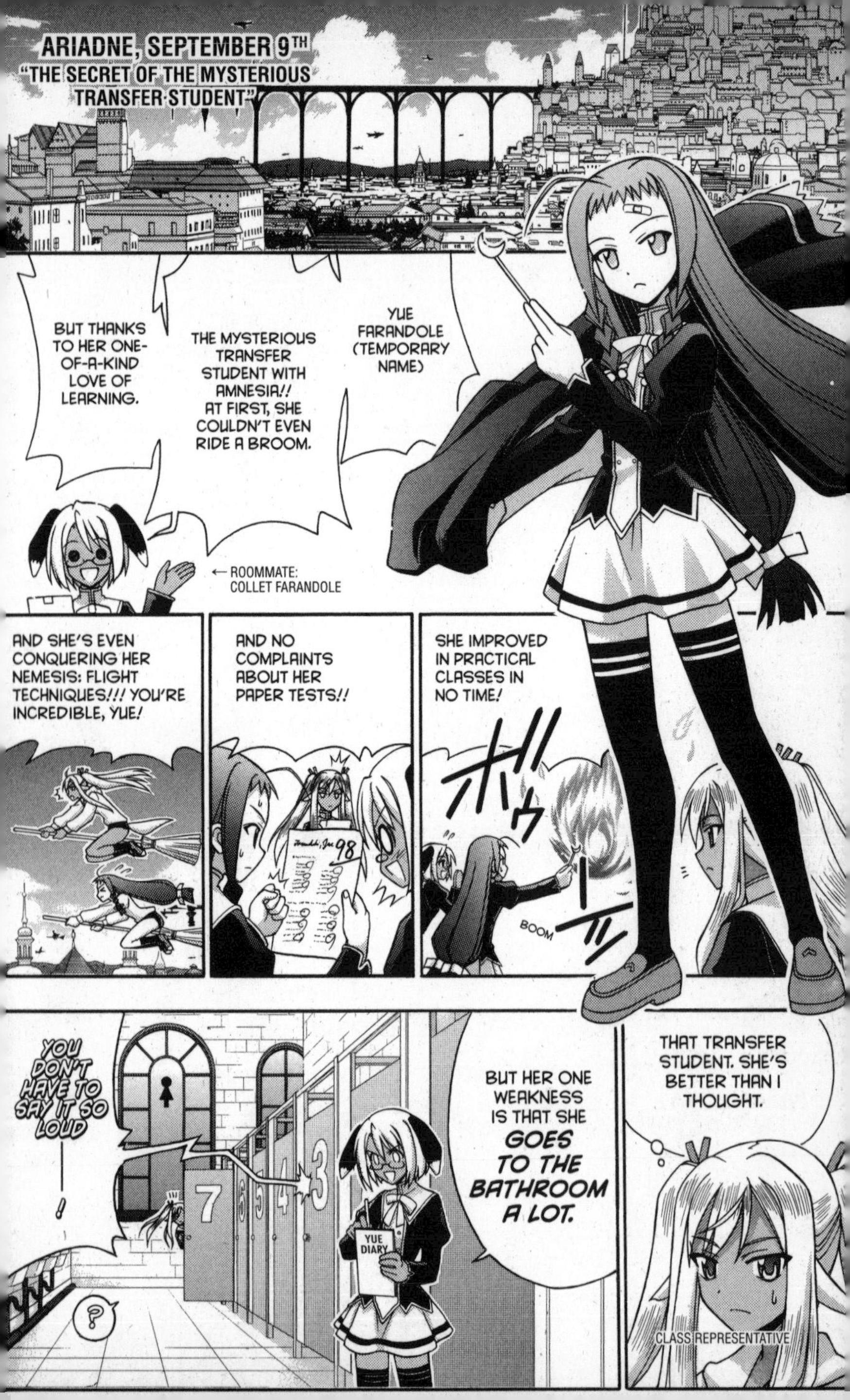

ARIADNE, SEPTEMBER 9TH
"THE SECRET OF THE MYSTERIOUS TRANSFER STUDENT"
YUE FARANDOLE (TEMPORARY NAME)
THE MYSTERIOUS TRANSFER STUDENT WITH AMNESIA!! AT FIRST, SHE COULDN'T EVEN RIDE A BROOM.
BUT THANKS TO HER ONE-OF-A-KIND LOVE OF LEARNING.
← ROOMMATE: COLLET FARANDOLE
SHE IMPROVED IN PRACTICAL CLASSES IN NO TIME!
BOOM
AND NO COMPLAINTS ABOUT HER PAPER TESTS!!
98
AND SHE'S EVEN CONQUERING HER NEMESIS: FLIGHT TECHNIQUES!!! YOU'RE INCREDIBLE, YUE!
THAT TRANSFER STUDENT. SHE'S BETTER THAN I THOUGHT.
CLASS REPRESENTATIVE
BUT HER ONE WEAKNESS IS THAT SHE GOES TO THE BATHROOM A LOT.
YUE DIARY
YOU DON'T HAVE TO SAY IT SO LOUD
!
?

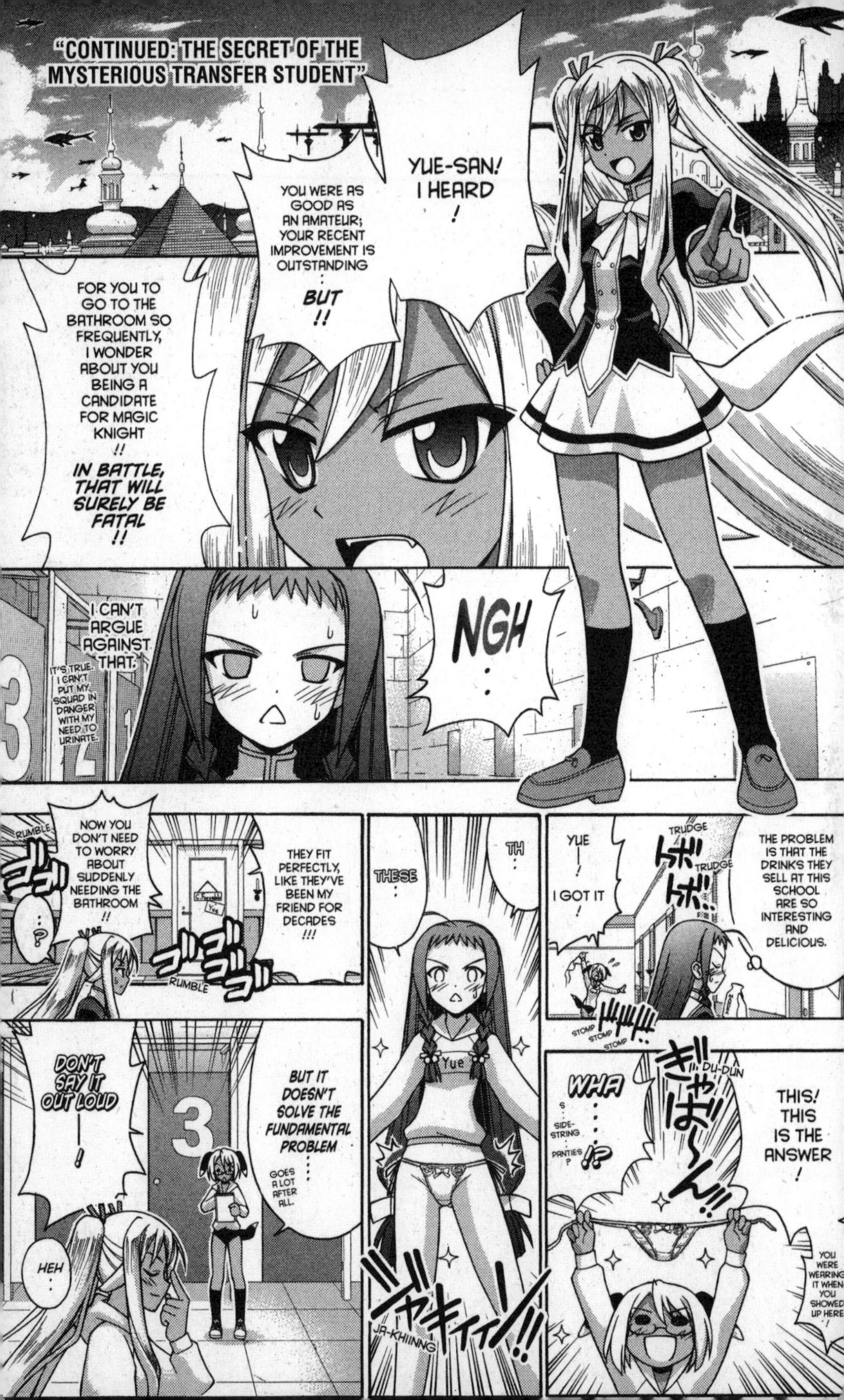
"CONTINUED: THE SECRET OF THE MYSTERIOUS TRANSFER STUDENT"
YUE-SAN! I HEARD!
YOU WERE AS GOOD AS AN AMATEUR; YOUR RECENT IMPROVEMENT IS OUTSTANDING... BUT!!
FOR YOU TO GO TO THE BATHROOM SO FREQUENTLY, I WONDER ABOUT YOU BEING A CANDIDATE FOR MAGIC KNIGHT!! IN BATTLE, THAT WILL SURELY BE FATAL!!
NGH...
I CAN'T ARGUE AGAINST THAT.
IT'S TRUE. I CAN'T PUT MY SQUAD IN DANGER WITH MY NEED TO URINATE.
THE PROBLEM IS THAT THE DRINKS THEY SELL AT THIS SCHOOL ARE SO INTERESTING AND DELICIOUS.
TRUDGE
TRUDGE
YUE! I GOT IT!
STOMP STOMP STOMP
TH..
THESE..
THEY FIT PERFECTLY, LIKE THEY'VE BEEN MY FRIEND FOR DECADES!!!
NOW YOU DON'T NEED TO WORRY ABOUT SUDDENLY NEEDING THE BATHROOM!!
RUMBLE
...?
RUMBLE
THIS! THIS IS THE ANSWER!
DU-DUN
WHA.....!?
S... SIDE-STRING PANTIES?
YOU WERE WEARING IT WHEN YOU SHOWED UP HERE!
JA-KHIING
BUT IT DOESN'T SOLVE THE FUNDAMENTAL PROBLEM....
GOES A LOT AFTER ALL.
DON'T SAY IT OUT LOUD—!
HEH..

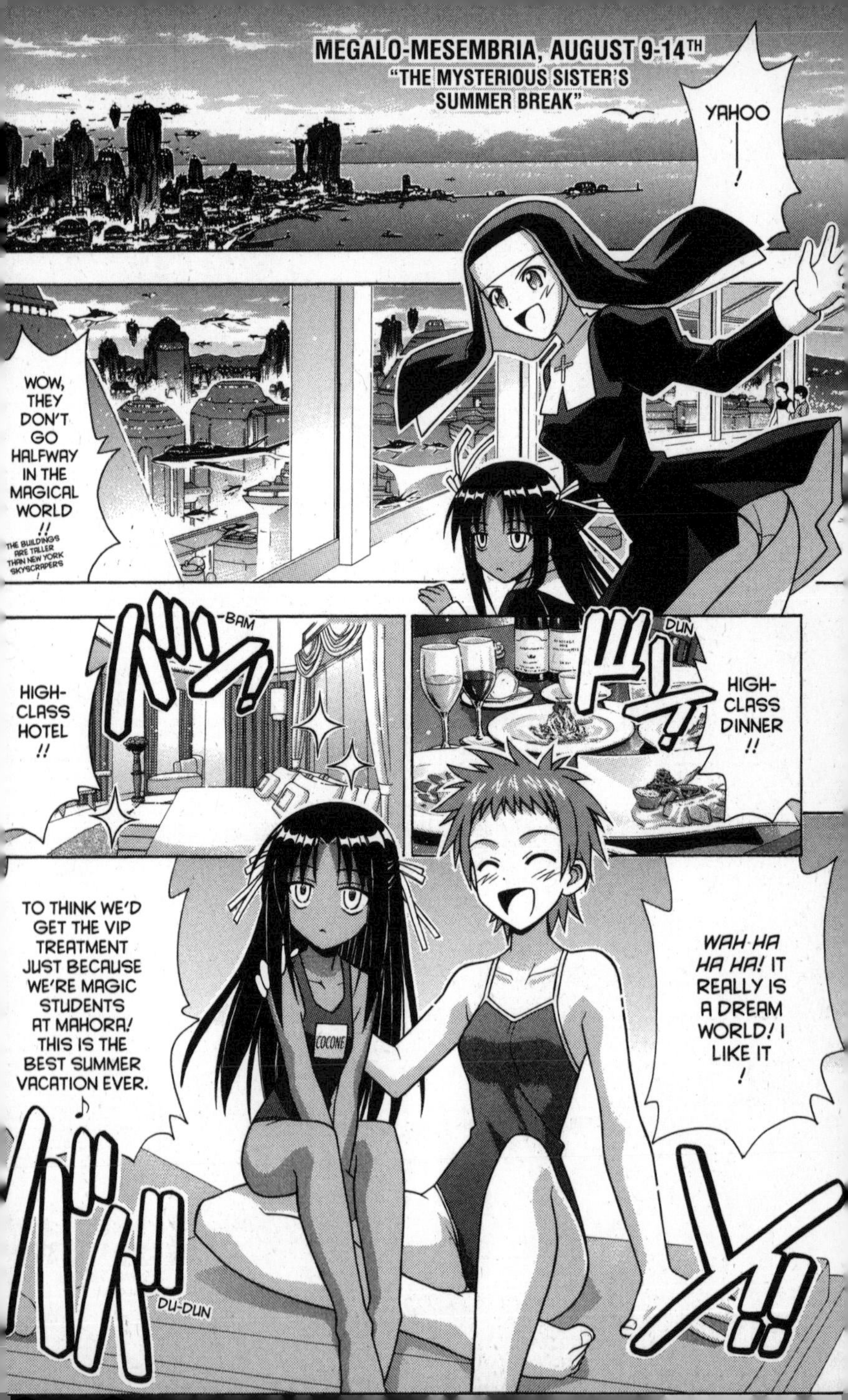
MEGALO-MESEMBRIA, AUGUST 9-14TH
"THE MYSTERIOUS SISTER'S SUMMER BREAK"
YAHOO—!
WOW, THEY DON'T GO HALFWAY IN THE MAGICAL WORLD!!
THE BUILDINGS ARE TALLER THAN NEW YORK SKYSCRAPERS!
DUN
HIGH-CLASS DINNER!!
BAM
HIGH-CLASS HOTEL!!
WAH HA HA HA! IT REALLY IS A DREAM WORLD! I LIKE IT!
TO THINK WE'D GET THE VIP TREATMENT JUST BECAUSE WE'RE MAGIC STUDENTS AT MAHORA! THIS IS THE BEST SUMMER VACATION EVER. ♪
COCONE
DU-DUN

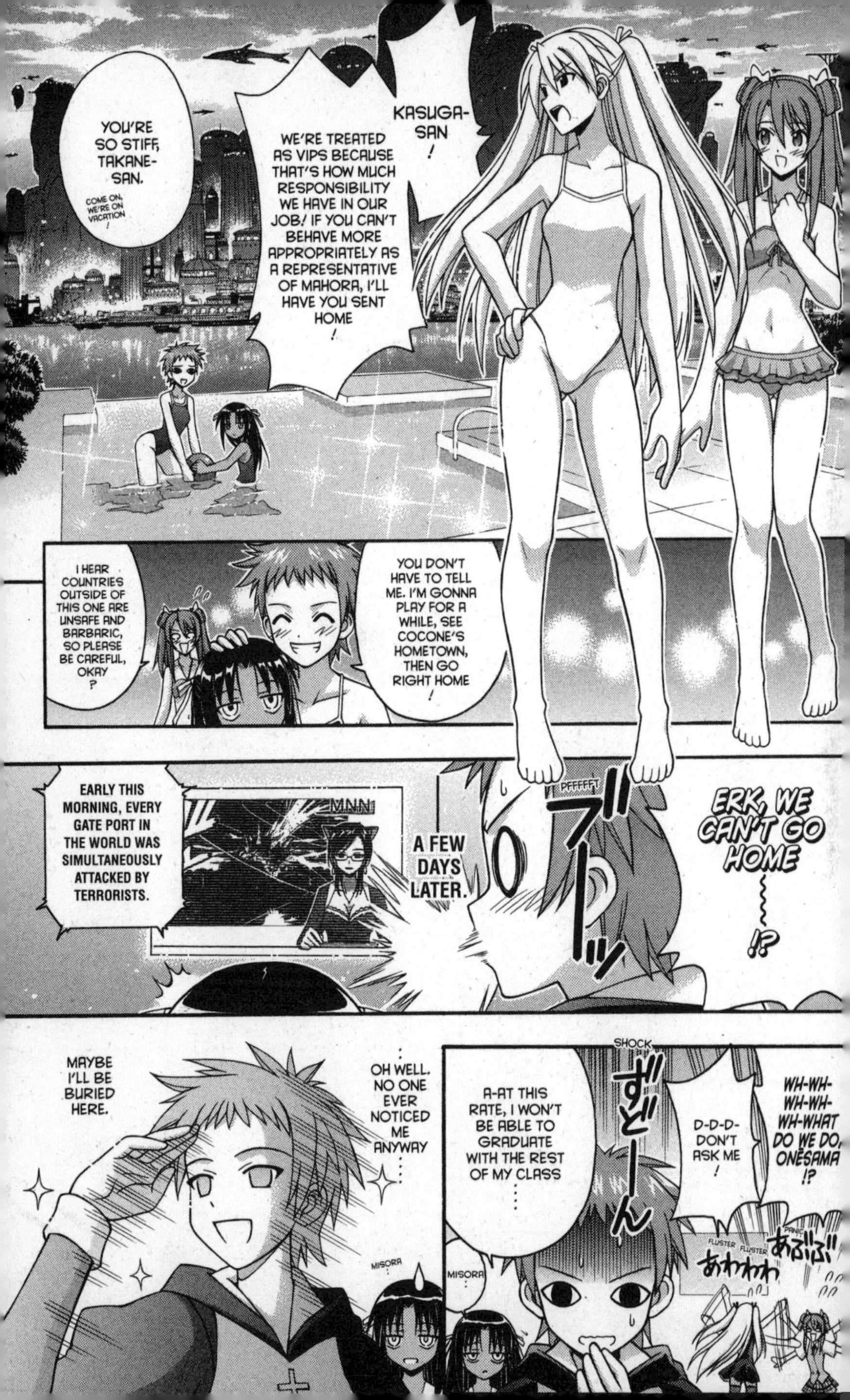

KASUGA-SAN!
WE'RE TREATED AS VIPS BECAUSE THAT'S HOW MUCH RESPONSIBILITY WE HAVE IN OUR JOB! IF YOU CAN'T BEHAVE MORE APPROPRIATELY AS A REPRESENTATIVE OF MAHORA, I'LL HAVE YOU SENT HOME!
YOU'RE SO STIFF, TAKANE-SAN.
COME ON, WE'RE ON VACATION!
YOU DON'T HAVE TO TELL ME. I'M GONNA PLAY FOR A WHILE, SEE COCONE'S HOMETOWN, THEN GO RIGHT HOME!
I HEAR COUNTRIES OUTSIDE OF THIS ONE ARE UNSAFE AND BARBARIC, SO PLEASE BE CAREFUL, OKAY?
ERK, WE CAN'T GO HOME~~~!?
PFFFFFT
ブーッ
A FEW DAYS LATER.
MNN
EARLY THIS MORNING, EVERY GATE PORT IN THE WORLD WAS SIMULTANEOUSLY ATTACKED BY TERRORISTS.
WH-WH-WH-WH-WH-WHAT DO WE DO, ONĒSAMA!?
D-D-D-DON'T ASK ME!
PANIC
あぶぶ
FLUSTER FLUSTER
あわわわ
SHOCK
ずどーん
A-AT THIS RATE, I WON'T BE ABLE TO GRADUATE WITH THE REST OF MY CLASS...
MISORA...
MISORA...
OH WELL. NO ONE EVER NOTICED ME ANYWAY...
MAYBE I'LL BE BURIED HERE.

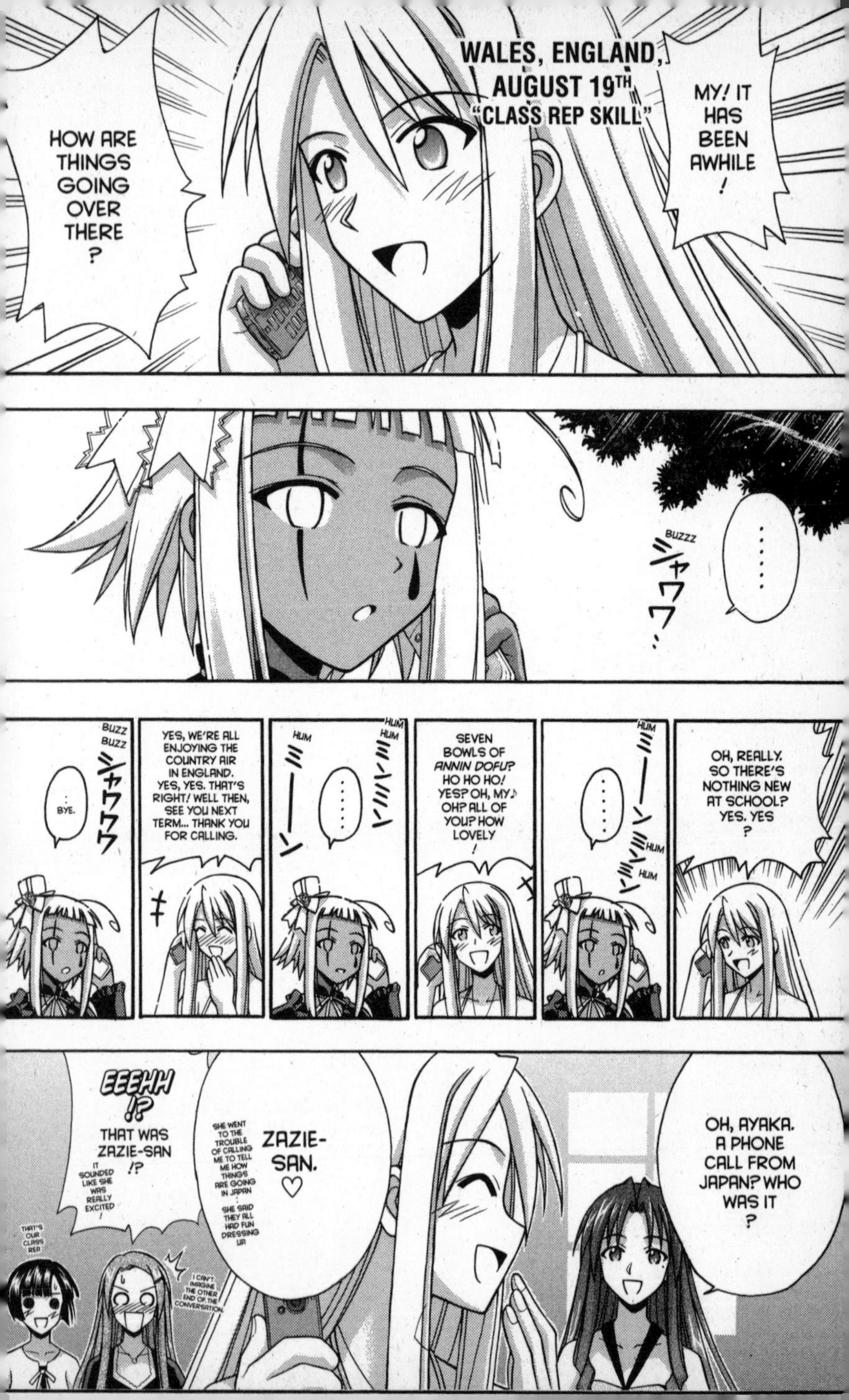
WALES, ENGLAND, AUGUST 19TH "CLASS REP SKILL"
MY! IT HAS BEEN AWHILE!
HOW ARE THINGS GOING OVER THERE?
......
BUZZZ シャワワ
OH, REALLY. SO THERE'S NOTHING NEW AT SCHOOL? YES. YES?
HUM HUM ミーンミンミン HUM HUM
......
SEVEN BOWLS OF *ANNIN DOFU*? HO HO HO! YES? OH, MY♪ OH? ALL OF YOU? HOW LOVELY!
HUM HUM ミンミンミン
HUM ミーン
......
YES, WE'RE ALL ENJOYING THE COUNTRY AIR IN ENGLAND. YES, YES. THAT'S RIGHT! WELL THEN, SEE YOU NEXT TERM... THANK YOU FOR CALLING.
BUZZ BUZZ シャワワワ
...BYE.
OH, AYAKA. A PHONE CALL FROM JAPAN? WHO WAS IT?
ZAZIE-SAN. ♡
SHE WENT TO THE TROUBLE OF CALLING ME TO TELL ME HOW THINGS ARE GOING IN JAPAN: SHE SAID THEY ALL HAD FUN DRESSING UP.
EEEHH!? THAT WAS ZAZIE-SAN!?
IT SOUNDED LIKE SHE WAS REALLY EXCITED!
I CAN'T IMAGINE THE OTHER END OF THE CONVERSATION.
THAT'S OUR CLASS REP.

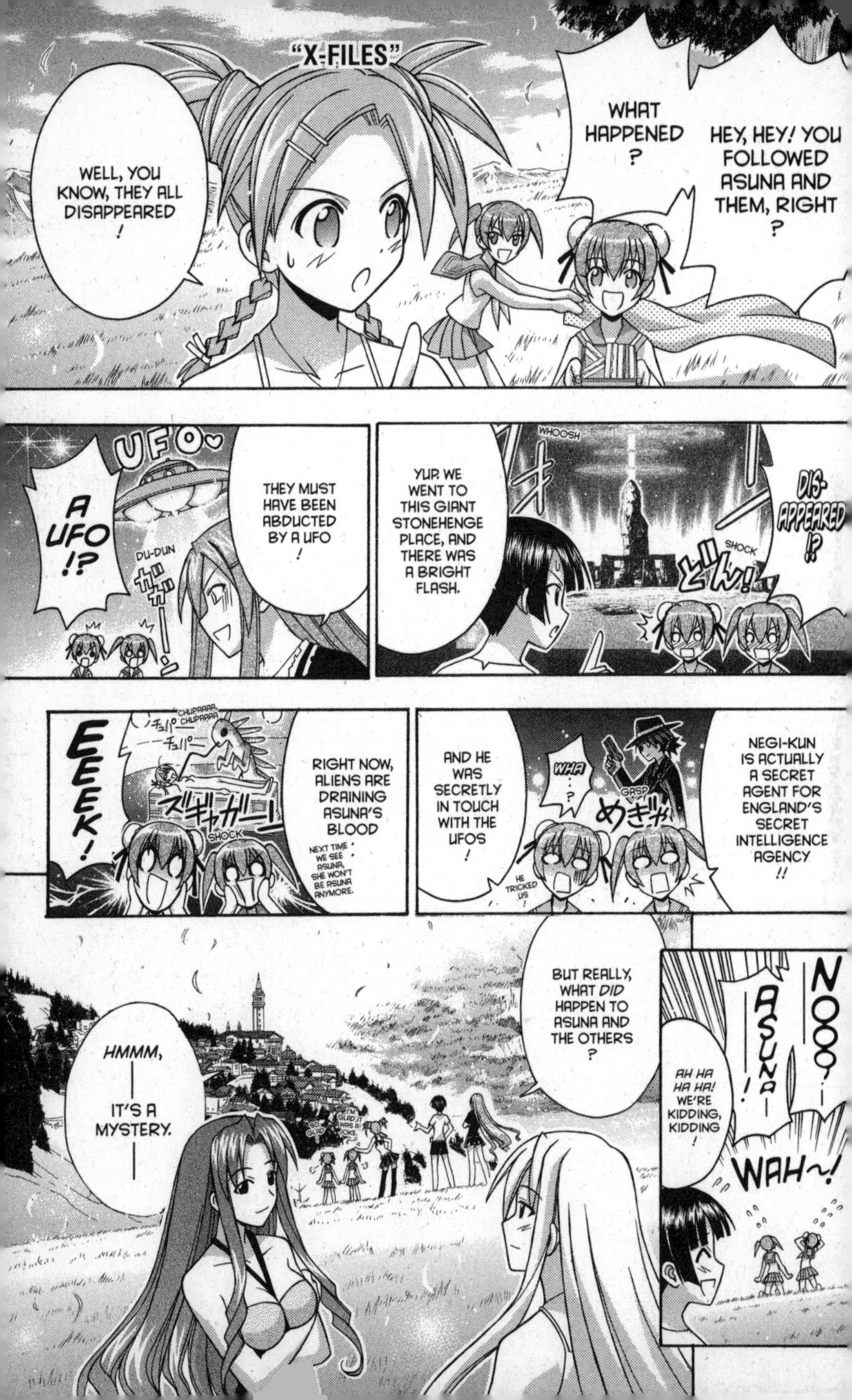
"X-FILES"
HEY, HEY! YOU FOLLOWED ASUNA AND THEM, RIGHT?
WHAT HAPPENED?
WELL, YOU KNOW, THEY ALL DISAPPEARED!
DIS-APPEARED!?
SHOCK
どん!
WHOOSH
YUP. WE WENT TO THIS GIANT STONEHENGE PLACE, AND THERE WAS A BRIGHT FLASH.
THEY MUST HAVE BEEN ABDUCTED BY A UFO!
UFO♡
A UFO!?
DU-DUN
ガガー!
NEGI-KUN IS ACTUALLY A SECRET AGENT FOR ENGLAND'S SECRET INTELLIGENCE AGENCY!!
WHA...?
GASP
めぎゃ
HE TRICKED US!
AND HE WAS SECRETLY IN TOUCH WITH THE UFOS!
RIGHT NOW, ALIENS ARE DRAINING ASUNA'S BLOOD
NEXT TIME WE SEE ASUNA, SHE WON'T BE ASUNA ANYMORE.
CHUPAAAA, CHUPAAAA
ズギャガー!
SHOCK
EEEEK!
NOOO! ASUNA!
WAH~!
AH HA HA HA! WE'RE KIDDING, KIDDING!
BUT REALLY, WHAT DID HAPPEN TO ASUNA AND THE OTHERS?
I'M GLAD IT WAS A JOKE.
SO GLAD
HMMM, IT'S A MYSTERY.

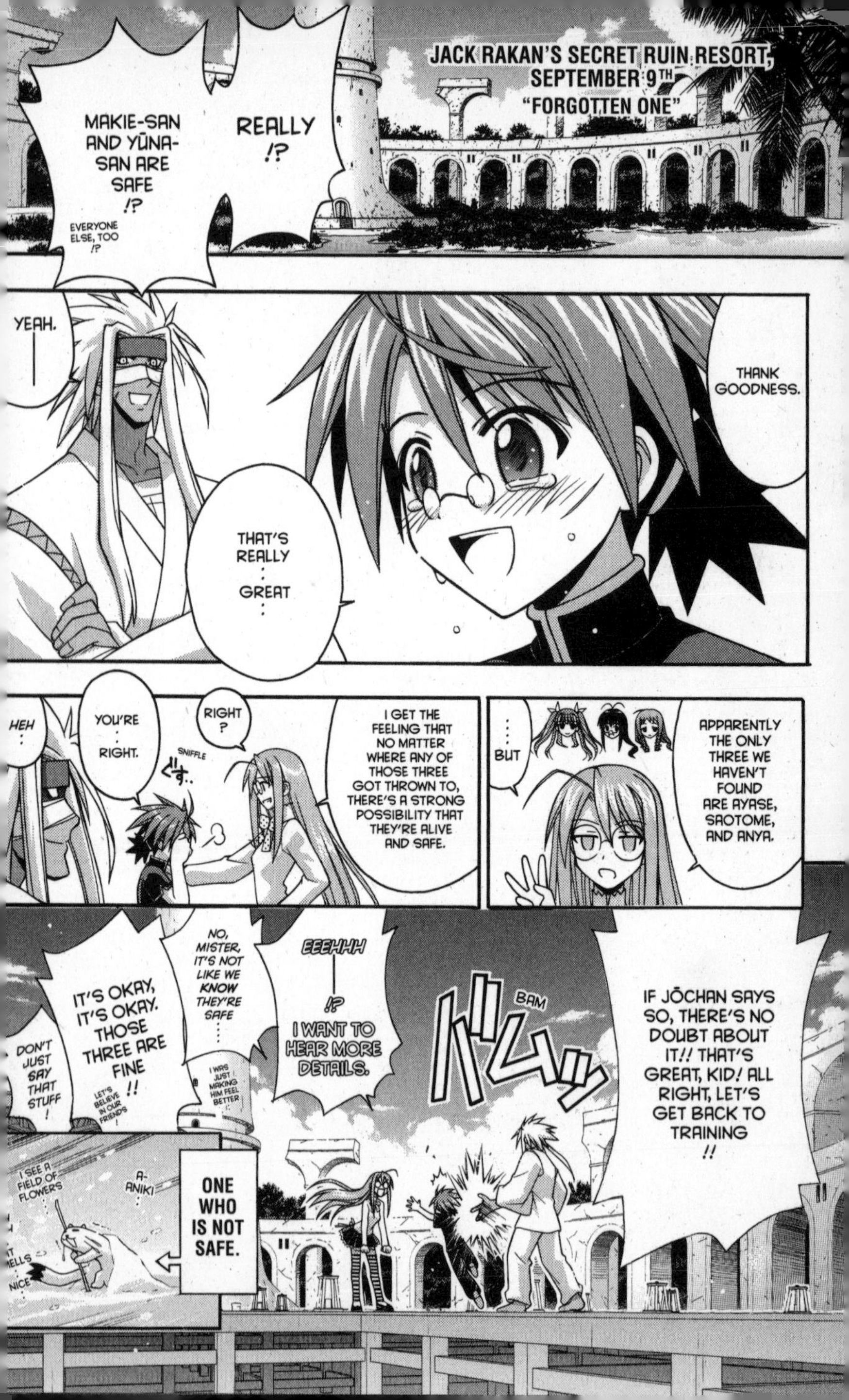
JACK RAKAN'S SECRET RUIN RESORT, SEPTEMBER 9TH
"FORGOTTEN ONE"
REALLY !?
MAKIE-SAN AND YŪNA-SAN ARE SAFE !?
EVERYONE ELSE, TOO !?
THANK GOODNESS.
THAT'S REALLY ... GREAT ...
YEAH.
APPARENTLY THE ONLY THREE WE HAVEN'T FOUND ARE AYASE, SAOTOME, AND ANYA.
... BUT
I GET THE FEELING THAT NO MATTER WHERE ANY OF THOSE THREE GOT THROWN TO, THERE'S A STRONG POSSIBILITY THAT THEY'RE ALIVE AND SAFE.
RIGHT ?
SNIFFLE
ぐす..
YOU'RE ... RIGHT.
HEH ...
IF JŌCHAN SAYS SO, THERE'S NO DOUBT ABOUT IT!! THAT'S GREAT, KID! ALL RIGHT, LET'S GET BACK TO TRAINING !!
BAM
ドムッ
EEEHHH !?
I WANT TO HEAR MORE DETAILS.
NO, MISTER, IT'S NOT LIKE WE KNOW THEY'RE SAFE ...
I WAS JUST MAKING HIM FEEL BETTER
IT'S OKAY, IT'S OKAY. THOSE THREE ARE FINE !!
LET'S BELIEVE IN OUR FRIENDS
DON'T JUST SAY THAT STUFF !
ONE WHO IS NOT SAFE.
A- ANIKI ...
I SEE A FIELD OF FLOWERS

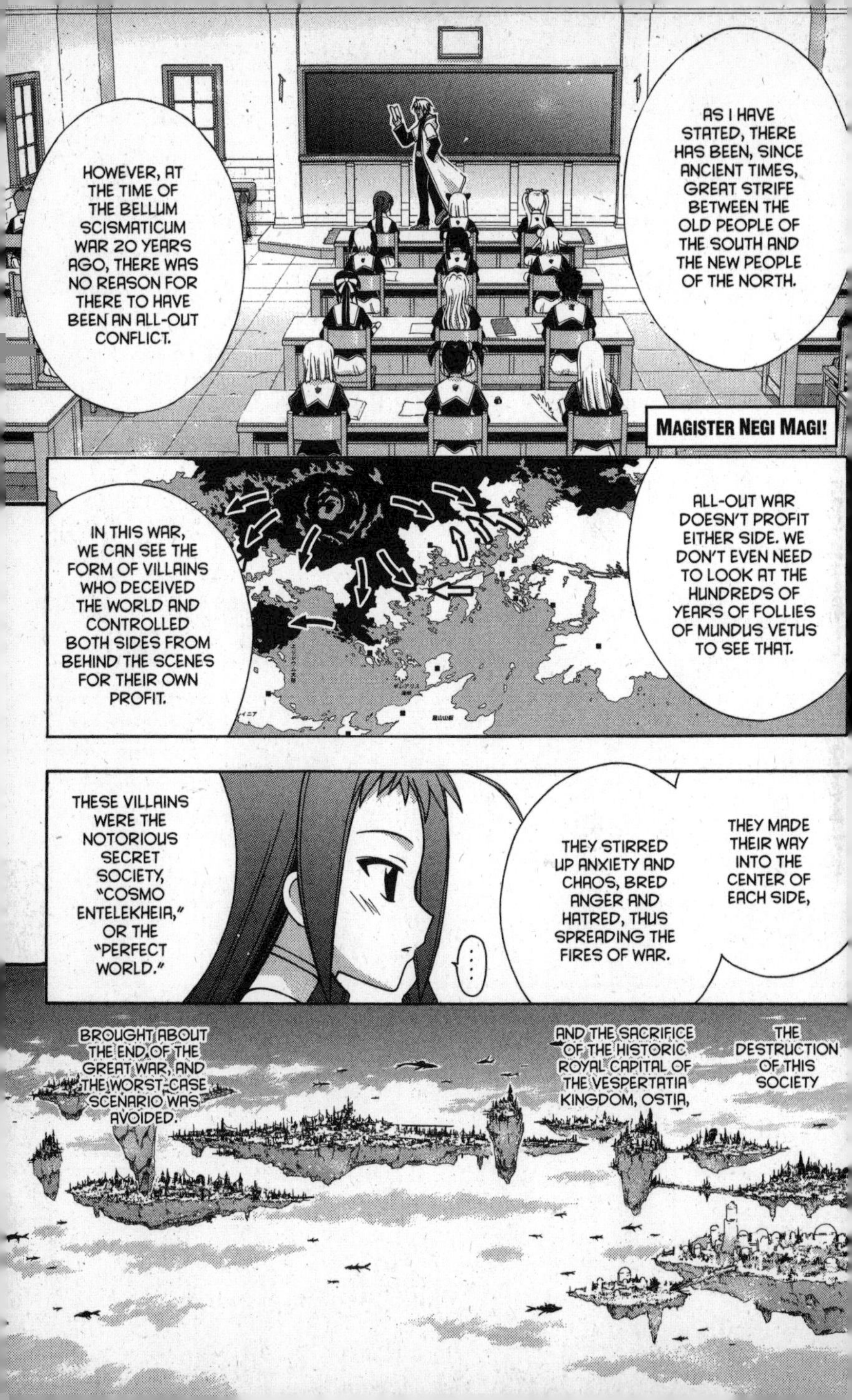
AS I HAVE STATED, THERE HAS BEEN, SINCE ANCIENT TIMES, GREAT STRIFE BETWEEN THE OLD PEOPLE OF THE SOUTH AND THE NEW PEOPLE OF THE NORTH.
HOWEVER, AT THE TIME OF THE BELLUM SCISMATICUM WAR 20 YEARS AGO, THERE WAS NO REASON FOR THERE TO HAVE BEEN AN ALL-OUT CONFLICT.
MAGISTER NEGI MAGI!
ALL-OUT WAR DOESN'T PROFIT EITHER SIDE. WE DON'T EVEN NEED TO LOOK AT THE HUNDREDS OF YEARS OF FOLLIES OF MUNDUS VETUS TO SEE THAT.
IN THIS WAR, WE CAN SEE THE FORM OF VILLAINS WHO DECEIVED THE WORLD AND CONTROLLED BOTH SIDES FROM BEHIND THE SCENES FOR THEIR OWN PROFIT.
THESE VILLAINS WERE THE NOTORIOUS SECRET SOCIETY, "COSMO ENTELEKHEIA," OR THE "PERFECT WORLD."
THEY MADE THEIR WAY INTO THE CENTER OF EACH SIDE,
THEY STIRRED UP ANXIETY AND CHAOS, BRED ANGER AND HATRED, THUS SPREADING THE FIRES OF WAR.
....
THE DESTRUCTION OF THIS SOCIETY
AND THE SACRIFICE OF THE HISTORIC ROYAL CAPITAL OF THE VESPERTATIA KINGDOM, OSTIA,
BROUGHT ABOUT THE END OF THE GREAT WAR, AND THE WORST-CASE SCENARIO WAS AVOIDED.

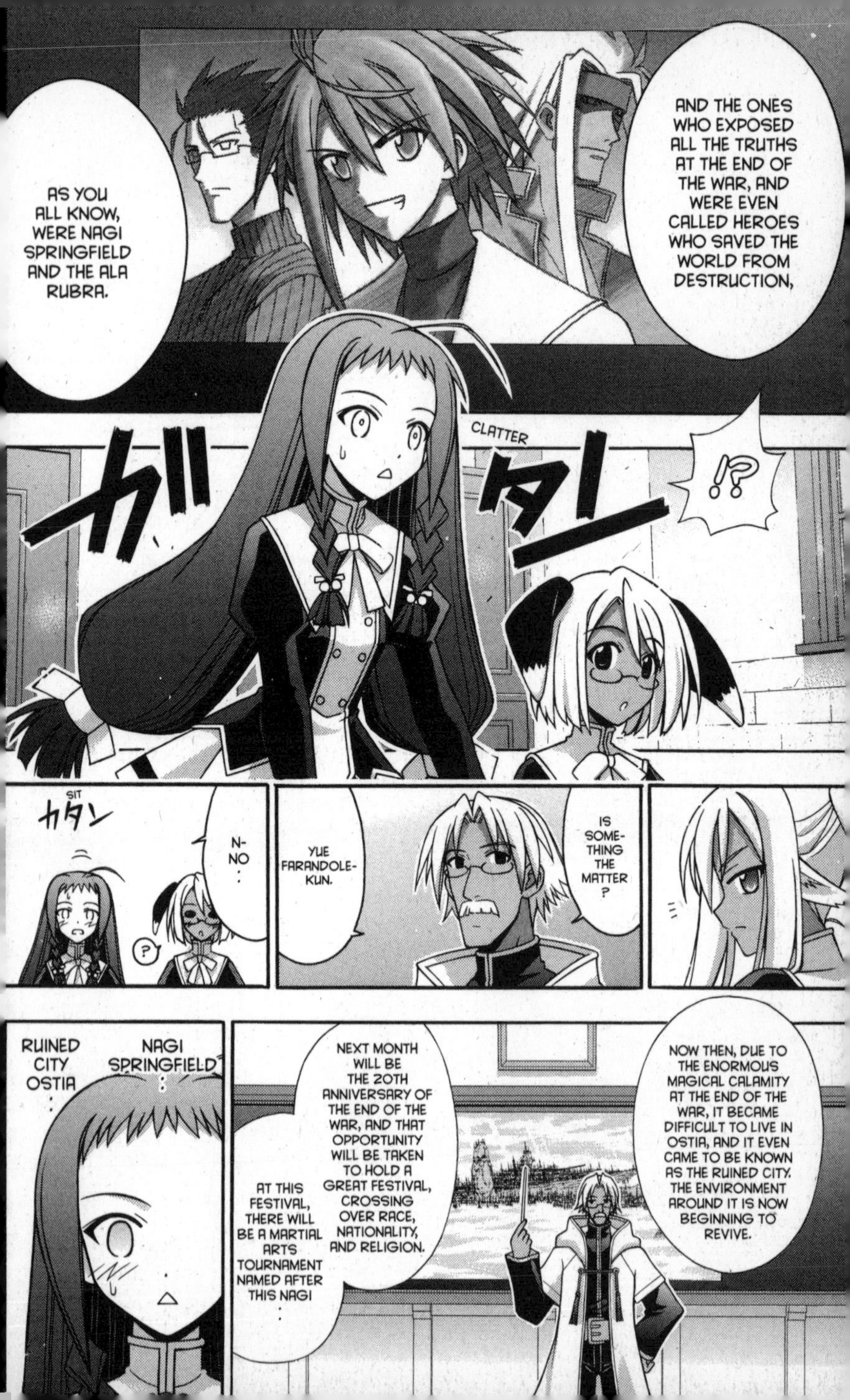
AND THE ONES WHO EXPOSED ALL THE TRUTHS AT THE END OF THE WAR, AND WERE EVEN CALLED HEROES WHO SAVED THE WORLD FROM DESTRUCTION,
AS YOU ALL KNOW, WERE NAGI SPRINGFIELD AND THE ALA RUBRA.
!?
ガタン
CLATTER
IS SOMETHING THE MATTER?
YUE FARANDOLE-KUN.
N-NO...
カタン
SIT
?
NOW THEN, DUE TO THE ENORMOUS MAGICAL CALAMITY AT THE END OF THE WAR, IT BECAME DIFFICULT TO LIVE IN OSTIA, AND IT EVEN CAME TO BE KNOWN AS THE RUINED CITY. THE ENVIRONMENT AROUND IT IS NOW BEGINNING TO REVIVE.
NEXT MONTH WILL BE THE 20TH ANNIVERSARY OF THE END OF THE WAR, AND THAT OPPORTUNITY WILL BE TAKEN TO HOLD A GREAT FESTIVAL, CROSSING OVER RACE, NATIONALITY, AND RELIGION.
AT THIS FESTIVAL, THERE WILL BE A MARTIAL ARTS TOURNAMENT NAMED AFTER THIS NAGI...
NAGI SPRINGFIELD...
RUINED CITY OSTIA...

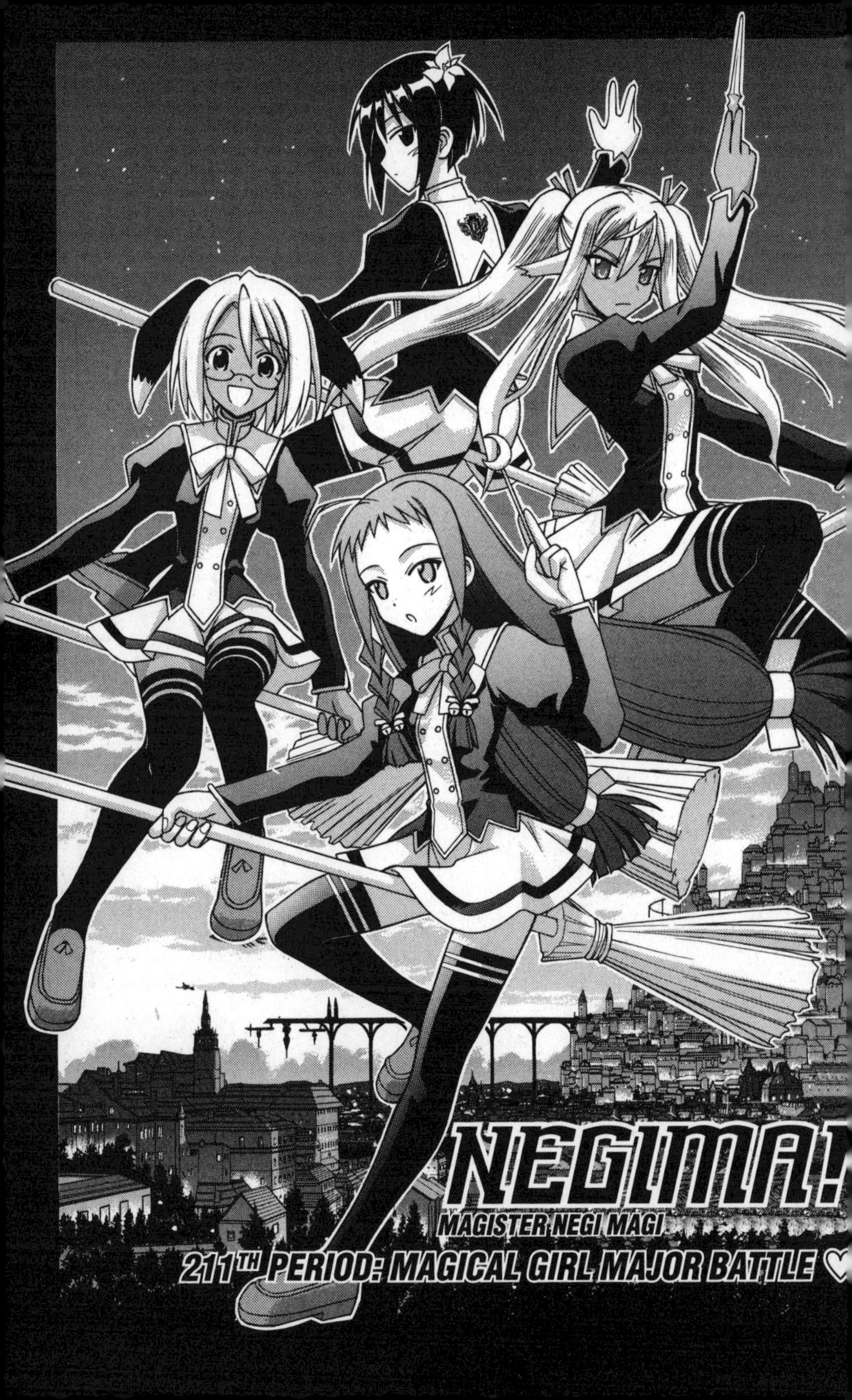
NEGIMA!
MAGISTER NEGI MAGI
211TH PERIOD: MAGICAL GIRL MAJOR BATTLE ♡

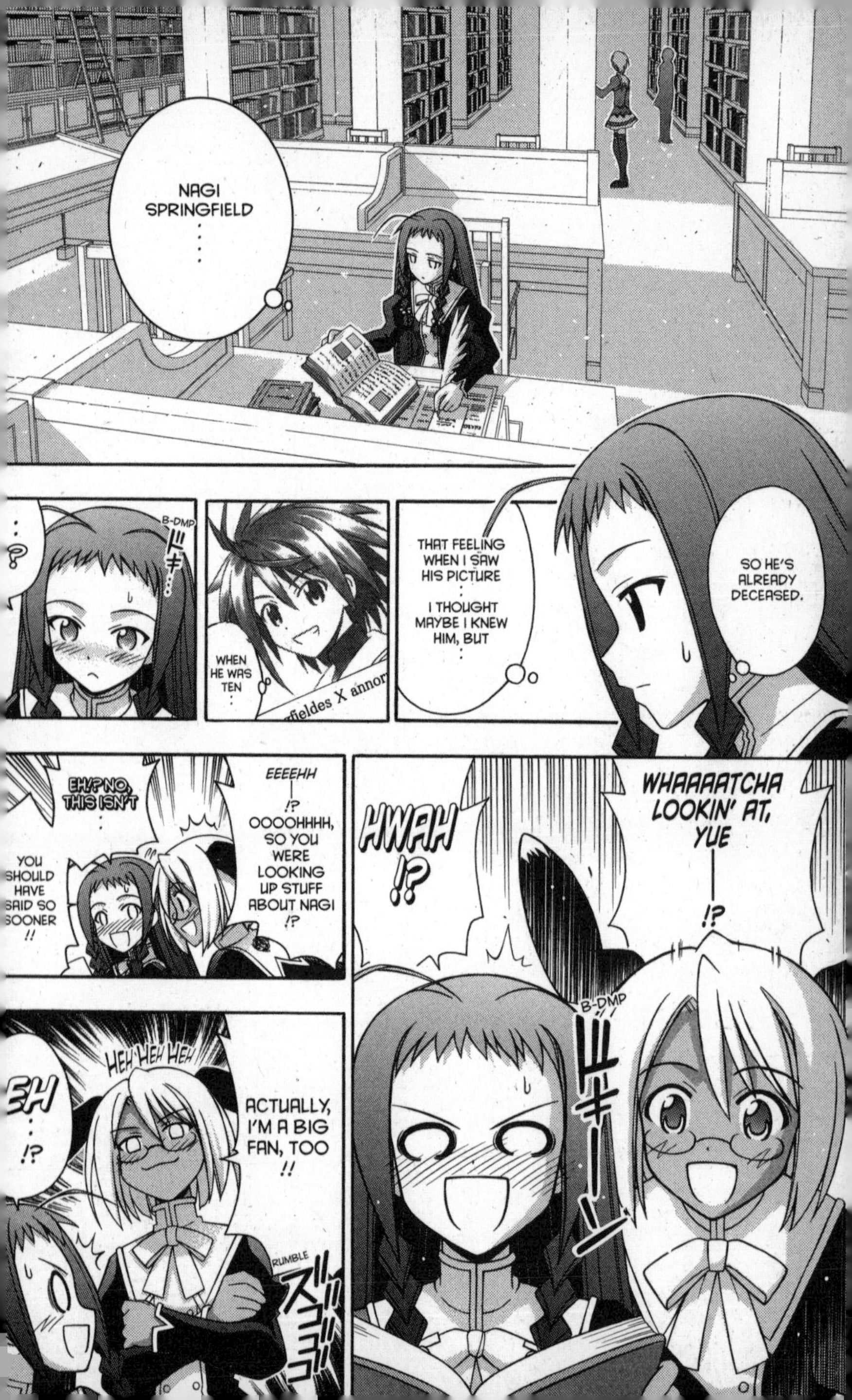
NAGI SPRINGFIELD
...
SO HE'S ALREADY DECEASED.
THAT FEELING WHEN I SAW HIS PICTURE...
I THOUGHT MAYBE I KNEW HIM, BUT...
WHEN HE WAS TEN...
fieldes X annor
...?
B-DMP
WHAAAATCHA LOOKIN' AT, YUE—!?
HWAH!?
B-DMP
EEEEHH—!?
OOOOHHHH, SO YOU WERE LOOKING UP STUFF ABOUT NAGI!?
EH!? NO, THIS ISN'T...
YOU SHOULD HAVE SAID SO SOONER!!
HEH HEH HEH
ACTUALLY, I'M A BIG FAN, TOO!!
EH...!?
RUMBLE

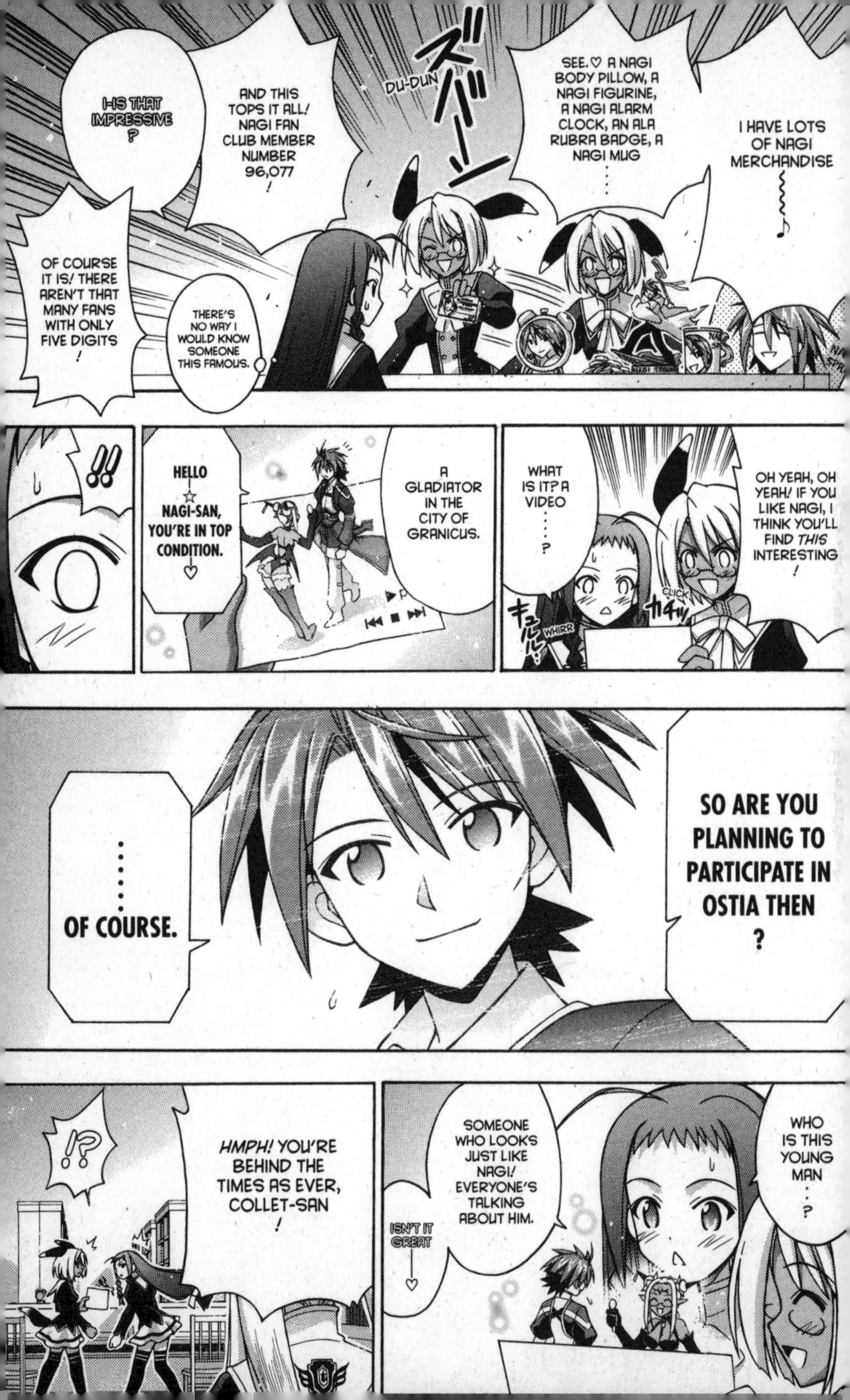
I HAVE LOTS OF NAGI MERCHANDISE ~♪
SEE.♡ A NAGI BODY PILLOW, A NAGI FIGURINE, A NAGI ALARM CLOCK, AN ALA RUBRA BADGE, A NAGI MUG...
DU-DUN
AND THIS TOPS IT ALL! NAGI FAN CLUB MEMBER NUMBER 96,077!
I-IS THAT IMPRESSIVE?
THERE'S NO WAY I WOULD KNOW SOMEONE THIS FAMOUS.
OF COURSE IT IS! THERE AREN'T THAT MANY FANS WITH ONLY FIVE DIGITS!
OH YEAH, OH YEAH! IF YOU LIKE NAGI, I THINK YOU'LL FIND *THIS* INTERESTING!
WHAT IS IT? A VIDEO...?
CLICK
WHIRR
A GLADIATOR IN THE CITY OF GRANICUS.
HELLO☆ NAGI-SAN, YOU'RE IN TOP CONDITION.♡
!!
SO ARE YOU PLANNING TO PARTICIPATE IN OSTIA THEN?
......OF COURSE.
WHO IS THIS YOUNG MAN...?
SOMEONE WHO LOOKS JUST LIKE NAGI! EVERYONE'S TALKING ABOUT HIM.
ISN'T IT GREAT♡
HMPH! YOU'RE BEHIND THE TIMES AS EVER, COLLET-SAN!
!?

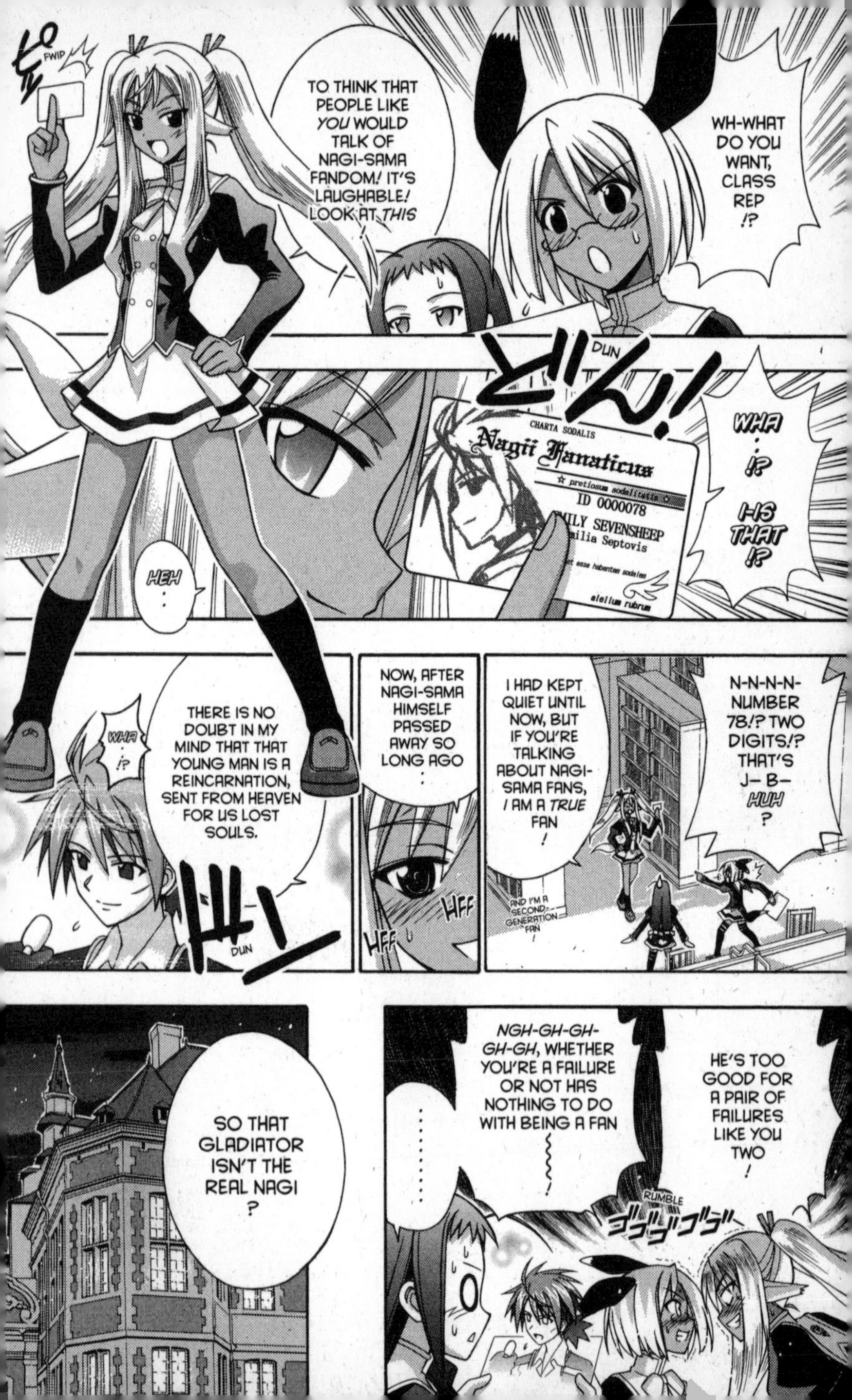
WH-WHAT DO YOU WANT, CLASS REP!?
TO THINK THAT PEOPLE LIKE *YOU* WOULD TALK OF NAGI-SAMA FANDOM! IT'S LAUGHABLE! LOOK AT *THIS*!
FWIP
DUN
WHA...!? I-IS THAT!?
CHARTA SODALIS
Nagii Fanaticus
☆ pretiosum sodalitatis ☆
ID 0000078
MILY SEVENSHEEP
milia Septovis
HEH...
N-N-N-N-NUMBER 78!? TWO DIGITS!? THAT'S J— B— *HUH*?
I HAD KEPT QUIET UNTIL NOW, BUT IF YOU'RE TALKING ABOUT NAGI-SAMA FANS, I AM A *TRUE* FAN!
AND I'M A SECOND-GENERATION FAN!
NOW, AFTER NAGI-SAMA HIMSELF PASSED AWAY SO LONG AGO...
HFF HFF
THERE IS NO DOUBT IN MY MIND THAT THAT YOUNG MAN IS A REINCARNATION, SENT FROM HEAVEN FOR US LOST SOULS.
WHA...!?
DUN
HE'S TOO GOOD FOR A PAIR OF FAILURES LIKE YOU TWO!
NGH-GH-GH-GH-GH, WHETHER YOU'RE A FAILURE OR NOT HAS NOTHING TO DO WITH BEING A FAN~~~!
......
RUMBLE
SO THAT GLADIATOR ISN'T THE REAL NAGI?

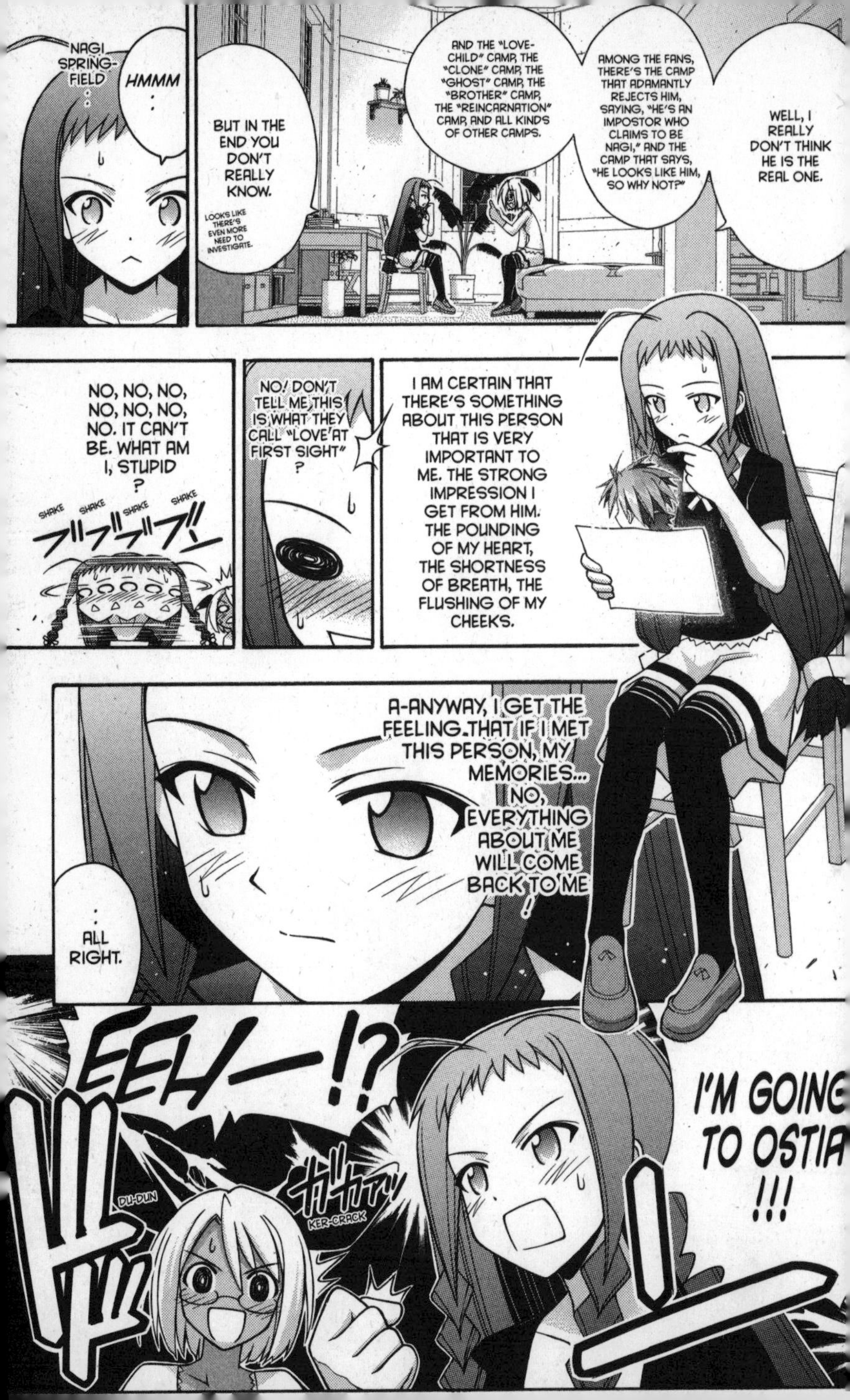
WELL, I REALLY DON'T THINK HE IS THE REAL ONE.
AMONG THE FANS, THERE'S THE CAMP THAT ADAMANTLY REJECTS HIM, SAYING, "HE'S AN IMPOSTOR WHO CLAIMS TO BE NAGI," AND THE CAMP THAT SAYS, "HE LOOKS LIKE HIM, SO WHY NOT?"
AND THE "LOVE-CHILD" CAMP, THE "CLONE" CAMP, THE "GHOST" CAMP, THE "BROTHER" CAMP, THE "REINCARNATION" CAMP, AND ALL KINDS OF OTHER CAMPS.
BUT IN THE END YOU DON'T REALLY KNOW.
LOOKS LIKE THERE'S EVEN MORE NEED TO INVESTIGATE.
HMMM :
NAGI SPRING-FIELD : :
I AM CERTAIN THAT THERE'S SOMETHING ABOUT THIS PERSON THAT IS VERY IMPORTANT TO ME. THE STRONG IMPRESSION I GET FROM HIM. THE POUNDING OF MY HEART, THE SHORTNESS OF BREATH, THE FLUSHING OF MY CHEEKS.
NO! DON'T TELL ME THIS IS WHAT THEY CALL "LOVE AT FIRST SIGHT" ?
NO, NO, NO, NO, NO, NO, NO. IT CAN'T BE. WHAT AM I, STUPID ?
SHAKE SHAKE SHAKE SHAKE
A-ANYWAY, I GET THE FEELING THAT IF I MET THIS PERSON, MY MEMORIES... NO, EVERYTHING ABOUT ME WILL COME BACK TO ME !
: ALL RIGHT.
I'M GOING TO OSTIA !!!
KER-CRACK
EEH—!?
DU-DUN

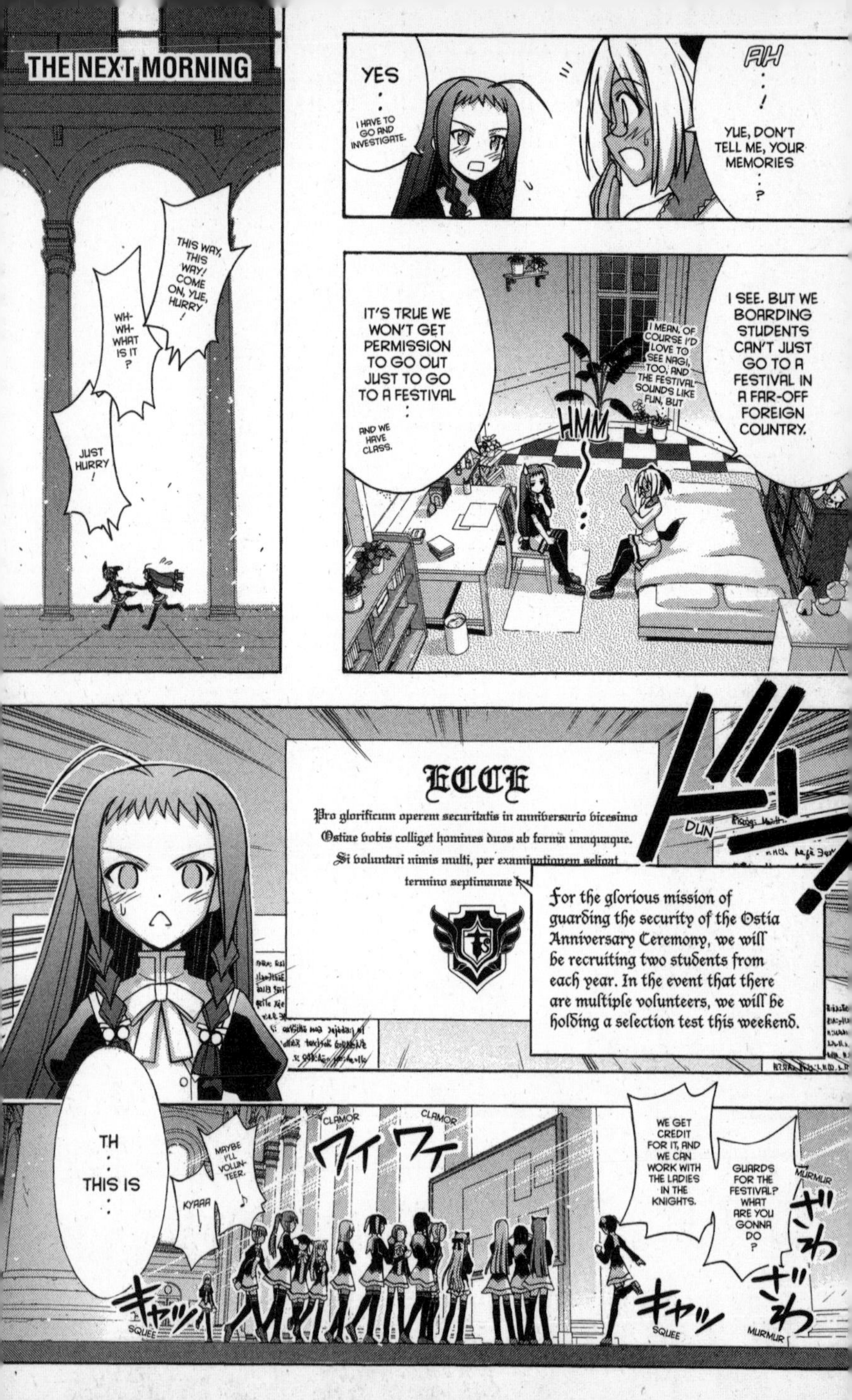

AH . . !
YUE, DON'T TELL ME, YOUR MEMORIES . . ?
YES . . I HAVE TO GO AND INVESTIGATE.
I SEE. BUT WE BOARDING STUDENTS CAN'T JUST GO TO A FESTIVAL IN A FAR-OFF FOREIGN COUNTRY.
I MEAN, OF COURSE I'D LOVE TO SEE NAGI, TOO, AND THE FESTIVAL SOUNDS LIKE FUN, BUT
HMM
IT'S TRUE WE WON'T GET PERMISSION TO GO OUT JUST TO GO TO A FESTIVAL . .
AND WE HAVE CLASS.
THE NEXT MORNING
THIS WAY, THIS WAY! COME ON, YUE, HURRY!
WH- WH- WHAT IS IT?
JUST HURRY!
DUN
ECCE
Pro glorificum operem securitatis in anniversario bicesimo
Ostiae bobis colliget homines duos ab forma unaquaque.
Si boluntari nimis multi, per examinationem seliont
termino septimanae h
For the glorious mission of guarding the security of the Ostia Anniversary Ceremony, we will be recruiting two students from each year. In the event that there are multiple volunteers, we will be holding a selection test this weekend.
MURMUR
MURMUR
GUARDS FOR THE FESTIVAL? WHAT ARE YOU GONNA DO?
WE GET CREDIT FOR IT, AND WE CAN WORK WITH THE LADIES IN THE KNIGHTS.
SQUEE
CLAMOR
CLAMOR
MAYBE I'LL VOLUNTEER. ♪
KYAAA!
SQUEE
TH . . THIS IS . .

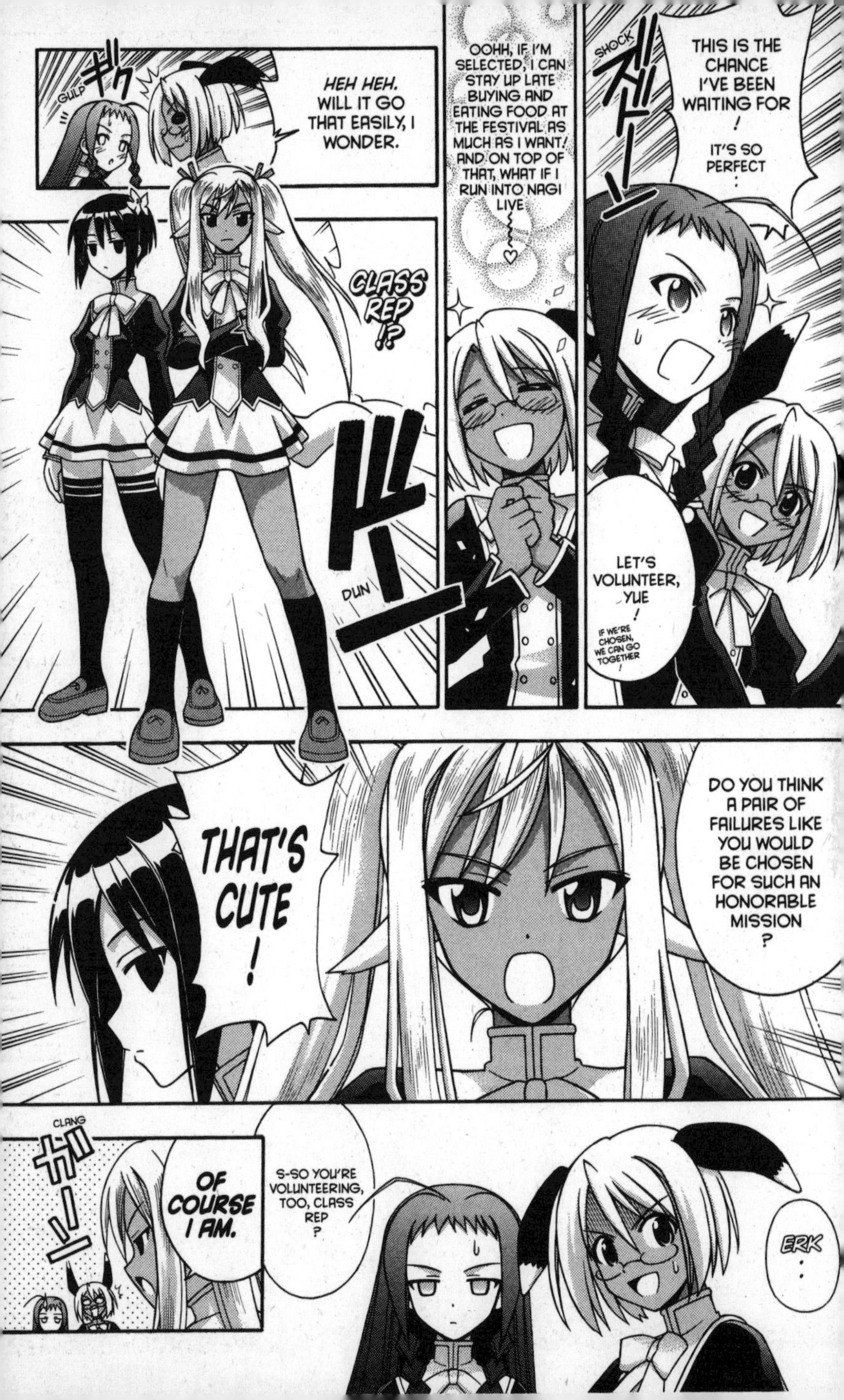
SHOCK
THIS IS THE CHANCE I'VE BEEN WAITING FOR!
IT'S SO PERFECT...
LET'S VOLUNTEER, YUE!
IF WE'RE CHOSEN, WE CAN GO TOGETHER!
OOHH, IF I'M SELECTED, I CAN STAY UP LATE BUYING AND EATING FOOD AT THE FESTIVAL AS MUCH AS I WANT! AND ON TOP OF THAT, WHAT IF I RUN INTO NAGI LIVE~♡
GULP
HEH HEH. WILL IT GO THAT EASILY, I WONDER.
CLASS REP!?
DUN
DO YOU THINK A PAIR OF FAILURES LIKE YOU WOULD BE CHOSEN FOR SUCH AN HONORABLE MISSION?
THAT'S CUTE!
S-SO YOU'RE VOLUNTEERING, TOO, CLASS REP?
ERK...
CLANG
OF COURSE I AM.

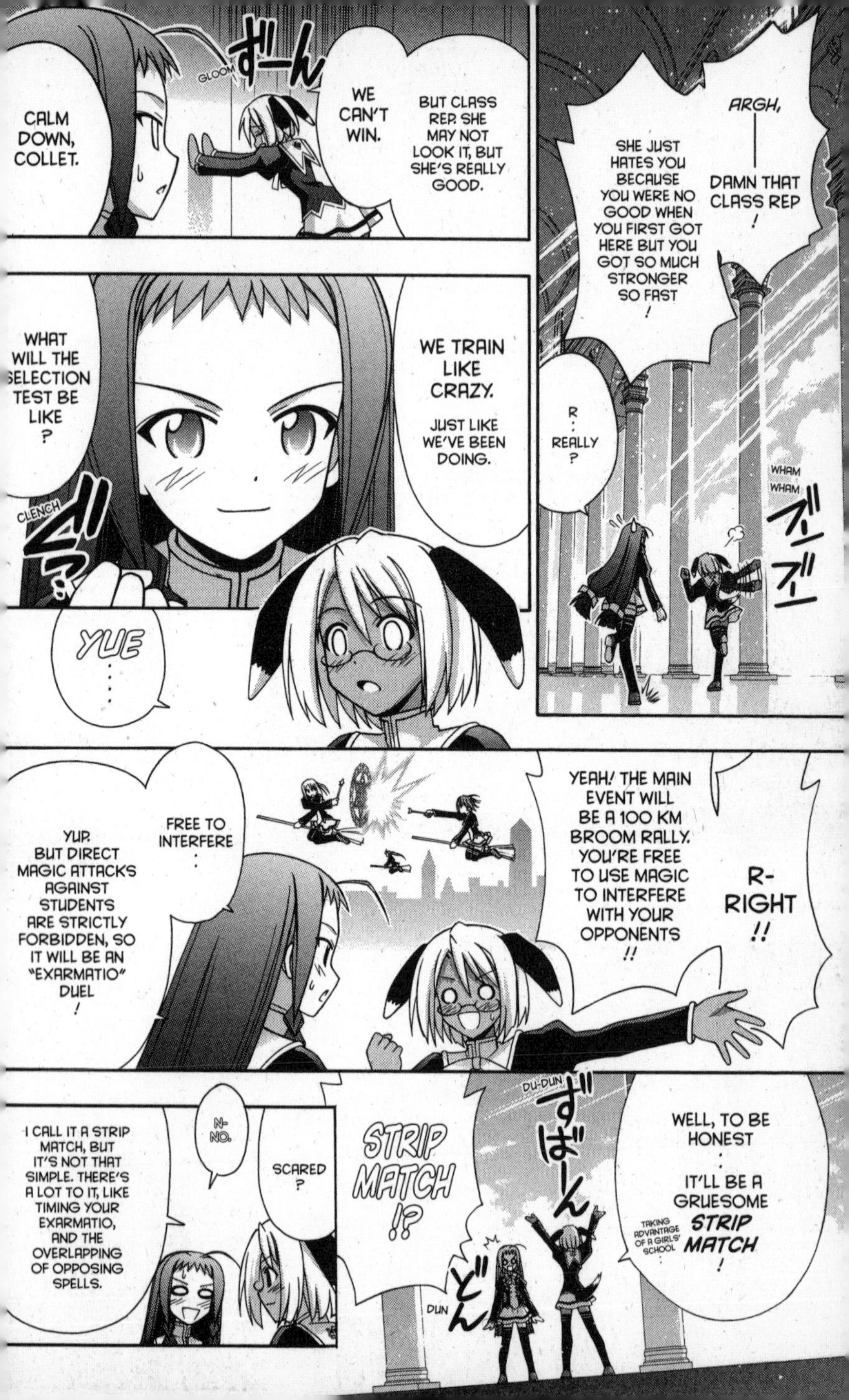
ARGH, DAMN THAT CLASS REP!
SHE JUST HATES YOU BECAUSE YOU WERE NO GOOD WHEN YOU FIRST GOT HERE BUT YOU GOT SO MUCH STRONGER SO FAST!
R... REALLY?
WHAM WHAM
GLOOM
WE CAN'T WIN. BUT CLASS REP. SHE MAY NOT LOOK IT, BUT SHE'S REALLY GOOD.
CALM DOWN, COLLET.
WE TRAIN LIKE CRAZY. JUST LIKE WE'VE BEEN DOING.
WHAT WILL THE SELECTION TEST BE LIKE?
CLENCH
YUE...
R-RIGHT!!
YEAH! THE MAIN EVENT WILL BE A 100 KM BROOM RALLY. YOU'RE FREE TO USE MAGIC TO INTERFERE WITH YOUR OPPONENTS!!
FREE TO INTERFERE...
YUP. BUT DIRECT MAGIC ATTACKS AGAINST STUDENTS ARE STRICTLY FORBIDDEN, SO IT WILL BE AN "EXARMATIO" DUEL!
WELL, TO BE HONEST... IT'LL BE A GRUESOME STRIP MATCH!
TAKING ADVANTAGE OF A GIRLS' SCHOOL...
DU-DUN
DUN
STRIP MATCH!?
SCARED?
N-NO.
I CALL IT A STRIP MATCH, BUT IT'S NOT THAT SIMPLE. THERE'S A LOT TO IT, LIKE TIMING YOUR EXARMATIO, AND THE OVERLAPPING OF OPPOSING SPELLS.

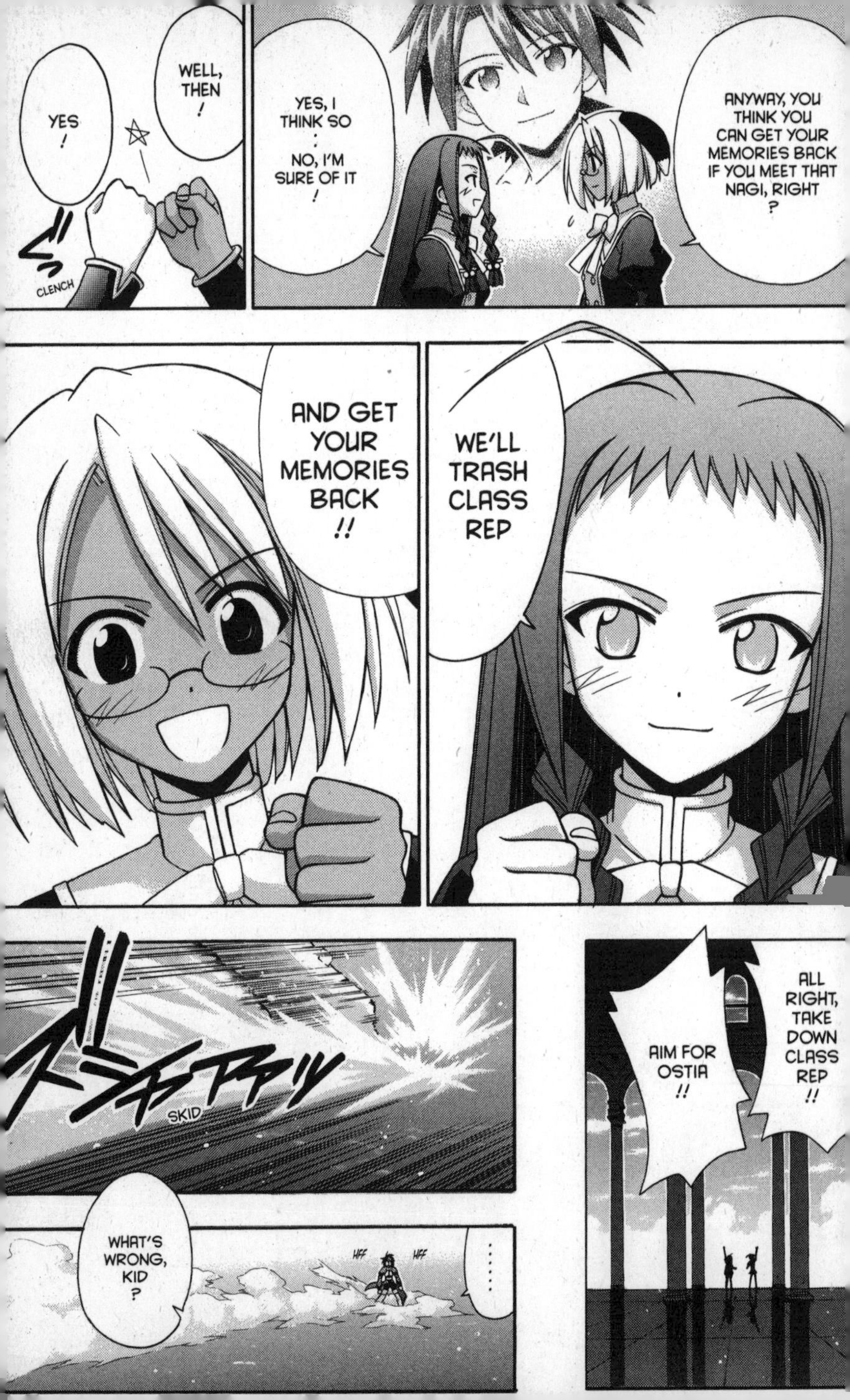
ANYWAY, YOU THINK YOU CAN GET YOUR MEMORIES BACK IF YOU MEET THAT NAGI, RIGHT?
YES, I THINK SO: NO, I'M SURE OF IT!
WELL, THEN!
YES!
CLENCH
WE'LL TRASH CLASS REP
AND GET YOUR MEMORIES BACK!!
ALL RIGHT, TAKE DOWN CLASS REP!!
AIM FOR OSTIA!!
SKID
......
HFF HFF
WHAT'S WRONG, KID?

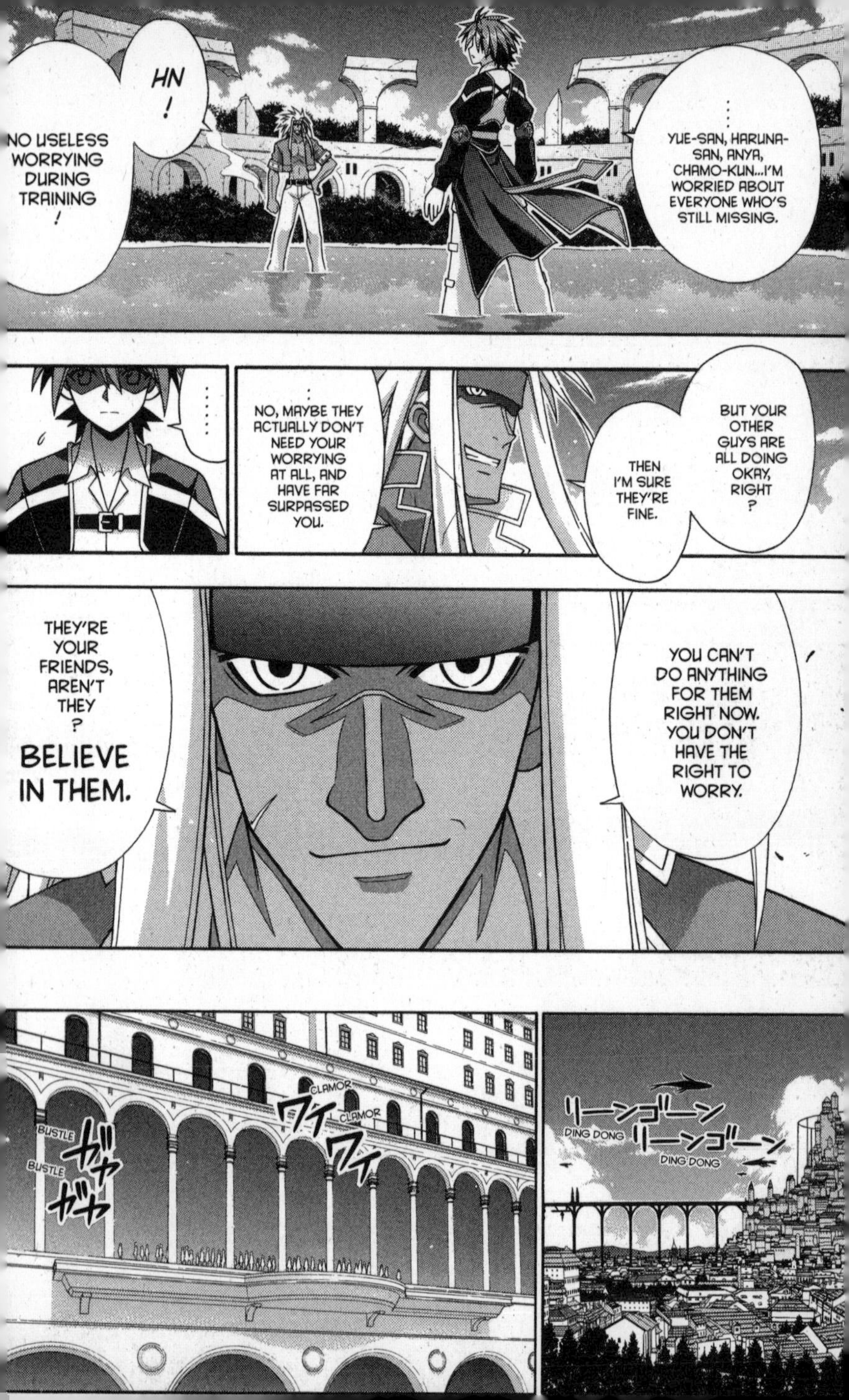
......YUE-SAN, HARUNA-SAN, ANYA, CHAMO-KUN...I'M WORRIED ABOUT EVERYONE WHO'S STILL MISSING.
HN!
NO USELESS WORRYING DURING TRAINING!
BUT YOUR OTHER GUYS ARE ALL DOING OKAY, RIGHT?
THEN I'M SURE THEY'RE FINE.
...NO, MAYBE THEY ACTUALLY DON'T NEED YOUR WORRYING AT ALL, AND HAVE FAR SURPASSED YOU.
......
YOU CAN'T DO ANYTHING FOR THEM RIGHT NOW. YOU DON'T HAVE THE RIGHT TO WORRY.
THEY'RE YOUR FRIENDS, AREN'T THEY?
BELIEVE IN THEM.
リーンゴーン DING DONG
リーンゴーン DING DONG
ワイ CLAMOR
ワイ CLAMOR
ガヤ BUSTLE
ガヤ BUSTLE

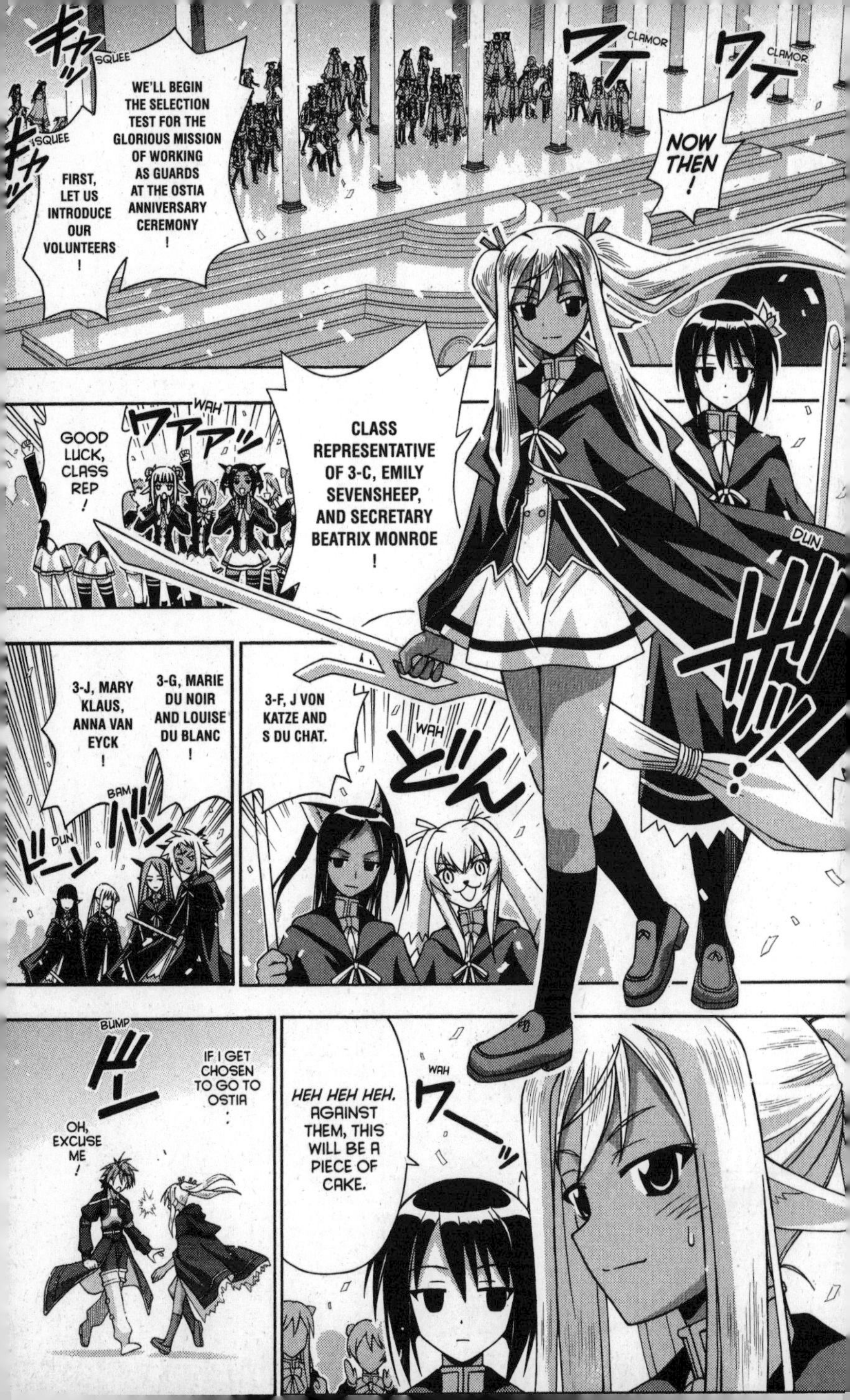
ワァ CLAMOR
ワァ CLAMOR
NOW THEN!
WE'LL BEGIN THE SELECTION TEST FOR THE GLORIOUS MISSION OF WORKING AS GUARDS AT THE OSTIA ANNIVERSARY CEREMONY!
FIRST, LET US INTRODUCE OUR VOLUNTEERS!
ギャッ SQUEE
ギャッ SQUEE
CLASS REPRESENTATIVE OF 3-C, EMILY SEVENSHEEP, AND SECRETARY BEATRIX MONROE!
ザザッ DUN
ワアアッ WAH
GOOD LUCK, CLASS REP!
3-F, J VON KATZE AND S DU CHAT.
どん WAH
3-G, MARIE DU NOIR AND LOUISE DU BLANC!
3-J, MARY KLAUS, ANNA VAN EYCK!
バン BAM
ドーン DUN
HEH HEH HEH. AGAINST THEM, THIS WILL BE A PIECE OF CAKE.
ワーッ WAH
IF I GET CHOSEN TO GO TO OSTIA
OH, EXCUSE ME!
ドー BUMP

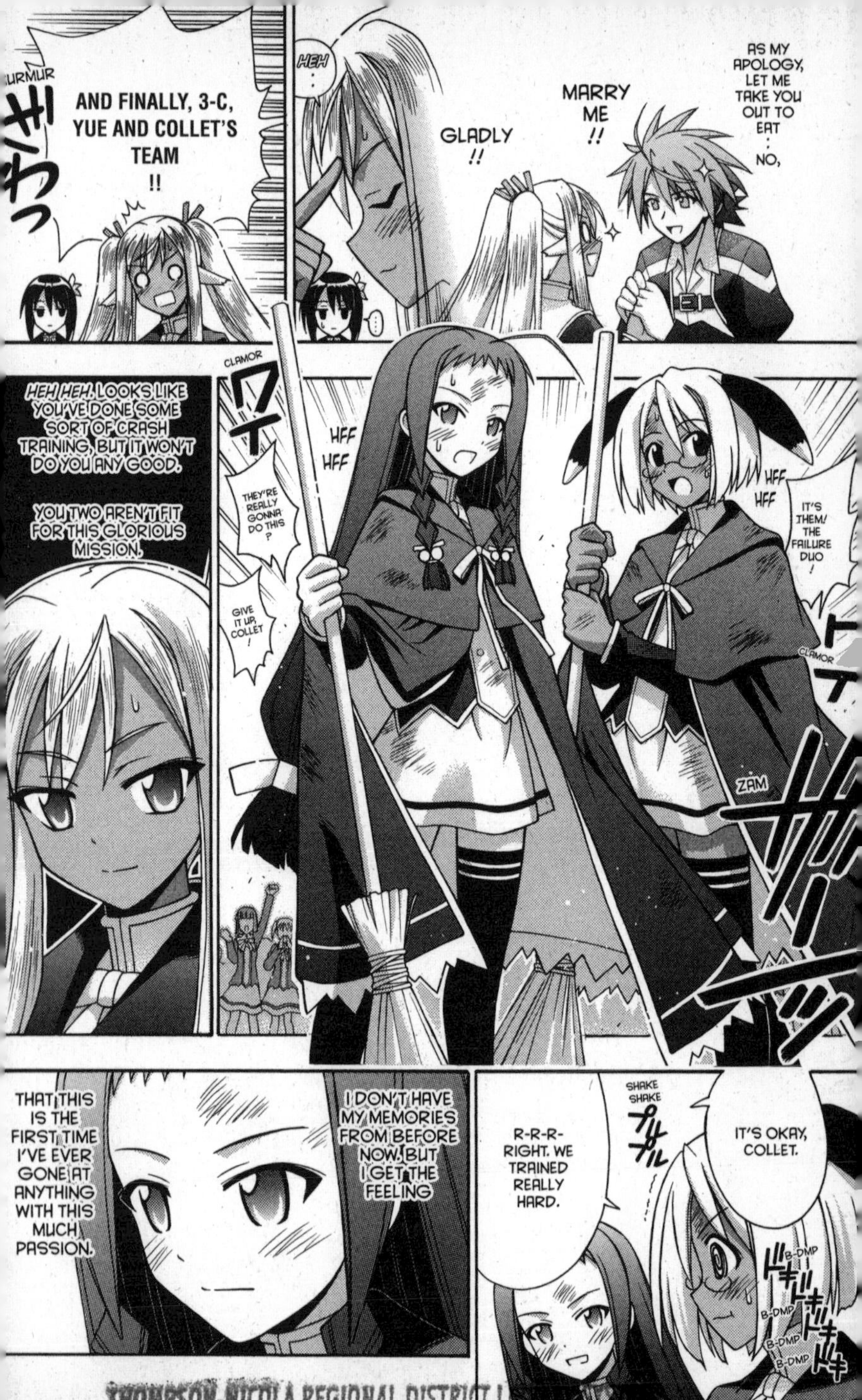
AS MY APOLOGY, LET ME TAKE YOU OUT TO EAT... NO,
MARRY ME!!
GLADLY!!
HEH...
URMUR
AND FINALLY, 3-C, YUE AND COLLET'S TEAM!!
CLAMOR
IT'S THEM! THE FAILURE DUO!
HFF HFF
ZAM
HFF HFF
THEY'RE REALLY GONNA DO THIS?
GIVE IT UP, COLLET!
CLAMOR
HEH HEH. LOOKS LIKE YOU'VE DONE SOME SORT OF CRASH TRAINING, BUT IT WON'T DO YOU ANY GOOD.
YOU TWO AREN'T FIT FOR THIS GLORIOUS MISSION.
IT'S OKAY, COLLET.
SHAKE SHAKE
R-R-R-RIGHT. WE TRAINED REALLY HARD.
B-DMP B-DMP B-DMP B-DMP
I DON'T HAVE MY MEMORIES FROM BEFORE NOW, BUT I GET THE FEELING
THAT THIS IS THE FIRST TIME I'VE EVER GONE AT ANYTHING WITH THIS MUCH PASSION.

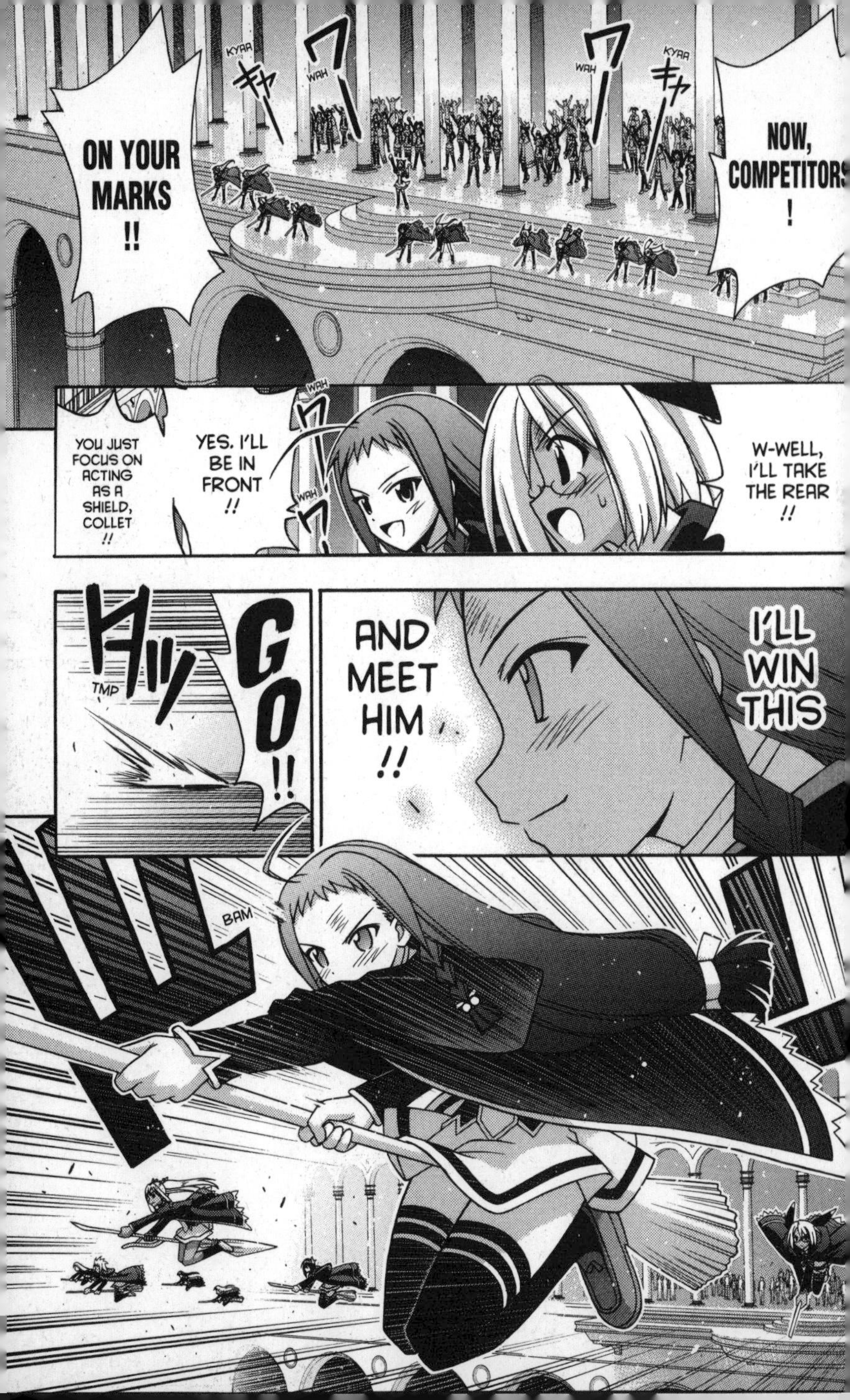
KYAA
WAH
NOW, COMPETITORS!
WAH
KYAA
ON YOUR MARKS!!
W-WELL, I'LL TAKE THE REAR!!
WAH
WAH
YES. I'LL BE IN FRONT!!
YOU JUST FOCUS ON ACTING AS A SHIELD, COLLET!!
I'LL WIN THIS
AND MEET HIM!!
GO!!
TMP
BAM

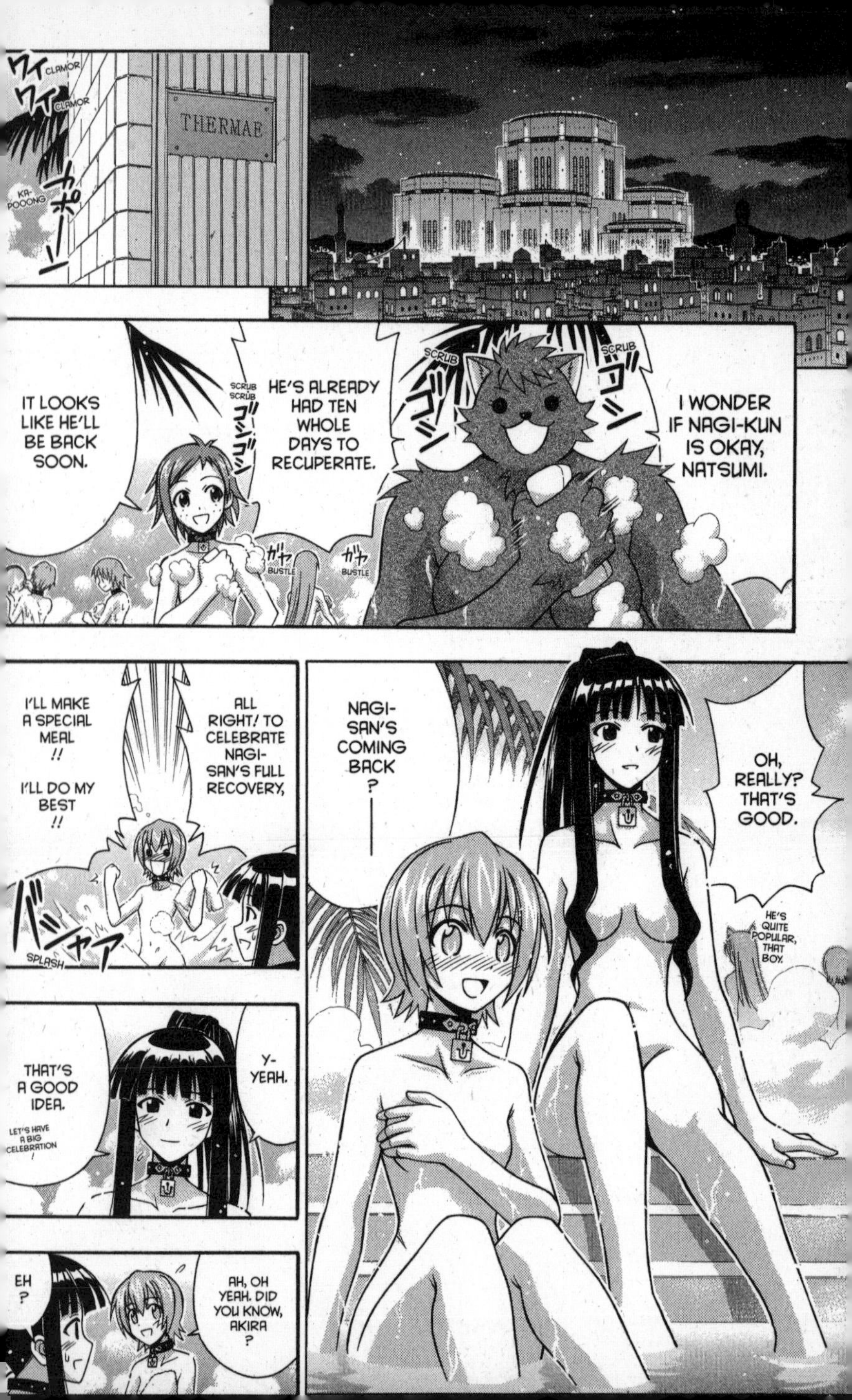
ワイ CLAMOR
ワイ CLAMOR
THERMAE
カポーン KA-POOONG
I WONDER IF NAGI-KUN IS OKAY, NATSUMI.
ゴシ SCRUB
ゴシ SCRUB
HE'S ALREADY HAD TEN WHOLE DAYS TO RECUPERATE.
ゴシゴシ SCRUB SCRUB
IT LOOKS LIKE HE'LL BE BACK SOON.
ガヤ BUSTLE
ガヤ BUSTLE
OH, REALLY? THAT'S GOOD.
NAGI-SAN'S COMING BACK? ——
HE'S QUITE POPULAR, THAT BOY.
ALL RIGHT! TO CELEBRATE NAGI-SAN'S FULL RECOVERY,
I'LL MAKE A SPECIAL MEAL!!
I'LL DO MY BEST!!
バシャア SPLASH
Y-YEAH.
THAT'S A GOOD IDEA.
LET'S HAVE A BIG CELEBRATION!
AH, OH YEAH. DID YOU KNOW, AKIRA?
EH?

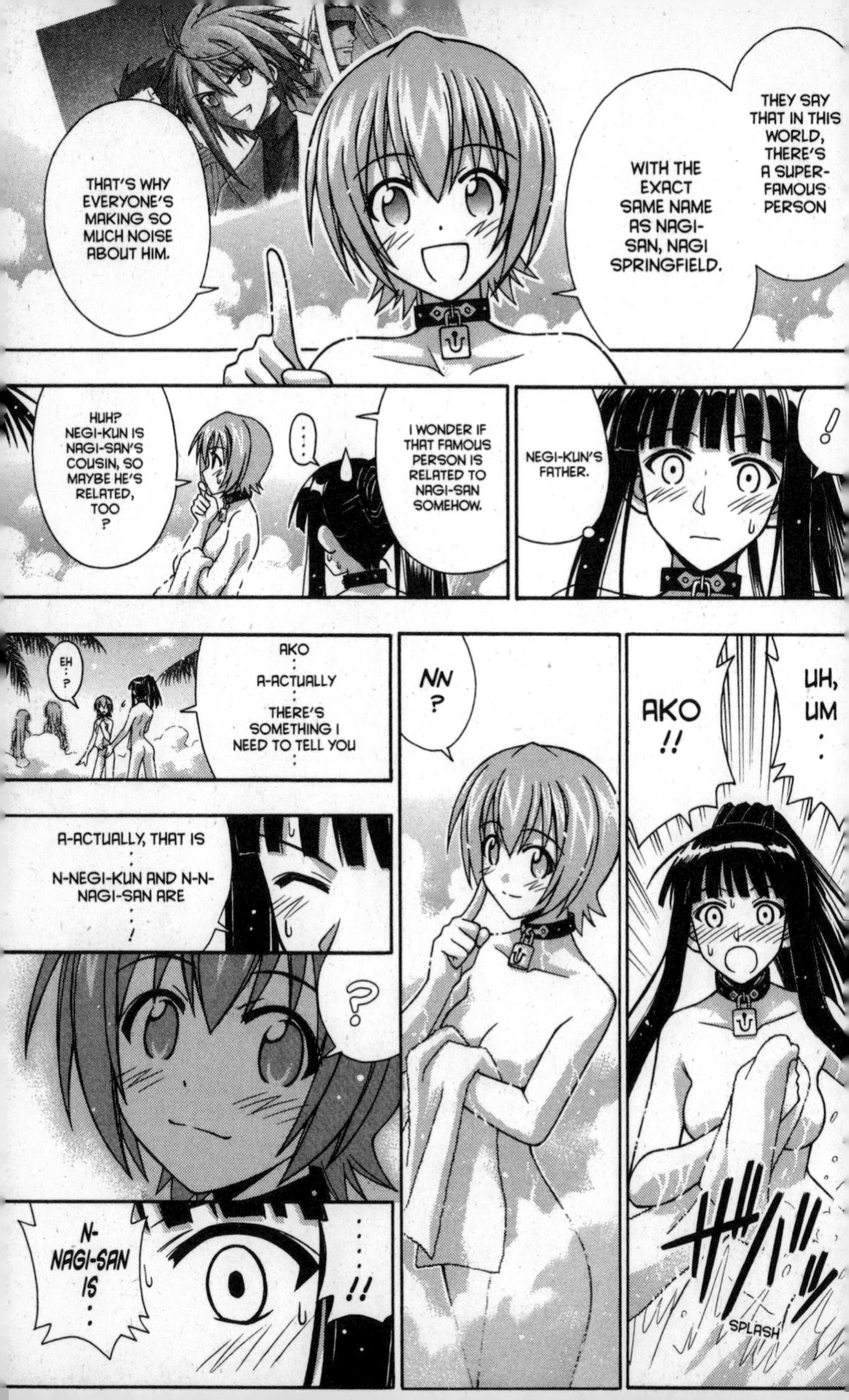
THEY SAY THAT IN THIS WORLD, THERE'S A SUPER-FAMOUS PERSON
WITH THE EXACT SAME NAME AS NAGI-SAN, NAGI SPRINGFIELD.
THAT'S WHY EVERYONE'S MAKING SO MUCH NOISE ABOUT HIM.
!
NEGI-KUN'S FATHER.
I WONDER IF THAT FAMOUS PERSON IS RELATED TO NAGI-SAN SOMEHOW.
...
HUH? NEGI-KUN IS NAGI-SAN'S COUSIN, SO MAYBE HE'S RELATED, TOO?
UH, UM...
AKO!!
SPLASH
NN?
AKO... A-ACTUALLY... THERE'S SOMETHING I NEED TO TELL YOU...
EH..?
A-ACTUALLY, THAT IS... N-NEGI-KUN AND N-N-NAGI-SAN ARE...!
?
N-NAGI-SAN IS...
......!!

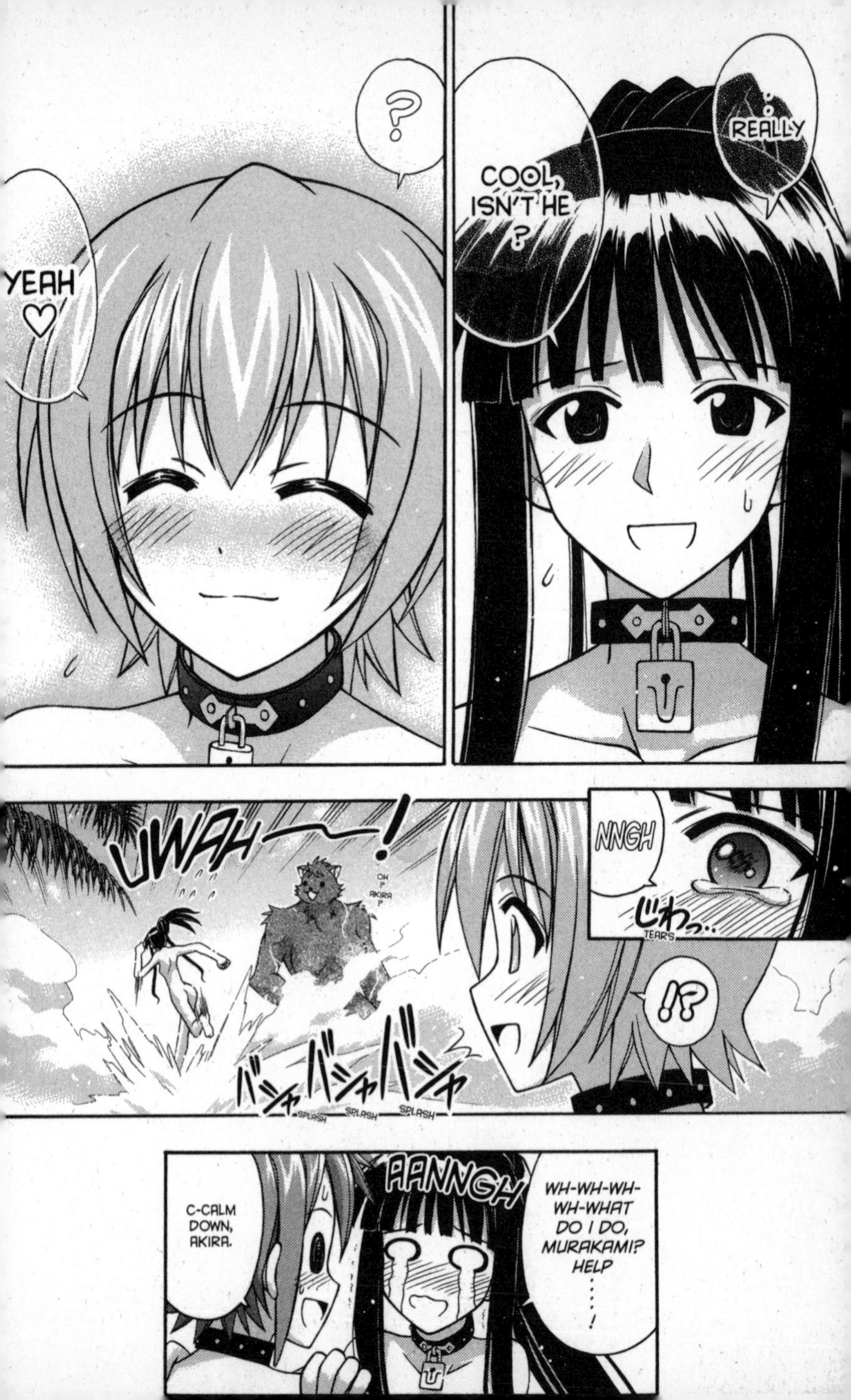

...REALLY
COOL, ISN'T HE ?
?
YEAH ♡
NNGH
じわっ…
TEARS
!?
UWAH——!
OH ♪ AKIRA ♪
バシャバシャバシャ
SPLASH SPLASH SPLASH
WH-WH-WH-WH-WHAT DO I DO, MURAKAMI? HELP.....!
AANNGH
C-CALM DOWN, AKIRA.

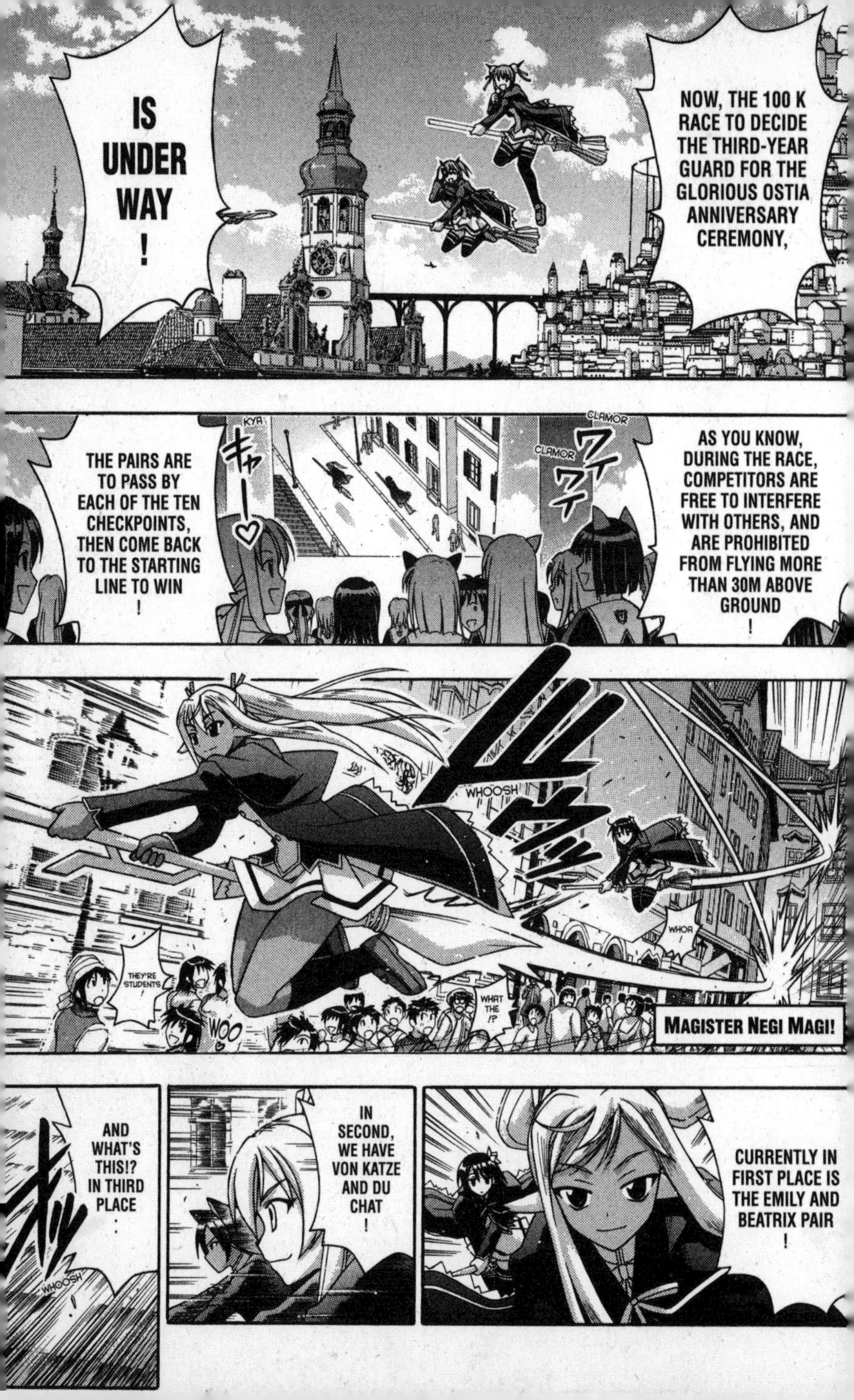
NOW, THE 100 K RACE TO DECIDE THE THIRD-YEAR GUARD FOR THE GLORIOUS OSTIA ANNIVERSARY CEREMONY,
IS UNDER WAY!
AS YOU KNOW, DURING THE RACE, COMPETITORS ARE FREE TO INTERFERE WITH OTHERS, AND ARE PROHIBITED FROM FLYING MORE THAN 30M ABOVE GROUND!
CLAMOR
CLAMOR
KYA
THE PAIRS ARE TO PASS BY EACH OF THE TEN CHECKPOINTS, THEN COME BACK TO THE STARTING LINE TO WIN!
WHOOSH
WHOA!
WHAT THE !?
THEY'RE STUDENTS!
WOO
MAGISTER NEGI MAGI!
CURRENTLY IN FIRST PLACE IS THE EMILY AND BEATRIX PAIR!
IN SECOND, WE HAVE VON KATZE AND DU CHAT!
AND WHAT'S THIS!? IN THIRD PLACE...
WHOOSH!

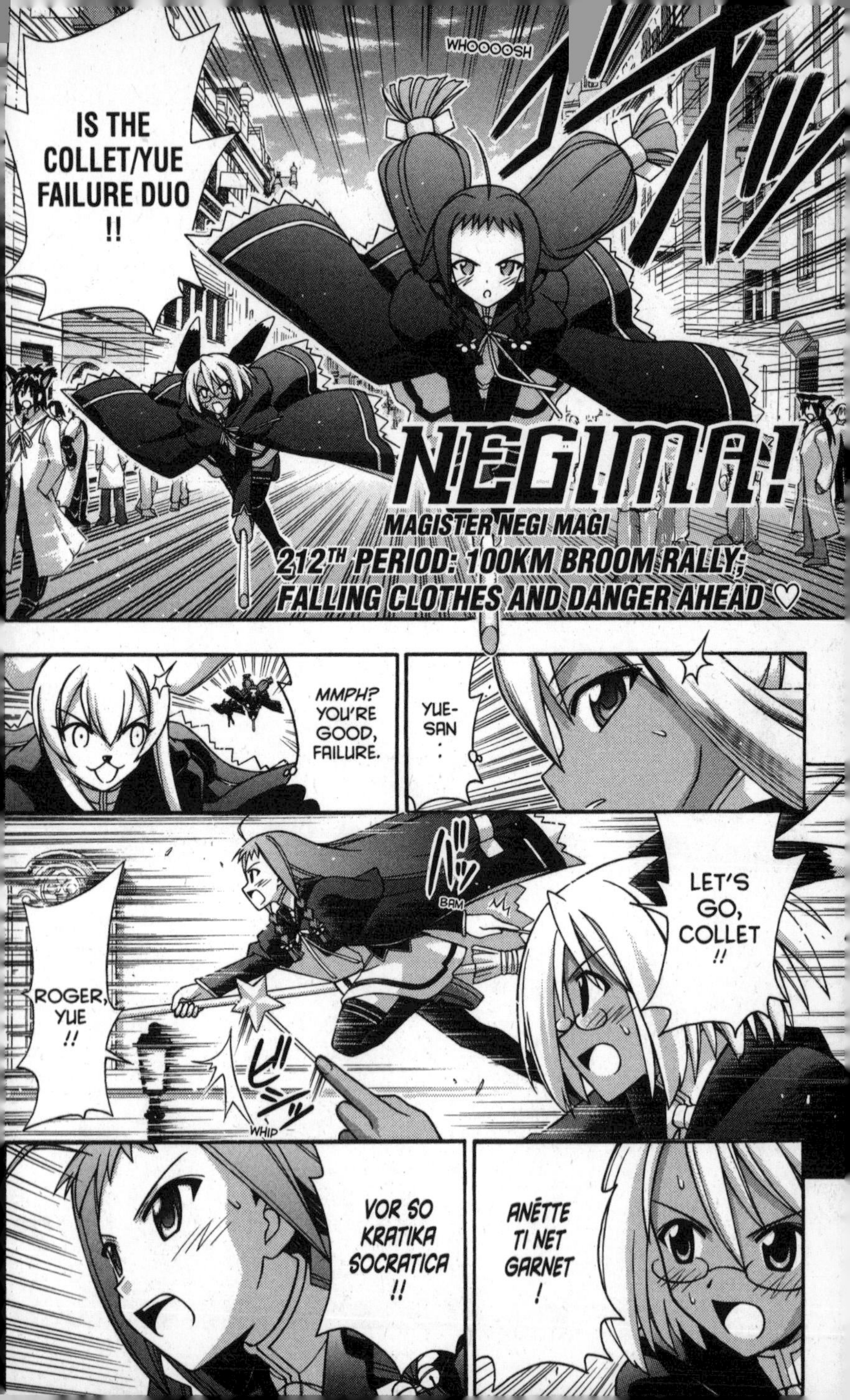
WHOOOOSH
NEGIMA!
MAGISTER NEGI MAGI
212TH PERIOD: 100KM BROOM RALLY; FALLING CLOTHES AND DANGER AHEAD ♡
IS THE COLLET/YUE FAILURE DUO !!
YUE-SAN :
MMPH? YOU'RE GOOD, FAILURE.
LET'S GO, COLLET !!
BAM
WHIP
ROGER, YUE !!
ANÉTTE TI NET GARNET !
VOR SO KRATIKA SOCRATICA !!

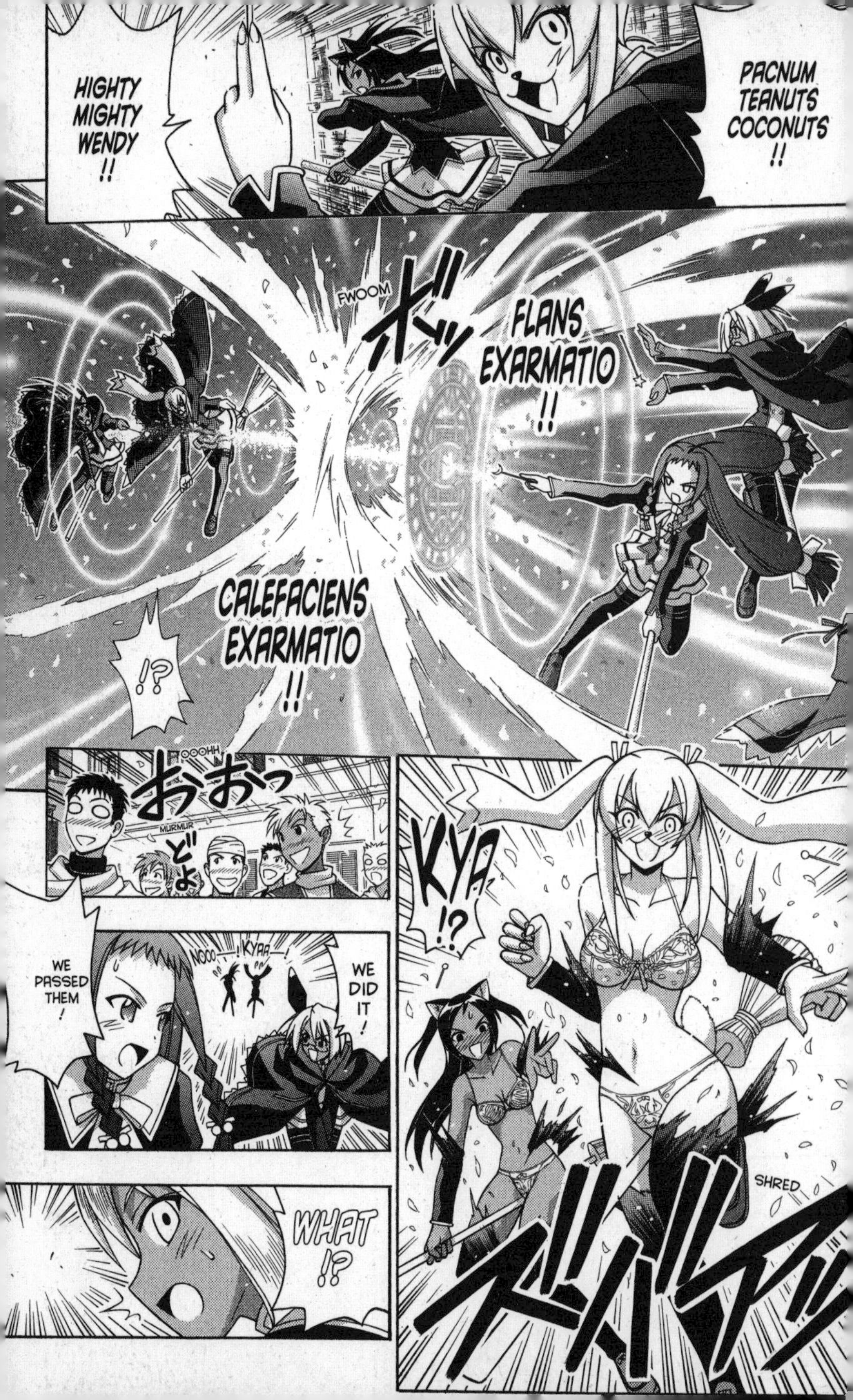
PACNUM TEANUTS COCONUTS !!
HIGHTY MIGHTY WENDY !!
FWOOM
FLANS EXARMATIO !!
CALEFACIENS EXARMATIO !!
!?
KYA !?
SHRED
OOOHH
おおっ
MURMUR
どよ
WE DID IT!
NOOO—!
KYAA—!
WE PASSED THEM!
WHAT !?

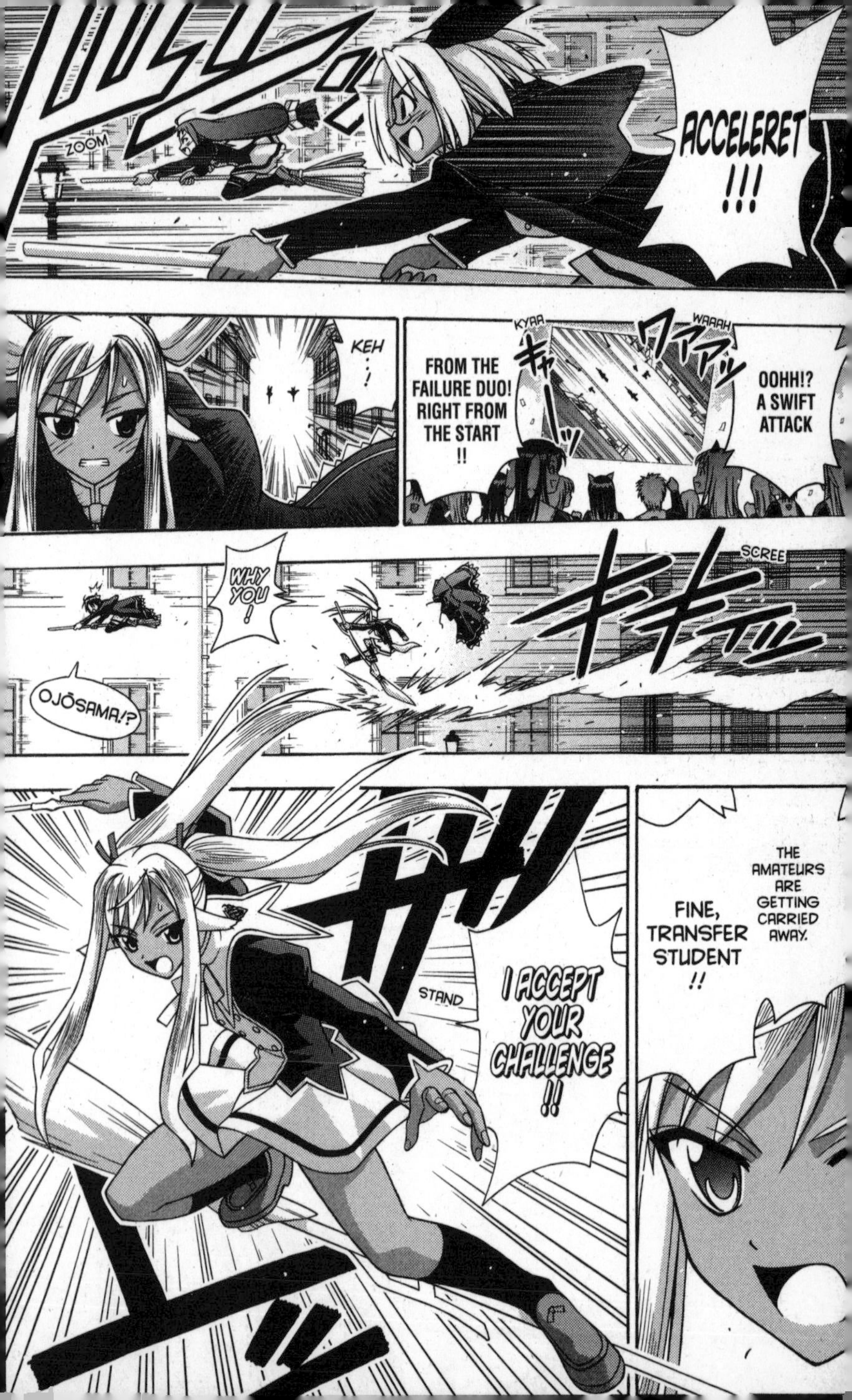
ACCELERET !!!
ZOOM
OOHH!? A SWIFT ATTACK
WAAAH
ワァアッ
KYAA
ギャーッ
FROM THE FAILURE DUO! RIGHT FROM THE START !!
KEH ...!
SCREE
キキィッ
WHY YOU !
OJŌSAMA!?
THE AMATEURS ARE GETTING CARRIED AWAY.
FINE, TRANSFER STUDENT !!
I ACCEPT YOUR CHALLENGE !!
STAND

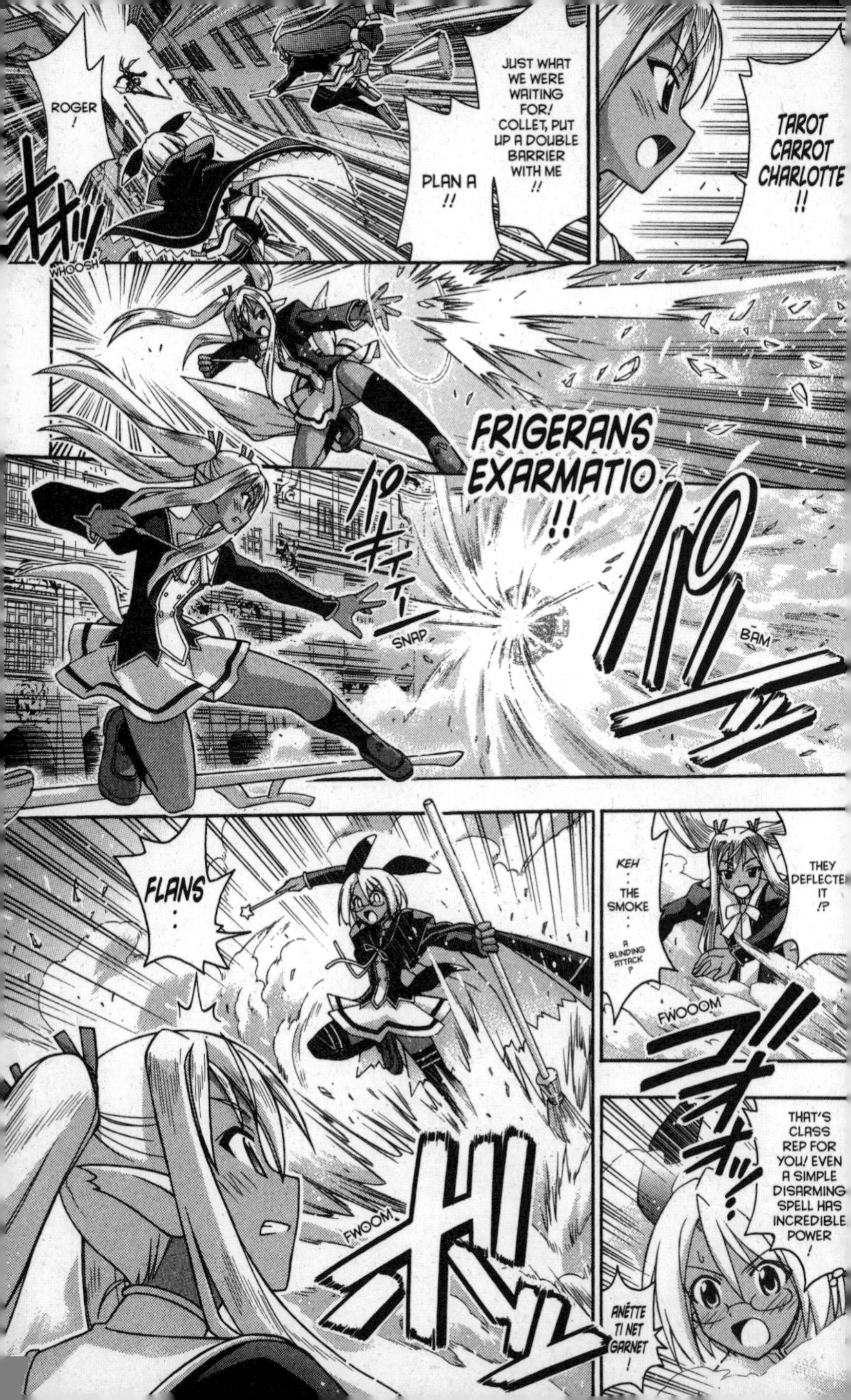
TAROT CARROT CHARLOTTE!!
JUST WHAT WE WERE WAITING FOR! COLLET, PUT UP A DOUBLE BARRIER WITH ME!!
PLAN A!!
ROGER!
WHOOSH
FRIGERANS EXARMATIO!!
BAM
SNAP
THEY DEFLECTE IT!?
KEH... THE SMOKE...
A BLINDING ATTACK?
FWOOOM
THAT'S CLASS REP FOR YOU! EVEN A SIMPLE DISARMING SPELL HAS INCREDIBLE POWER!
ANÉTTE TI NET GARNET!
FLANS...
FWOOM

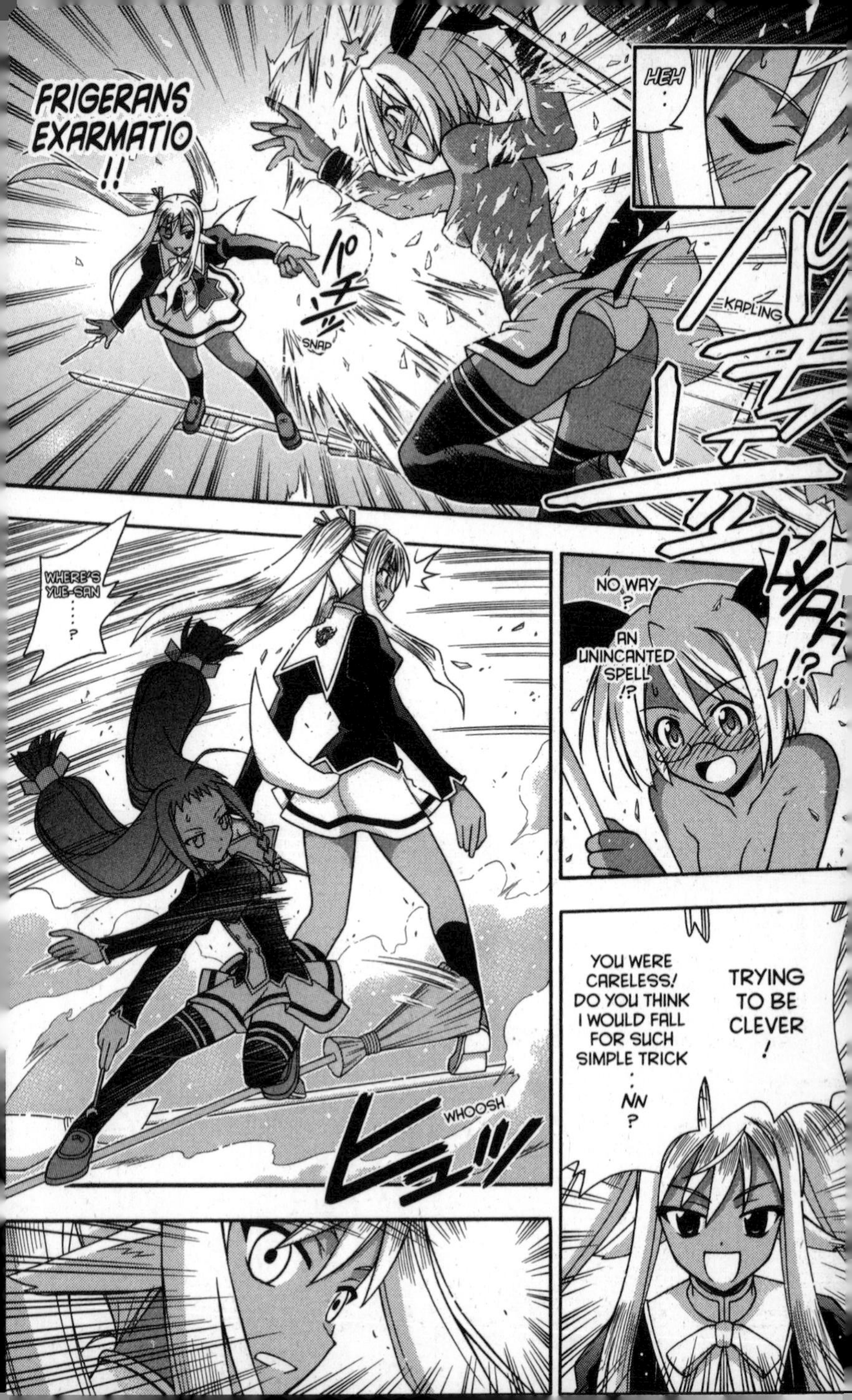
HEH...
FRIGERANS EXARMATIO!!
SNAP
KAPLING
NO WAY?
AN UNINCANTED SPELL!?
KYAA!?
TRYING TO BE CLEVER!
YOU WERE CARELESS! DO YOU THINK I WOULD FALL FOR SUCH SIMPLE TRICK..
NN?
WHERE'S YUE-SAN.....?
WHOOSH

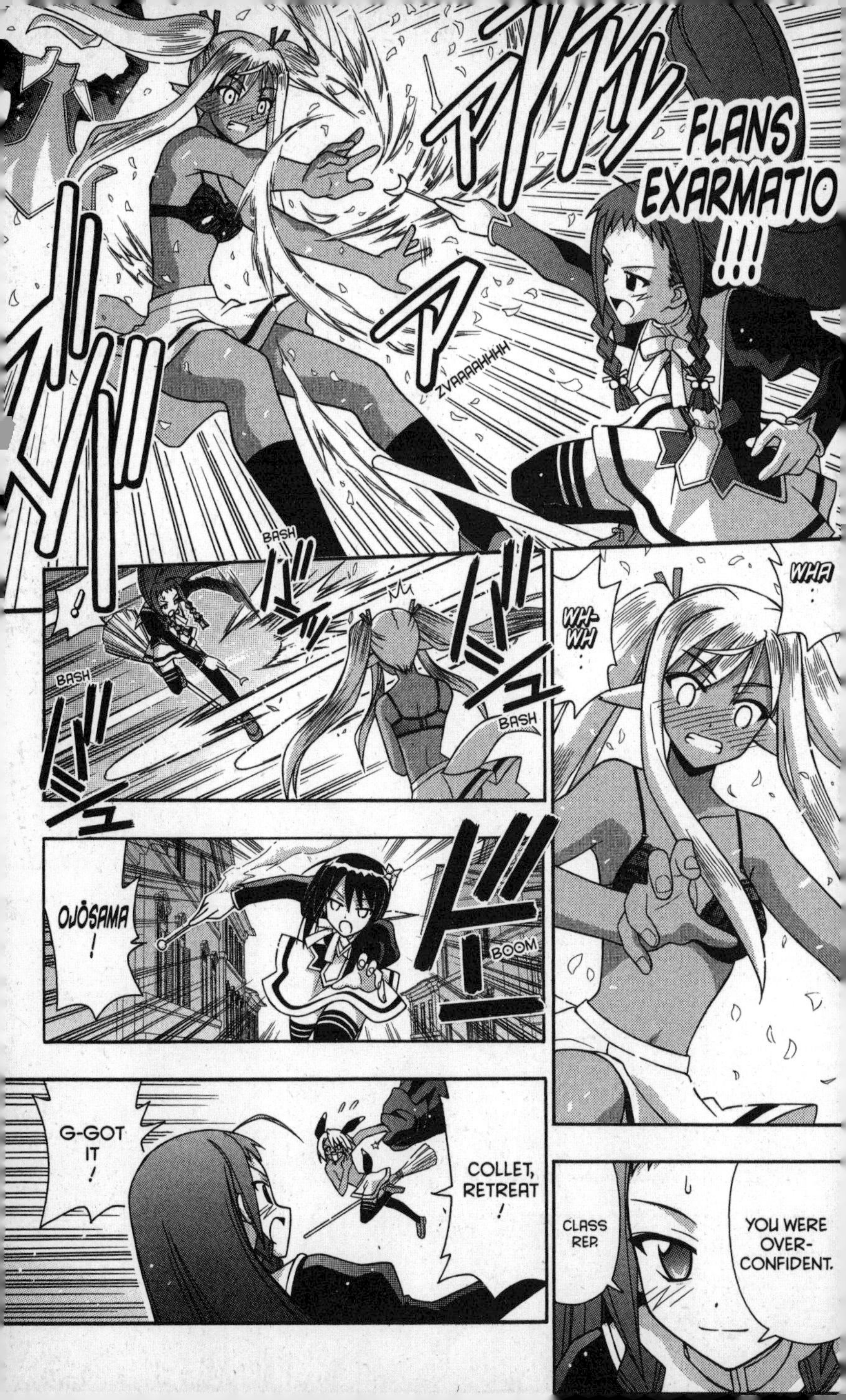
FLANS EXARMATIO !!!
ZVAAAAHHHH
WHA
WH-WH
BASH
BASH
BASH
OJŌSAMA !
BOOM
CLASS REP.
YOU WERE OVER-CONFIDENT.
COLLET, RETREAT !
G-GOT IT !

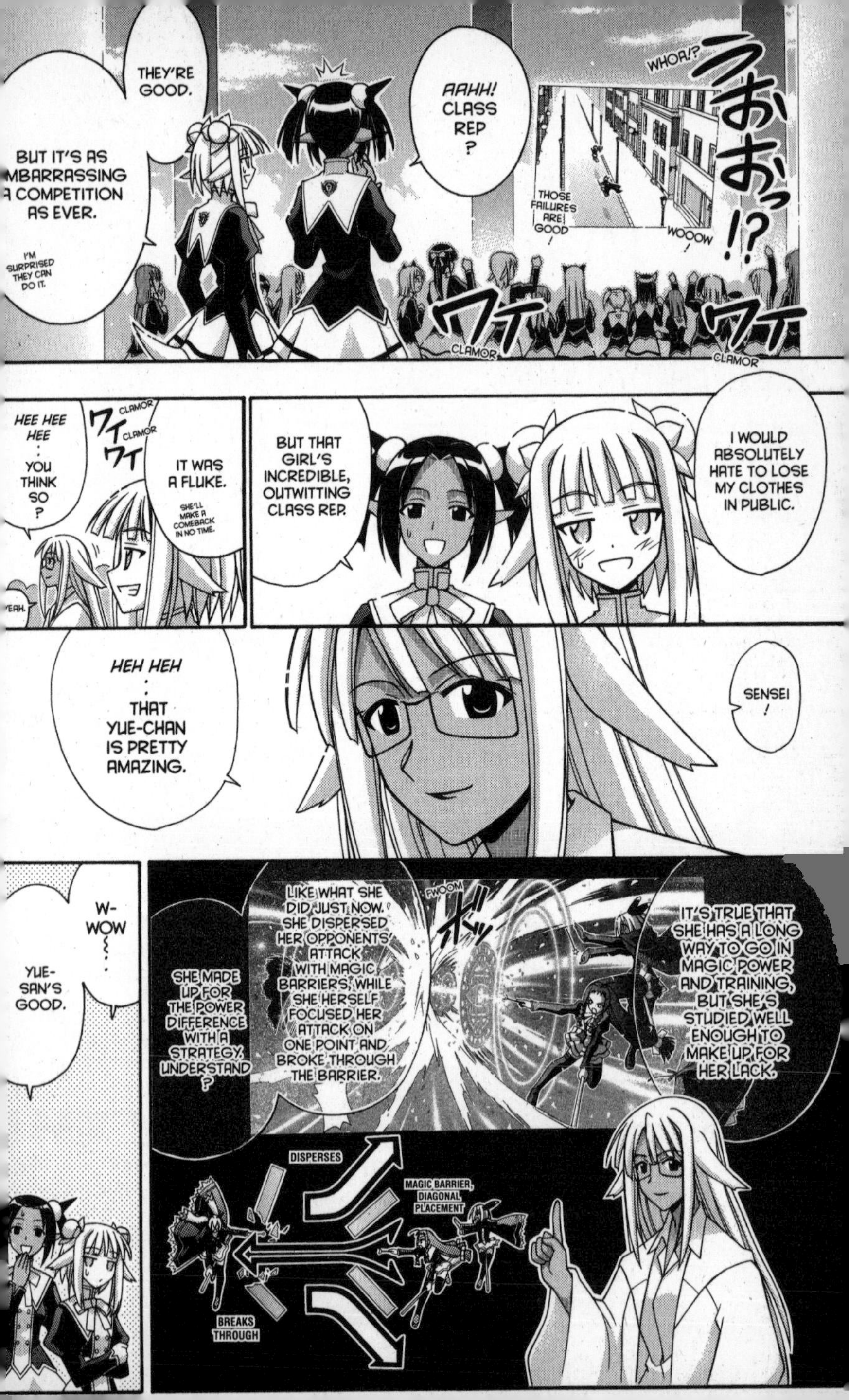
WHOA!?
うおおっ!?
THOSE FAILURES ARE GOOD!
WOOOW!
AAHH! CLASS REP?
THEY'RE GOOD.
BUT IT'S AS MBARRASSING A COMPETITION AS EVER.
I'M SURPRISED THEY CAN DO IT.
ワイ CLAMOR
ワイ CLAMOR
I WOULD ABSOLUTELY HATE TO LOSE MY CLOTHES IN PUBLIC.
BUT THAT GIRL'S INCREDIBLE, OUTWITTING CLASS REP.
IT WAS A FLUKE.
SHE'LL MAKE A COMEBACK IN NO TIME.
ワイ CLAMOR
ワイ CLAMOR
HEE HEE HEE... YOU THINK SO?
YEAH.
SENSEI!
HEH HEH... THAT YUE-CHAN IS PRETTY AMAZING.
IT'S TRUE THAT SHE HAS A LONG WAY TO GO IN MAGIC POWER AND TRAINING, BUT SHE'S STUDIED WELL ENOUGH TO MAKE UP FOR HER LACK.
FWOOM
LIKE WHAT SHE DID JUST NOW. SHE DISPERSED HER OPPONENTS' ATTACK WITH MAGIC BARRIERS, WHILE SHE HERSELF FOCUSED HER ATTACK ON ONE POINT AND BROKE THROUGH THE BARRIER.
SHE MADE UP FOR THE POWER DIFFERENCE WITH A STRATEGY. UNDERSTAND?
DISPERSES
MAGIC BARRIER, DIAGONAL PLACEMENT
BREAKS THROUGH
W-WOW~...
YUE-SAN'S GOOD.

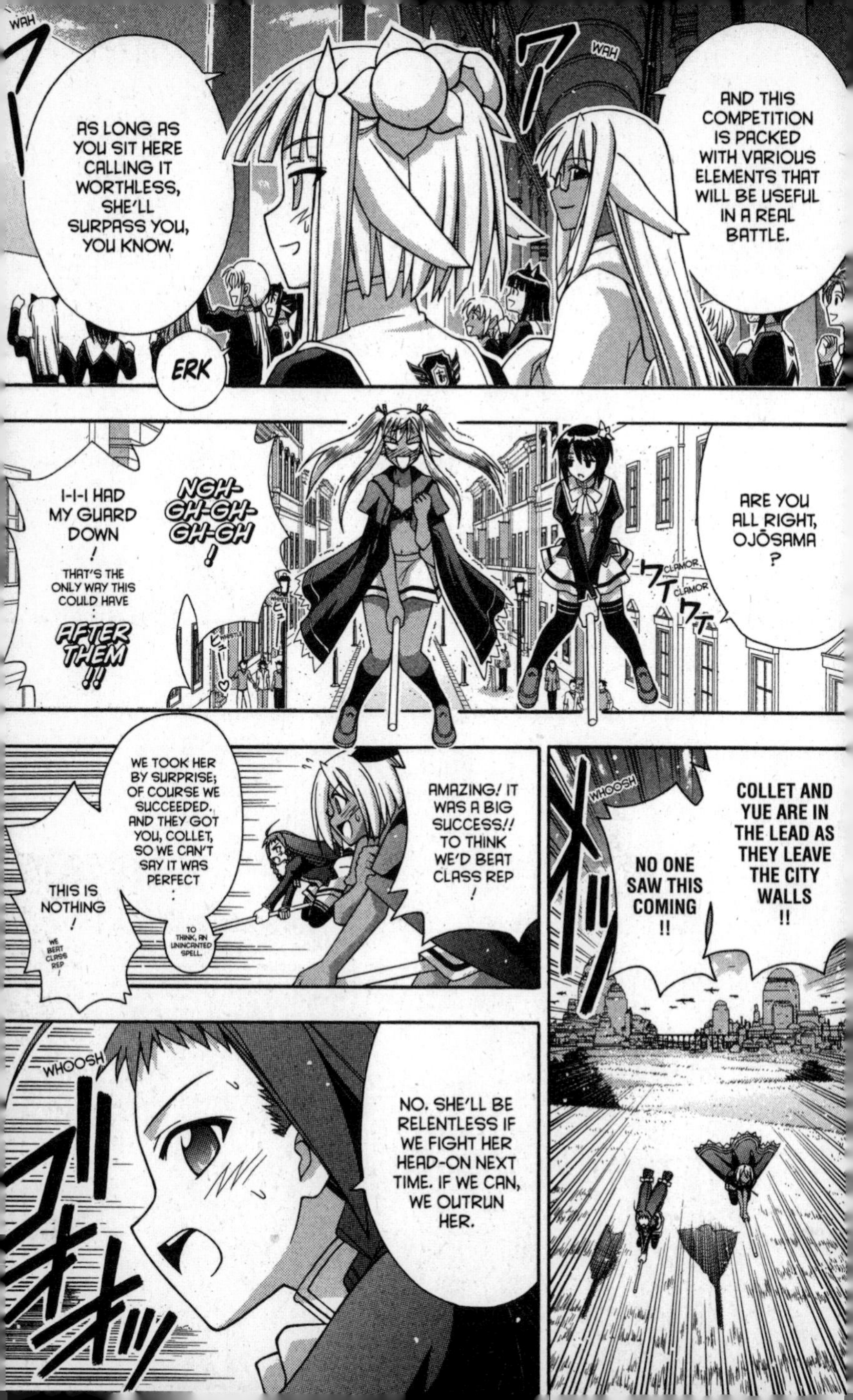
WAH
AND THIS COMPETITION IS PACKED WITH VARIOUS ELEMENTS THAT WILL BE USEFUL IN A REAL BATTLE.
WAH
AS LONG AS YOU SIT HERE CALLING IT WORTHLESS, SHE'LL SURPASS YOU, YOU KNOW.
ERK
ARE YOU ALL RIGHT, OJŌSAMA?
CLAMOR
CLAMOR
NGH-GH-GH-GH!
I-I-I HAD MY GUARD DOWN!
THAT'S THE ONLY WAY THIS COULD HAVE...
AFTER THEM!!
WHOOSH
COLLET AND YUE ARE IN THE LEAD AS THEY LEAVE THE CITY WALLS!!
NO ONE SAW THIS COMING!!
AMAZING! IT WAS A BIG SUCCESS!! TO THINK WE'D BEAT CLASS REP!
WE TOOK HER BY SURPRISE; OF COURSE WE SUCCEEDED. AND THEY GOT YOU, COLLET, SO WE CAN'T SAY IT WAS PERFECT...
TO THINK, AN UNINCANTED SPELL.
THIS IS NOTHING!
WE BEAT CLASS REP!
NO. SHE'LL BE RELENTLESS IF WE FIGHT HER HEAD-ON NEXT TIME. IF WE CAN, WE OUTRUN HER.
WHOOSH

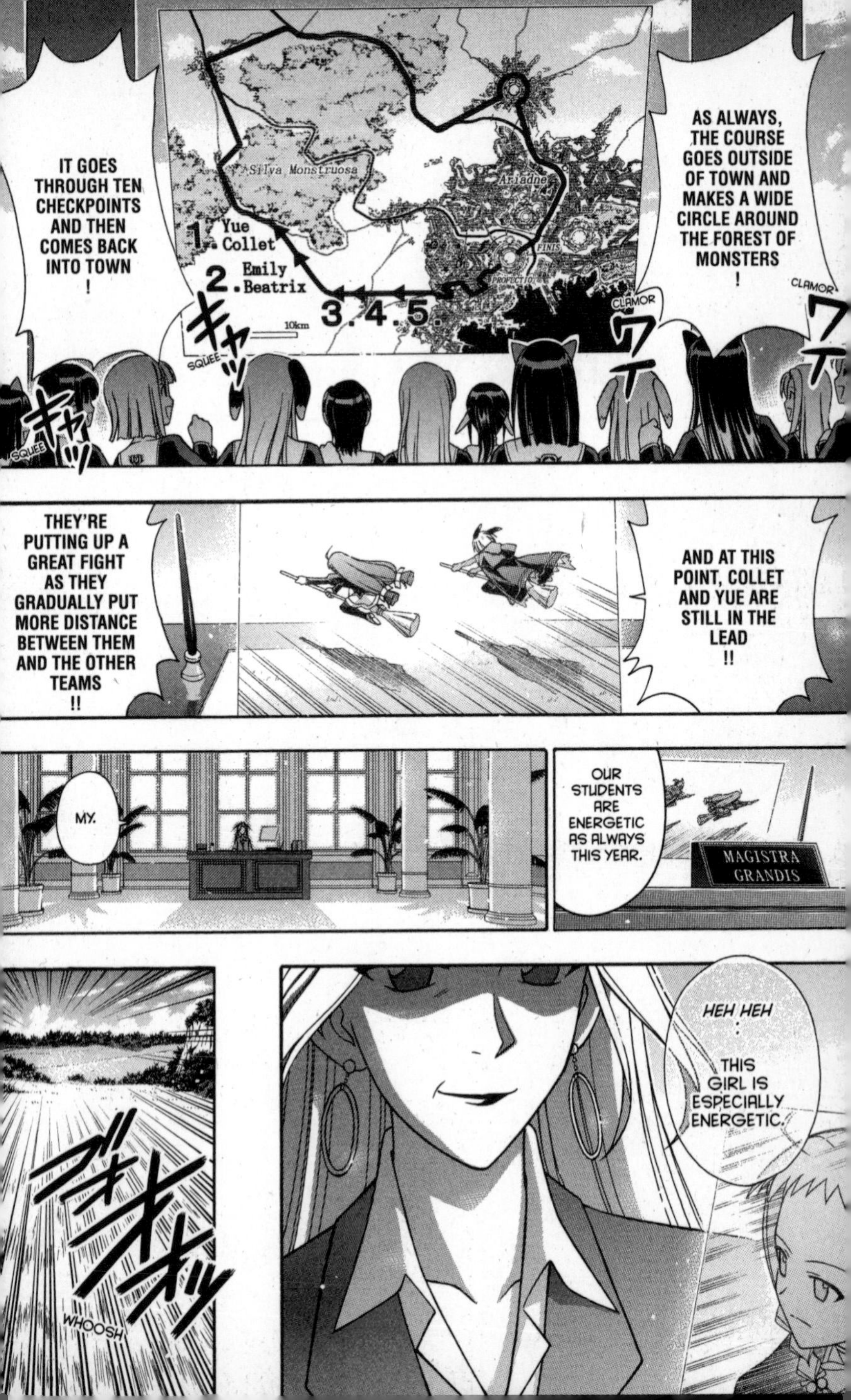
AS ALWAYS, THE COURSE GOES OUTSIDE OF TOWN AND MAKES A WIDE CIRCLE AROUND THE FOREST OF MONSTERS!
CLAMOR
ワァ
CLAMOR
ワァ
Ariadne
FINIS
PROFECTIO
Silva Monstruosa
1. Yue Collet
2. Emily Beatrix
3. 4. 5.
10km
IT GOES THROUGH TEN CHECKPOINTS AND THEN COMES BACK INTO TOWN!
キャッ
SQUEE
キャッ
SQUEE
AND AT THIS POINT, COLLET AND YUE ARE STILL IN THE LEAD!!
THEY'RE PUTTING UP A GREAT FIGHT AS THEY GRADUALLY PUT MORE DISTANCE BETWEEN THEM AND THE OTHER TEAMS!!
OUR STUDENTS ARE ENERGETIC AS ALWAYS THIS YEAR.
MAGISTRA GRANDIS
MY.
HEH HEH: THIS GIRL IS ESPECIALLY ENERGETIC.
WHOOSH

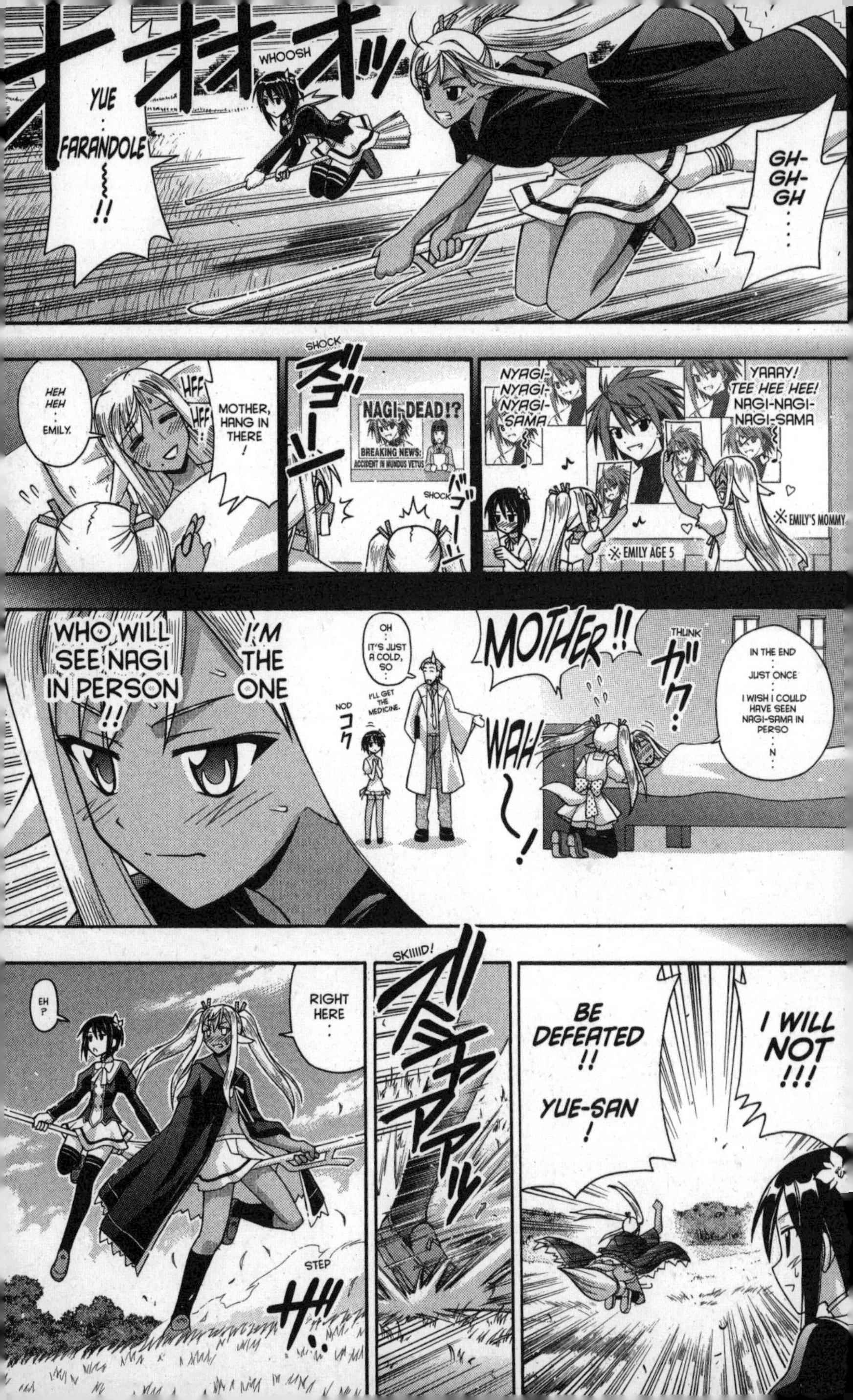
GH-GH-GH....
WHOOSH
YUE... FARANDOLE~~~!!
YAAAY! TEE HEE HEE! NAGI-NAGI-NAGI-SAMA~
NYAGI-NYAGI-NYAGI-SAMA
※EMILY'S MOMMY
※EMILY AGE 5
SHOCK
NAGI DEAD!?
BREAKING NEWS: ACCIDENT IN MUNDUS VETUS
SHOCK
MOTHER, HANG IN THERE!
HFF HFF
HEH HEH... EMILY.
IN THE END... JUST ONCE... I WISH I COULD HAVE SEEN NAGI-SAMA IN PERSO...N
THUNK
MOTHER!!
WAH~!
OH... IT'S JUST A COLD, SO...
I'LL GET THE MEDICINE.
NOD
I'M THE ONE
WHO WILL SEE NAGI IN PERSON!!
I WILL NOT!!!
BE DEFEATED!!
YUE-SAN!
SKIIIID!
RIGHT HERE...
EH?
STEP

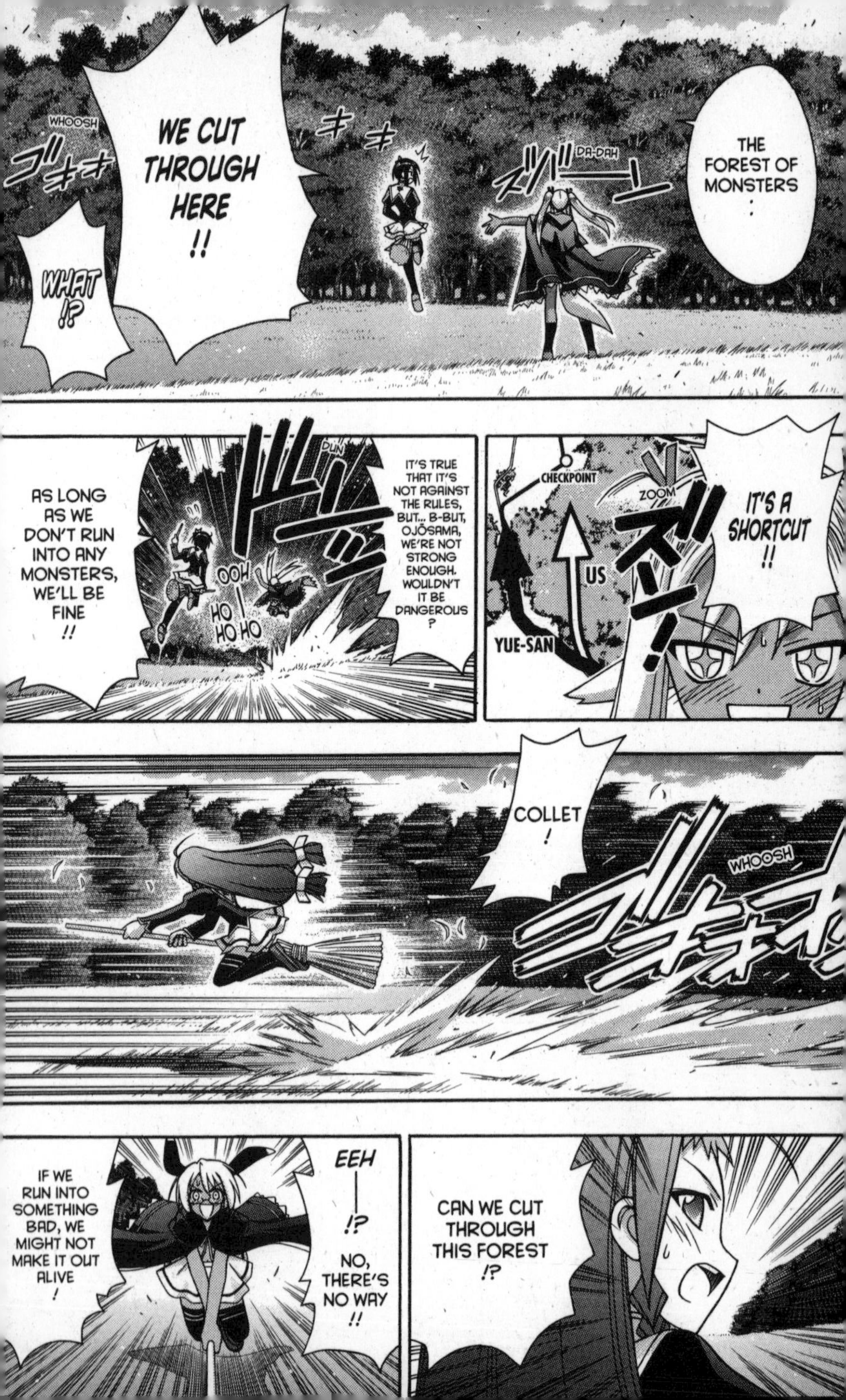
THE FOREST OF MONSTERS :
DA-DAH
WE CUT THROUGH HERE !!
WHOOSH
WHAT !?
IT'S A SHORTCUT !!
ZOOM
CHECKPOINT
US
YUE-SAN
IT'S TRUE THAT IT'S NOT AGAINST THE RULES, BUT... B-BUT, OJŌSAMA, WE'RE NOT STRONG ENOUGH. WOULDN'T IT BE DANGEROUS ?
DUN
OOH HO HO HO
AS LONG AS WE DON'T RUN INTO ANY MONSTERS, WE'LL BE FINE !!
COLLET !
WHOOSH
CAN WE CUT THROUGH THIS FOREST !?
EEH — !?
NO, THERE'S NO WAY !!
IF WE RUN INTO SOMETHING BAD, WE MIGHT NOT MAKE IT OUT ALIVE !

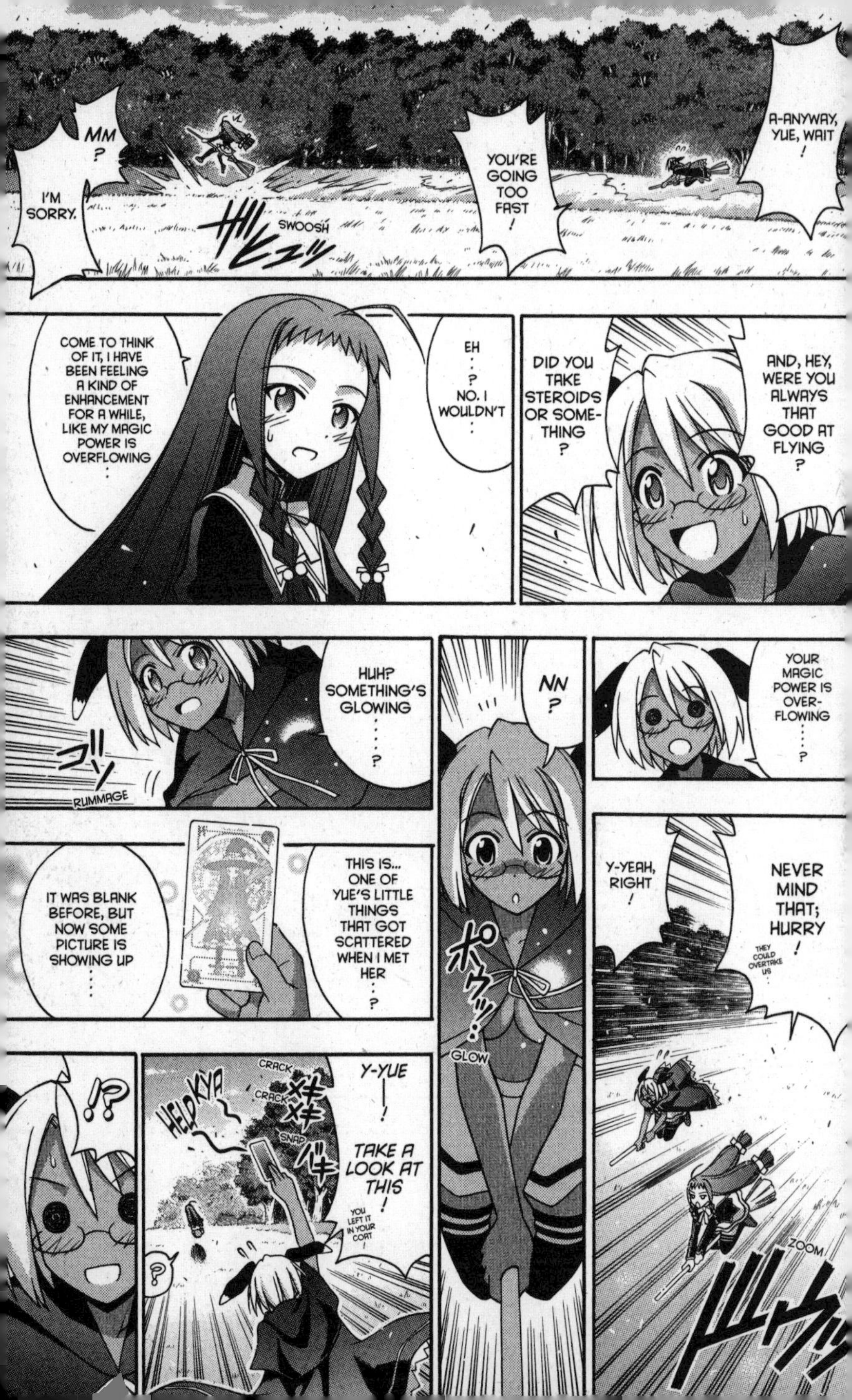

A-ANYWAY, YUE, WAIT!
YOU'RE GOING TOO FAST!
SWOOSH
MM?
I'M SORRY.
AND, HEY, WERE YOU ALWAYS THAT GOOD AT FLYING?
DID YOU TAKE STEROIDS OR SOMETHING?
EH...? NO. I WOULDN'T...
COME TO THINK OF IT, I HAVE BEEN FEELING A KIND OF ENHANCEMENT FOR A WHILE, LIKE MY MAGIC POWER IS OVERFLOWING...
YOUR MAGIC POWER IS OVERFLOWING....?
NEVER MIND THAT; HURRY!
THEY COULD OVERTAKE US...
Y-YEAH, RIGHT!
ZOOM
NN?
GLOW
HUH? SOMETHING'S GLOWING....?
RUMMAGE
THIS IS... ONE OF YUE'S LITTLE THINGS THAT GOT SCATTERED WHEN I MET HER...?
IT WAS BLANK BEFORE, BUT NOW SOME PICTURE IS SHOWING UP...
Y-YUE—!
TAKE A LOOK AT THIS!
YOU LEFT IT IN YOUR COAT!
CRACK
CRACK
SNAP
KYA~
HELP
!?
?

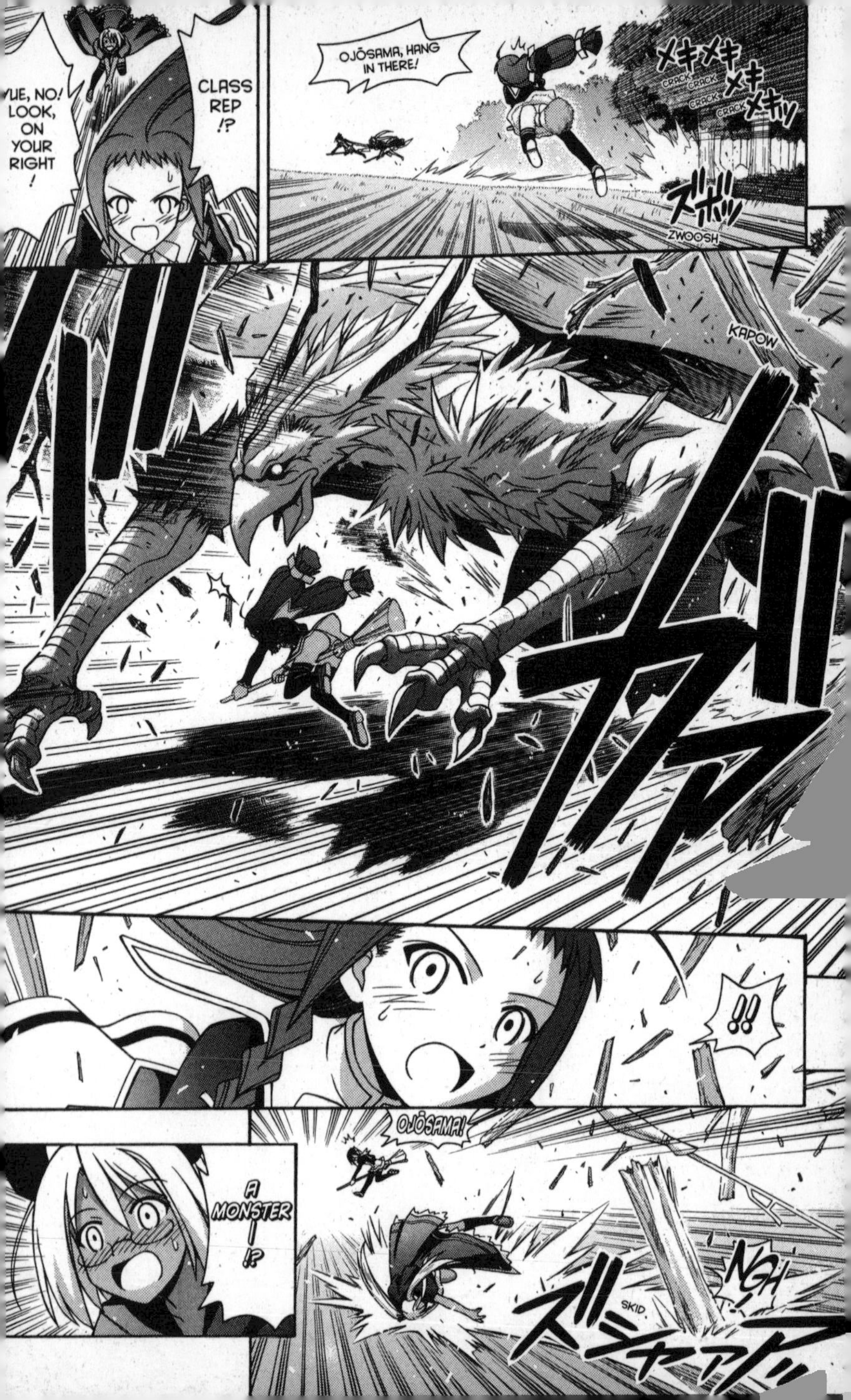

メキメキメキメキッ
CRACK CRACK CRACK CRACK
OJŌSAMA, HANG IN THERE!
ズボッ
ZWOOSH
CLASS REP!?
YUE, NO! LOOK, ON YOUR RIGHT!
KAPOW
ズガァ
!!
OJŌSAMA!
NGH!
SKID
ズシャアッ
A MONSTER!?

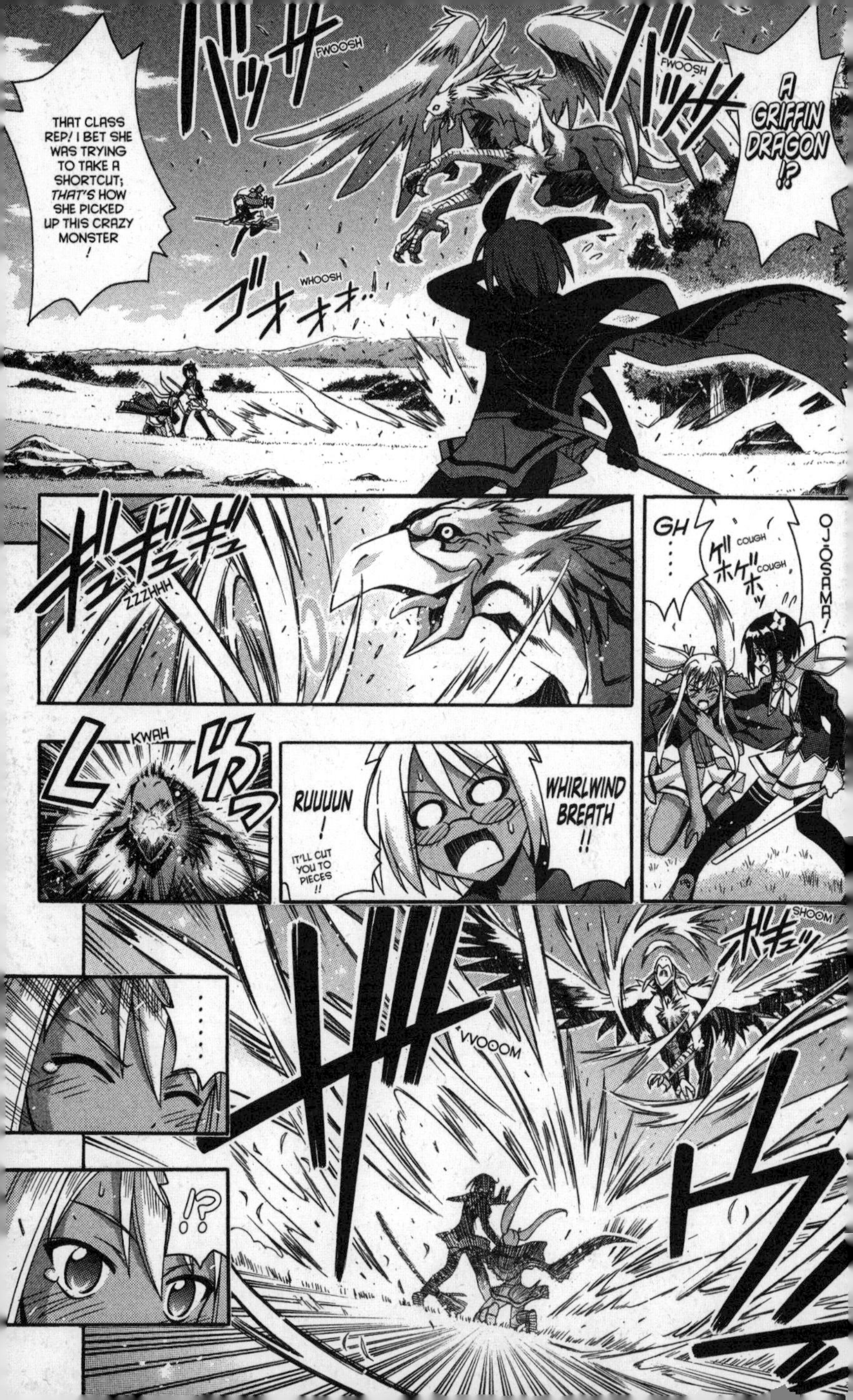

A GRIFFIN DRAGON!?
バッサ
FWOOSH
バッサ
FWOOSH
THAT CLASS REP! I BET SHE WAS TRYING TO TAKE A SHORTCUT; *THAT'S* HOW SHE PICKED UP THIS CRAZY MONSTER!
ゴオオオ..
WHOOSH
OJŌSAMA!
ゲホゲホッ
COUGH COUGH
GH......
ギュギュギュ
ZZZHHH
WHIRLWIND BREATH!!
RUUUUN!
IT'LL CUT YOU TO PIECES!!
KWAH
SHOOM
VVOOOM
......
!?

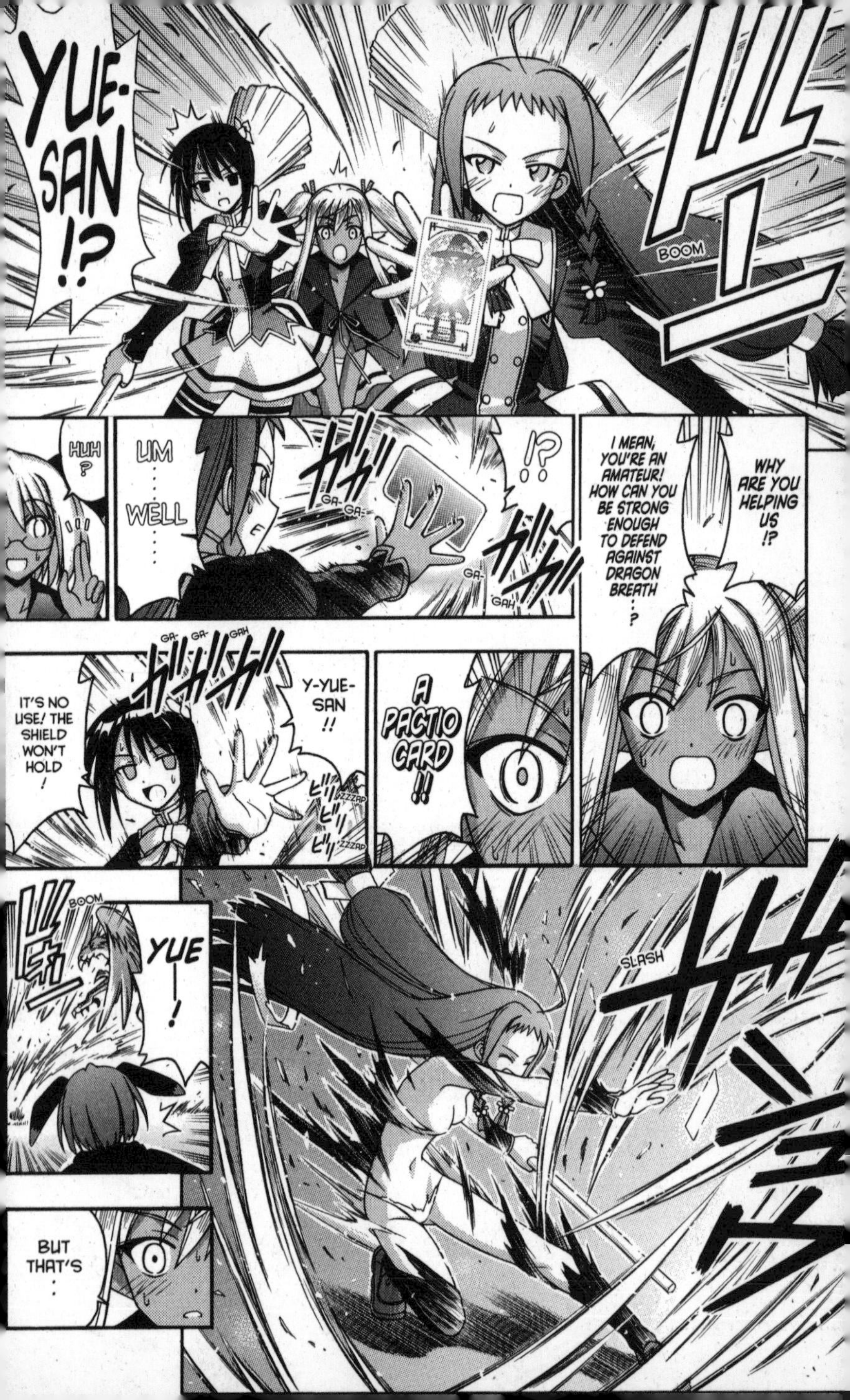
BOOM
YUE-SAN !?
WHY ARE YOU HELPING US !?
I MEAN, YOU'RE AN AMATEUR! HOW CAN YOU BE STRONG ENOUGH TO DEFEND AGAINST DRAGON BREATH ...?
!?
GA-GA-
GA-GAH
UM ... WELL ...
HUH ?
A PACTIO CARD !!
GA-GA-GAH
Y-YUE-SAN !!
IT'S NO USE! THE SHIELD WON'T HOLD!
ZZZAP
ZZZAP
SLASH
BOOM
YUE—!
BUT THAT'S ...

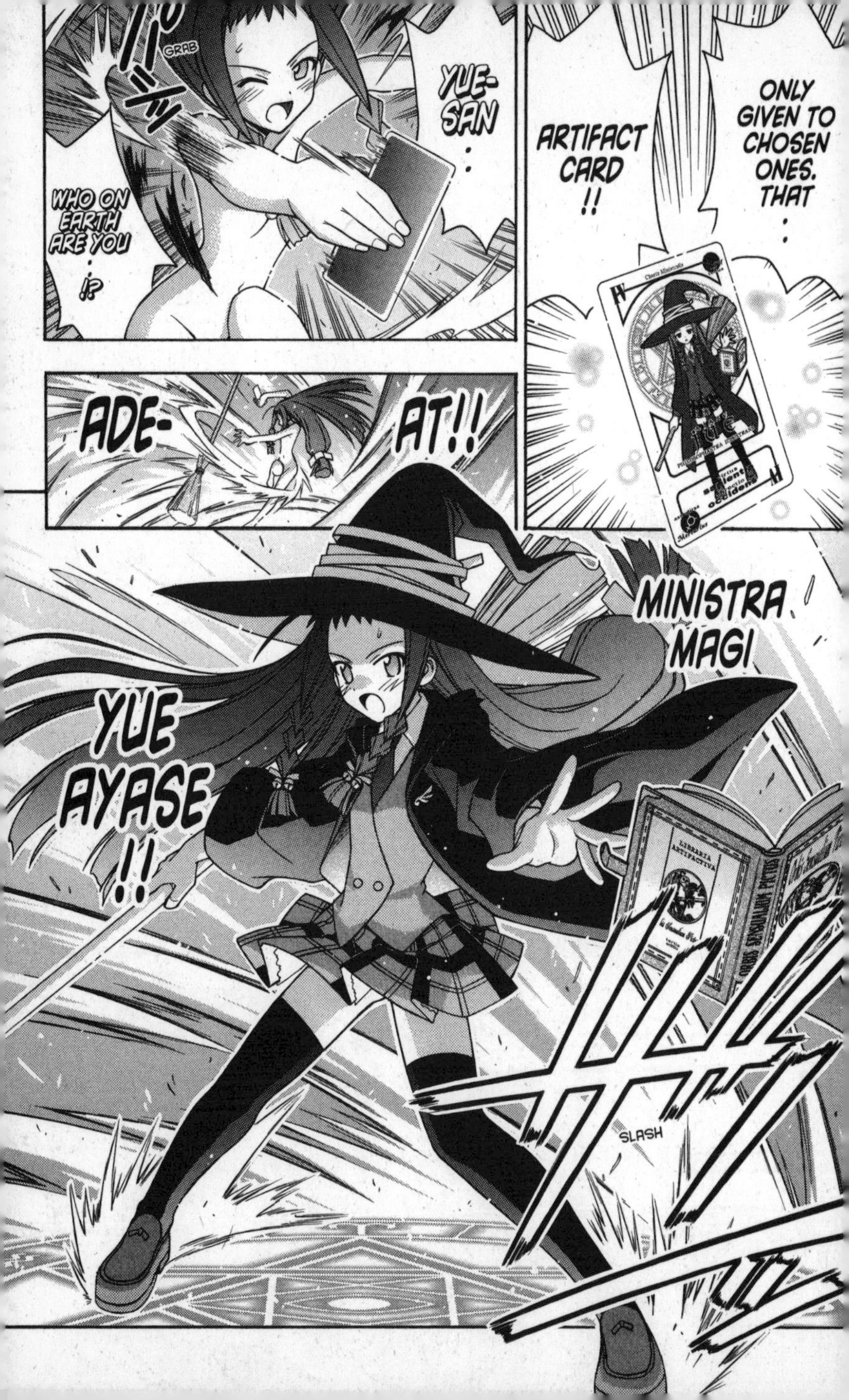

ONLY GIVEN TO CHOSEN ONES. THAT...
ARTIFACT CARD!!
GRAB
YUE-SAN...
WHO ON EARTH ARE YOU...!?
ADE-
AT!!
MINISTRA MAGI
YUE AYASE!!
LIBRARIA ARTIFACTIVA
ORBIS SENSUALIUM PICTUS
SLASH

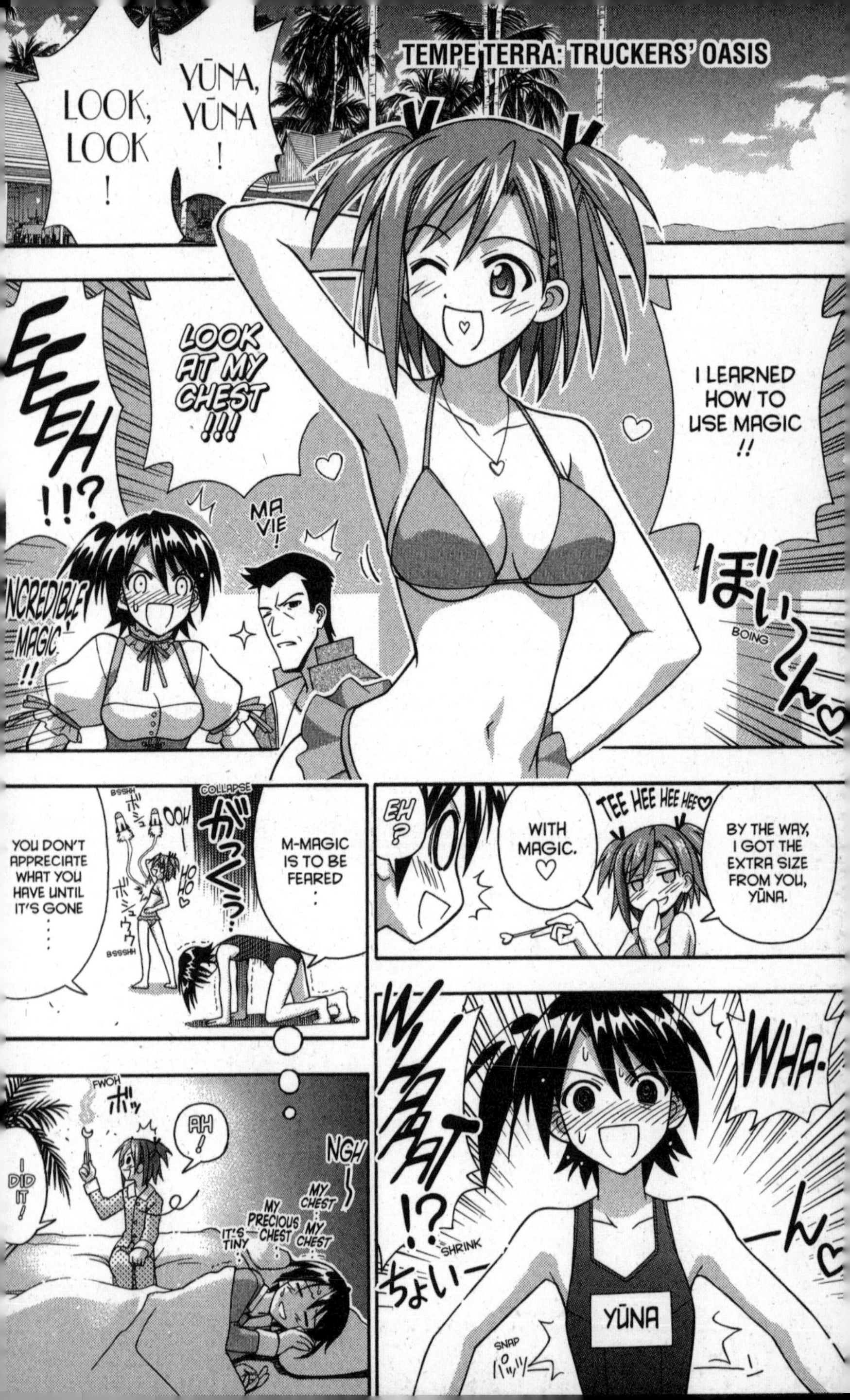
TEMPE TERRA: TRUCKERS' OASIS
YŪNA, YŪNA!
LOOK, LOOK!
I LEARNED HOW TO USE MAGIC!!
ぼいーん♡
BOING
LOOK AT MY CHEST!!!
EEEEH!!?
MA VIE!
INCREDIBLE MAGIC!!
BY THE WAY, I GOT THE EXTRA SIZE FROM YOU, YŪNA.
TEE HEE HEE HEE♡
WITH MAGIC. ♡
EH?
M-MAGIC IS TO BE FEARED...
がっくぅ…
COLLAPSE
OOH HO HO♡
ボシュ
BSSHH
ボシュウウ
BSSSHH
YOU DON'T APPRECIATE WHAT YOU HAVE UNTIL IT'S GONE....
WHA-
ーん♡
WHAAAT!?
ちょいー
SHRINK
パッ
SNAP
YŪNA
NGH~
MY CHEST... MY CHEST
MY PRECIOUS CHEST...
IT'S TINY
AH!
ボッ
FWOH
I DID IT!

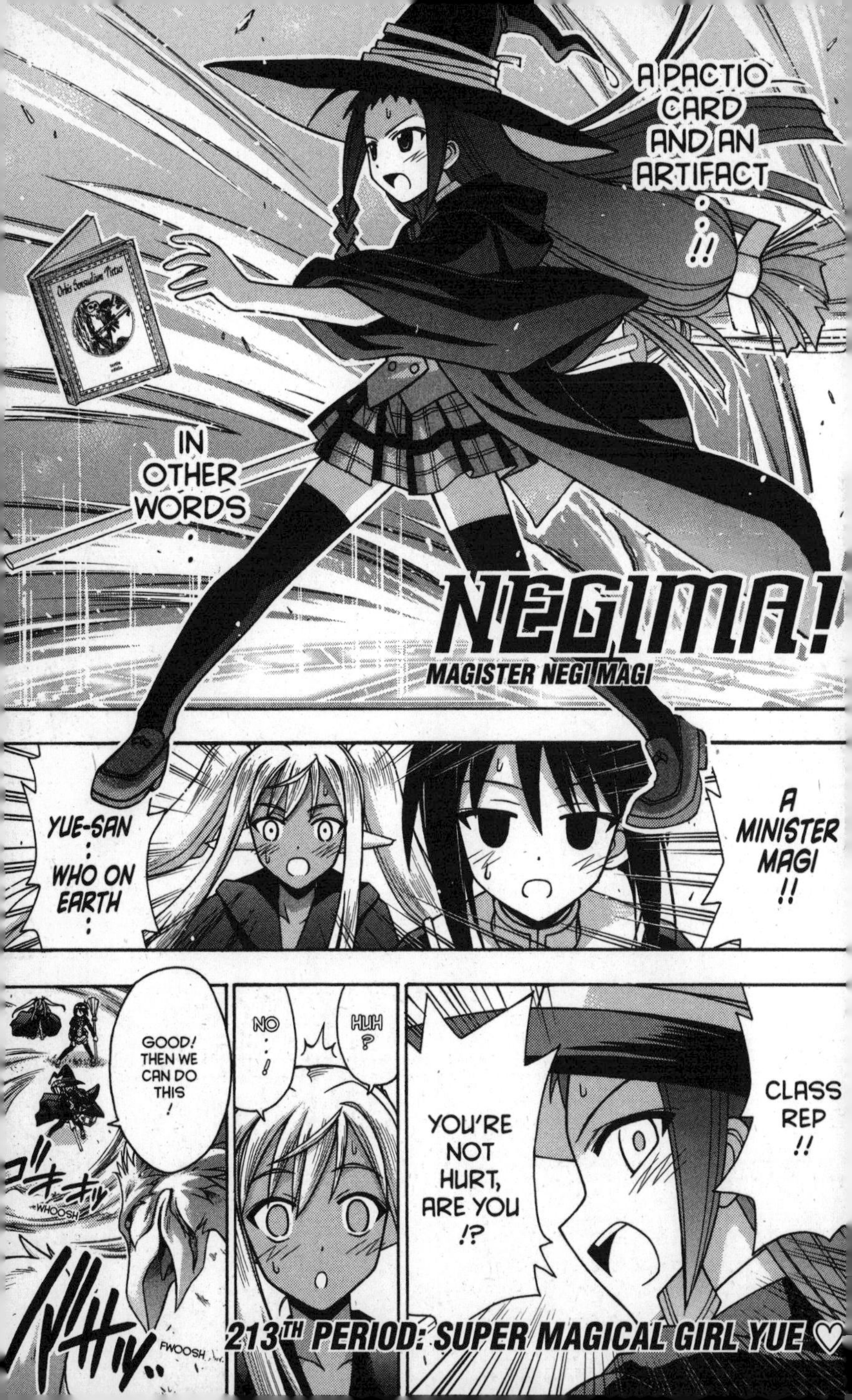
A PACTIO CARD AND AN ARTIFACT...!!
IN OTHER WORDS...
NEGIMA!
MAGISTER NEGI MAGI
A MINISTER MAGI!!
YUE-SAN... WHO ON EARTH...
CLASS REP!!
YOU'RE NOT HURT, ARE YOU!?
HUH?
NO...!
GOOD! THEN WE CAN DO THIS!
WHOOSH
FWOOSH
213TH PERIOD: SUPER MAGICAL GIRL YUE ♡

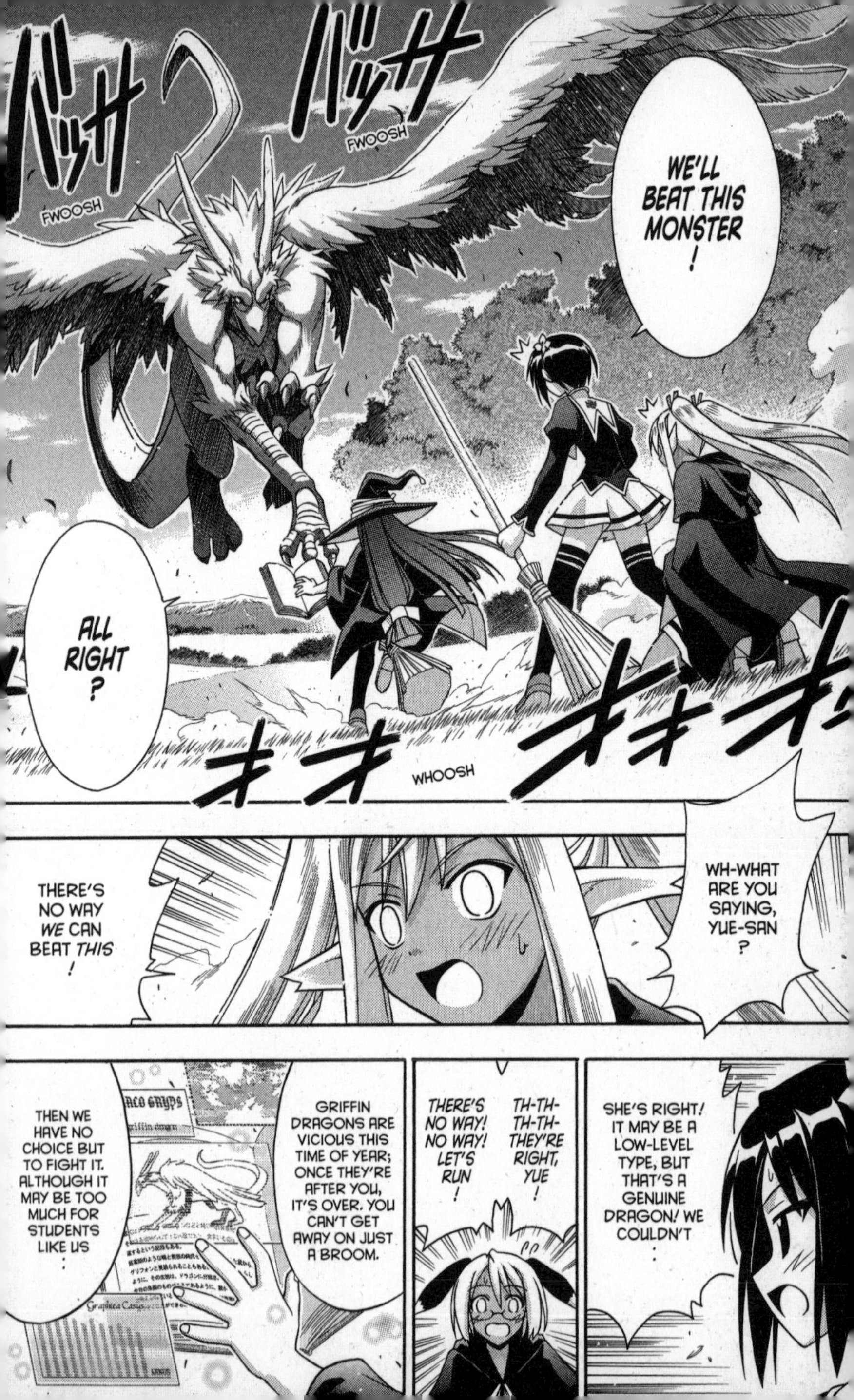
FWOOSH
FWOOSH
WE'LL BEAT THIS MONSTER!
ALL RIGHT?
WHOOSH
WH-WHAT ARE YOU SAYING, YUE-SAN?
THERE'S NO WAY *WE* CAN BEAT *THIS*!
SHE'S RIGHT! IT MAY BE A LOW-LEVEL TYPE, BUT THAT'S A GENUINE DRAGON! WE COULDN'T...
TH-TH-TH-TH-THEY'RE RIGHT, YUE!
THERE'S NO WAY! NO WAY! LET'S RUN!
GRIFFIN DRAGONS ARE VICIOUS THIS TIME OF YEAR; ONCE THEY'RE AFTER YOU, IT'S OVER. YOU CAN'T GET AWAY ON JUST A BROOM.
THEN WE HAVE NO CHOICE BUT TO FIGHT IT. ALTHOUGH IT MAY BE TOO MUCH FOR STUDENTS LIKE US...

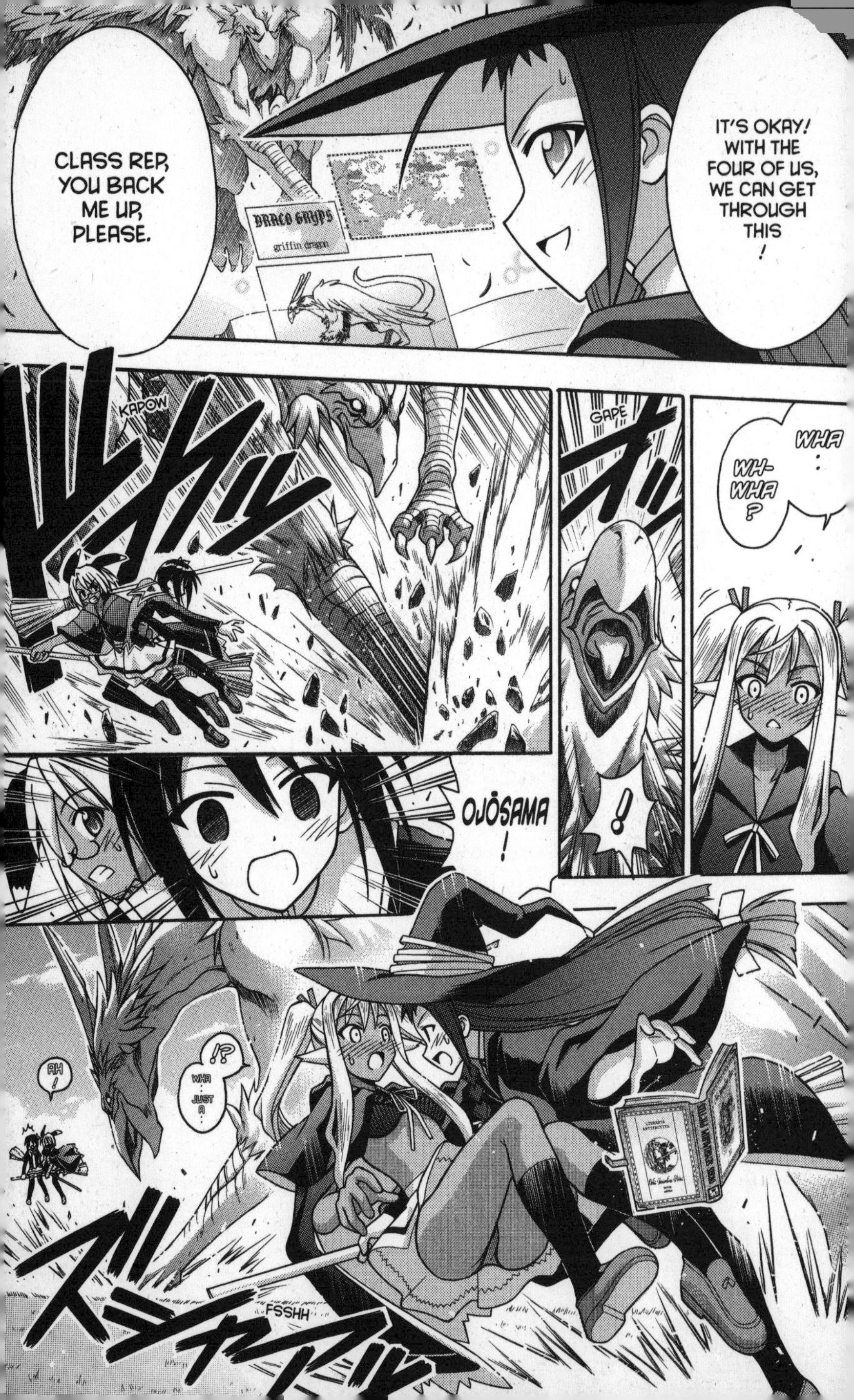

IT'S OKAY! WITH THE FOUR OF US, WE CAN GET THROUGH THIS!
DRACO GRYPS
griffin dragon
CLASS REP, YOU BACK ME UP, PLEASE.
WHA...
WH-WHA?
GAPE
!
KAPOW
OJŌSAMA!
!?
WHA... JUST A...
AH!
FSSHH

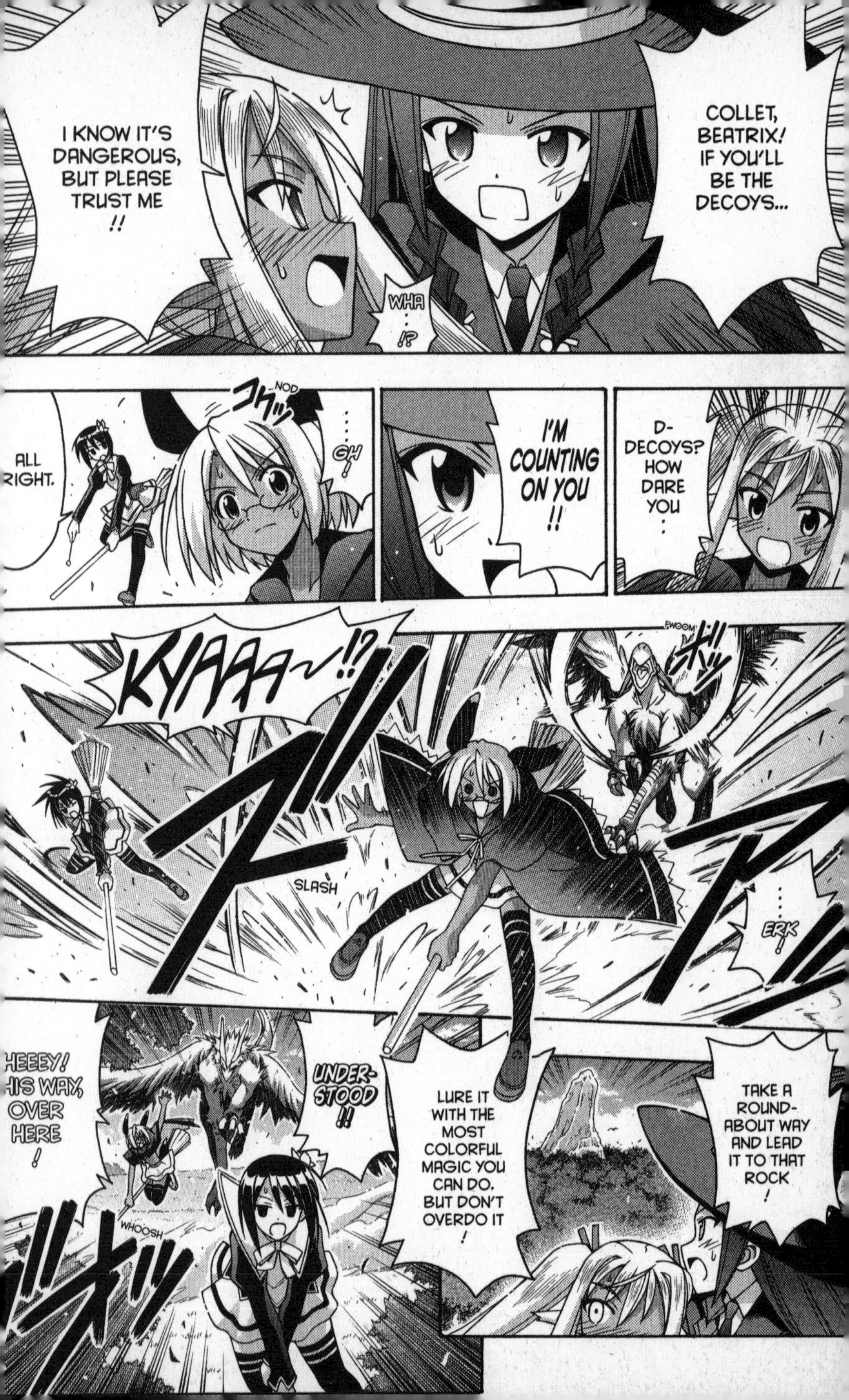
COLLET, BEATRIX! IF YOU'LL BE THE DECOYS...
WHA...!?
I KNOW IT'S DANGEROUS, BUT PLEASE TRUST ME!!
D-DECOYS? HOW DARE YOU...
I'M COUNTING ON YOU!!
NOD
...GH!
ALL RIGHT.
FWOOM
KYAAAA~!!?
SLASH
...ERK!
TAKE A ROUND-ABOUT WAY AND LEAD IT TO THAT ROCK!
LURE IT WITH THE MOST COLORFUL MAGIC YOU CAN DO. BUT DON'T OVERDO IT!
UNDER-STOOD!!
HEEEY! HIS WAY, OVER HERE!
WHOOSH

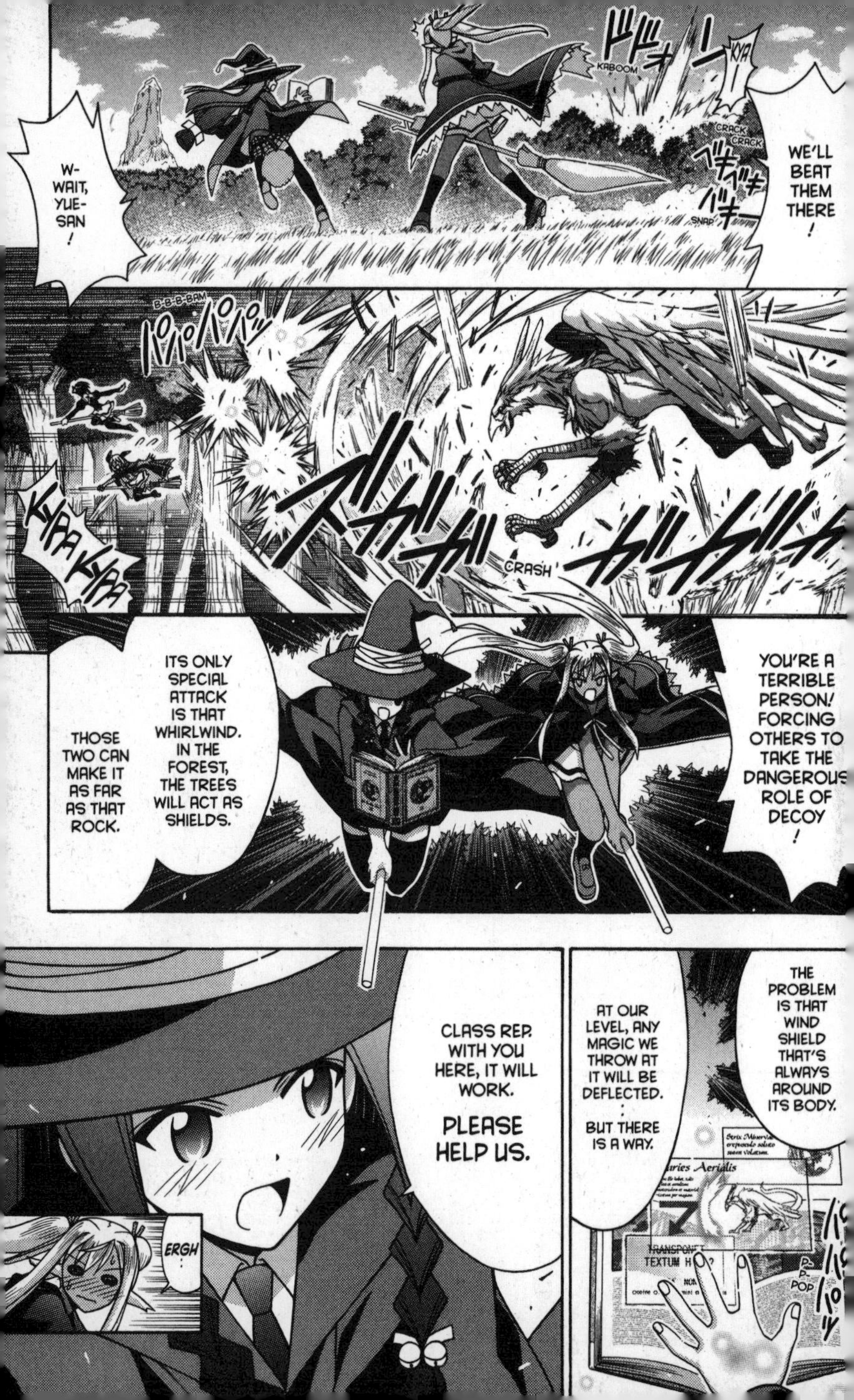
KYA!
KABOOM
WE'LL BEAT THEM THERE!
CRACK CRACK
SNAP
W-WAIT, YUE-SAN!
CRASH
B-B-B-BAM
KYAA KYAA
YOU'RE A TERRIBLE PERSON! FORCING OTHERS TO TAKE THE DANGEROUS ROLE OF DECOY!
ITS ONLY SPECIAL ATTACK IS THAT WHIRLWIND. IN THE FOREST, THE TREES WILL ACT AS SHIELDS.
THOSE TWO CAN MAKE IT AS FAR AS THAT ROCK.
THE PROBLEM IS THAT WIND SHIELD THAT'S ALWAYS AROUND ITS BODY.
AT OUR LEVEL, ANY MAGIC WE THROW AT IT WILL BE DEFLECTED.
BUT THERE IS A WAY.
P-P-POP
CLASS REP. WITH YOU HERE, IT WILL WORK.
PLEASE HELP US.
ERGH...

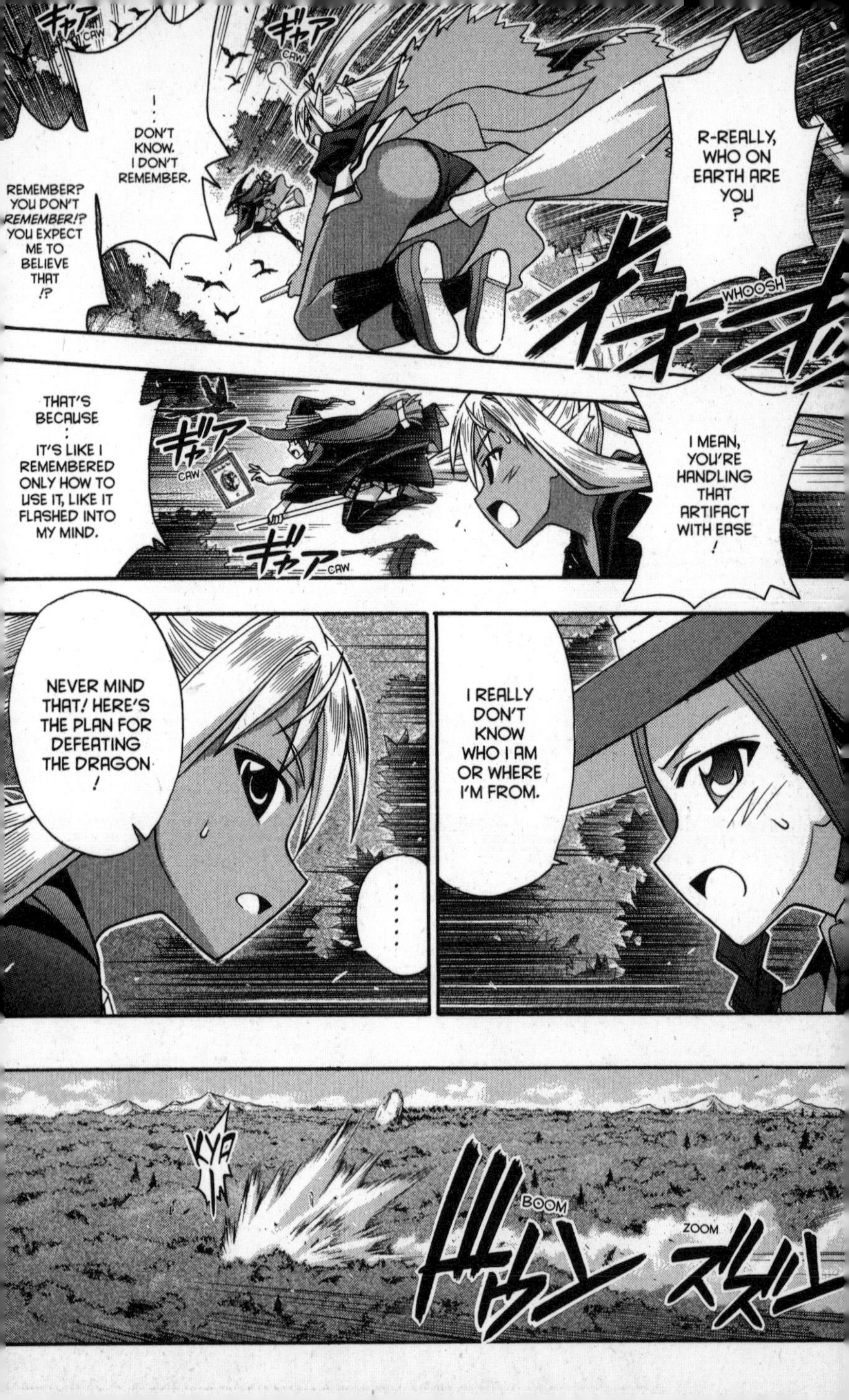
ギャア
CAW
ギャア
CAW
R-REALLY, WHO ON EARTH ARE YOU?
WHOOSH
...
DON'T KNOW. I DON'T REMEMBER.
REMEMBER? YOU DON'T *REMEMBER!?* YOU EXPECT ME TO BELIEVE THAT!?
I MEAN, YOU'RE HANDLING THAT ARTIFACT WITH EASE!
THAT'S BECAUSE...
IT'S LIKE I REMEMBERED ONLY HOW TO USE IT, LIKE IT FLASHED INTO MY MIND.
ギャア
CAW
ギャア
CAW
I REALLY DON'T KNOW WHO I AM OR WHERE I'M FROM.
......
NEVER MIND THAT! HERE'S THE PLAN FOR DEFEATING THE DRAGON!
ZOOM
BOOM
KYA!

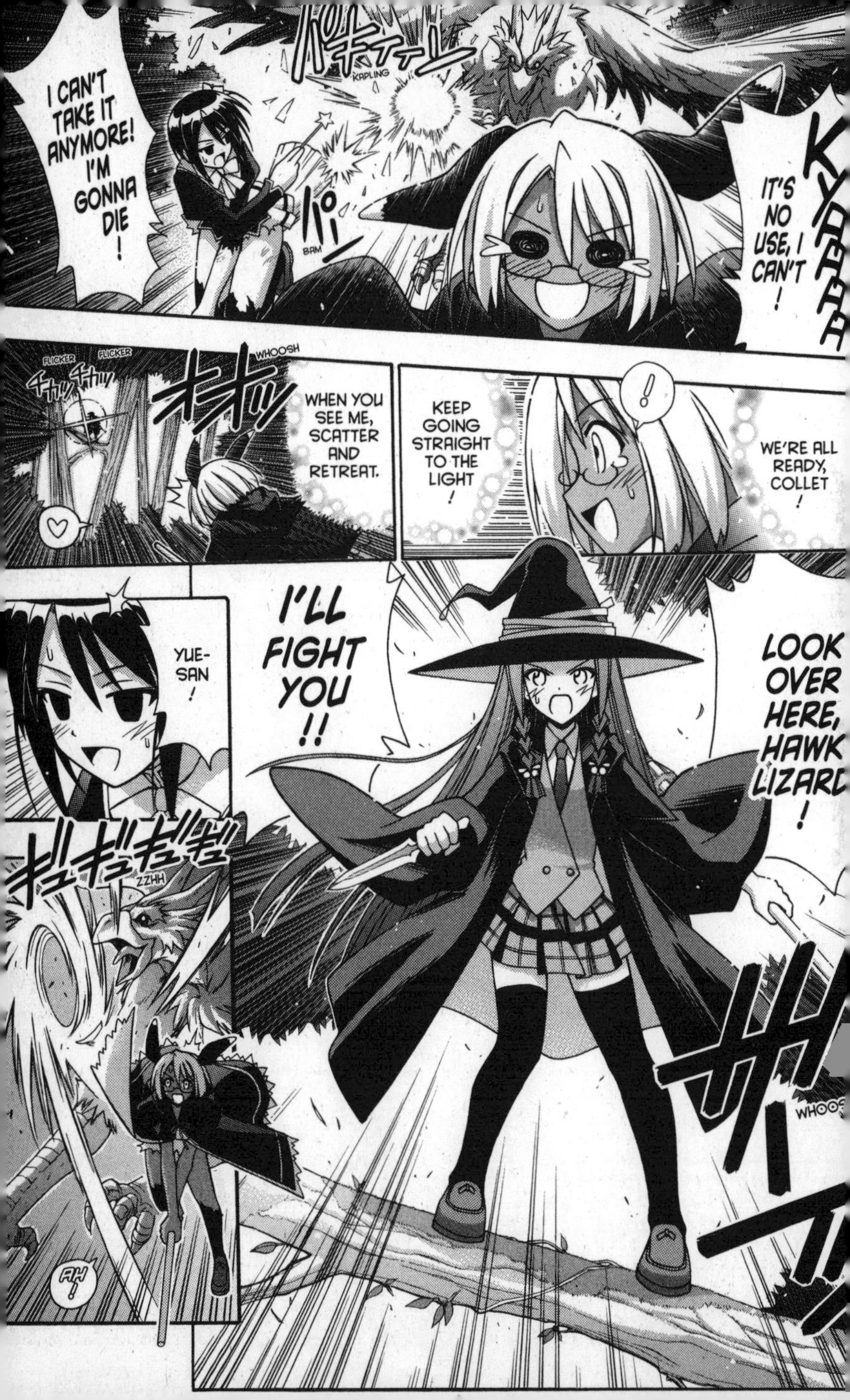
KAPLING
KYAAAAA
IT'S NO USE, I CAN'T!
I CAN'T TAKE IT ANYMORE! I'M GONNA DIE!
BAM
!
WE'RE ALL READY, COLLET!
KEEP GOING STRAIGHT TO THE LIGHT!
WHEN YOU SEE ME, SCATTER AND RETREAT.
WHOOSH
FLICKER
FLICKER
LOOK OVER HERE, HAWK LIZARD!
I'LL FIGHT YOU!!
YUE-SAN!
ZZHH
AH!

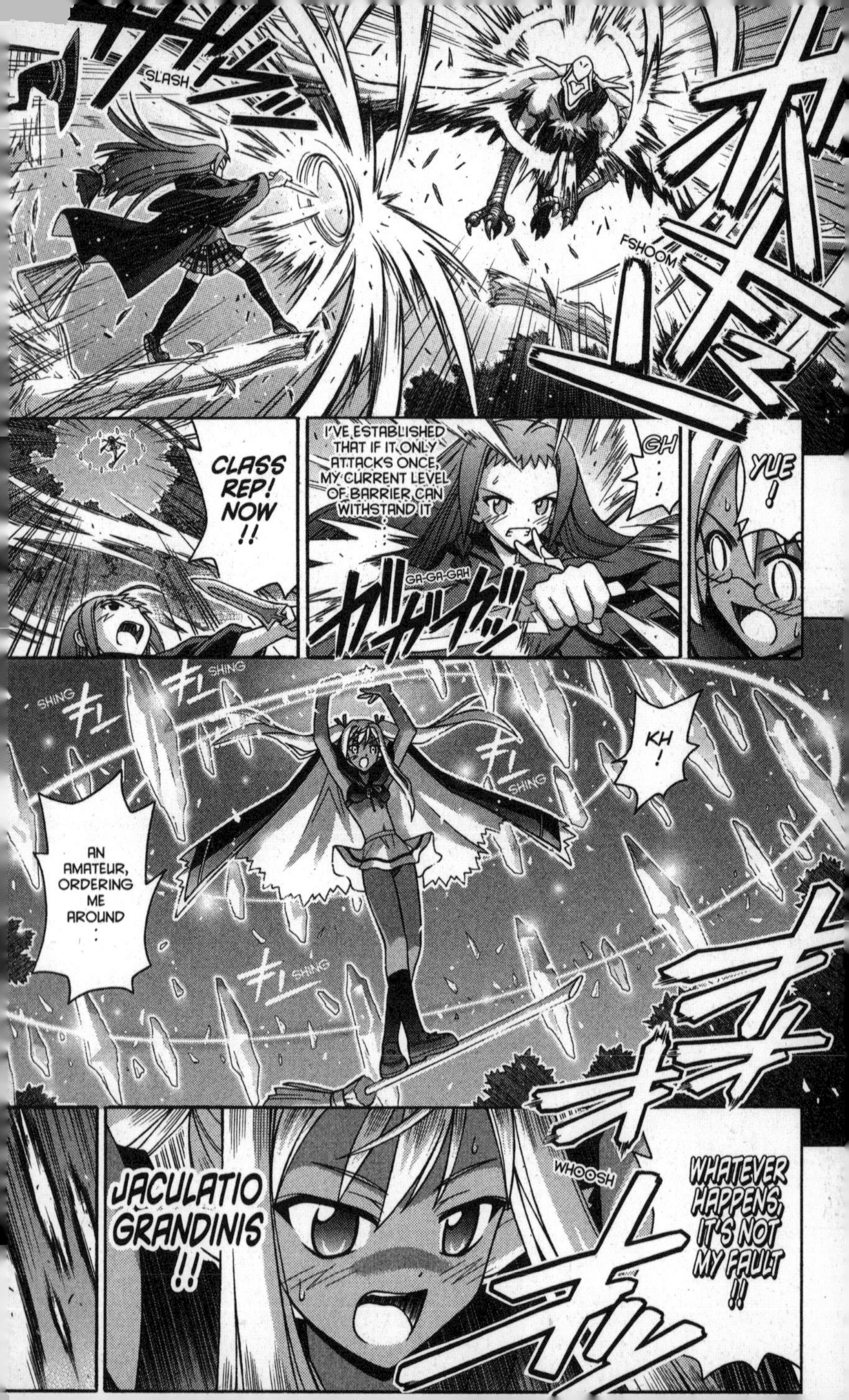
SLASH
FSHOOM
YUE!
GH...!
I'VE ESTABLISHED THAT IF IT ONLY ATTACKS ONCE, MY CURRENT LEVEL OF BARRIER CAN WITHSTAND IT...
GA-GA-GAH
CLASS REP! NOW!!
KH!
SHING
SHING
SHING
SHING
AN AMATEUR, ORDERING ME AROUND...
WHATEVER HAPPENS, IT'S NOT MY FAULT!!
WHOOSH
JACULATIO GRANDINIS!!

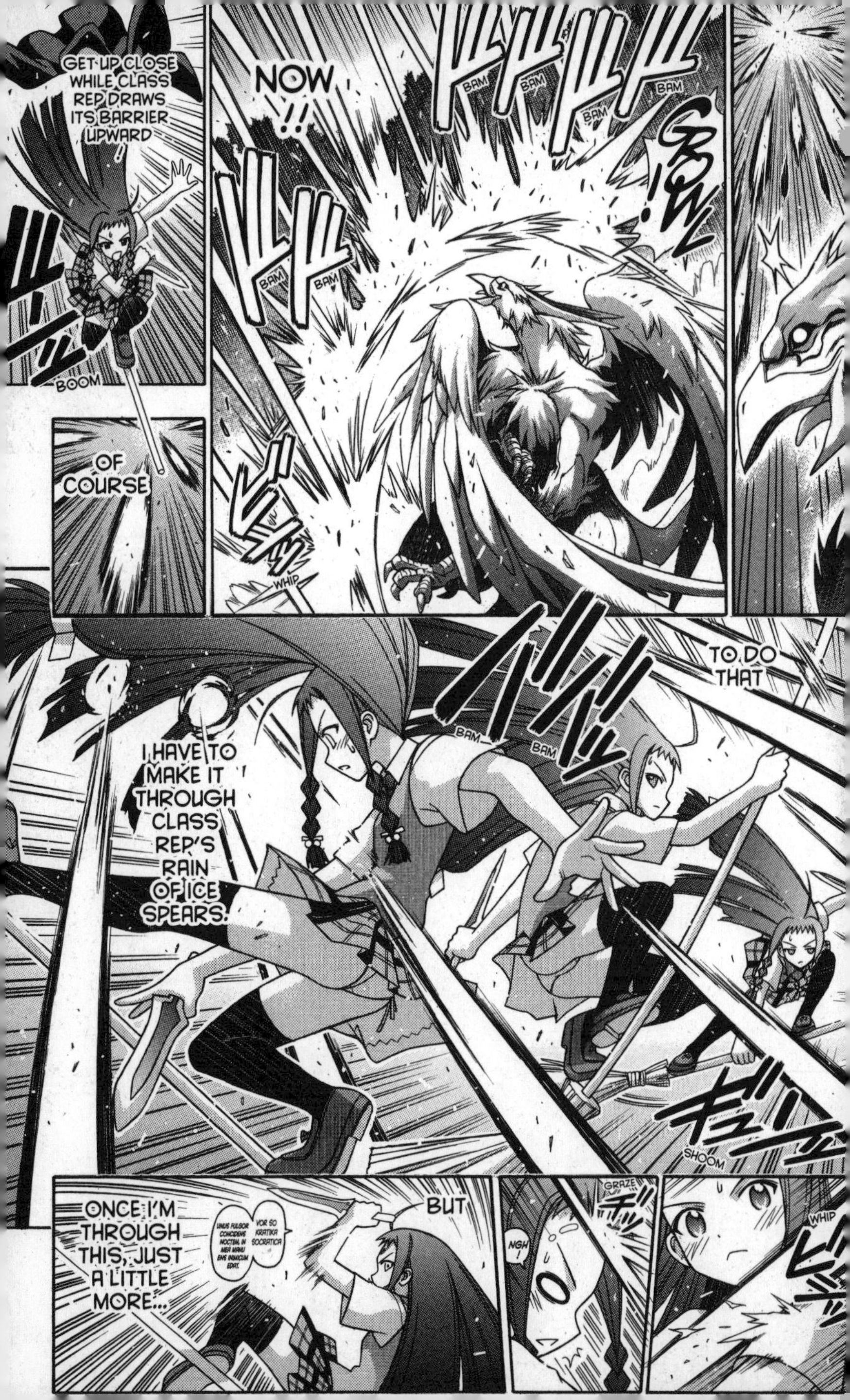
NOW!!
BAM
BAM
BAM
BAM
BAM
GROWL!
BAM
BAM
WHIP
GET UP CLOSE WHILE CLASS REP DRAWS ITS BARRIER UPWARD
BOOM
OF COURSE
TO DO THAT
BAM
BAM
I HAVE TO MAKE IT THROUGH CLASS REP'S RAIN OF ICE SPEARS.
SHOOM
WHIP
GRAZE
NGH!
BUT
VOR SO KRATIKA SOCRATICA
UNUS FULGOR CONCIDENS NOCTEM, IN MEA MANU ENS INIMICUM EDAT.
ONCE I'M THROUGH THIS, JUST A LITTLE MORE...

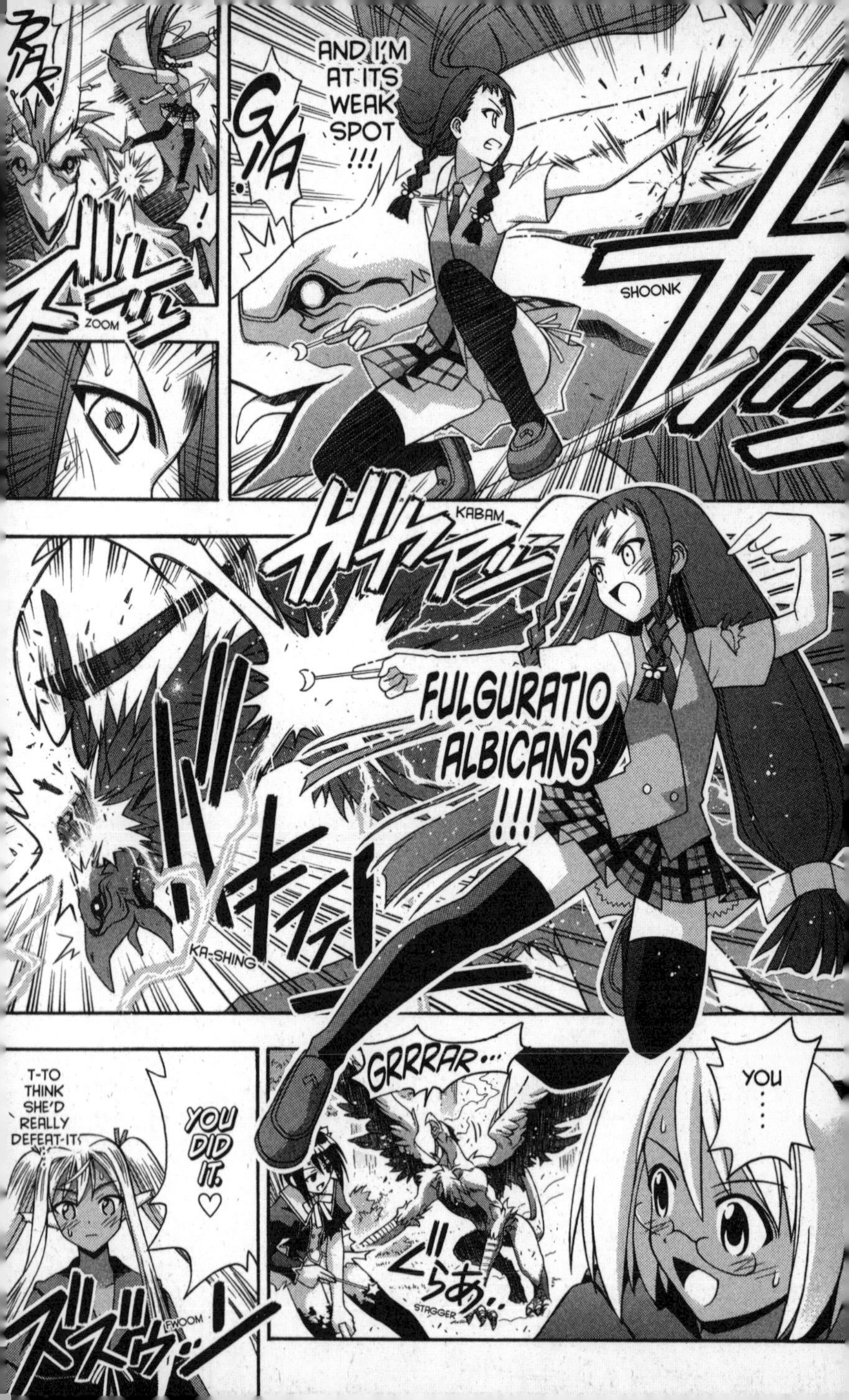

AND I'M AT ITS WEAK SPOT !!!
GYA
SHOONK
ZOOM
KABAM
FULGURATIO ALBICANS !!!
KA-SHING
YOU ....
GRRRAR...
STAGGER
T-TO THINK SHE'D REALLY DEFEAT IT
YOU DID IT. ♡
FWOOM

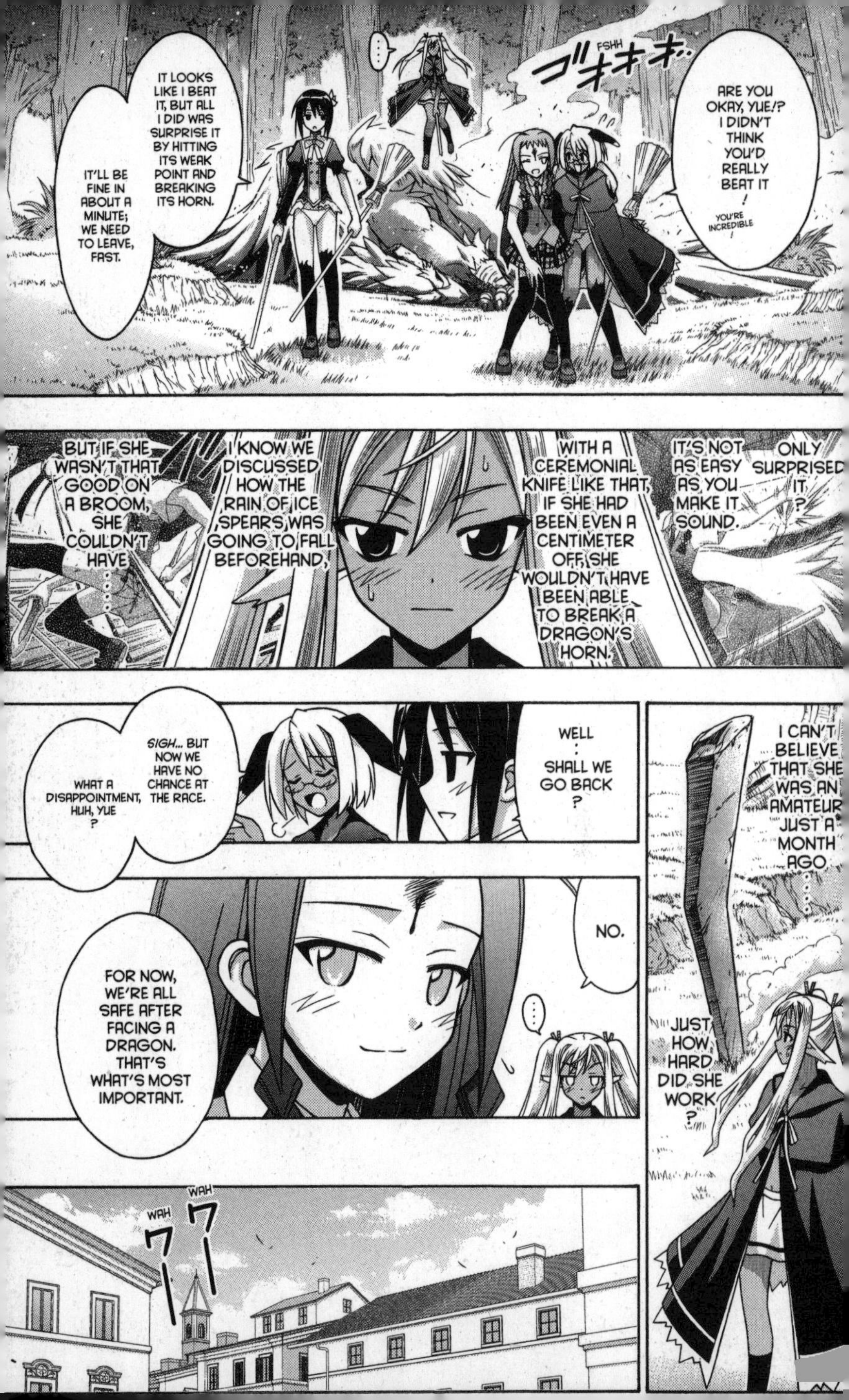
FSHH
ARE YOU OKAY, YUE!? I DIDN'T THINK YOU'D REALLY BEAT IT!
YOU'RE INCREDIBLE!
...
IT LOOKS LIKE I BEAT IT, BUT ALL I DID WAS SURPRISE IT BY HITTING ITS WEAK POINT AND BREAKING ITS HORN.
IT'LL BE FINE IN ABOUT A MINUTE; WE NEED TO LEAVE, FAST.
ONLY SURPRISED IT?
IT'S NOT AS EASY AS YOU MAKE IT SOUND.
WITH A CEREMONIAL KNIFE LIKE THAT, IF SHE HAD BEEN EVEN A CENTIMETER OFF, SHE WOULDN'T HAVE BEEN ABLE TO BREAK A DRAGON'S HORN.
I KNOW WE DISCUSSED HOW THE RAIN OF ICE SPEARS WAS GOING TO FALL BEFOREHAND,
BUT IF SHE WASN'T THAT GOOD ON A BROOM, SHE COULDN'T HAVE......
I CAN'T BELIEVE THAT SHE WAS AN AMATEUR JUST A MONTH AGO......
JUST HOW HARD DID SHE WORK?
WELL: SHALL WE GO BACK?
SIGH... BUT NOW WE HAVE NO CHANCE AT THE RACE.
WHAT A DISAPPOINTMENT, HUH, YUE?
NO.
FOR NOW, WE'RE ALL SAFE AFTER FACING A DRAGON. THAT'S WHAT'S MOST IMPORTANT.
...
WAH
WAH

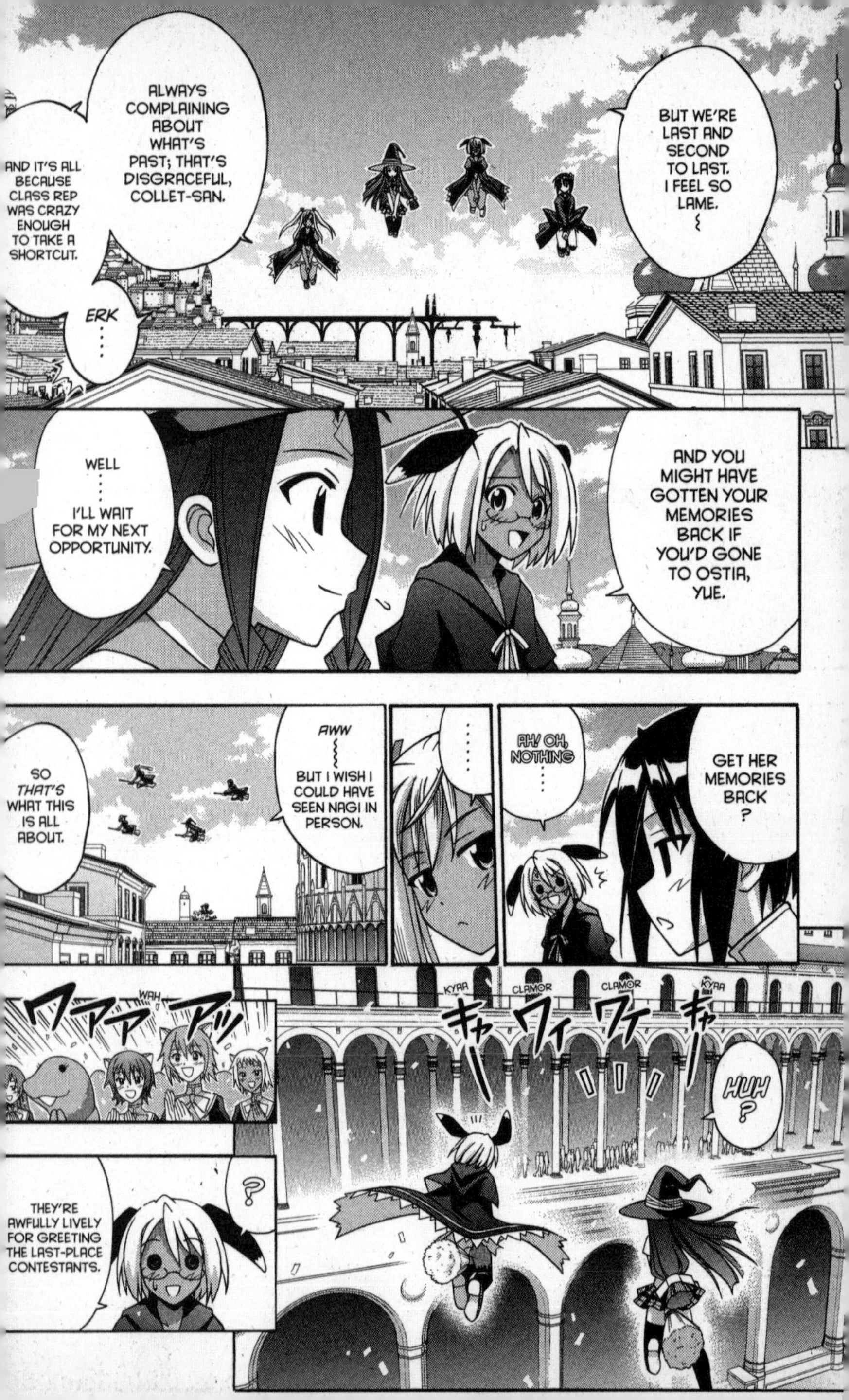

BUT WE'RE LAST AND SECOND TO LAST. I FEEL SO LAME.
AND IT'S ALL BECAUSE CLASS REP WAS CRAZY ENOUGH TO TAKE A SHORTCUT.
ALWAYS COMPLAINING ABOUT WHAT'S PAST; THAT'S DISGRACEFUL, COLLET-SAN.
ERK....
AND YOU MIGHT HAVE GOTTEN YOUR MEMORIES BACK IF YOU'D GONE TO OSTIA, YUE.
WELL... I'LL WAIT FOR MY NEXT OPPORTUNITY.
GET HER MEMORIES BACK?
AH! OH, NOTHING.....
......
AWW~ BUT I WISH I COULD HAVE SEEN NAGI IN PERSON.
SO *THAT'S* WHAT THIS IS ALL ABOUT.
KYAA
CLAMOR
CLAMOR
KYAA
HUH?
WAH
?
THEY'RE AWFULLY LIVELY FOR GREETING THE LAST-PLACE CONTESTANTS.

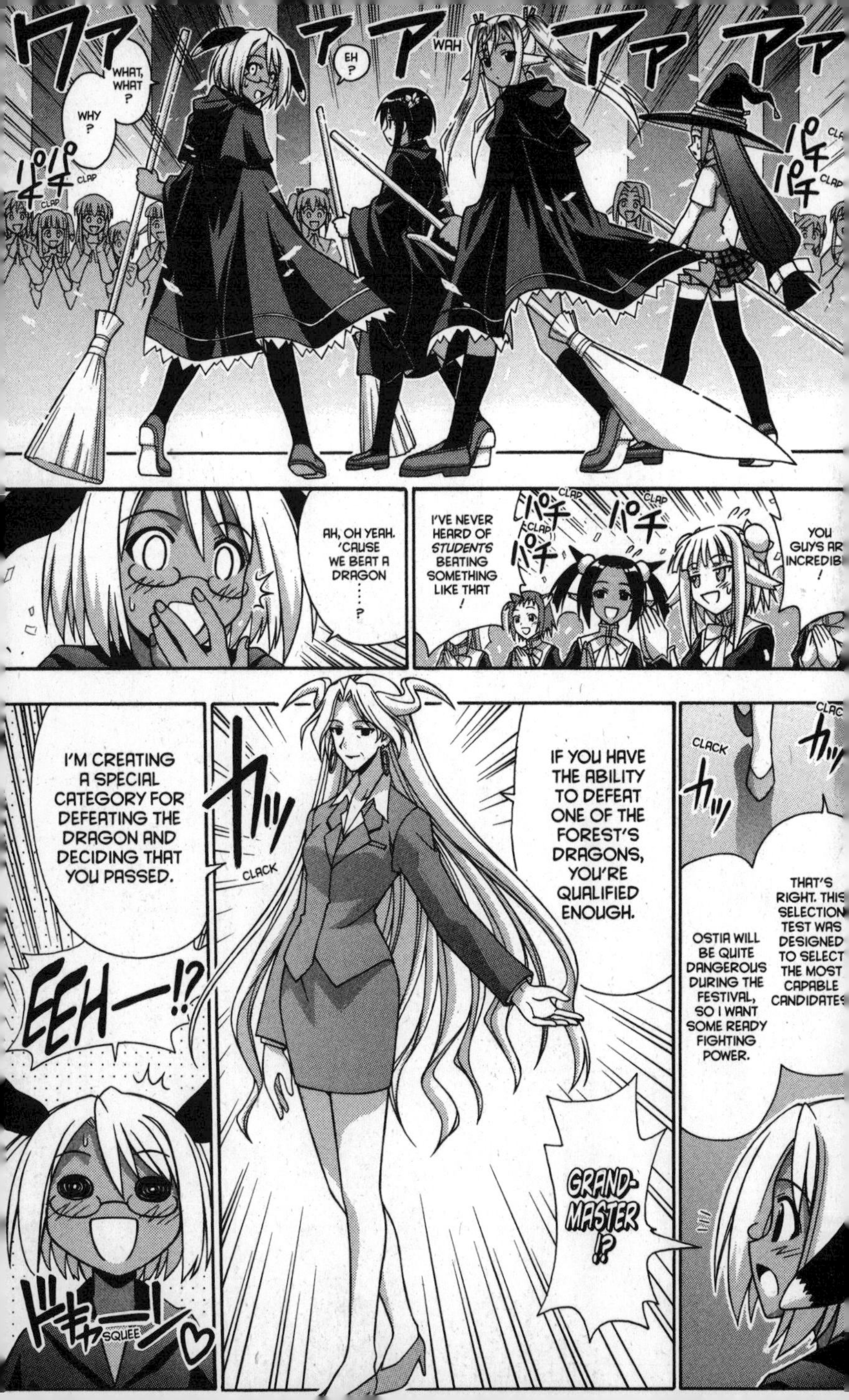
パチ CLAP
パチ CLAP
WAH
EH?
WHAT, WHAT? WHY?
パチパチ CLAP CLAP
YOU GUYS AR INCREDIB !
パチ CLAP パチ CLAP パチ CLAP
I'VE NEVER HEARD OF *STUDENTS* BEATING SOMETHING LIKE THAT!
AH, OH YEAH. 'CAUSE WE BEAT A DRAGON ......?
カッ CLACK
カッ CLACK
THAT'S RIGHT. THIS SELECTION TEST WAS DESIGNED TO SELECT THE MOST CAPABLE CANDIDATES
OSTIA WILL BE QUITE DANGEROUS DURING THE FESTIVAL, SO I WANT SOME READY FIGHTING POWER.
IF YOU HAVE THE ABILITY TO DEFEAT ONE OF THE FOREST'S DRAGONS, YOU'RE QUALIFIED ENOUGH.
カッ CLACK
GRAND-MASTER!?
I'M CREATING A SPECIAL CATEGORY FOR DEFEATING THE DRAGON AND DECIDING THAT YOU PASSED.
EEH—!?
ドキャー SQUEE ♡

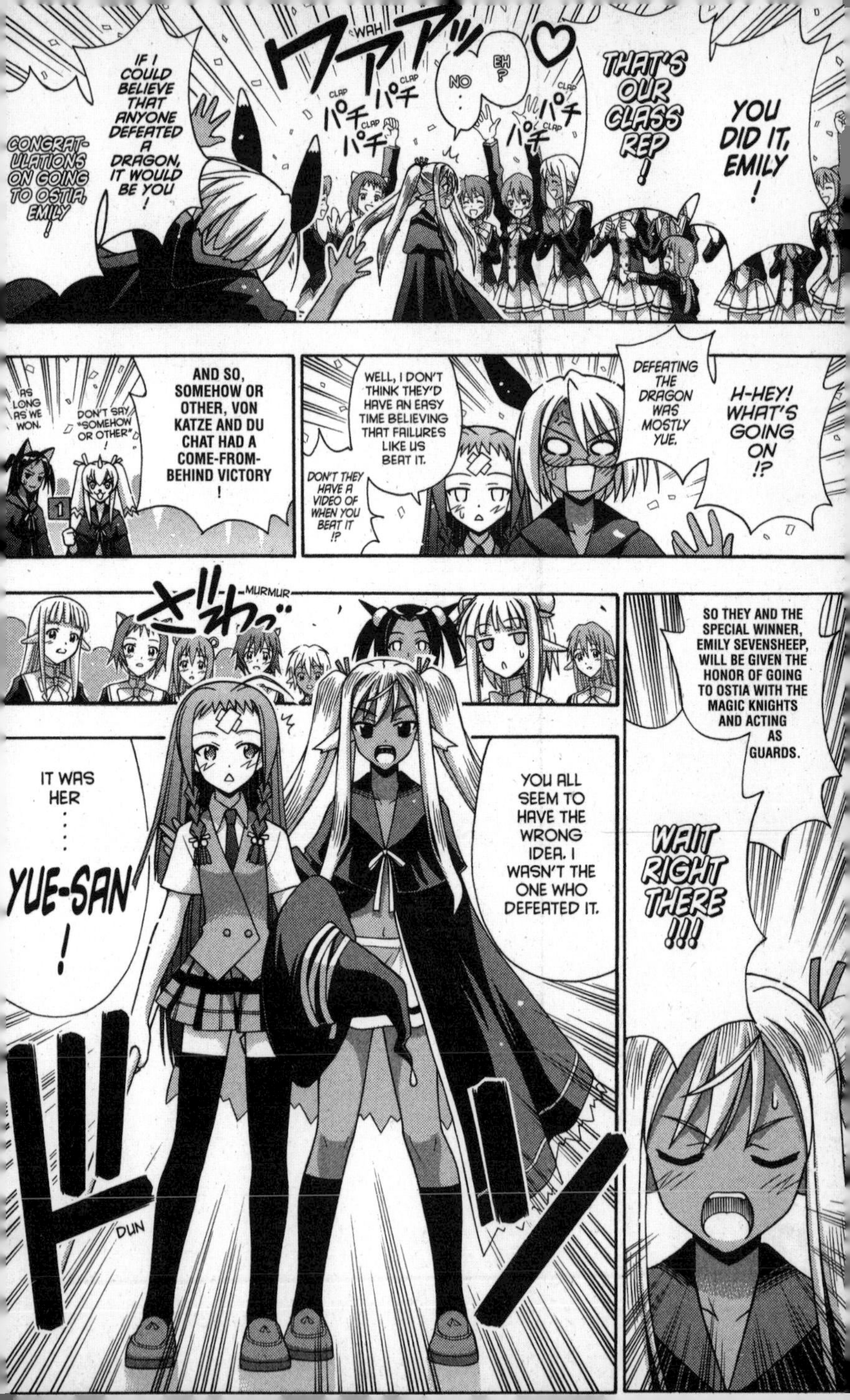
YOU DID IT, EMILY!
THAT'S OUR CLASS REP!
CLAP CLAP
EH?
NO...
CLAP CLAP
WAH
IF I COULD BELIEVE THAT ANYONE DEFEATED A DRAGON, IT WOULD BE YOU!
CONGRATULATIONS ON GOING TO OSTIA, EMILY!
H-HEY! WHAT'S GOING ON!?
DEFEATING THE DRAGON WAS MOSTLY YUE.
WELL, I DON'T THINK THEY'D HAVE AN EASY TIME BELIEVING THAT FAILURES LIKE US BEAT IT.
DON'T THEY HAVE A VIDEO OF WHEN YOU BEAT IT!?
AND SO, SOMEHOW OR OTHER, VON KATZE AND DU CHAT HAD A COME-FROM-BEHIND VICTORY!
DON'T SAY "SOMEHOW OR OTHER"!
AS LONG AS WE WON.
SO THEY AND THE SPECIAL WINNER, EMILY SEVENSHEEP, WILL BE GIVEN THE HONOR OF GOING TO OSTIA WITH THE MAGIC KNIGHTS AND ACTING AS GUARDS.
WAIT RIGHT THERE!!!
MURMUR
YOU ALL SEEM TO HAVE THE WRONG IDEA. I WASN'T THE ONE WHO DEFEATED IT.
IT WAS HER... YUE-SAN!
DUN

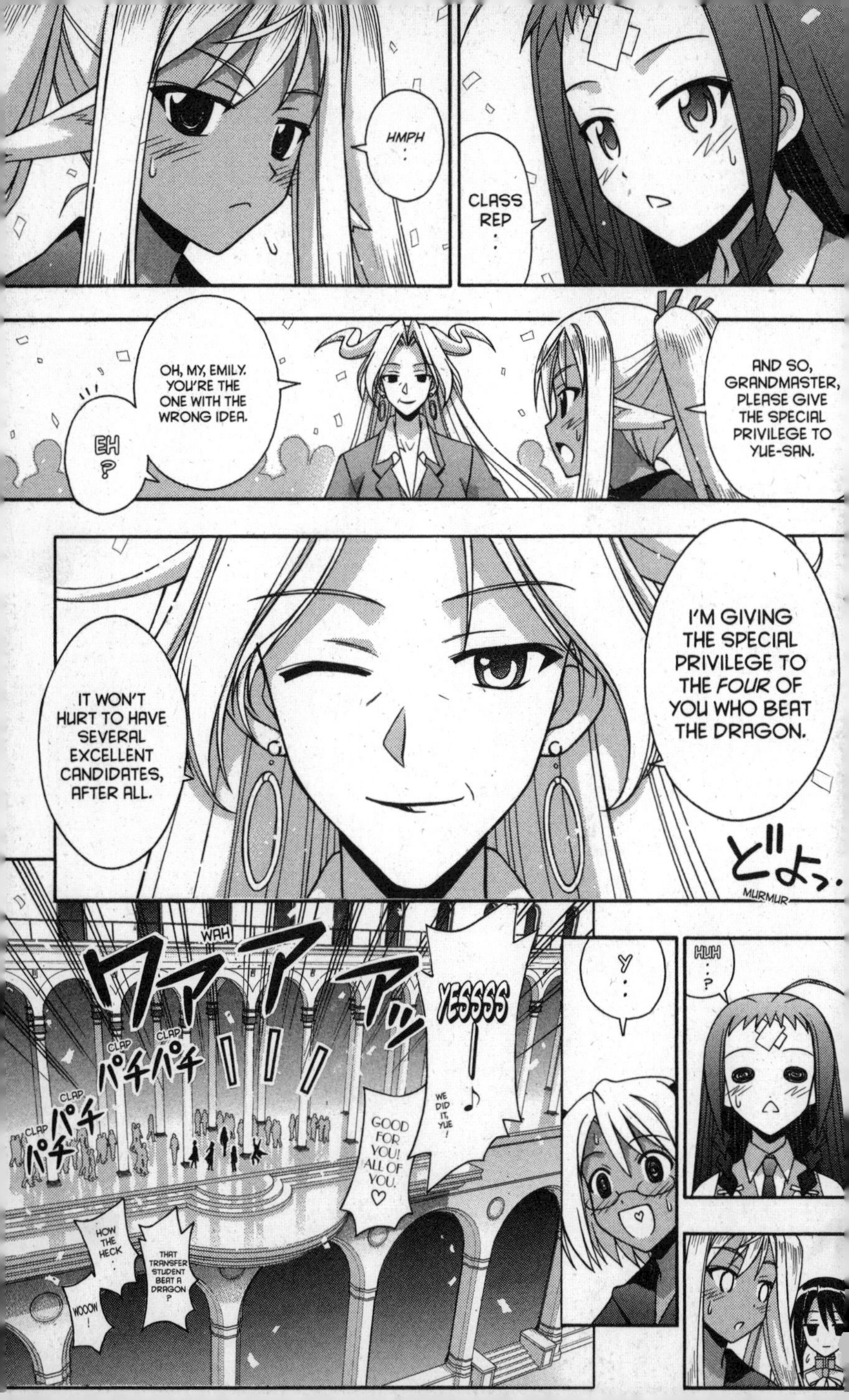

CLASS REP...
HMPH...
AND SO, GRANDMASTER, PLEASE GIVE THE SPECIAL PRIVILEGE TO YUE-SAN.
OH, MY, EMILY. YOU'RE THE ONE WITH THE WRONG IDEA.
EH?
I'M GIVING THE SPECIAL PRIVILEGE TO THE *FOUR* OF YOU WHO BEAT THE DRAGON.
IT WON'T HURT TO HAVE SEVERAL EXCELLENT CANDIDATES, AFTER ALL.
どよっ
MURMUR
HUH...?
Y...
YESSSS! ♪
WE DID IT, YUE!
GOOD FOR YOU! ALL OF YOU. ♡
ワアアッ!!!
WAH
パチパチ
CLAP CLAP
パチパチ
CLAP CLAP
HOW THE HECK...
THAT TRANSFER STUDENT BEAT A DRAGON?
WOOOW!

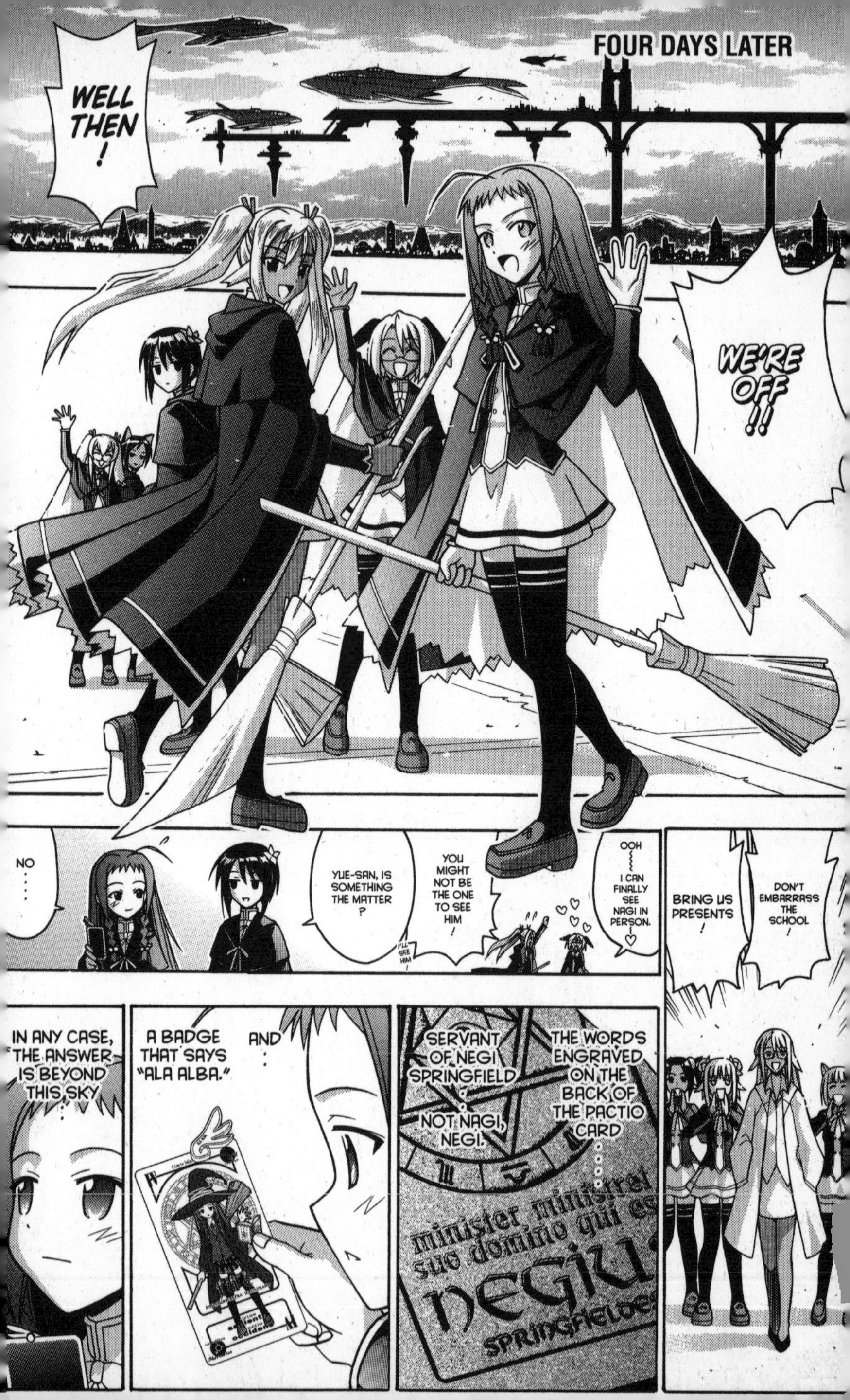
FOUR DAYS LATER
WELL THEN!
WE'RE OFF!!
DON'T EMBARRASS THE SCHOOL!
BRING US PRESENTS!
OOH I CAN FINALLY SEE NAGI IN PERSON. ♡
I'LL SEE HIM!
YOU MIGHT NOT BE THE ONE TO SEE HIM!
YUE-SAN, IS SOMETHING THE MATTER?
NO...
THE WORDS ENGRAVED ON THE BACK OF THE PACTIO CARD......
SERVANT OF NEGI SPRINGFIELD...
NOT NAGI, NEGI.
minister ministrel suo domino qui es
NEGIU SPRINGFIELDE
AND...
A BADGE THAT SAYS "ALA ALBA."
IN ANY CASE, THE ANSWER IS BEYOND THIS SKY...

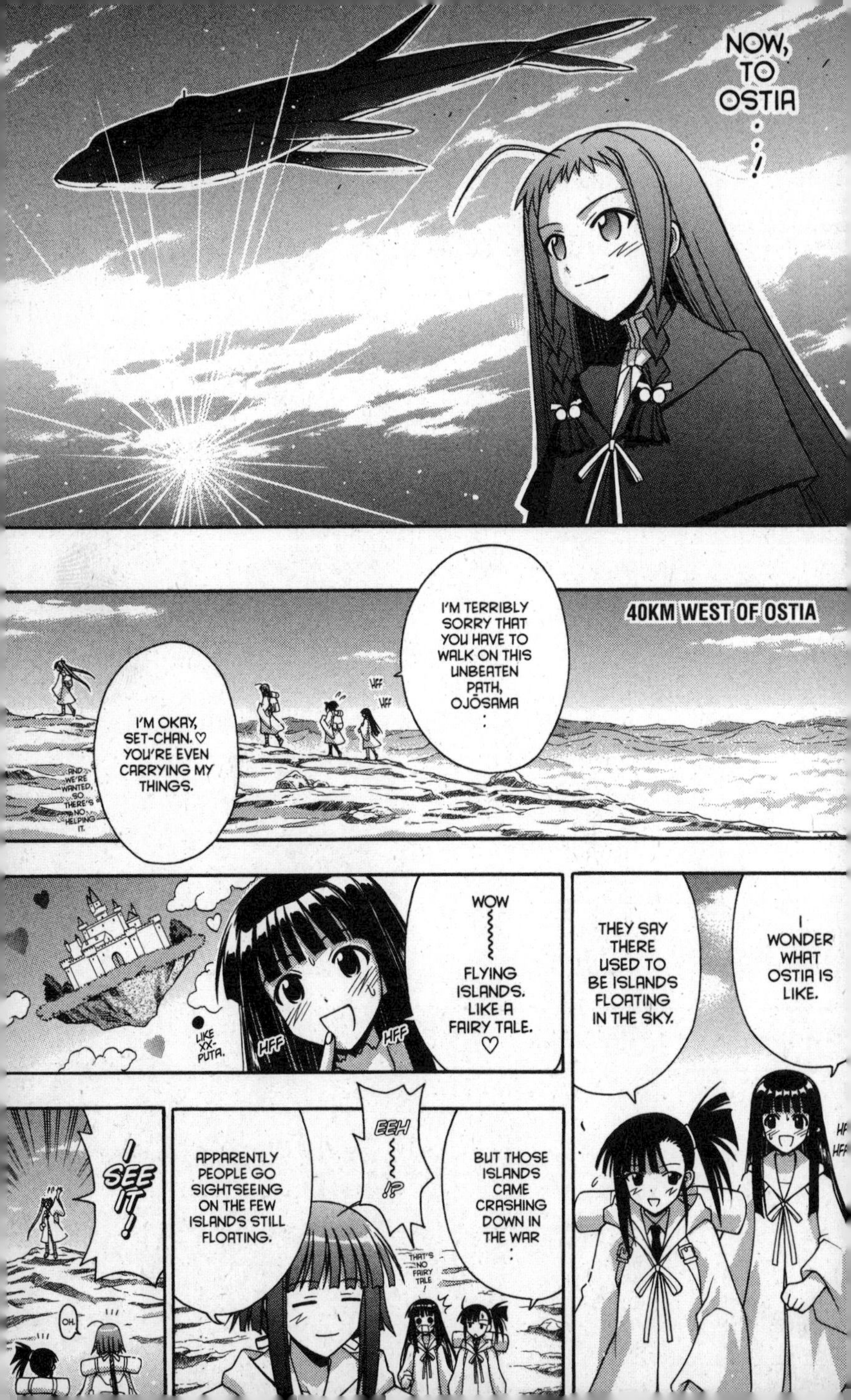
NOW, TO OSTIA...!
40KM WEST OF OSTIA
I'M TERRIBLY SORRY THAT YOU HAVE TO WALK ON THIS UNBEATEN PATH, OJŌSAMA...
HFF HFF
I'M OKAY, SET-CHAN. ♡ YOU'RE EVEN CARRYING MY THINGS.
AND WE'RE WANTED, SO THERE'S NO HELPING IT.
I WONDER WHAT OSTIA IS LIKE.
THEY SAY THERE USED TO BE ISLANDS FLOATING IN THE SKY.
HF HFF
WOW~ FLYING ISLANDS. LIKE A FAIRY TALE. ♡
HFF HFF
LIKE XX-PUTA.
BUT THOSE ISLANDS CAME CRASHING DOWN IN THE WAR...
EEH~!?
APPARENTLY PEOPLE GO SIGHTSEEING ON THE FEW ISLANDS STILL FLOATING.
THAT'S NO FAIRY TALE
I SEE IT!
OH.

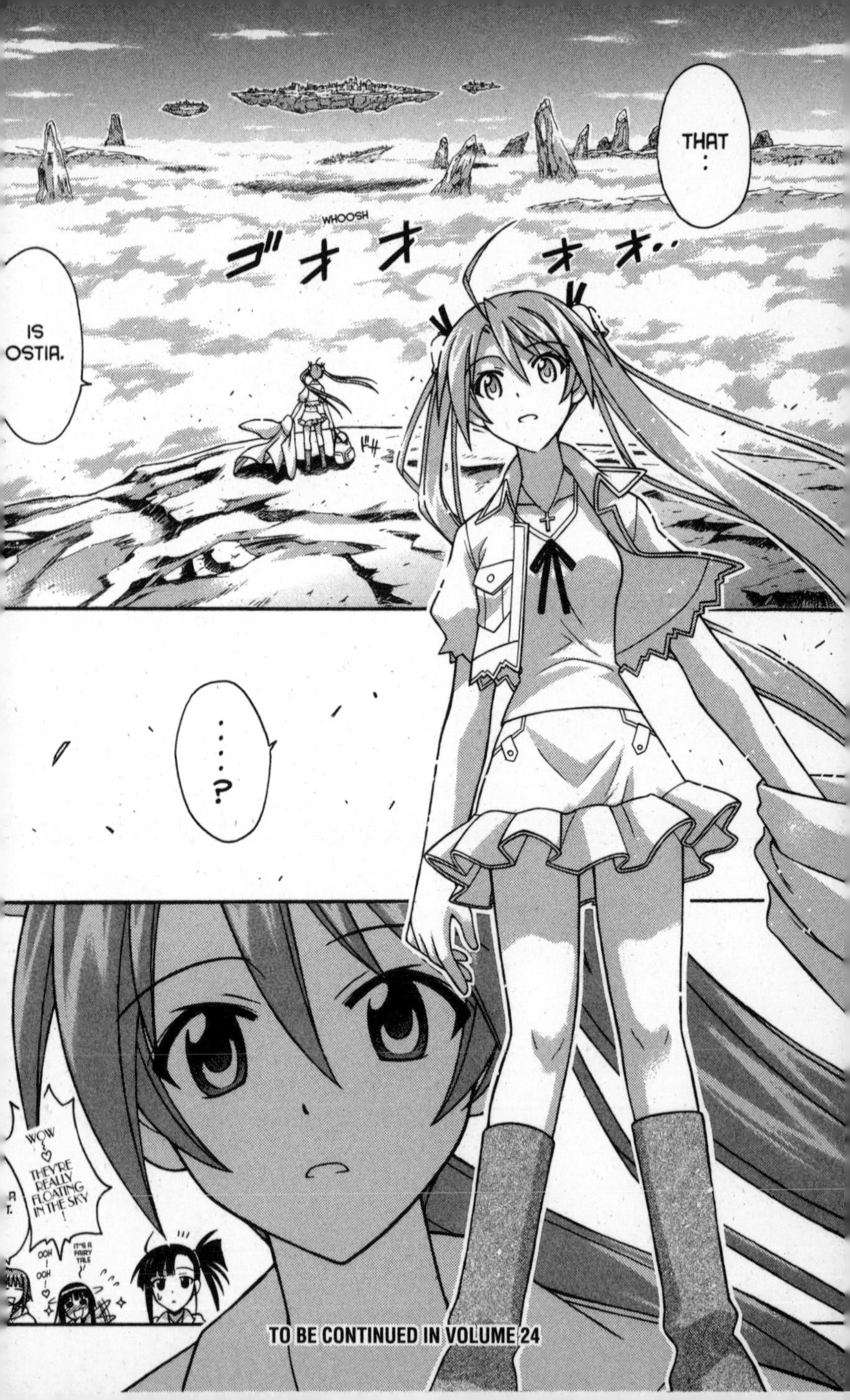
THAT...
WHOOSH
ゴオオ オオ..
IS OSTIA.
....?
WOW ♡ THEY'RE REALLY FLOATING IN THE SKY!
IT'S A FAIRY TALE
OOH! OOH! ♡
TO BE CONTINUED IN VOLUME 24

— STAFF —

Ken Akamatsu
Takashi Takemoto
Kenichi Nakamura
Masaki Ohyama
Keiichi Yamashita
Tadashi Maki
Tohru Mitsuhashi

Thanks To

Ran Ayanaga

NEGIMA!
FAN ART CORNER

OH! THE FATE POWER HAS EMERGED. NO, SOME KIND OF VAGUE FORCE IS GRADUALLY MAKING ITS WAY IN (LAUGH). I GOT TO SEE A LOT OF PICTURES THAT WERE OF MULTIPLE CHARACTERS, BUT NOT COUPLES. ANYHOW, LET'S GET STARTED.

TEXT BY MAX

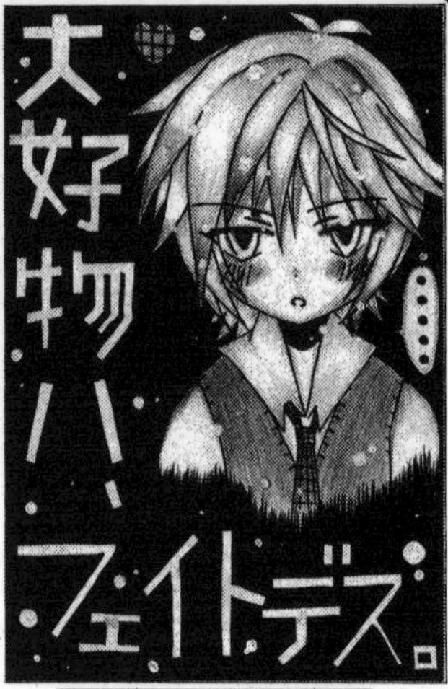
大好物ハ、フェイトデス。
I MIGHT WANT TO PROTECT A FATE LIKE THIS (LAUGH)

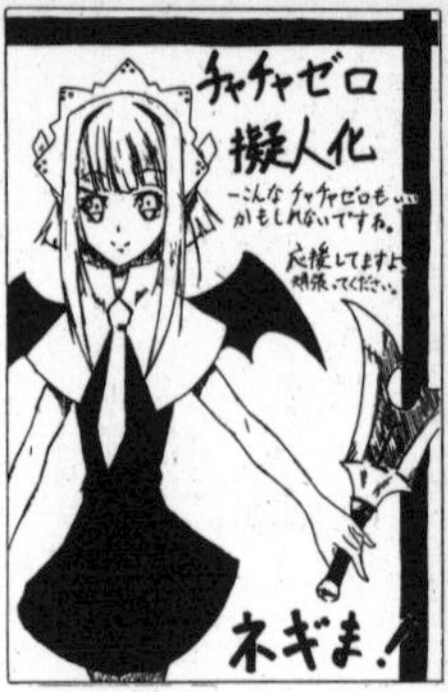
チャチャゼロ
擬人化
ネギま!
A BEAUTIFUL GIRL? (LAUGH)

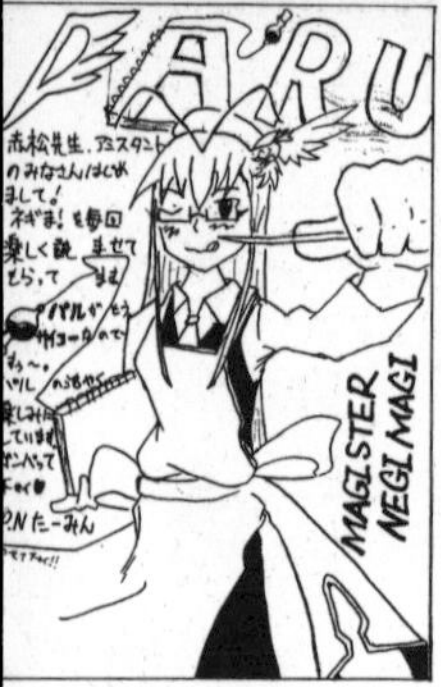
MAGISTER NEGI MAGI
SHE'S READY FOR SOMETHING ☆

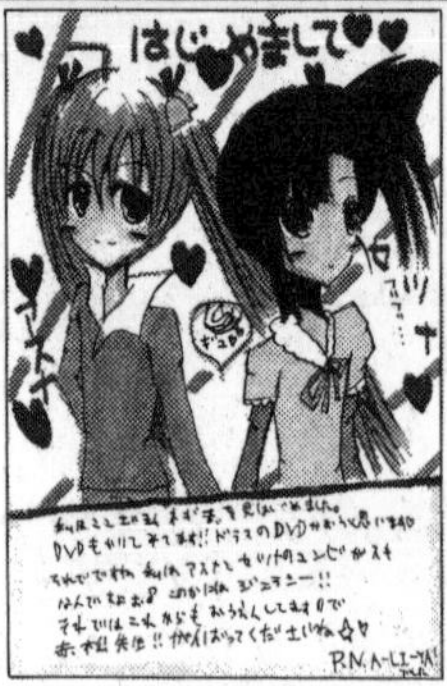
はじめまして
IT KINDA PLUCKS AT YOUR HEARTSTRINGS.

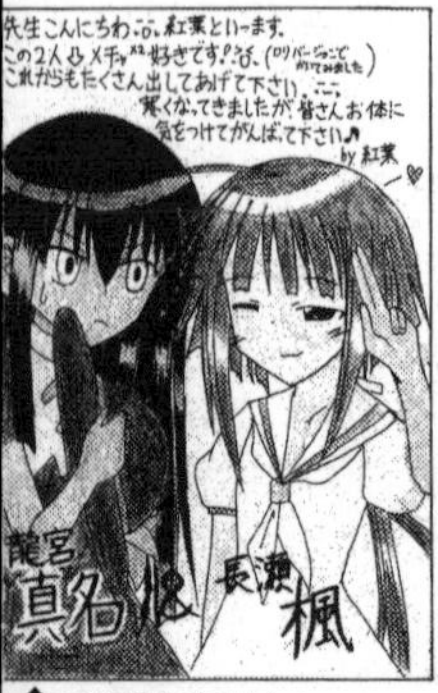
龍宮
真名
長瀬
楓
BATTLE TEAM ☆

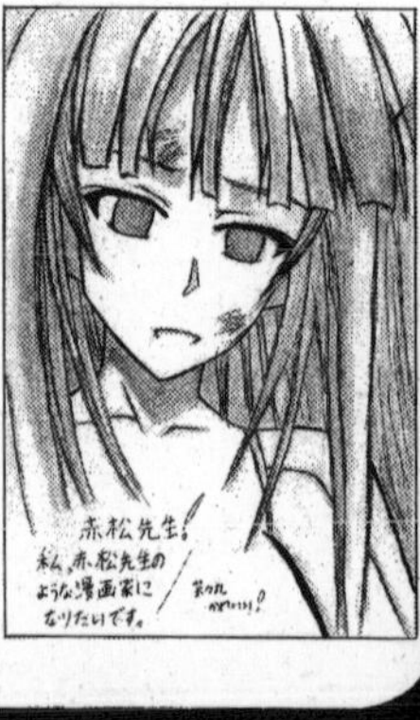
赤松先生!
GOOD EYES.

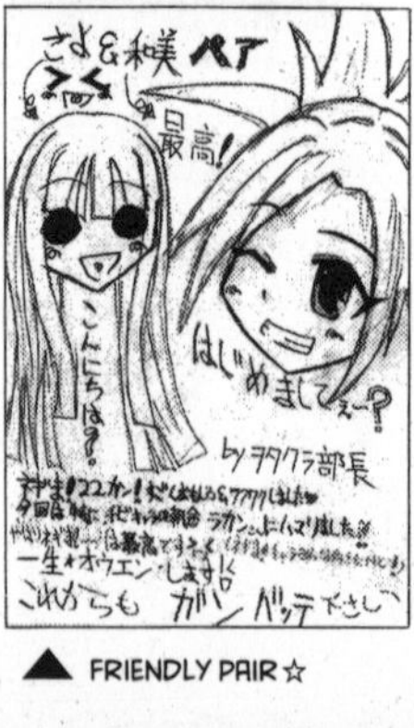
さよ&楓ペア
最高!
はじめまして
FRIENDLY PAIR ☆

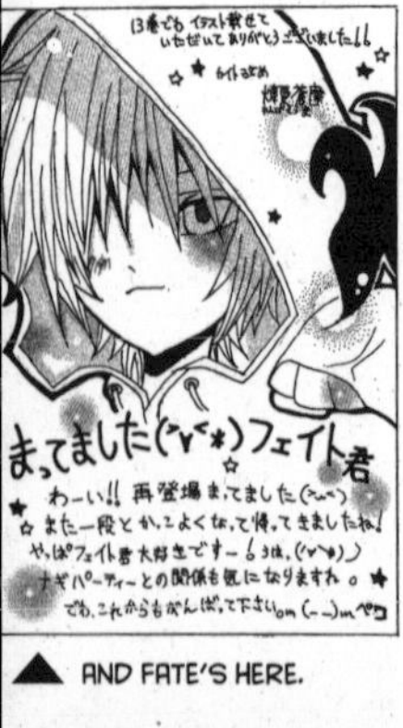
まってました
AND FATE'S HERE.

MAGISTER NEGI MAGI

MAHORA

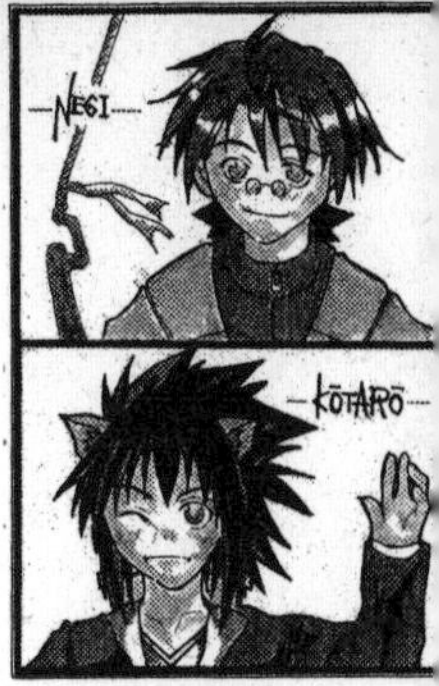

NEGI
KOTARO

KOTA-NEGI★

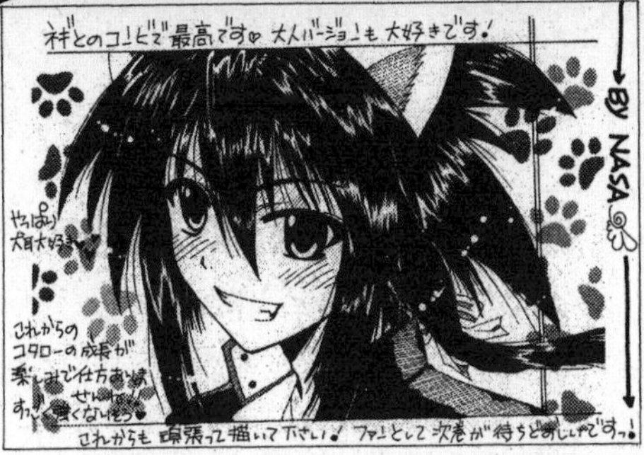

ネギとのコンビで最高です♥ 大人バージョンも大好きです!
BY NASA
やっぱり犬耳大好き
これからのコタローの成長が楽しみで仕方ありません
これからも頑張って描いて下さい! ファンとして次巻が待ちどおしいです!

THIS...IS TOO CUTE (LAUGH)

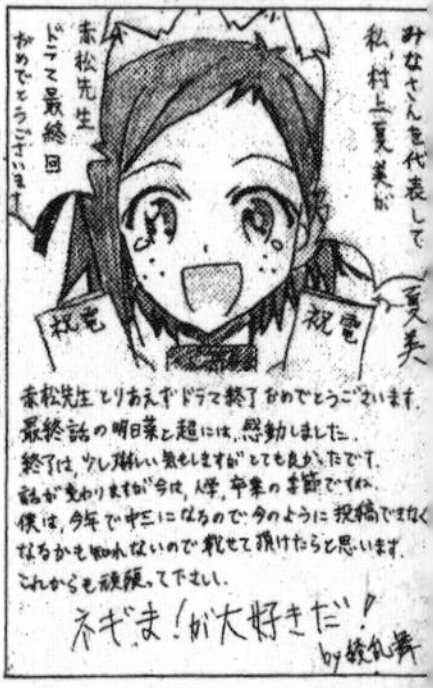

みなさん色代表して私、村上夏美が
赤松先生 ドラマ最終回 おめでとうございます
祝電
祝電
夏美
赤松先生とりあえずドラマ終了おめでとうございます。
最終話の明日菜と超には、感動しました。
終了は、少し寂しい気もしますがとても良かったです。
話が変わりますが今は、入学、卒業の季節ですね。
僕は、今年で中三になるので、今のように投稿できなくなるかも知れないので載せて頂けたらと思います。
これからも頑張って下さい。
ネギま!が大好きだ!

SHE HAS CONGRATULATORY TELEGRAMS (LAUGH)

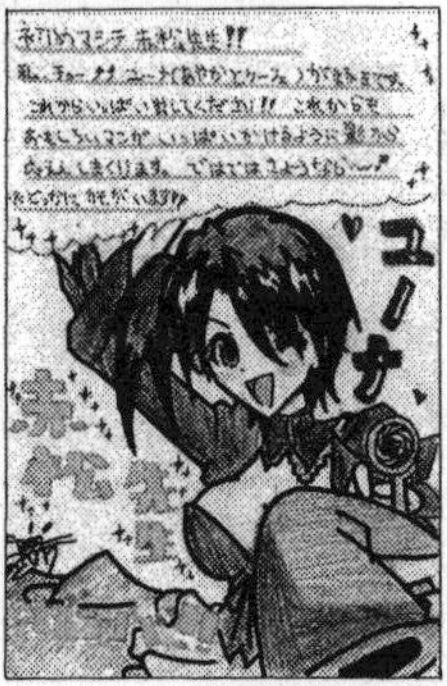

初めまして 赤松先生!!
ユーナ

YŪNA SURE IS ENERGETIC.

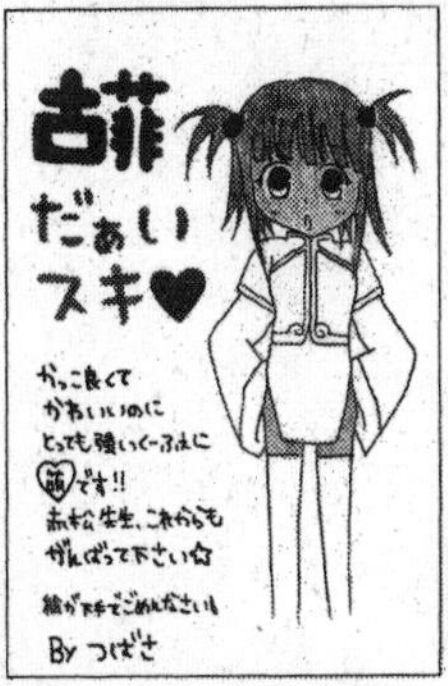

古菲
だぁいスキ♥
かっこ良くて かわいいのに とっても強いくーふぇに 萌です!!
赤松先生、これからも がんばって下さい☆
絵が下手でごめんなさい
By つばさ

IT'S LIKE SHE'S SAYING "HAYO?" ("HUH?")

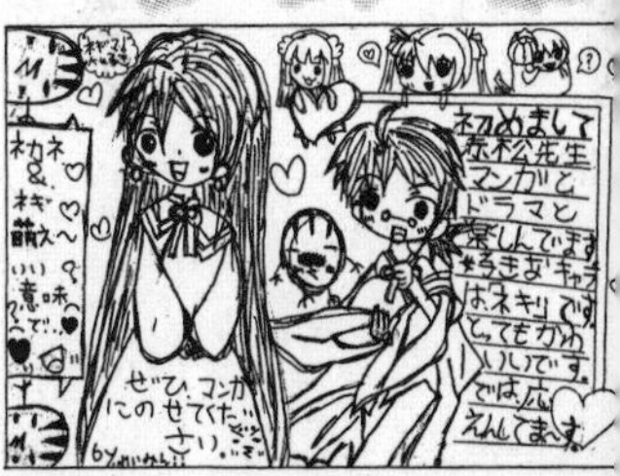

初めまして 赤松先生 マンガとドラマと楽しんでます
とってもかわいいです。
ぜひ、マンガにのせてください。

NEKANE. THAT'S UNUSUAL.

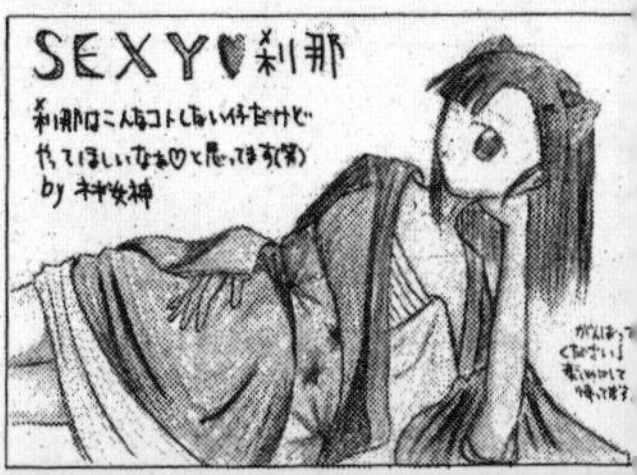

SEXY♥刹那
刹那はこんなコトしない子だけど やってほしいなぁ♥と思ってます(笑)
by ネギ女神

THAT IS SEXY.

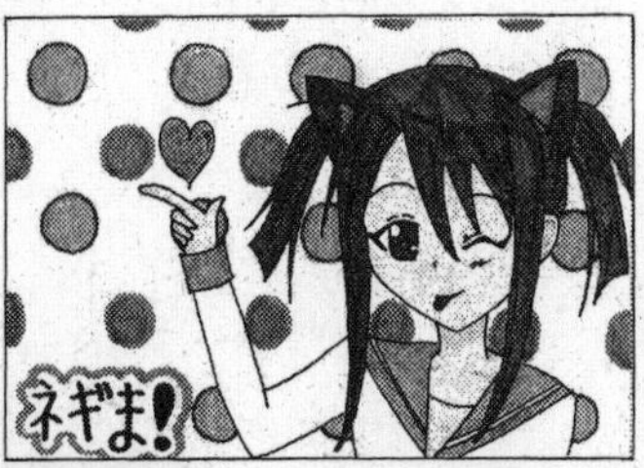

ネギま!

HER TONGUE IS SO CUTE.

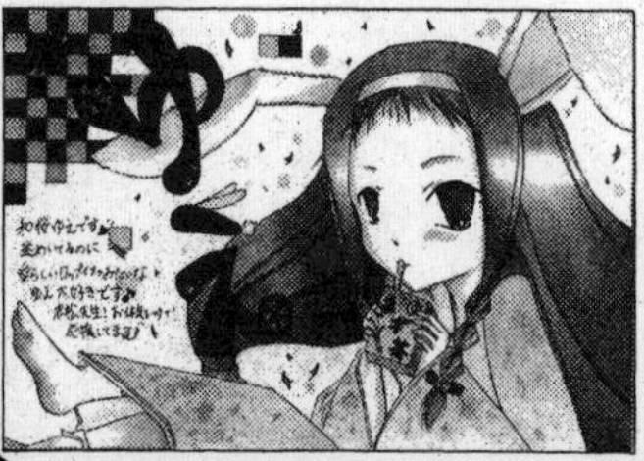

IS THE NEGI (GREEN ONION) TEA ANY GOOD?

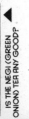

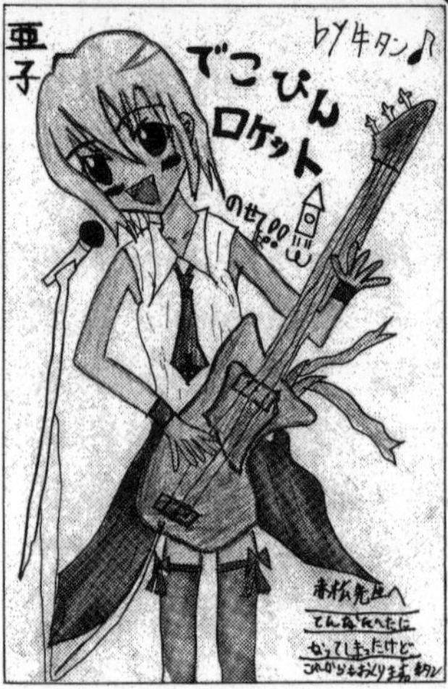
亜子
でこぴんロケット
by牛タン♪

▲ THOSE DOUBLE TEETH ARE NICE, HUH, AKO?

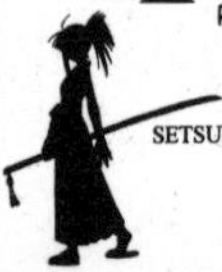

SETSUNA SAKURAZAKI

▼ HAKASE FETISH

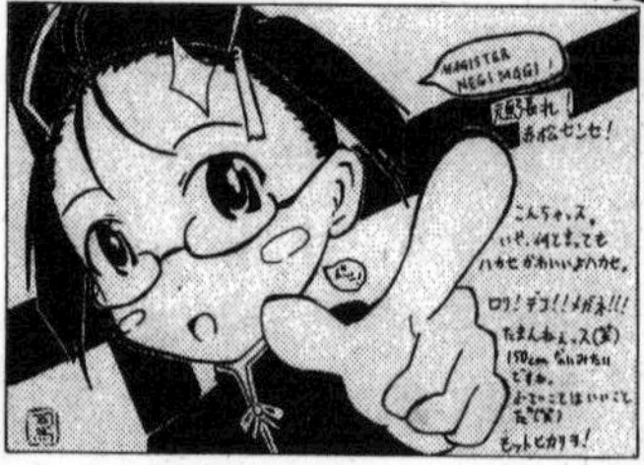
MAGISTER NEGI MAGI!

▼ SUPERCUTE ZAZI-SAN

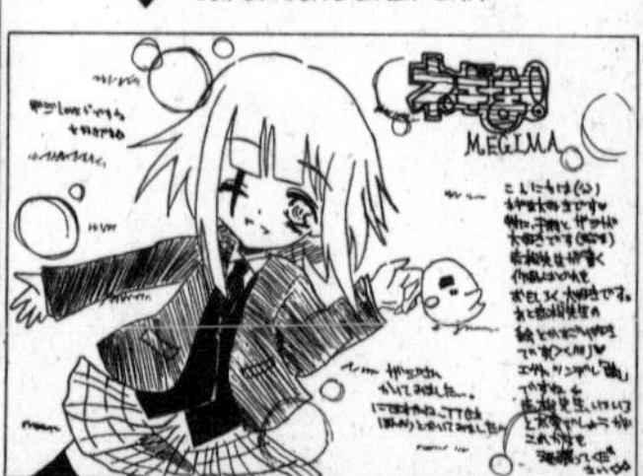
MEGIMA

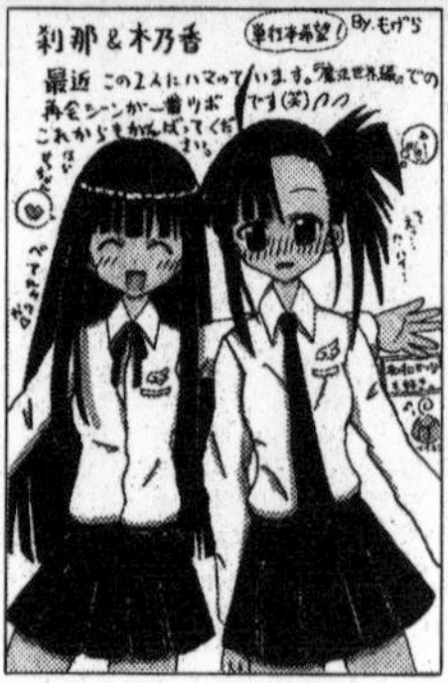
刹那＆木乃香

▲ NICE ATMOSPHERE.

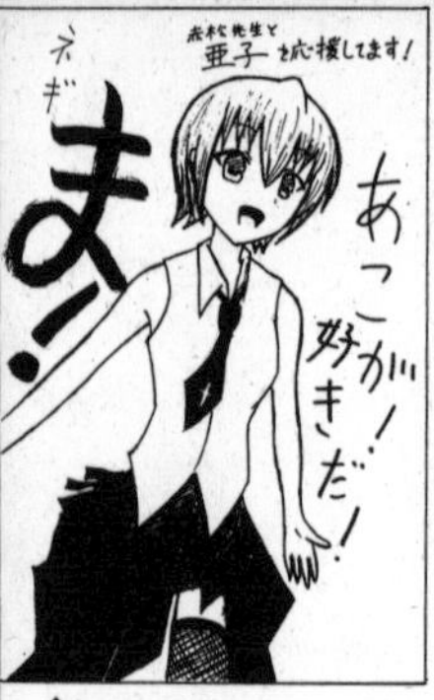
亜子を応援してます!
ま!
あっこが!好きだ!

▲ AKO'S GETTING CUTER AND CUTER.

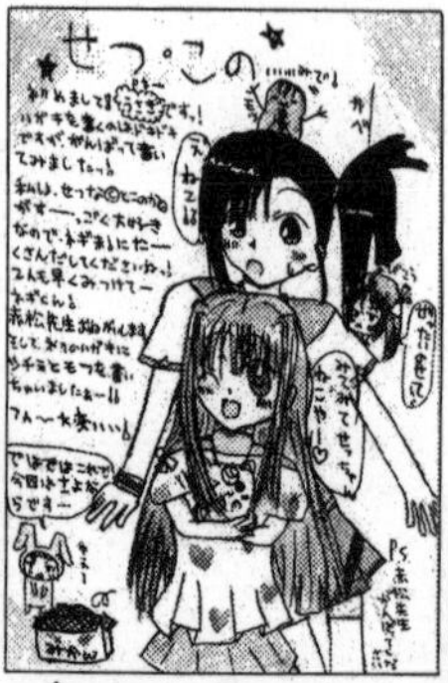
せつこの

▲ THERE ARE A LOT OF THESE.

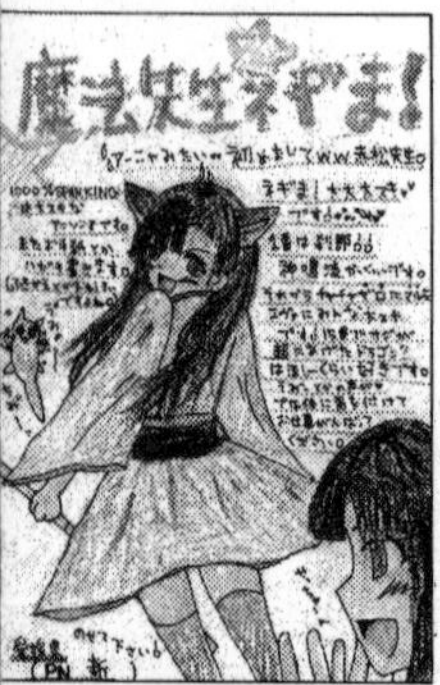
魔法先生ネギま!

▲ CUTE SETSUNA

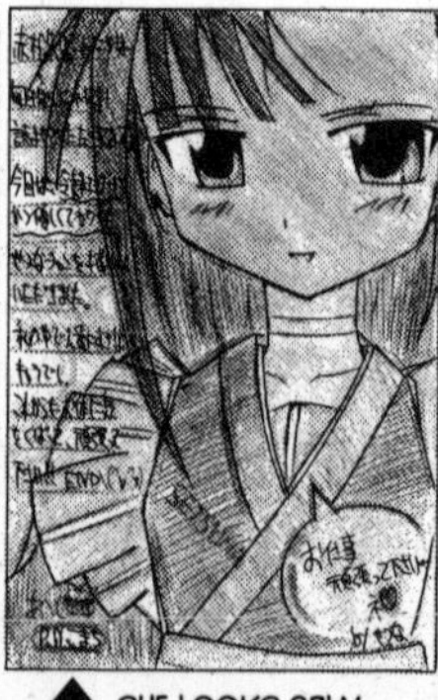

▲ SHE LOOKS CALM.

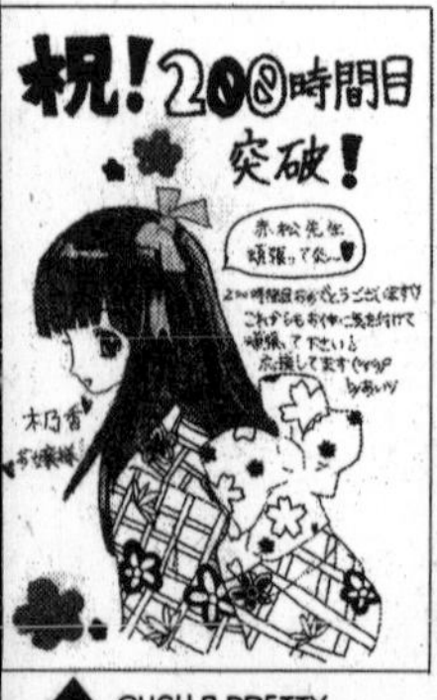
祝!200時間目
突破!

▲ SUCH A PRETTY KIMONO.

THIS VOLUME'S

FEATURED CHARACTER

ASUNA KAGURAZAKA

RANKING

NEGI MAGI MAGISTER

FIRST PLACE

祝! 200話!!

AN ENERGETIC AND CUTE ASUNA.♡ THE WAY SHE HOLDS HER ARTIFACT AND THE WAY HER HAIR FALLS ARE ALL GOOD!

(AKAMATSU)

SECOND PLACE

・あすな・
NEGIMA

ASUNA'S SOMEHOW INCREDIBLY SEXY. IT'S TRUE, NEGI X ASU DOES SEEM LIKELY, MAYBE?

THIRD PLACE

ネギま!
魔法世界
すごく
楽しそうです!

IF YOU ACTUALLY WENT TO THE MAGICAL WORLD, IT MIGHT BE PRETTY TOUGH. (LAUGH) THERE'S LOTS OF DRAGONS AND STUFF LIKE THAT...

3-D BACKGROUNDS EXPLANATION CORNER

PRESENTED ALONG WITH THINGS I COULDN'T
INTRODUCE IN THE LAST VOLUME.

• RAKAN'S CASTLE

SCENE NAME: RAKAN'S TOWER   POLYGON COUNT: 92,856

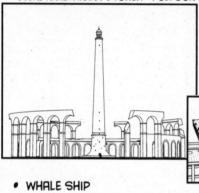

RAKAN'S HOME, STANDING IN THE MIDDLE OF
THE DESERT. APPROXIMATELY 320M TALL, WORD
IS IT STARTED OUT AS AN ANCIENT RUIN.
THE REASON HE LIVES HERE IS UNKNOWN, BUT
IT DOES SEEM LIKE A CONVENIENT PLACE FOR
RAKAN, WHO HAS EXTRAORDINARY POWER, TO
TRAIN.

• PIER & BED

APPARENTLY HE
BROUGHT A BED OUT
HERE SO THEY WOULDN'T
HAVE TO MOVE NEGI
TOO MUCH. THAT'S
RAKAN FOR YOU—HE'S
REALLY STRONG.
(LAUGH)

• WHALE SHIP

SCENE NAME: WHALE SHIP POLYGON COUNT: 66,114

THE VIEWING DECK ON THE
WHALE SHIP ASAKURA AND
CHACHAMARU ARE RIDING. IT'S
WIDE AND SPACIOUS, AND IT
LOOKS LIKE THEY CAN ENJOY A
REFINED JOURNEY.
INCIDENTALLY, FOR THE DESIGN
I REFERRED TO ORDINARY
VIEWING PLATFORMS.

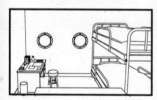

• CABINS

ON THE OTHER HAND, THEIR CABIN IS
SIMPLE. IS IT TO SAVE ON TRAVEL EXPENSES?

• RURAL MOUNTAIN VILLAGE

SCENE NAME: VILLAGE
POLYGON COUNT: 503,511

THE MOUNTAIN VILLAGE WHERE
ASUNA AND KONOKA WERE REUNITED.
IT'S NOT A VERY BIG VILLAGE, BUT
IT'S A RELAY POINT FOR TRAVELERS
CROSSING THE MOUNTAINS, SO IT
GETS A LOT OF VISITORS.
I MADE THE WOOD HOUSES BY
REMODELING EVA'S HOUSE. OR WAS
THAT OBVIOUS? (LAUGH)

— ARIADNE MAGIC SCHOOL —

• CLASSROOM

SCENE NAME: MS CLASSROOM
POLYGON COUNT: 32,900

THE ROOM WHERE YUE, COLLET, AND THE OTHERS LEARN. FITTING OF AN ILLUSTRIOUS SCHOOL OF THE MAGICAL ACADEMIC CITY ARIADNE, YOU CAN FEEL THE HISTORY IN THE WAY IT WAS MADE. BUT ACTUALLY, THE DESKS AND CHAIRS ARE JUST REUSED, SO I HAD A RELATIVELY EASY TIME MAKING IT.

• NURSE'S OFFICE

SCENE NAME: MS HEALTH ROOM
POLYGON COUNT: 91,914

THE NURSE'S OFFICE THAT APPEARED IN VOLUME 22. THERE ARE ALL KINDS OF MEDICINAL HERBS INSIDE THE LARGE MEDICINE CABINET. THE MEDICINE BOTTLES STAND OUT, TOO.

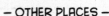

• COLLET'S ROOM

SCENE NAME: COLLET'S ROOM
POLYGON COUNT: 58,279

COLLET'S ROOM IN THE STUDENT DORMS. THERE ARE A LOT OF POTTED PLANTS, MAYBE BECAUSE SHE'S GROWING THE MEDICINAL HERBS THAT SHE USES IN CLASS.
ALSO, IF YOU LOOK CLOSELY, YOU CAN SEE A WEIRD STUFFED ANIMAL. (LAUGH)

— OTHER PLACES —

• GRANDMASTER'S OFFICE

I ONLY USED IT FOR THIS ONE PANEL, BUT FOR SOMETHING LIKE THIS, IT'S ACTUALLY FASTER TO MAKE IT IN 3-D.

• LIBRARY

THE LIBRARY'S READING AREA. I MADE IT COMPLETELY NEW, BUT MAYBE IT'S NOT MUCH BETTER THAN THE MAHORA LIBRARY? (^_^;)

• GIRLS' BATHROOM

THERE'S A "LADIES'" SYMBOL ON IT; APPARENTLY THAT DESIGN IS THE SAME IN THE OLD WORLD AND IN THE MAGICAL WORLD. (LAUGH)

LEXICON NEGIMARIUM

[*Negima!* 205th Period Lexicon Negimarium]

■ Dark Magic

Magia Erebea

"Magia" is Latin for "magic." "Erebea" is the feminine singular nominative case of the adjective meaning "of Erebos." According to Hesiod, Erebos (ʼΕρεβος) is the god of darkness in Greek mythology, the son of one of the original gods, Chaos. The children that Erebos begat with his twin sister Nyx (night) were Aether (shining air)*[1] and Hemera (day), (cf. *Theogony* 123–125), and, being darkness and night, they are the divine beings that precede light. In the words of the German romantic philosopher F. W. J. Schelling (1775–1854), "All birth is birth from darkness to light." (*Investigations of Human Freedom,* SW360; but according to Hesiod, it wasn't that everything was born from Chaos and darkness—the heavens, the oceans, and many others were born from Gaia, who was born at the same time as Chaos.)

Thus, light cannot give birth to darkness, but darkness can give birth to light. Darkness is not in opposition to light. Darkness is a source that holds all things within it, and is tremendously broad-minded. And this broad-mindedness becomes a power that takes in all opposites such as good and evil, superiority and inferiority, self and others, etc. This is because *light* is the basis of opposition and disparity. Schelling says, "Light's advance on the dark aspiration to create something . . . is due to the thoughts that are mingled in chaos becoming distinct . . . and unity being erected" (ibid. SW361). If light is the basis of opposition and disparity, darkness is the basis of nondiscrimination. Therefore, dark magic has the tremendous broad-mindedness to take in all power without discriminating between self and others.

However, things are not that simple. Within darkness, all disparity becomes invisible; the difference between self and others vanishes as well, and the spellcaster loses sight of himself. But magic spells are never anything more than techniques the caster uses to accomplish his willful purposes; their purpose is not to reach some kind of absolute truth. As stated by Schelling's school colleague, G. W. F. Hegel (1770–1830),

---

*[1]: Aether (αθήρ) is the "ether" that we speak of in modern language. In premodern cosmology, it is said to be one of the five elements that makes up things in the heavens. However, going further back and looking at mythological texts, Aether was thought of as the air in the clear sky. The Aether that Hesiod speaks of is one of the twins of light born from the twins of darkness. Because the genealogy of the goddesses goes from night (Nyx) to day (Hemera), the male gods' genealogy would go from darkness to light (however, because the Greek word "aether" does not mean light, but is translated to "*kirameku kūki,*" meaning "bright upper air" in Japanese, it was translated to the single word "*kōki,*" shining air.)

"To pit this single assertion, that 'In the Absolute, all is one,' against the organized whole of determinate and complete knowledge, or of knowledge which at least aims at and demands complete development—to give out its Absolute as the night, in which, as we say, all cows are black—that is the very naivete of emptiness of knowledge." (*Phenomenology of Spirit,* preface). In order to use a technique as a technique, especially within darkness, one must make sure not to lose sight of one's self.

What is needed then is a "confrontation with one's shadow," or "an encounter with one's anima." The battle Negi fights in Phantasmagoria is none other than a "confrontation with his shadow," or "encounter with his anima."

The Swiss psychiatrist C. G. Jung (1875–1961) said the following in regards to encounters with one's self and encounters with one's shadow: "A meeting with one's self first means a meeting with one's shadow. By shadow, I mean none other than a single narrow path, a single gate. . . . What comes after that gate is, unsurprisingly, a limitless, unprecedented uncertainty. There, it is believed there is neither inside nor outside, up nor down, far nor near, self nor other, good nor evil.

That is a world of water, and approximately everything with life there is floating, drifting" *2 (*The Archetypes and the Collective Unconscious*). By encountering one's shadow, one enters into his own soul and, as Hegel points out, enters into an obscure darkness. Jung states the following: "There, I am joined directly and firmly to the world, and it's all too simple to forget who I am in actuality. If I were to characterize this condition, the most appropriate phrase would be 'lost within oneself'" (ibid.). Thus, if one goes through their shadow into darkness, they face the fundamental danger of losing sight of oneself.

What is needed to conquer this danger is an "encounter with one's anima." Those who pass through their shadow selves and search out their souls, (as explained above) enter into a "world of water," but inside this water, people (especially men) meet their anima. "What one who gazes into the water first sees is a form of himself, but soon a living entity surfaces from beneath it. . . . It is a unique kind of water creature. Sometimes a water sprite, or a mermaid caught in a fisherman's net. . . . The water sprite is an early, instinctive stage of the mystical, feminine entity called anima." (ibid.) It is said that the anima's early stage sometimes takes the form of erotic spirits, such as demon girls or vampire women (Lamie). And it is said that "anima appear in the form of goddesses or witches." (ibid.) The Evangeline that Negi encounters in Phantasmagoria in this story is this early stage, this anima. Evangeline first appears in the nude, and we don't even have to point out that she is a vampire and also a witch. And this encounter with an anima results in a certain wisdom. "Indeed the anima is a chaotic life impulse, but on the other hand, in a mysterious sense, it has on hand secret knowledge and concealed wisdom, and is in the most peculiar opposition to one's illogical, spiritual nature. . . . This wisdom aspect appears only to one who confronts his anima. This is an intense labor . . . and can more strongly indicate that something like a secret intention hides behind all cruelty that plays with man's fate. This unpredictable thing, this

---

*2: According to *Archetypes* (Kinokuniya Shoten), take Tode as Tor.

chaotic thing that brings anxiety is precisely what exposes deep meaning. As one becomes aware of this meaning, the anima loses its aggressive personality. The embankments that hold off the flood of chaos gradually build up." (ibid.) When the one who has passed through his shadow and set foot into darkness confronts his anima and touches on that wisdom, he conquers the fundamental danger of losing sight of himself in the darkness and chaos, and obtains a way to use dark magic, or, in other words, the original broad-mindedness that encompasses all opposites.

[*Negima!* 205th Period Lexicon Negimarium]

■ Demon's Nursery Rhyme
(Comptina Daemonia)

A magical item that can learn the names of others. In magical culture, it is believed to be extremely dangerous to have one's name known to others (cf. *The Golden Bough,* ch.XXII, §1).

For example, there is an old story from Isawa District in Iwate Prefecture of Japan. A carpenter took on the job of building a bridge over some swift rapids. But the job was too difficult, and he sat near the river, at a loss for what to do. A demon appeared and said he would build the bridge in exchange for the carpenter's eyes. Two days later, the carpenter went to the river, and the bridge was built. The demon appeared and demanded the carpenter's eyes. The carpenter panicked and escaped into the mountains, where he heard a song in the distance: "I hope Oniroku brings the eyes soon" (this song varies depending on tradition; there is a version where it is a nursery rhyme sung by demon children, and a version where it is a lullaby sung to lull demon children to sleep). The next day, the carpenter met the demon, who told him that if he could guess the demon's name, he would not have to give up his eyes. When the carpenter said "Oniroku," the demon was destroyed (Keigo Seki's *Japanese Folktales III,* Iwanami Shoten). The story tells us that even if you are facing a type of demon, if you know their name, you can hold their life in your hands. Furthermore, it also tells us that true names are hidden in nursery rhymes and lullabies. The name "Demon's Nursery Rhyme" means that the item will inform its user of those hidden names.

[*Negima!* 206th Period Lexicon Negimarium]

■ 文
(man)

In Ryōfu Nankoku Sanzō Mandara Sen's translation of *Manjushiri Shosetsu Maka Hannya Haramikkyō*, it says, "Mañjuśrī said, 'I do not see the form of truth in all things. Buddha naturally perceives that all things are emptiness. This is precisely what can prove wisdom.' Buddha said to Mañjuśrī, 'That is correct. Enlightened ones truly perceive and naturally prove the truth of emptiness.'" Mañjuśrī is known as a bodhisattva, one who vows to save all beings before becoming a Buddha, who excelled in wisdom, or prajñā (Sanskrit). Mañjuśrī is his Sanskrit name.

The character "man" is Mañjuśrī's seed syllable (the first syllable of a mantra, in which is contained all meaning), and is said to come from the first character in Mañjuśrī. This seed is written on Kaede's blindfold to share in the good luck of the words of Mañjuśrī, where he says, "I do not see truth in all things, I naturally perceive the truth (that all things are emptiness)," and gain extraordinary perceptive powers.

■ 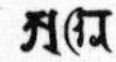

(agni)

A word that means "fire," or "god of fire," in Sanskrit (to be more precise, its root and singular noun form is "agnis"). In order to make use of the ninja techniques (or rather Buddhist techniques) that come from explosive fire, Kaede makes a chain of charms with that name written on them in Sanskrit.

■ 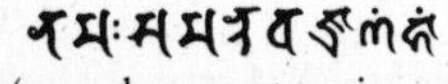

(namak samanta vajra nan han)

The mantra said by *Fudō Myō-ō*, Acala the Immovable One, called the "*fudō-ichijishu*." According to a summary of notes on the Mahāvairocana Tantra, "*Dainichikyō Somyōinshō*," "*Fudō Myō-ō* is namely the Great Buddha's embodiment of injunction." That is to say, *Fudō Myō-ō* is believed to be the form Buddha takes to force his sworn enemies into submission (embodiment of injunction), and is the most aggressive of his various personalities. In Esoteric Buddhism, these three embodiments, *Myō-ō* (embodiment of injunction), *Bosatsu* (embodiment of the true way), and *Nyorai* (embodiment of self), unite to complete the mandala circle (cakram), or chakra (Sanskrit). We can assume that Kaede chanted the mantra of the Immovable in order to use Buddhist techniques with high attack power.

[*Negima!* 207th Period Lexicon Negimarium]

■ Artemisia Leaves

(folium Artemisiae)

According to the ancient Roman military commander Pliny the Elder (AD 23–79), the plant called artemisia is also known as parthenis, ambrosia, botrys, etc. (cf. *Naturalis Historia XXVII*). According to Pliny's work, the name "artemisia" was taken from the queen of Caria in Asia Minor. "The plant that had been called 'parthenis' adopted the name of Maussollos's wife, Artemisia. There are also some who believe the plant gets its name from Artemis Eileithyia. This is because this plant was used especially to heal the afflictions of women. . . . Some call it botrys, and others call it ambrosia, but these grow in Cappadocia." (ibid. XXV)

Pliny also tells of the Magi's view of Artemisia: "It is said that poison, vicious beasts, not even the sun can harm one who carries artemisia on him." (ibid. XXV) From this legend and others (cf. ibid. XXVI), we can assume that the plant artemisia has mysterious power. Further, though not recorded in Pliny, artemisia leaves are well-known for staunching bleeding. However, artemisia leaves are not shaped like trident maple leaves as depicted in this work (those who are interested can observe the wild plants in their neighborhood). Nevertheless, as Pliny points out, artemisia is used for the name of various plants, and many of the plants belonging to the artemisia genus in the aster family are called in Latin "Artemisia...." Perhaps it is because of that that artemisia does not necessarily mean Artemisia vulgaris, common artemisia. Incidentally, artemisia is mugwort.

[*Negima!* 210th Period Lexicon Negimarium]

■ Read-Aloud Ear
(auris recitans)
A magical item used by those with visual disabilities to read texts. They are marketed in the Magical World. It reads what is in the texts via thought waves, so even those with hearing disabilities can use it.

[*Negima!* 212th Period Lexicon Negimarium]

■ anétte ti net garnet
Activation key of Collet Farandole, a trainee at the Magical Academic City Ariadne.

■ vor so kratika socratica
Activation key of Yue Farandole, a trainee at the Magical Academic City Ariadne.

■ Heatwave Disarmament
(CALEFACIENS EXARMATIO)
A magic spell that uses extreme heat to evaporate the enemy's equipment without burning them, thus disarming them. Of course it can't evaporate equipment made of metal, earthenware, or the like, but because its aim is disarmament, it is a complex spell that not only bathes the enemy in heat, but protects the enemy's body by casting heat-resistant magic on them.

■ tarot carrot charlotte
Activation key of Emily Sevensheep, a trainee at the Magical Academic City Ariadne.

■ Hail of Ice Spears
(JACULATIO GRANDINIS)
An attack spell that causes javelins made of ice to fall like hail. Because the warheads it releases are spears and not arrows, each individual warhead is more powerful than magic arrows made of ice. However, because the basis of the spell is warheads that fall from above, the spell is harder to put into practical use than magic arrows.

FIRST, LET'S LOOK AT THE TAIWANESE VERSION OF THE GREETING BETWEEN CLASS REP AND NEGI THAT WE COMPARED IN THE OTHER DIFFERENT LANGUAGES IN VOLUME 20!

IN CASES SUCH AS PROPER NOUNS THAT CAN'T BE TRANSLATED AND SPELLS, WHERE THE WAY A WORD SOUNDS IS MORE IMPORTANT THAN THE MEANING, THE CHINESE LANGUAGE VERSIONS USE CHARACTERS TO REPRESENT SOUNDS THAT ARE READ (PRONOUNCED) THE SAME WAY IN JAPANESE. THESE CHARACTERS, "涅吉(BLACK, GOOD LUCK)," ARE READ "NEGI." NAGI IS 納吉(OBTAIN GOOD LUCK); THEY DON'T USE THE KANJI THAT WE PRONOUNCE *NEGI* (葱) IN JAPANESE, WHICH MEANS "GREEN ONION."

POINT 1

POINT 2

BECAUSE IT'S CHINESE, THEY USE KANJI*. FROM WORDS THAT ARE WRITTEN THE SAME IN JAPANESE (LIKE 昨晩, LAST NIGHT) TO WORDS THAT YOU CAN KIND OF UNDERSTAND (LIKE 班長 (GROUP LEADER: CLASS REP) AND 早安 (EARLY PEACE: GOOD MORNING)), TO THINGS WHERE THE MEANING IN JAPANESE IS DIFFERENT (老師, RŌSHI, MASTER IN JAPANESE, MEANS TEACHER, *LĂOSHI,* IN CHINESE). IF YOU'VE READ THE ORIGINAL *NEGIMA!,* YOU CAN GET THE GIST OF WHAT THEY'RE SAYING.

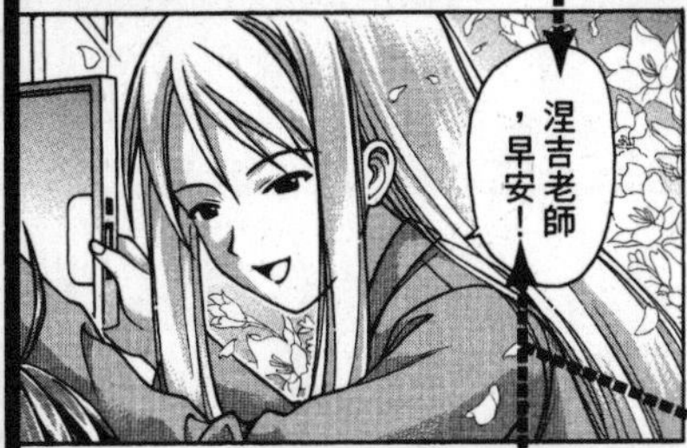

涅吉老師，早安！

GOOD MORNING, NEGI-SENSEI.

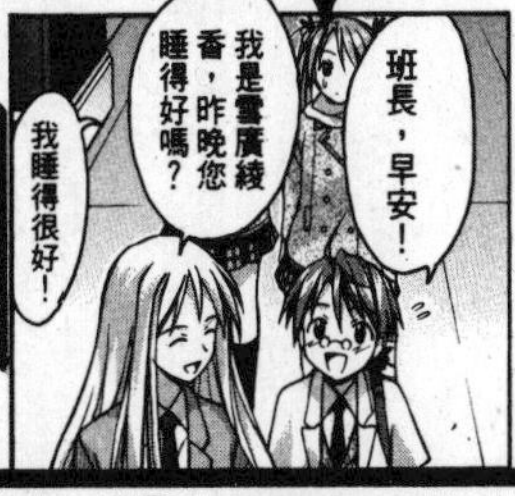

班長，早安！
我是雪廣綾香，昨晚您睡得好嗎？
我睡得很好！

GOOD MORNING, CLASS REP-SAN.

I'M AYAKA YUKIHIRO. DID YOU SLEEP WELL LAST NIGHT?

YES, VERY WELL.

POINT 3

IN THE JAPANESE VERSION, SOME OF THE JARGON BORROWS ENGLISH WORDS, SUCH AS "ARTIFACT" AND "*NUDE*-BEAM (OR STRIP-BEAM, 'NAKED RAY' IN THE ENGLISH VERSION)." THE TAIWANESE VERSION CHANGES THOSE TO CHINESE CHARACTERS THAT WE CAN READ LIKE, 道具 (*DŌGU,* TOOL) AND 脱衣光線 (*DATSUI KOUSEN,* STRIP-BEAM), MAKING THE JARGON FRESH AND NEW. IN THE BUBBLE IN THE PICTURE BELOW, THE ORIGINAL CALLED THEM THE *NAGI & AKO PAIR,* BORROWING "PAIR" FROM ENGLISH, BUT A "PAIR" IS ALSO A "組 (*KUMI*)" IN JAPANESE...KANJI SURE CAN HOLD A LOT OF INFORMATION.

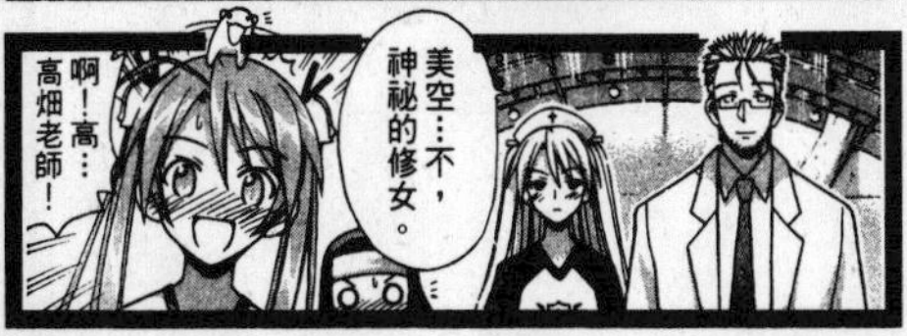

美空…不，神秘的修女。
啊！高…高畑老師！

美空…不、 MISORA-KU... I MEAN

神秘的修女 MYSTERIOUS SISTER-KUN

啊！高… AH! TA...

高畑老師！ TAKAHATA-SENSEI!

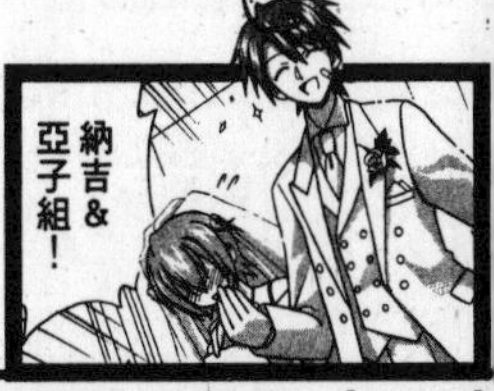

納吉&亞子組！

WORK: SHONEN MAGAZINE EDITORIAL DEPARTMENT, COOPERATION: JŪBEI YAGYŪ

*"IN TAIWAN, THEY CALL JAPANESE KANJI "漢字 (HÀNZÌ)," USING THE SAME CHARACTERS WE DO IN JAPAN. THE CHINESE KANJI THAT THEY USE IN TAIWAN ARE CALLED "國字 (GÚOZÌ, NATIVE CHARACTERS)."

INCIDENTALLY, AS FOR TWO CHINESE GIRLS, “CHAO LINGSHEN” IS A NAME THAT SEEMS KIND OF UNLIKELY (AS OF THE PRESENT DAY), BUT APPARENTLY KŪ FEI IS A POSSIBLE NAME. THE SETUP STILL HOLDS.

BATTLE TERMS & NAMES

戰鬥関係用語&名字集錦

READY? OK! JACULATOR!!!

一、二、三！攻擊敵人吧

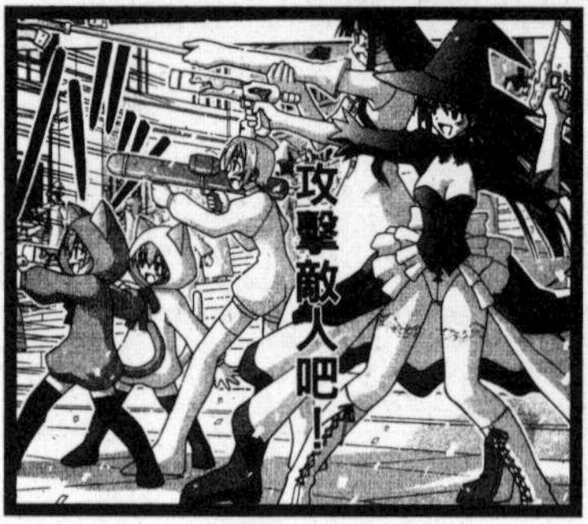
攻擊敵人吧！

佐倉愛衣 = MEI SAKURA

道具 = ARTIFACT

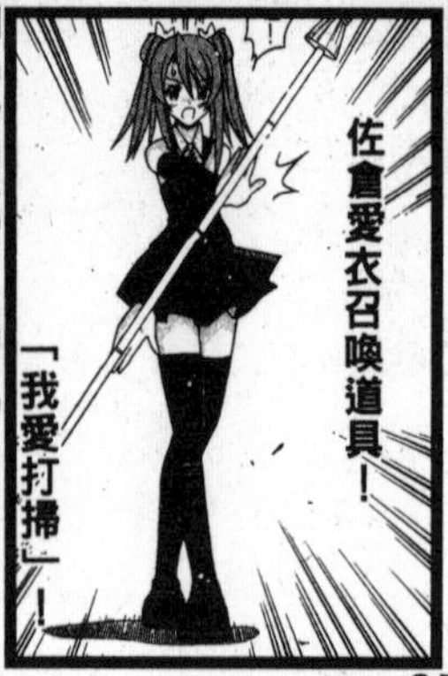
佐倉愛衣召喚道具！「我愛打掃」！

「我愛打掃」 = I LOVE CLEANING

愛書狂・紅色支配者

BIBLIO ROULIN ROUGE

雙重愛書狂死光 = (DOUBLE BOOK FREAK DEATH LIGHT) =DOUBLE BIBLIO COLLIDER

愛書狂水之狂想曲 = (BOOK FREAK WATER RHAPSODY) =BIBLIO AQUA RHAPSODY

愛書狂・粉紅鬱金香

BIBLIO PINK TULIP

BIBLIO • SPIRAL SHOOT

愛書狂螺旋奔流

BOOK FREAK SPIRAL CASCADE

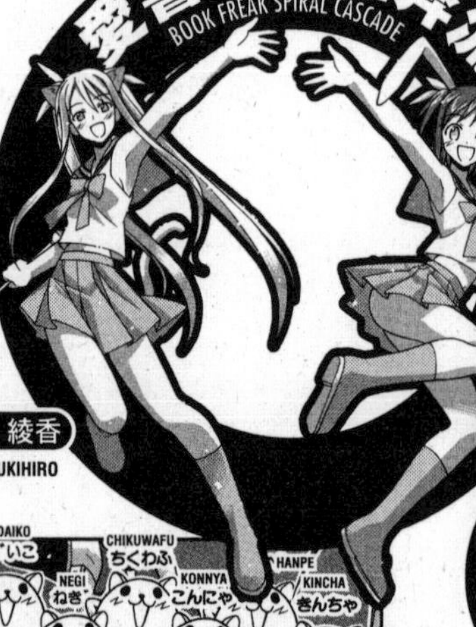
佐佐木蒔繪
MAKIE SASAKI
雪廣 綾香
AYAKA YUKIHIRO

愛書狂・紅玫瑰

BIBLIO RED ROSE

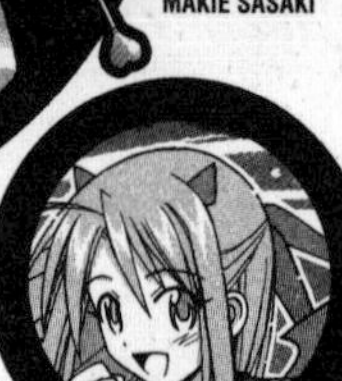
長谷川 千雨
CHISAME HASEGAWA

ETERNAL NEGI FEVER

永恆涅吉狂熱

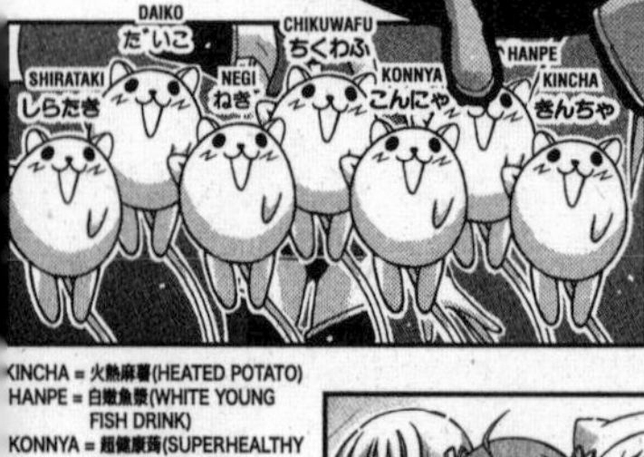
DAIKO
だいこ
CHIKUWAFU
ちくわふ
SHIRATAKI
しらたき
NEGI
ねぎ
KONNYA
こんにゃ
HANPE
KINCHA
きんちゃ

KINCHA = 火熱麻薯(HEATED POTATO)
HANPE = 白嫩魚漿(WHITE YOUNG FISH DRINK)
KONNYA = 超健康蒟(SUPERHEALTHY DEVIL'S TONGUE)
CHIKUWAFU = 美味竹輪(DELICIOUS CHIKUWA)
NEGI = 蔥(GREEN ONION)
DAIKO = 好吃白蘿(DAIKON)
SHIRATAKI = 蒟蒻絲(KONNYAKU THREAD)

NEGI BEAM

涅吉光波

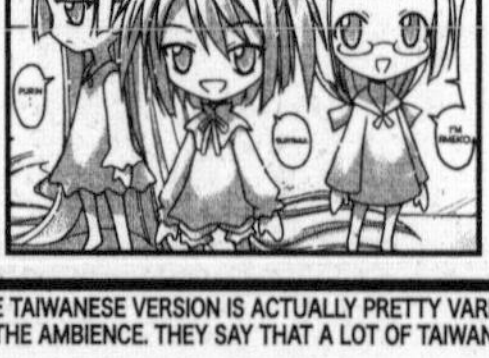

AMEKO = 雨子
SURAMUI = 史萊姆
PURIN = 布丁

NEGI KAISER

涅吉超大光波

AS YOU CAN SEE TO THE LEFT, THE TAIWANESE VERSION IS ACTUALLY PRETTY VARIEGATED, WITH LETTERS OF THE ALPHABET, AND HANDWRITTEN CHARACTERS LEFT IN JAPANESE TO BRING OUT THE AMBIENCE. THEY SAY THAT A LOT OF TAIWANESE READERS CAN READ THE SOUND EFFECTS WITH NO PROBLEM.

モー ファー ラオ スー

魔法老師!

MAGISTER NEGI MAGI

MÓFÂ LÂOSHI!

"NEGIMA! TERMS" COMPARISON 魔法老師用語對照翻譯

FINALLY, LET'S GIVE YOU PRONUNCIATIONS AND STUDY CHINESE. TRANSLATING THE TAIWANESE TITLE, "*MÓFÂ LÂOSHI!*" DIRECTLY INTO JAPANESE, IT'S "*MAHŌ SENSEI!*," OR "MAGIC TEACHER!" IN ENGLISH (IN CHINESE, THE KANJI THAT READ *-SENSEI* IN JAPANESE ARE THE EQUIVALENT TO *-SAN* USED FOR MALES). NOW THAT WE KNOW THAT *LÂOSHI* MEANS *SENSEI*, WE CAN USE IT FOR AKAMATSU-SENSEI.

↓

NOW, BECAUSE NEGI'S FULL NAME IS THE SAME IN JAPANESE, CHINESE, AND ENGLISH, LET'S PROVIDE THE NAME OF THE HEROINE. AND WE ALSO PUT CHACHAMARU, BECAUSE HER NAME SOUNDS NICE. (WHEN THEY CALL HER CHACHA-CHAN, IT SOUNDS LIKE TSAA-TSAA.)

LET'S USE THEIR TAIWANESE NAMES!

赤松 健先生 =KEN AKAMATSU-SENSEI=

赤松 健老師 CHÌSONG JIÀN-LÂOSHI

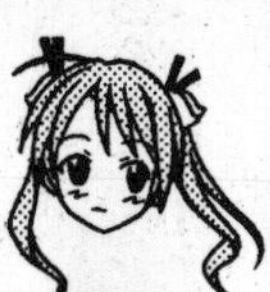

神樂坂 明日菜 SHÉNLÈBÂN MÍNGRÌCÀI

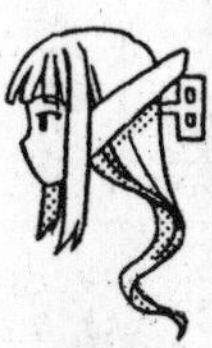

茶茶丸 CHÁCHÁWÁN

愛書狂火焰 → 火焰 IS ANOTHER WAY OF WRITING 火炎 (*KAEN*, BLAZE). THIS IS A BIBLION MOVE, SO... → BIBLIO FIRE

朗讀耳 (MELODY READING EAR) → IN JAPANESE KANJI, THAT BECOMES 朗読耳 (*RŌDOKUMIMI*). ANOTHER WORD FOR THE NAME OF THE ITEM THAT APPEARS IN VOLUME 23. → READ-ALOUD EAR

火星機器人軍團 (MARS MACHINE-MAN ARMY) → 軍團 = 軍団 (*GUNDAN*, ARMY). 火星 IS MARS, THE SAME AS IN JAPANESE. → MARTIAN ROBOT ARMY

涅吉魔社 (NEGI MAGIC SOCIETY) → THE FIRST TWO CHARACTERS ARE "NEGI." ITS OTHER NAME IS "白色之翼 (WHITE WINGS)." → NEGIMA CLUB

茶茶零號 (TEA TEA ZERO NUMBER) → 號 = 号, *GŌ*, A JAPANESE WORD INDICATING THE NAME OF A SHIP, PLANE, ROBOT, ETC. BUT IN JAPANESE, THE *GŌ* IS TAKEN OFF OF HER NAME... → CHACHAZERO

年齡詐稱藥 (AGE-FALSIFYING DRUG) → WITHOUT THESE, THE COVER OF VOLUME 22 WOULDN'T WORK. → AGE-MISREPRESENTATION PASTILLES

小夜仔 → SAYO AISAKA IS 相坂小夜, AND THIS ISN'T A DIRECT TRANSLATION, BUT A LIBERAL TRANSLATION BASED ON THE MEANING...AN ADAPTATION. → SAYO-BŌ

ALSO, KUGIMĪ BECOMES 釘仔.

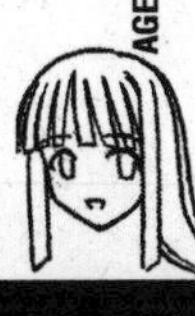

SEE KANJI IN A NEW LIGH

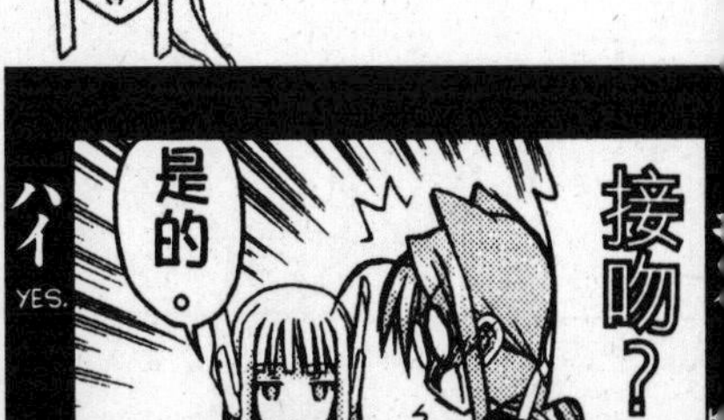
接吻？
是的。
ハイ
YES.

魔法先生 ネギま! MAGISTER NEGI MAGI

赤松 健 SHONEN MAGAZINE COMICS KEN AKAMATSU

23

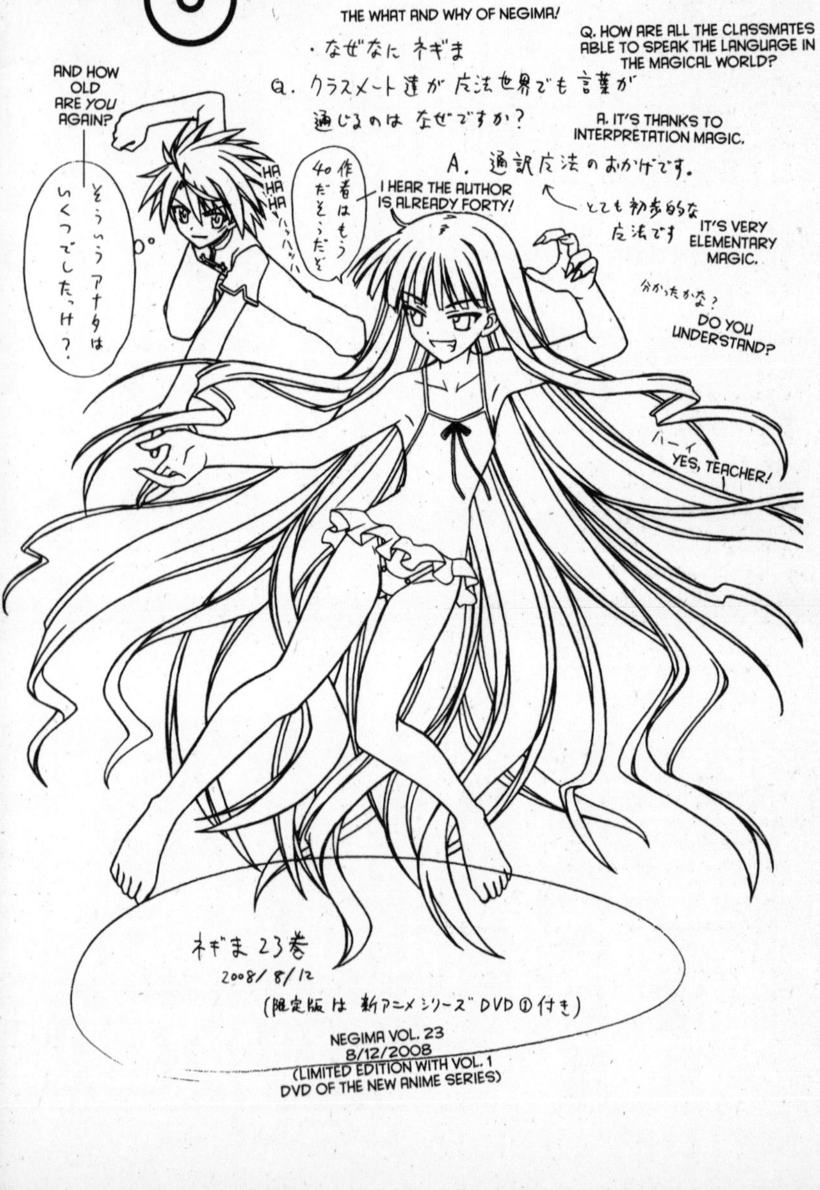

THE WHAT AND WHY OF NEGIMA!
・なぜなに ネギま
Q. クラスメート達が 魔法世界でも 言葉が 通じるのは なぜですか?
Q. HOW ARE ALL THE CLASSMATES ABLE TO SPEAK THE LANGUAGE IN THE MAGICAL WORLD?
A. 通訳魔法のおかげです。
A. IT'S THANKS TO INTERPRETATION MAGIC.
とても初歩的な魔法です
IT'S VERY ELEMENTARY MAGIC.
分かったかな?
DO YOU UNDERSTAND?
ハーイ
YES, TEACHER!
作者はもう40だそうだぞ
I HEAR THE AUTHOR IS ALREADY FORTY!
HA HA HA
ハッハッハ
そういうアナタはいくつでしたっけ?
AND HOW OLD ARE YOU AGAIN?
ネギま 23巻
2008/8/12
(限定版は 新アニメシリーズ DVD① 付き)
NEGIMA VOL. 23
8/12/2008
(LIMITED EDITION WITH VOL. 1 DVD OF THE NEW ANIME SERIES)

キャラ解説

CHARACTER PROFILE

⑦ 柿崎美砂

⑦ MISA KAKIZAKI

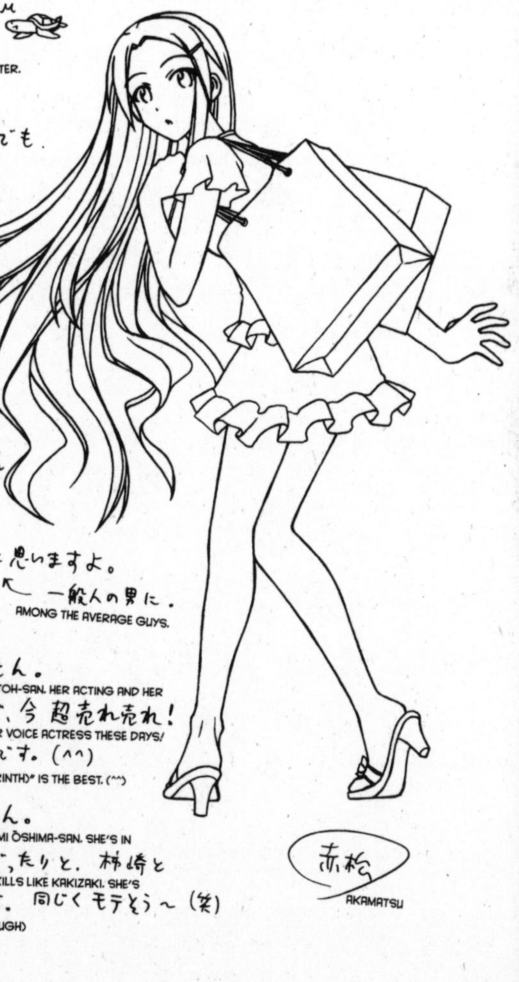

名前は マクロスのキャラから。
I GOT HER NAME FROM A MACROSS CHARACTER.
(漢字ちがいますけど…)
(BUT WITH DIFFERENT KANJI...)

スタイルの良い チア3人組の中でも
OF THE THREE NICE-BODIED CHEERLEADERS,
最も 色気というか Hっぽさが
SHE IS THE SEXIEST, OR RATHER,
高い彼女。(笑)
THE HOOCHIEST. (LAUGH)

4巻で
THE EXISTENCE OF
彼氏の存在が確認
HER BOYFRIEND WAS CONFIRMED IN
されましたが、今も
VOLUME FOUR, BUT IT IS UNKNOWN
付き合ってるかどうかは
WHETHER OR NOT SHE IS STILL GOING OUT
不明です。(もうフッちゃったん
WITH HIM. (I THINK SHE MIGHT HAVE DUMPED HIM
じゃないかな～)(^^;)
ALREADY...) (^^;) OF ALL THE GIRLS IN
3-Aで 一番モテる女だと思いますよ。
3-A, I THINK SHE'S THE MOST POPULAR.
← 一般人の男に。
AMONG THE AVERAGE GUYS.

アニメ版CVは 伊藤静さん。
HER VOICE IN THE ANIME IS PROVIDED BY SHIZUKA ITOH-SAN. HER ACTING AND HER
演技も歌もパーフェクトな人で、今超売れ売れ！
SINGING ARE PERFECT, AND SHE'S A SUPERPOPULAR VOICE ACTRESS THESE DAYS!
「せつなくてラビリンス」とか 最高です。(^^)
"SETSUNAKUTE LABYRINTH (HEARTBREAKING LABYRINTH)" IS THE BEST. (^^)

ドラマ版は 大島あすみさん。
IN THE LIVE-ACTION DRAMA, SHE'S PLAYED BY ASUMI ŌSHIMA-SAN. SHE'S IN
キャンギャルだったり モデルだったりと、柿崎と
COMMERCIALS AND DOES MODELING, AND HAS SKILLS LIKE KAKIZAKI. SHE'S
似たようなスキルを持ちます。同じくモテそう～(笑)
PROBABLY JUST AS POPULAR WITH THE BOYS! (LAUGH)

赤松

AKAMATSU

About the Creator

Negima! is only Ken Akamatsu's third manga, although he started working in the field in 1994 with *AI Ga Tomaranai* (released in the United States with the title *A.I. Love You*). Like all of Akamatsu's work to date, it was published in Kodansha's *Shonen Magazine*. *AI Ga Tomaranai* ran for five years before concluding in 1999. In 1998, however, Akamatsu began the work that would make him one of the most popular manga artists in Japan: *Love Hina*. *Love Hina* ran for four years, and before its conclusion in 2002, it would cause Akamatsu to be granted the prestigious Manga of the Year award from Kodansha, as well as going on to become one of the bestselling manga in the United States.

Translation Notes

Japanese is a tricky language for most Westerners, and translation is often more art than science. For your edification and reading pleasure, here are notes on some of the places where we could have gone in a different direction with our translation of the work, or where a Japanese cultural reference is used.

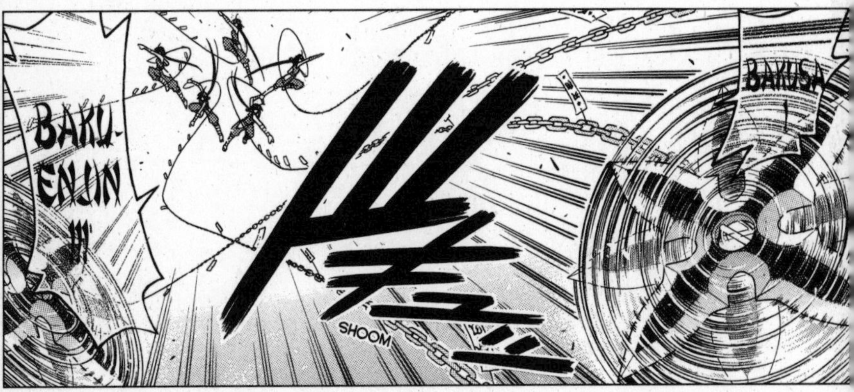
BAKUSA
BAKU-ENJIN
SHOOM

Bakusa and bakuenjin, page 22

Bakusa means binding chain. Kaede uses it to restrain the dragon before using *bakuenjin*, which means "exploding flame army."

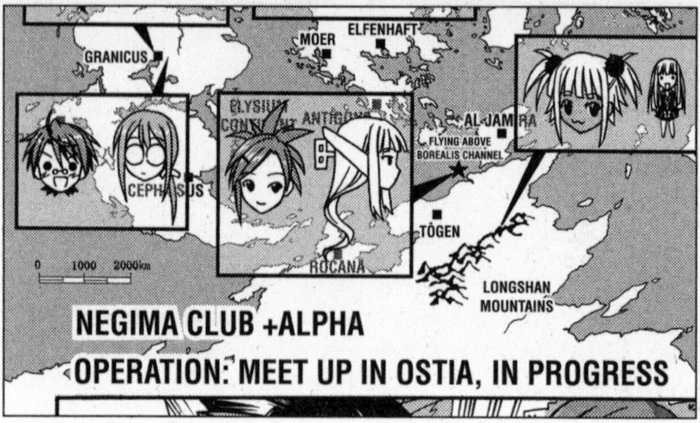
GRANICUS
MOER
ELFENHAFT
ANTIGONE
AL-JAMRA
FLYING ABOVE
BOREALIS CHANNEL
CEPHASUS
TŌGEN
ROCANA
0 1000 2000km
LONGSHAN MOUNTAINS
NEGIMA CLUB +ALPHA
OPERATION: MEET UP IN OSTIA, IN PROGRESS

Negima Club +alpha, page 52

The Greek letter alpha is used to represent an unknown factor. In Japan, when something comes with extras, sometimes they say the name of the thing "+(plus) alpha." In this case, the +alpha refers to the girls who are not in the Negima Club, and Negima Club +alpha means "Negima Club and some others."

Chibisuke, page 52

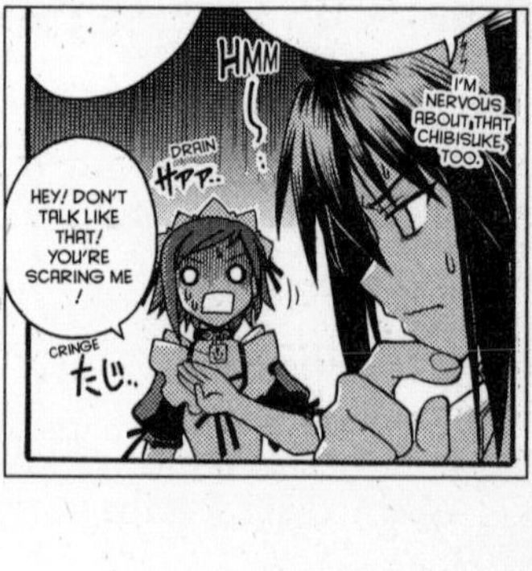
I'M NERVOUS ABOUT THAT CHIBISUKE, TOO.
HMM
DRAIN
HEY! DON'T TALK LIKE THAT! YOU'RE SCARING ME!
CRINGE

Kotarō can't let go of the fact that Yue is very short (maybe it makes him feel better about himself?), so he calls her Chibisuke. *Chibi* roughly means "shorty," and adding *suke* to it makes it a boy's name. Incidentally, Yuekichi, another of Yue's nicknames, is also more masculine.

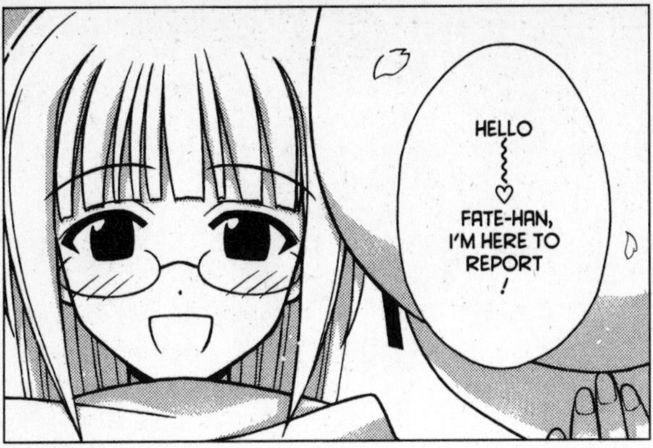
HELLO ♡ FATE-HAN, I'M HERE TO REPORT!

Fate-han, page 88

Tsukuyomi, being from the Kansai region of Japan, uses a thick Kansai dialect—so thick that she uses "*han*" instead of "*san*."

Annin dofu, page 92

Annin dofu is a kind of dessert made with a jelly made from *annin* (apricot seeds), fruit, and syrup.

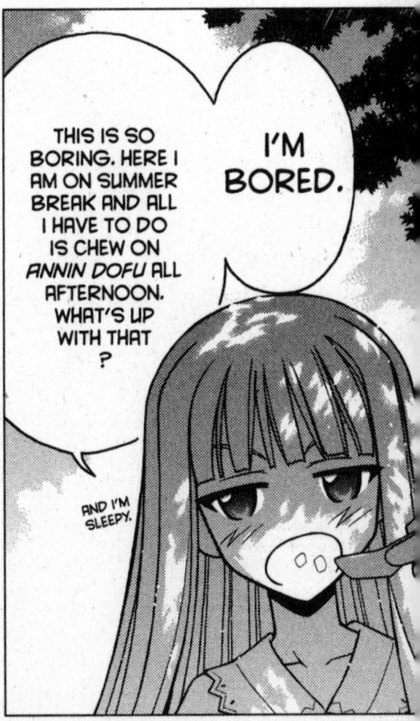
I'M BORED.
THIS IS SO BORING. HERE I AM ON SUMMER BREAK AND ALL I HAVE TO DO IS CHEW ON ANNIN DOFU ALL AFTERNOON. WHAT'S UP WITH THAT?
AND I'M SLEEPY.

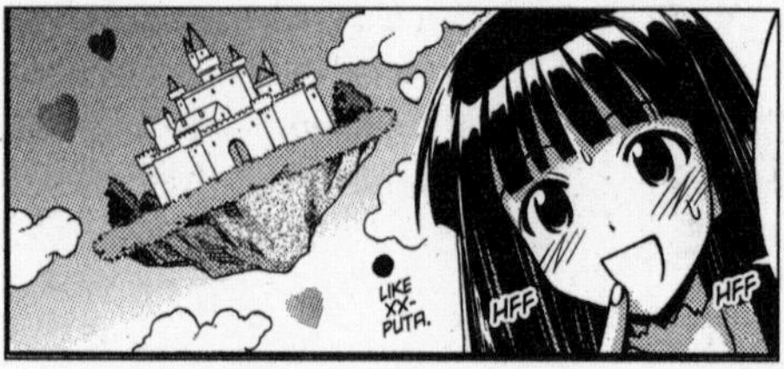
LIKE XX-PUTA.
HFF
HFF

XX-puta, page 157

What Konoka is preventing herself from saying (most likely for copyright reasons) is the name of a certain castle in the sky, featured in a film by Studio Ghibli. We won't tell you what it is, but it starts with L and rhymes with "Laputa."

Setsunakute Labyrinth, page 175

This is the title of a song from the third Negima!? PS2 game, sung, as mentioned, by Shizuka Itoh, the voice actress who plays Misa Kakizaki.

Preview of *Negima!* Volume 24

We're pleased to present you a preview from volume 24. Please check our website, www.delreymanga.com, to see when this volume will be available in English. For now you'll have to make do with Japanese!

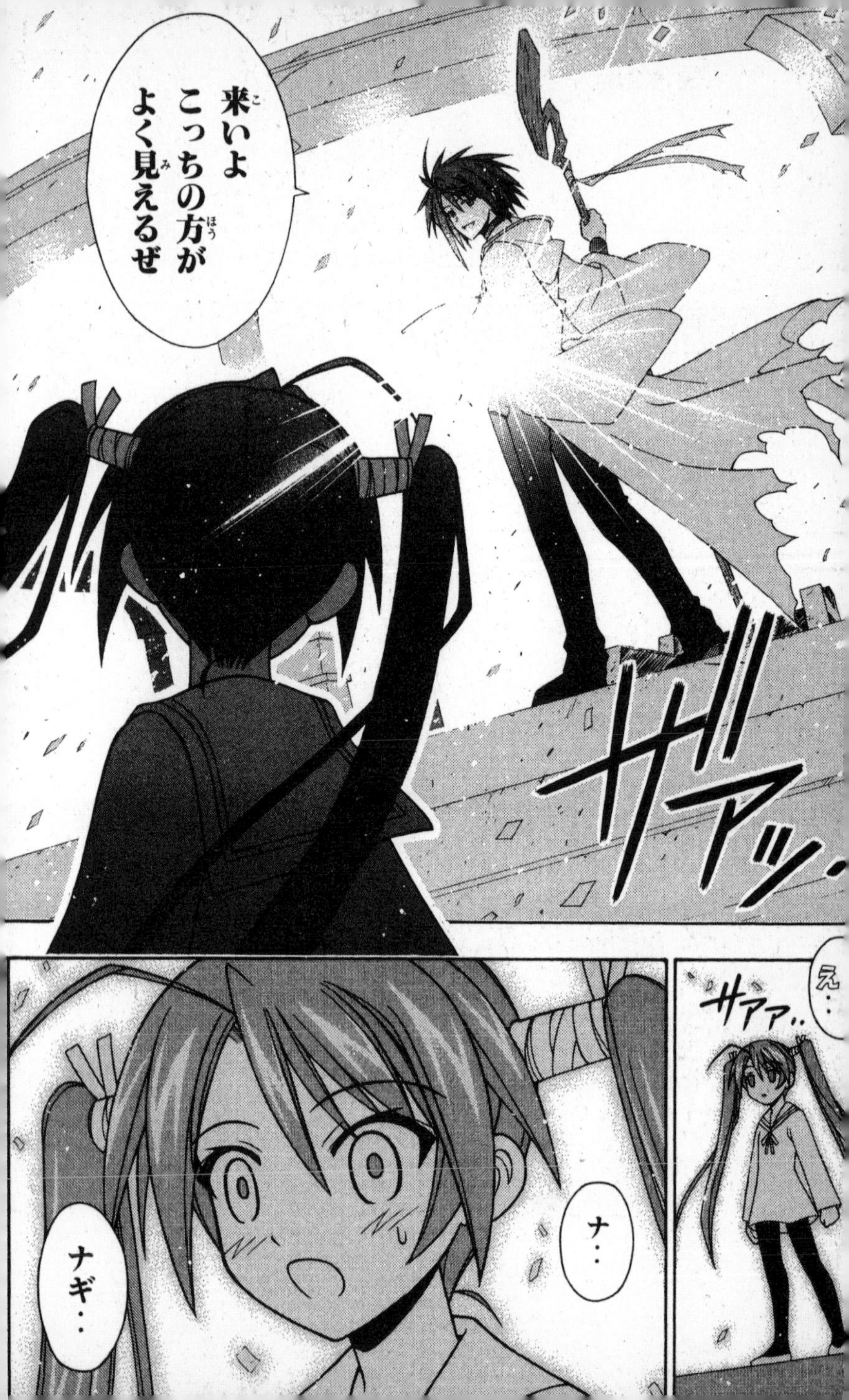
来いよ こっちの方が よく見えるぜ
ザアッ
え・・
サアア・・
ナ・・
ナギ・・

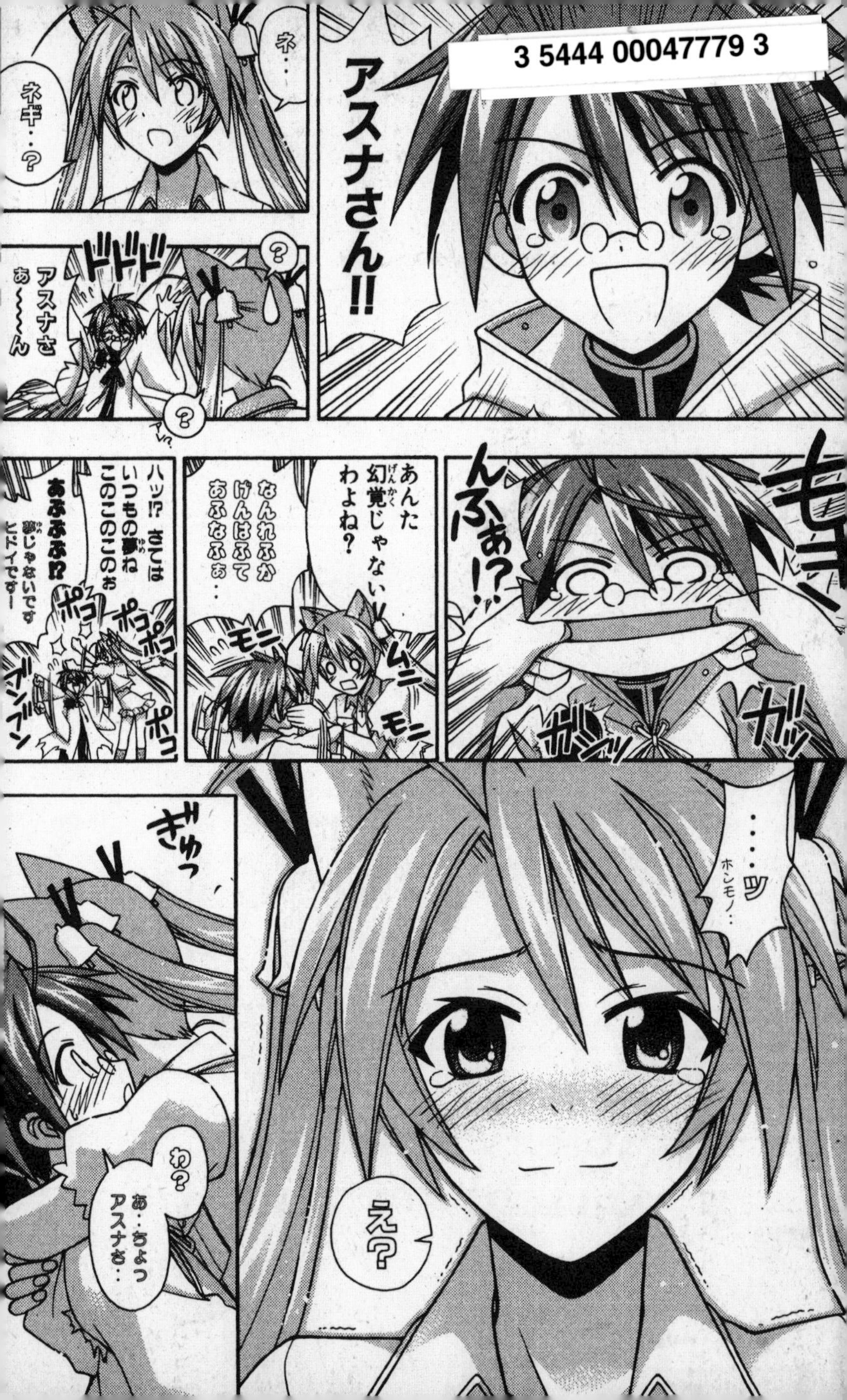
アスナさん!!
ネ・・・
ネギ・・・?
ドドド
アスナさあ〜〜〜ん
?
?
んふぁ!?
ガッ
ガシッ
あんた幻覚じゃないわよね?
なんれふかげんはふてあふなふぁ・・・
モニ
ムニ
モニ
ハッ!? さては いつもの夢ね このこのこのぉ
あぶぶぶ!? 夢じゃないです ヒドイですー
ポコ
ポコ
ポコ
ポコ
ブンブン
・・・ッ
ホンモノ・・・
え?
ぎゅっ
わ?
あ・・・ちょっ アスナさ・・・

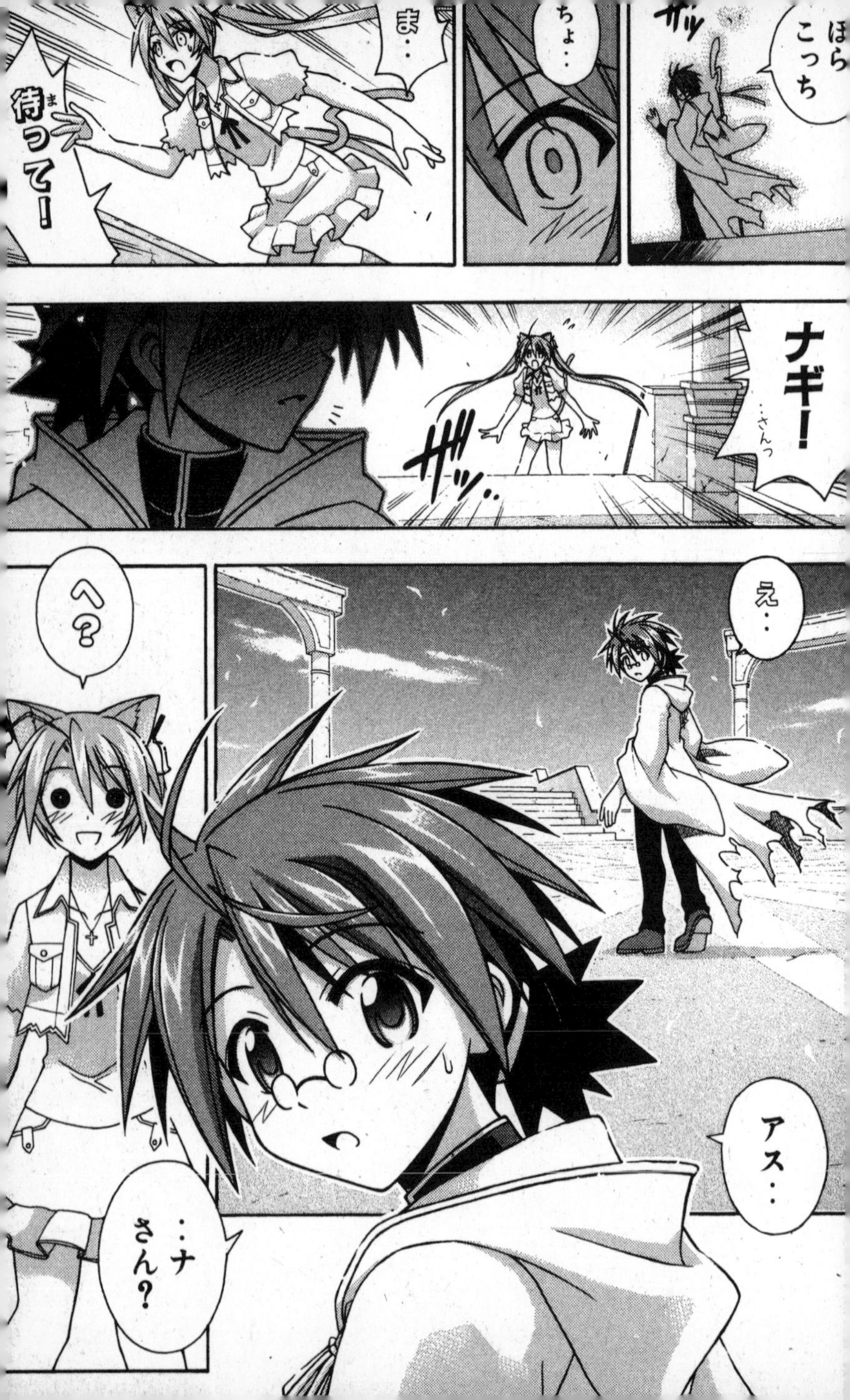
ほら
こっち
ザッ
ちょ・・・
ま・・・
待って！
ナギ！
・・・さんっ
ザザッ
え・・・
アス・・・
・・ナ
さん？
へ？

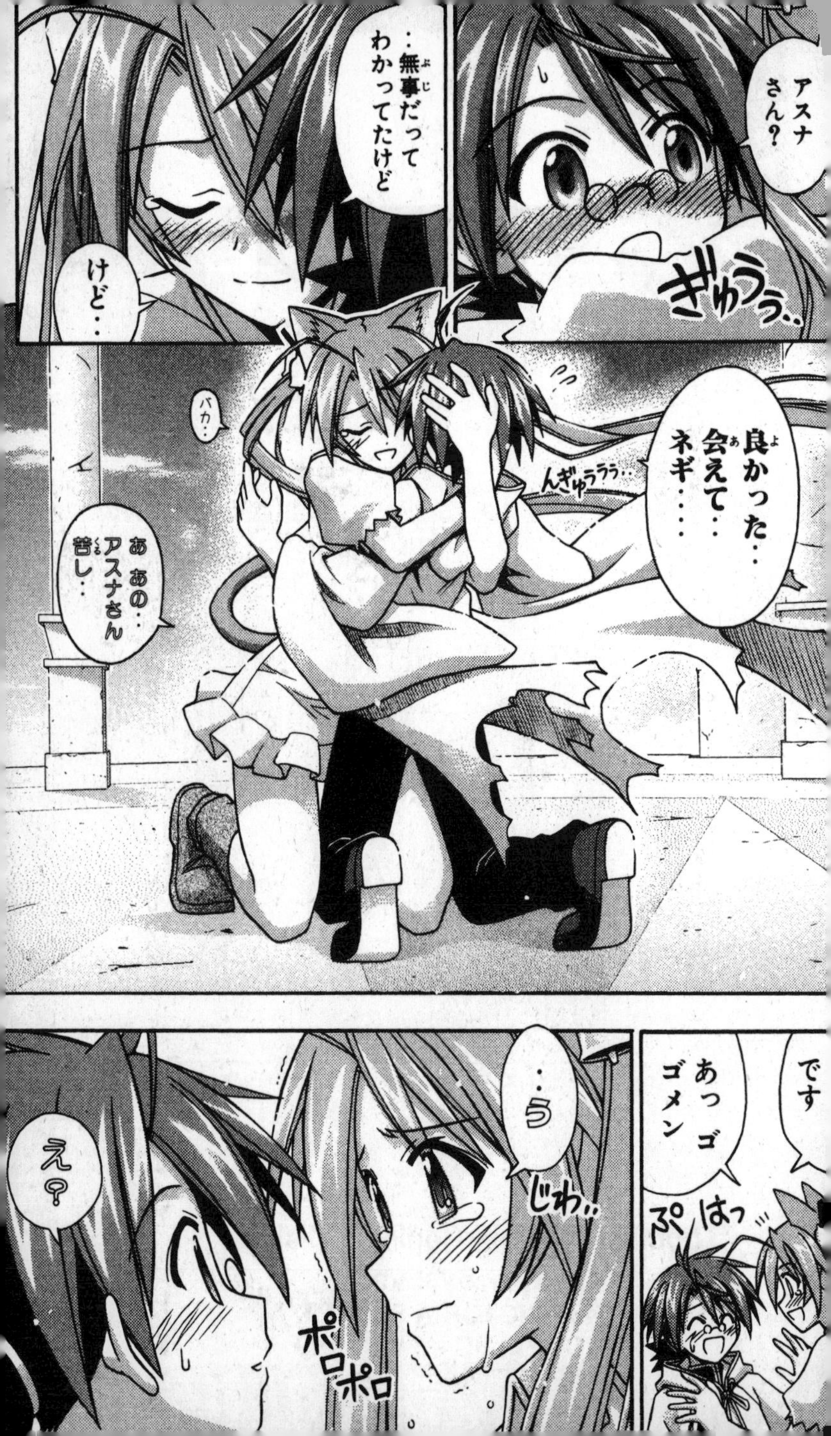
アスナさん？
ぎゅうう…
…無事だってわかってたけど
けど…
良かった…会えて…ネギ……
んぎゅううう…
バカ…
あ あの…アスナさん苦し…
です
あっゴメン
ぷはっ
…う
じわ…
ポロポロ
え？

35444000477793
GN YA 741.5952 AKA
Akamatsu, Ken.
Negima! : Magister Negi
Magi Vol. 23

WITHDRAWN

TOMARE!

[STOP!]

You're going the wrong way!

Manga is a completely different type of reading experience.

To start at the *beginning*, go to the *end*!

That's right! Authentic manga is read the traditional Japanese way—from right to left, exactly the *opposite* of how American books are read. It's easy to follow: Just go to the other end of the book, and read each page—and each panel—from right side to left side, starting at the top right. Now you're experiencing manga as it was meant to be.

Thompson-Nicola Regional District
Library System
300-465 VICTORIA STREET
KAMLOOPS, BC   V2C 2A9